Business Models for Sustainability Transitions

"The business model lens and the recognition of our institutionalized 'unsustainable' business models, such as the take-make-dispose linear business model in sustainability transitions, provide a new and exciting perspective. The book *Business Models for Sustainability Transitions* presents multiple interdisciplinary perspectives on the focus areas of business models and sustainability transitions, including various case studies and lenses to investigate the topic. In this way, this edited book provides a unique pathway forward for theory and practice on sustainability transitions and the potential positive role of business."

—Nancy Bocken, Professor in Sustainable Business, *Maastricht Sustainability Institute, Maastricht University, the Netherlands*

"Research on business models for sustainability has become a field in its own right. This book is taking the next step and connects the firm-level with socio-technical systems in which the business is embedded. A much needed step to understand how business models can contribute to a sustainable development of markets, the economy, society and the planet!"

—Stefan Schaltegger, *Professor for Sustainability Management, Centre for Sustainability Management (CSM), Leuphana University, Germany*

Annabeth Aagaard
Florian Lüdeke-Freund • Peter Wells
Editors

Business Models for Sustainability Transitions

How Organisations Contribute to Societal Transformation

palgrave
macmillan

Editors
Annabeth Aagaard
Business Development & Technology
Aarhus University
Herning, Denmark

Florian Lüdeke-Freund
European Sustainability Department
ESCP Business School
Berlin, Germany

Peter Wells
Cardiff Business School
Cardiff University
Cardiff, UK

ISBN 978-3-030-77579-7 ISBN 978-3-030-77580-3 (eBook)
https://doi.org/10.1007/978-3-030-77580-3

This Palgrave Macmillan imprint is published by the registered company Springer Nature Switzerland AG.
The registered company address is: Gewerbestrasse 11, 6330 Cham, Switzerland

Foreword: A Transitions Perspective

We are confronted with a large variety of major sustainability challenges such as climate change, loss of biodiversity, lack of clean water, waste production, inequality, poverty, and modern slavery. Many of these issues are connected to unsustainable business models. They are not just the unwanted side effects of doing business but the result of a systematic optimization of organizational strategies and processes to increase profitability. Take fast fashion, for example. Leading brands have built globally operating business networks, based on the systematic exploitation of human and natural resources, and adversely affecting almost all of the above sustainability issues. Even more, fast fashion has managed to instil a new need in consumers to buy clothes in short cycles and to discard them as 'out of fashion' equally rapidly.

Firms such as Patagonia have shown that there are alternative and successful business models which benefit a wide range of stakeholders. The outdoor clothing specialist sells long-lasting products; uses organic, fair trade materials; actively supports repair and second-hand use; supports social movements; and even promotes alternative consumption practices and lifestyles.

A key question is how such alternative approaches can be multiplied and used to change entire industries—in clothing and beyond. How can we connect firm and supply chain level change processes with larger sectoral transformations?

This book brings together a compelling set of contributions that explore the intersection of transition studies and business model innovation with the aspiration to bridge the two strands of research and to open new and impactful avenues for research.

Research on sustainability transitions seeks to address grand challenges through radical changes in socio-technical systems. It analyses how innovations can be mobilized to transform systems of provision, such as energy supply, transport, or agri-food, and explores how unsustainable practices can be phased-out. For example, building a novel energy system based on renewables such as wind and solar energy to combat climate change. Transitions research studies the interplay of changes in technologies, infrastructures, institutions, policies and organizations, typically with a sectoral focus. However, it tends to miss out on non-technical innovations, transformations of entire supply chains, or change processes at the organizational level.

Research on business model innovation for sustainability goes beyond the financial profitability of firms as it includes the social and environmental purposes of strategy making. It also looks beyond the boundaries of the individual firm, studying how businesses can become key orchestrators of changes towards sustainability in larger supply chains or industries. At the same time, business model studies may find it challenging to connect specific firm and supply chain level activities to larger sectoral and system level transformation processes or to systematically address the political dimension of sustainability transitions.

It is in exploring the complementarities of business model innovation and sustainability transitions where this book makes a major contribution. Many of the chapters emphasize the coordinating character of innovative business models and analyze how organizational decision makers can find new ways of engaging with the wider systems context that is characterized by a multitude of different types of actors, a pivotal role for (sustainability) policy making, and a strong influence of consumers, needs and lifestyles.

Bridging related but so far separate areas of research and generating new insights for strategy and policy-making is key to destabilizing unsustainable business practices and to accelerate processes of transformative and sustainable change. This book is an important stepping-stone in a much larger journey toward more sustainable modes of production and consumption.

Zurich, Switzerland Jochen Markard

Foreword: A Business Models Perspective

Increasing pressure on the environment and society indicate that a rapid sustainability transition is needed worldwide. Biodiversity has experienced a rapid decline, climate change has accelerated, and under pressure of the COVID-19 pandemic, equality and poverty reduction have only worsened (UN, 2020). The impact of human activity on the world has been so tremendous that this era is dubbed the 'Anthropocene', where human impacts occur at such a scale that these are outcompeting natural processes (Crutzen, 2006).

What is the answer to accelerating sustainability transitions? Transitions researchers have noted the importance of multiple actors driving the transition in conjunction and the required changes at the micro-, meso- and macro-levels (Geels, 2002). In this edited book titled *Business Models for Sustainability Transitions,* the focus is on the role of business and specifically of business models, as the world economy is dominated by business and business practice. Rather than seeing business as the main culprit for unsustainability, how can it be the driver for positive change and innovation?

This idea of business as a force for good in driving sustainability transitions is not new. The sustainable development agenda by Brundtland et al. (1987) has been translated into positive goals and actions by leading thinkers. Corporate Social Responsibility (CSR) became popular in the 1990s as a way for companies to meet economic as well as legal and ethical responsibilities. Elkington (1997) coined the term 'triple bottom line' of people, profit, and planet to broaden the business focus beyond profits. Hart (2007) defined 'sustainable value' as a way for business to create societal, economic, and environmental value in conjunction. Yunus pioneered work on social businesses: rather than optimizing shareholder value, social businesses create broader stakeholder value, focusing on issues such as poverty reduction, while being financially viable (Yunus et al., 2010). Recently, the topic of Circular Economy – again based on older thinking (Blomsma & Brennan, 2017) – became an important driver for the sustainability transitions, in which companies take responsibility for resource use and ultimately the climate and biodiversity.

So, what is the role of business and business models specifically in sustainability transitions? In the past, much of the transitions research has focused on how companies put forward technical niches, supporting, for example, the renewable energy or electric vehicle transitions. More recently, researchers have observed that non-technical niches and dominant patterns such as the unsustainable business model (Bidmon & Knab, 2018; Sarasini & Linder, 2018) form the core blockages in sustainability transitions (Hernandez Chea et al., 2020). Consider the take-make-use model that extracts resources at an unsustainable rate dependent on disposing the product prematurely or the 'addictive consumption' model which drives an unsustainable level of consumption as the basis for a profitable model. Several researchers have started to understand the need to break through these institutionalized unsustainable models (Ritala et al., 2021). As sustainable business models take a holistic perspective on the way business is done, starting with the business purpose and taking into account multiple stakeholder perspectives such as the perspectives of the society and the environment (Bocken et al., 2013), sustainable business models provide a unique lens to investigate sustainability transitions from a business perspective.

Interdisciplinary insight from research and practice can help illuminate the solutions to drive these transitions. For example, the field of experimentation, explored in fields like transitions research, design, business and engineering studies, might be a promising avenue (Bocken et al., 2021). Through experimentation, companies can put forward new sustainable business models that challenge the status quo and may subsequently also stimulate new policy and legislation. Collaboration between different actors (business, policy, NGOs) will also become increasingly important, specifically because sustainability issues transcend corporate boundaries and new sustainable business models require a responsibility (yet) beyond the firm level. Collaboration allows firms to gain the required capabilities for innovation and jointly resolve issues beyond the firm, such as biodiversity regeneration initiatives that concern the business (who depend on the natural resources), the local communities and environments within which business operate, as well policymakers and NGOs. Finally, new platforms and digital technology developments will provide unprecedented business model opportunities similar to how smartphones – and the Internet more broadly – allowed for new successful service-oriented and sharing business models to flourish.

This book presents multiple perspectives on business models and sustainability transitions including various business cases and lenses on the topic. In this way, it should provide a fruitful pathway forward for theory and practice.

Maastricht, The Netherlands Nancy Bocken

References

Bidmon, C. M., & Knab, S. F. (2018). The three roles of business models in societal transitions: New linkages between business model and transition research. *Journal of Cleaner Production, 178*, 903–916.

Blomsma, F., & Brennan, G. (2017). The emergence of circular economy: A new framing around prolonging resource productivity. *Journal of Industrial Ecology, 21*(3), 603–614.

Bocken, N., Short, S., Rana, P., & Evans, S. (2013). A value mapping tool for sustainable business modelling. *Corporate Governance, 13*(5), 482–497.

Bocken, N., Weissbrod, I., & Antikainen, M. (2021). Business model experimentation for the circular economy: Definition and approaches. *Circular Economy and Sustainability*. https://doi.org/10.1007/s43615-021-00026-z

Brundtland, G. H., Khalid, M., Agnelli, S., Al-Athel, S., & Chidzero, B. J. N. Y. (1987). Our common future. New York, 8.
Crutzen, P. J. (2006). The "anthropocene". In *Earth system science in the anthropocene* (pp. 13–18). Springer.
Elkington, J. (1997). Cannibals with forks. The triple bottom line of 21st century, 73.
Geels, F. W. (2002). Technological transitions as evolutionary reconfiguration processes: A multi-level perspective and a case-study. *Research policy, 31*(8–9), 1257–1274.
Hart, S. L. (2007). *Capitalism at the crossoads: Aligning business, earth, and humanity*. Pearson Prentice Hall.
Hernandez Chea, R., Jain, A., & Bocken, N. (2020). A conceptualization of firm activities toward sustainability transitions. In *Academy of management proceedings* (Vol. 2020, No. 1, p. 21756). Academy of Management.
Ritala, P., Albareda, L., & Bocken, N. (2021). Value creation and appropriation in economic, social, and environmental domains: Recognizing and resolving the institutionalized asymmetries. *Journal of Cleaner Production, 290*, 125796.
Sarasini, S., & Linder, M. (2018). Integrating a business model perspective into transition theory: The example of new mobility services. *Environmental innovation and societal transitions, 27*, 16–31.
UN. (2020). Sustainable development goals report. https://unstats.un.org/sdgs/report/2020/. Accessed 21 Apr 2021.
Yunus, M., Moingeon, B., & Lehmann-Ortega, L. (2010). Building social business models: Lessons from the Grameen experience. *Long Range Planning, 43*(2–3), 308–325.

Contents

Notes on Contributors

Annabeth Aagaard is an associate professor and the founding director of Interdisciplinary Centre for Digital Business Development at Aarhus University, Denmark. Her research is focused on digital and sustainable business development, ecosystems, and innovation, from which she has (co)-authored 14 textbooks, including *Sustainable Business Models – Innovation, Implementation and Success* (Palgrave).

Andres Alcayaga, MSc, is a doctoral candidate and research associate at the Institute for Integrated Quality Design (IQD) at the Johannes Kepler University Linz (JKU), Austria. His research explores the intersection between the Circular Economy, the Internet of Things, and service business models. In particular, he aims to discover opportunities and challenges of smart products for life cycle management and business model innovation. He also focuses on understanding innovative business practices related to digital technologies and circular systems, as well as the consequences of novel value chain architectures for quality and environmental management systems. He graduated in Business Administration and holds a Master's degree in International Information Systems. He has previously worked as an IT Performance and Quality Manager and as an IT Consultant.

Karoline Augenstein is Junior Professor of Policy Analysis, Transformation Research and Sustainability at the University of Wuppertal, Germany. She is co-leader of the junior research group 'UrbanUp' (Upscaling Strategies for an Urban Sharing Society) at the Center for Transformation Research and Sustainability (transzent). In her research, she focuses on the role of narratives in sustainability transitions, the governance of urban transitions and transdisciplinary research approaches. She was a doctoral research fellow at the Wuppertal Institute (PhD thesis on 'E-mobility as a Sustainable System Innovation'), and she holds a BA in European Studies from Maastricht University and an MA in Sustainability Economics and Management from the University of Oldenburg.

Marjo Baeten is a lecturer-researcher at HAS and performs various coordinating roles in international projects and master classes within the university. Being, a TIAS School for Business and Society graduate from a farming family, Marjo is highly engaged in the agri-food transition.

P. J. Beers is Professor of New Business Models for Agri-food Transition at HAS University of Applied Sciences ('s-Hertogenbosch, the Netherlands; henceforth: HAS) and senior researcher at the Dutch Research Institute for Transitions (DRIFT, Erasmus University Rotterdam). He combines research on learning, reflexivity, and business in the context of agri-food transition.

Lara Anne Blasberg is an assistant professor and postdoctoral fellow in the Department of Management, Society and Communications (MSC) at Copenhagen Business School (CBS), focusing on the development of sustainability in the building sector. She is lead researcher for a joint industrial project with VELUX, CBS, and BLOXHUB on the topic of 'Smart Buildings and Cities Business Model Innovation.' The research project is supported by the Danish Innovation Fund and Realdania. Lara's research involves applied investigation into innovation processes for building organizations to adapt their business models to the increasing digitization and automation of buildings, with a focus on sustainability and user-centered design. It is enacted as part of the Science Forum at BLOXHUB, the Nordic building innovation centre, and the Sustainability Centre at CBS.

Erwin Bouwmans is a lecturer-researcher at HAS, and his expertise concerns leadership, new business models and food systems transition. He has a professional background in agricultural consultancy and finance (i.e. ABAB accountants, Rabobank, ZLTO).

Carolina Castaldi, PhD, is a full professor at Utrecht University, the Netherlands, where she holds the chair in Geography of Innovation. Her research focuses on innovation, in all its forms. She has extensively studied the service innovation and is interested in investigating the specific challenges of sustainable innovation.

Ignes A. Castro Contreiras de Carvalho is a PhD student and industrial engineer. She develops a thesis on sustainable business models strategies, focusing on a value-network to promote sustainable production and consumption.

Jacqueline Cramer is Professor of Sustainable Innovation at Utrecht University. Her background is primarily related to industry, working as a consultant for many years with more than 200 companies on the implementation of sustainable entrepreneurship, corporate social responsibility, and circular economy. Among others, she is member of the Amsterdam Economic Board, particularly in charge of the circular economy. From 2007 to 2010 she was Minister of Housing, Spatial Planning and the Environment for the Labour Party.

Krzysztof Dembek (PhD, Monash University) is Lecturer in Social Impact at the Centre for Social Impact—Swinburne University— an honorary fellow at the University of Melbourne, and visiting professor at the WSB University in Gdansk, Poland. His research interests focus on solving complex global problems and on using business models for creating positive social and environmental impact. His articles have appeared in journals such as *Business and Society*, *Journal of Business Ethics* and *Journal of Cleaner Production*.

Hanna Geyerlechner, MA, is quality manager at Salesianer Miettex GmbH, Austria. She previously worked in the customer service area for a firm that offers textile supply services in the healthcare industry. In this position, she dealt with service processes and related supply systems. She focused on the achievement of transparency in relation to the life cycle of textiles with embedded RFID technologies. She also managed internal processes improvement and effectiveness, and the identification of optimization measures across the entire value creation chain. She graduated in Process Management and Services of General Interest with a focus on Quality Management in the Services Sector at the University of Applied Sciences Upper Austria.

Erik G. Hansen is a full professor and head of the Institute of Integrated Quality Design (IQD) at the Johannes Kepler University (JKU) Linz, Austria. He is also a visiting researcher at the Centre for Sustainability Management (CSM), Leuphana University of Lüneburg, Germany. His research focuses on the management of circular, green-tech, and sustainability-oriented innovations at the level of products, product-service systems, business models, as well as management systems in support of these processes. He was appointed by acatech (Germany's National Academy of Science and Engineering) as scientific head of the Working Group on Circular Business Models and Digital Technologies and is a member of the editorial board of Business Strategy and the Environment.

Boukje Huijben, PhD, is an assistant professor at the Innovation, Technology Entrepreneurship and Marketing (ITEM) group of Eindhoven University of Technology, the Netherlands. Her research focuses on sustainable business model innovation in companies, preferably by working directly together with them to support their sustainability strategy making process.

Janne Huiskonen, D.Sc. (Tech), is Professor of Supply Chain Management in the School of Engineering Science at LUT University. His research focuses on sustainable business models and operations management in supply chains, networks, and service systems. He has published over 60 articles in scientific conferences and journals.

Nina Kinnunen, M.Sc. (Political science), is Sustainability, Brand and Communications Director at Kekkilä-BVB, which is the leading horticultural substrate company in Europe. She is responsible for sustainability, brand, and communications strategies. She has over five years' experience at Kekkilä Group. Formerly she worked almost ten years at K

Group, which is a Finnish trading sector pioneer operating in the grocery trade, the building and technical trade, and the car trade.

Maren Ingrid Kropfeld is a PhD candidate in the field of ecological economy at the University of Oldenburg, Germany. She holds a PhD scholarship by the German Academic Scholarship Foundation and works as a freelance lecturer at Karlshochschule International University in Karlsruhe. Before her PhD studies, she worked in the energy efficiency service sector and as coordinator for Research and Teaching at the Karlsruhe University of Applied Sciences. Her research focus is on sufficiency-oriented business models and consumer practices, where she discusses how business models change with a sufficiency orientation and how they can support consumers in living more sustainably. www.mareningrid.wordpress.com.

Minttu Laukkanen, D.Sc. (Tech), is a post-doctoral researcher in the School of Business and Management at LUT University. She defended her dissertation focusing on sustainable business models to advance system-level sustainability at the end of 2019. She is interested in finding ways to achieve sustainable business at the company level as well as how companies can act as agents within broader sustainability transformation. Further, she is interested in understanding how to recognize new sustainable business opportunities for companies and to build competitiveness through sustainable business models.

Florian Lüdeke-Freund is Professor of Corporate Sustainability and director of the MSc Sustainability Entrepreneurship & Innovation, at ESCP Business School, Berlin. He serves on the editorial boards of different journals, and he has authored or edited four books, including *Sustainable Business Model Design.* Florian founded the international research hub www.SustainableBusinessModel.org.

Kaisa Manninen, M.Sc. (Tech), is a junior researcher and PhD candidate in the School of Engineering Science at LUT University. She has a background in environmental technology and her current research interest focuses on sustainable business models, especially sustainable value creation. She aims to increase understanding of how companies can take conscious steps toward being sustainable and how companies can develop their business models to advance sustainability.

Ruth Mourik, PhD, holds a degree in Science, Society and Technology studies and in Anthropology. She is the CEO of Duneworks, a private research company located in Eindhoven, the Netherlands. She performs research and training activities with the aim to accelerate sustainable transitions and actual implementation and up-scaling of sustainable solutions. She does so by means of a transformative approach, with a strong focus on the end users.

Alexandra Palzkill is Junior Professor of Economics and Management, Transformation Research and Sustainability at the University of Wuppertal, Germany. She is co-leader of the junior research group 'UrbanUp' (Upscaling Strategies for an Urban Sharing Society) at the Center for Transformation Research and Sustainability (tranzent). Her research focuses are sustainable business models in urban sustainability transitions and alternative ways of doing business. She was a doctoral research fellow at the Wuppertal Institute (PhD thesis on 'Business Model Resilience') and studied Economics and Sociology at the University of Göttingen, Germany.

Brett John Mathew Petzer took degrees in Political Science and French (Rhodes University, 2007) and Architecture (University of Cape Town, 2011) before orienting himself toward an interest in the politics of urban planning, and particularly, urban mobility. This led him to a Masters in Urban and Regional Planning at the University of Cape Town in 2016. His dissertation sought to explore the tension between the cycling environment as captured in evaluation and planning guidelines, and in the experiences of users. In 2017, he started his PhD candidature as part of the Eindhoven University of Technology's Bicycle Challenges group, where his focus is on the role of cycling-based mobility systems (such as bikeshare) in the urban mobility transition of the Netherlands.

Julia Planko is Professor of Sustainable and Circular Business at University of Applied Sciences Leiden. Her research interest is on how businesses can contribute to sustainable development and to circular economy transitions, specifically how businesses collaborate in networks to build innovation ecosystems that bring about sustainability transitions. She has worked on applied research projects related to positive energy districts, sustainable textiles, circular building materials, circular urban spaces, e-charging poles for LEVs, bio-plastic packaging, and reduction of microplastics. She holds a PhD in innovation studies from the Copernicus Institute of Sustainable Development, Utrecht University.

Marcos Queiroz is an entrepreneur who promotes slow fashion practices stimulating sustainable production and consumption to avoid textiles waste. He develops solution based in co-creation processes.

André Reichel is Professor of International Management and Sustainability at the International School of Management (ISM), Germany. He has a university degree in management and a doctoral degree in economics and social sciences from Universität Stuttgart, Germany. Before his tenure at ISM he was Professor of Critical Management & Sustainable Development at Karlshochschule International University, research fellow at Zeppelin University and guest lecturer at the Environmental Change Institute at University of Oxford. Additionally, he serves as honorary director of elobau foundation in Leutkirch, Germany, and chairman of the supervisory board of Wirtschaftsförderung Region Stuttgart (Stuttgart Region Economic Development Corporation). His research focuses on sustainability and digital business, notions of postgrowth and degrowth from a business and civil society perspective, as well as building a new management theory based on the 'Laws of Form' by George Spencer Brown. www.andre-reichel.de.

Pascale Schwab Castella is a senior researcher in the industrial ecology group. Her research focuses on (i) the use of life cycle assessment and greenhouse gas accounting in prospective environmental planning projects, and (ii) the links between industrial and natural ecosystems.

Bram van Helvoirt is a lecturer-researcher at HAS and combines his expertise in international development studies (at Utrecht University) with his professional experience with sustainable agri-food business development in developing countries (Ministry of Foreign Affairs of the Netherlands).

Geert Verbong is a full professor and chair of System Innovations & Sustainability Transitions in the section of Technology Innovation & Society at Eindhoven University of Technology (TU/e). His areas of expertise include the history of technology, renewable energy technologies, power generation, energy, photovoltaics, distributed generation and grids. Geert's research focuses on the introduction of renewable energy technologies and the future of energy systems.

Peter Wells is Professor of Business and Sustainability and director of the Centre for Automotive Industry Research, at Cardiff Business School. He is author or editor of 11 books and is frequently quoted in *The New York Times*, *Forbes*, *Bloomberg*, *the BBC*, and other international news sources.

Jos Wesselink has worked at HAS University as a lecturer-researcher teaching about the role of animal husbandry in the global food system and guided transition-oriented dialogues in various courses. He is also one of the founding persons of the International Food and Agribusiness programme at HAS University.

Anna Wieczorek is a sustainability transition scholar with over 20 years' international experience in socio-technical system innovation, governance, and sustainable development and innovation. Within the geographical scope of Europe and the Global South and the empirical domains of smart energy, smart mobility and urban transitions, her work seeks to unpack upscaling, experimentation by communities, co-creation and new business and market models (e.g. P2P) and institutional arrangements. Using the field of transitions as a springboard for transdisciplinary collaboration aimed at real-world interventions, Wieczorek is involved in a number of major projects alongside work as guest speaker, guest editor, reviewer and an associate editor of the journal *Urban Transformations*. She is project leader of a € 7.1 M Interreg NWE project on community-based Virtual Power Plant (cVPP) as well as lead on an NWO-funded ORAKLE project on organizing learning and knowledge for the energy transition in the Dutch province of North Brabant.

Jodi C. York is a sociologist with a diverse interdisciplinary work history focused on how narrative and non-financial information are used to create and constrain progressive social and environmental change by capital providers, enterprises, government and civil society. She has published qualitative and quantitative research in sociology, economics, accounting, and management. Her focus is on social impact by enterprises and capital providers—how to fund it, how to create it, how to measure and report it, and how to leverage sustainable business models and networks to multiply it.

Ruud Zanders is a Dutch poultry entrepreneur. He is one of the four founders of Kipster, his third poultry business. Before Kipster, he was Professor of Healthy Poultry Farming at Aeres University of Applied Sciences Dronten, The Netherlands.

List of Figures

Sustainable Value Creation for Advancing Sustainability Transition: An Approach to Integrate Company- and System-level Sustainability

Building BOP Business Models for Sustainable Poverty Alleviation: System Tips and System Traps

The Business Model of Enough: Value Creation for Sufficiency-Oriented Businesses

Collaborative Business Models and Platforms in Shared Mobility Transitions: The Case of Bikeshare Integration

List of Tables

The Business Model of Enough: Value Creation for Sufficiency-Oriented Businesses

Collaborative Business Models and Platforms in Shared Mobility Transitions: The Case of Bikeshare Integration

Upscaling Sustainable Niches: How a User Perspective of Organizational Value Logics Can Help Translate Between Niche and System

IoT-Driven Reuse Business Models: The Case of Salesianer Textile Rental Services

Business Models for Smart Sustainability: A Critical Perspective on Smart Homes and Sustainability Transitions

Business Models for Energy Efficiency Services: Four Archetypes Based on User-Centeredness and Dynamic Capabilities

Reverse Logistics Process for Business Transitions: An Example from the Clothing Industry

Introduction to Business Models for Sustainability Transitions

Annabeth Aagaard, Florian Lüdeke-Freund, and Peter Wells

1 Why a Book on Business Models for Sustainability Transitions?

The prevalent literature on sustainability transitions has primarily been concerned with the long-term transformation towards sustainability of socio-technical systems of provision (e.g., transportation, water, and electricity supply) with the aim to satisfy basic human needs (e.g., food, heating, access to water) (Smith et al., 2010). A related strand of research has

---

A. Aagaard (✉)
Business Development & Technology, Aarhus University, Herning, Denmark
e-mail: aaa@btech.au.dk

F. Lüdeke-Freund
European Sustainability Department, ESCP Business School, Berlin, Germany
e-mail: fluedeke-freund@escp.eu

P. Wells
Cardiff Business School, Cardiff University, Cardiff, UK
e-mail: wellspe@cardiff.ac.uk

A. Aagaard et al. (eds.), *Business Models for Sustainability Transitions*,
https://doi.org/10.1007/978-3-030-77580-3_1

focused on the role of business models for sustainability, but with a strong emphasis on short-term and firm-level development and implementation of new business models in creating value through sustainable business models (e.g., Boons & Lüdeke-Freund, 2013). Recent years have witnessed a growing interest in exploring how these two research strands might be combined to offer new insights into how business model innovation may act as a catalyst for system-wide sustainability transitions (Bolton & Hannon, 2016; Foxon et al., 2015; Hannon, 2012; Hannon et al., 2013; Loorbach et al., 2010; Wells, 2013).

Thus, this book brings together in one volume the two streams of research that have hitherto been largely separate: sustainability transitions and business models for sustainability. These two realms of research and, increasingly, policy have their conceptual and epistemological roots in distinct and diverse traditions. Yet, there is scope for each tradition to learn from the other. This book therefore seeks a benign and mutually beneficial confluence of ideas, thereby contributing in an exploratory manner both to accelerated sustainable transitions and to flourishing business models for sustainability. The search for contributions to this book was guided by the question whether *business models and business model innovation can contribute to sustainability transitions*, that is, fundamental change at a societal level, and whether *change at the societal level can in turn contribute to the emergence of fundamentally different business models*. This book is meant to offer exemplary studies of *transformational and transformed business models*, which we simply call 'business models for sustainability transitions'. In contrast, business models may be contributory to transition failure (Turnheim & Sovacool, 2020), while influences from societal and system levels may inhibit more sustainable business models (Bidmon & Knab, 2018). Furthermore, the roles and behaviours of customers and users in collaborative value co-creation of sustainable business model innovation (Aagaard & Ritzén, 2019) are also critical to sustainability transitions in practice. However, as this book incorporates a business focus and emphasises 'successful' sustainability transitions, these aspects are beyond the scope of this book. However, they all point to important avenues for future research.

Sustainability transitions, understood as '… fundamental changes in socio-technical systems … to address grand challenges in a way that meets the needs of the present without compromising the ability of future generations to meet their own needs (Markard et al., 2020, p. 1)', are an increasingly important concern for policy-makers, business, and wider society. Today, humanity uses the equivalent of 1.7 Earths to provide the resources we use and to absorb our waste. This implies that it takes Planet Earth more than one year and eight months to regenerate what we use in just one year. Current resource use is only possible because of the continued depletion of finite stocks and biocapacity. Thus, continuing the current population and consumption trends will require the equivalent of two Earths by the 2030s (Global Footprint Network, 2020). There are multiple indicators of planetary system stress in which boundaries are being exceeded (Stoknes & Rockström, 2018). Governmental policy interventions together with the adoption of sustainability strategies by corporations and recurring wake-up calls for more sustainable consumption led to some improvements in terms of eco-efficiency gains and socio-economic progress, at least in some parts of the world. However, these improvements are constantly overwhelmed by population growth coupled with increased material prosperity, again, in some parts of the world.

Sustainability transitions are characterised by fundamental changes in the man-made systems of production and consumption (e.g., the socio-technical system of energy provision), an orientation towards grand sustainability challenges (e.g., climate change), and—typically in hindsight—radical innovations and the emergence of struggles within existing paradigms and system characteristics (Markard et al., 2020). Those fundamental innovations include, for example, novel technologies (e.g., solar energy), business models (e.g., product-service systems), and changes in social practices (e.g., sharing instead of owning), which implies that business has a role to play in sustainability transitions. It is just one force among many which make up today's socio-technical systems, yet it is a critical one. The way business is done has a fundamental influence on how goods and services are produced and consumed. Business also influences other system elements, including lifestyles, how the environment and other living species are treated, how policies are made, and so on. Hence, there are good reasons to dedicate a book to the question how business activities—here, mainly seen through a business model lens—relate to sustainability transitions, and vice versa. How business models can drive and inhibit sustainability transitions, and how, in turn, sustainability transitions can drive and inhibit new business models. In fact, various authors, at least implicitly, call for more research at the intersections of business model and sustainability transitions studies (e.g., Bidmon & Knab, 2018; Boons et al., 2013; Köhler et al., 2019; Markard et al., 2020).

2 Business Model for Sustainability Perspective

Over the recent decades, research on business models and business model innovation has received substantial attention from both academics and practitioners (e.g., Massa et al., 2017; Wirtz, Pistoia, et al., 2016; Zott et al., 2011). Taking a business model perspective offers holistic and systemic insights into how value is created, proposed, delivered, and captured by organisations (Massa et al., 2018; Teece, 2010), which, depending on the underlying theory or framework, includes strategy models, market models, or network and value chain models (Wirtz, Pistoia, et al., 2016). Acknowledging the fact that organisations are per se complex systems, respectively, systems of (sub-)systems, Massa et al. (2018) argue that a business model is 'a system level concept… centered on activities… spanning the boundaries of a focal organisation to include exchanges with a network of partners …, and overall trying to describe how that organisation functions in achieving its goals (p. 60)'.

This systems perspective invites looking beyond single organisations and considering their embeddedness in value chains, stakeholder networks, and inter-organisational collaboration. In other words, it invites going beyond the micro-level of single organisations into spheres of more complex social phenomena at meso- and macro-levels (cf. Starik et al., 2016). This offers various innovation opportunities, including new business infrastructures, customer offerings, and ways of connecting to stakeholders (Foss & Saebi, 2017; Lüdeke-Freund et al., 2018; Remane et al., 2017; Wirtz, Göttel, & Daiser, 2016), which can have effects far beyond a single organisation. Hence, it is reasonable to assume that business models and business model innovation offer promising pathways for incumbents and new entrants to develop and introduce more sustainable ways of doing business and, in the best case, create positive effects for the natural and social systems surrounding them (Aagaard, 2019; Lüdeke-Freund et al., 2020; Schaltegger, Lüdeke-Freund, & Hansen, 2016; Wells, 2013), and hence contribute to sustainability transitions.

Although growing circles in academia and business as well as at the political and societal levels are discussing sustainability (Dryzek, 2005), its influence on the ways that production and consumption are organised is still rather weak (Bansal, 2005; Schaltegger, Hansen, & Lüdeke-Freund, 2016; Stubbs & Cocklin, 2008). There are motivating success stories such as a growing number of green and social start-ups, the sustainable business model transformations of incumbents (e.g., US carpet manufacturer Interface), and even paradigm shifts in whole industries (e.g., Germany's exit from using nuclear power). However, there are also overwhelming indications that the 'greening of industry' and the proliferation of corporate social responsibility have failed to deliver substantial and enduring sustainability benefits.

The new quest for business models for sustainability transitions can be seen as a reaction to these (indeed dissatisfying) developments, which call for fundamental change at all levels and increasing transformation dynamics to leave business-as-usual behind (Markard et al., 2020). This quest integrates two dynamically growing, yet hardly connected, research fields: on the one hand research on responsible, inclusive, and circular business models, more broadly speaking business models for sustainability (e.g., Aagaard, 2019; Boons & Lüdeke-Freund, 2013; Lüdeke-Freund & Dembek, 2017; Wells, 2013), and on the other hand research on socio-technical and sustainability transitions (e.g., Geels, 2005; Geels et al., 2016; Grin et al., 2010; Köhler et al., 2019; Markard et al., 2020; Sovacool et al., 2020). Making both research communities talk to each other was also part of the motivation for this book. Maybe the most important part.

3 Sustainability Transitions Perspective

The grand sustainability challenges we encounter are global, multi-dimensional, multi-actor, and systemic in nature. Therefore, to achieve global long-term sustainability goals, the core systems of our societies will have to change dramatically (EEA, 2019). Our assumption is that business models for sustainability transitions have the potential to contribute to this transformation of economy and society. First, by enabling change within business operations, practices, and strategies (*transformed* business models), and second, by new ways for business to interact with markets, supply chains, policy-making, regulation, consumers, and many more (*transformational* business models). The latter speaks to the core issue of sustainability transitions studies, defined as 'long-term, multi-dimensional, and fundamental transformation processes through which established socio-technical systems shift to more sustainable modes of production and consumption' (Markard et al., 2012, p. 956).

In theories of socio-technical transition, an important question is that of how socio-technical systems change. That is, transitions are changes from one socio-technical regime to another, respectively, from one dynamic equilibrium to another. Subsidiary questions then revolve around the cause of the 'failure' of existing regimes, and of the emergence to dominance of new regimes. In this case, socio-technical transitions are conceptualised as the status of regimes in socio-technical systems that emerge as a result of the interrelationship of two modes: change and stability. This theoretical framing developed out of systems theory, evolutionary economics, and innovation studies. In consequence, Geels and Schot (2007) developed the concept of transition pathways, as a typology of ideal types, to describe pathways as more or less coherent sequences of change events over time. Constituent elements of a socio-technical regime exhibit a co-evolutionary dynamic that may alter under conditions of change along these pathways (Berkhout et al., 2004; Geels, 2005). The 'ideal types' identified by Geels and Schot (2007) comprise the following categories:

1. Reproduction in which the regime is said to be dynamically stable, changing but not so far as to disrupt the socio-technical system as a whole.

2. Transformation under which moderate external pressures for change may lead to modifications of development pathways and enhanced levels of innovation.
3. De-alignment and re-alignment in which large-scale and rapid changes in external pressures can undermine an existing regime (causing 'de-alignment') and, in the absence of a candidate nascent set of niche practices, can create the space for re-alignment.
4. Technological substitution. Under this pathway a pre-existing niche can rapidly flourish when there are large-scale and rapid changes in external pressures.
5. Reconfiguration. Here the established regime at the heart of the socio-technical system may seek to capture symbiotic innovations and thereby adjust the regime to changed circumstances without being destabilised.

Importantly, transition pathways are not regarded as simply conforming to these ideal types, particularly as regime transitions are considered to be highly contextualised and contested with uncertain outcomes. Contestation is played out within and between all the regime constituents (both incumbent and emergent). Pathways of change thus emerge out of market interactions (supply and demand, price signals, organisational competition) including of course businesses. However, transition is also an emergent property of technological innovation; regulation and governance; behavioural, cultural, and attitudinal norms; environmental imperatives; and political contestation. In consequence, the pathways or sequences are less coherent in practice than the ideal types suggest.

4 Business Model Innovation and Sustainability Transitions

As Sovacool et al. (2020, p. 7) note in their wide-ranging review, which referenced 447 publications from science and technology studies (STS): 'Research of whole system transition, however, requires a broader approach that simultaneously analyses multiple niche-innovations (including business model and social innovations)'. The diffusion of innovations is thus considered a process of societal embedding (Geels & Johnson, 2018) of which business strategies are a part. Business actors may perceive that technological innovations offer a new set of ways to define and then realise expectations. Yet complementary roles of business models may impact transition dynamics in multiple ways as stressed by Bidmon and Knab (2018): (1) As part of the socio-technical regime, existing business models hamper transitions by reinforcing the current regime's stability; (2) as intermediates between the technological niche and the socio-technical regime, business models drive transitions by facilitating the stabilisation process of technological innovation and supporting their breakthrough; and (3) as non-technological niche innovation, novel business models drive transitions by building up a substantial part of a new regime without relying on technological innovation.

It is probable that sustainability transitions theorisation such as that offered by Sovacool et al. (2020) underplays the power of corporate actors, who are often more than mere expendable niche experimenters. Businesses are, after all, the predominant mode of resource allocation in capitalist society, having privileged access to government, finance, and other key resources that need to be mobilised to enact societal change. The authors, considering the broader field of studies of technology and society with respect to energy, conclude that: The STS community needs to also reach beyond academic research as a whole to engage with other key stakeholders, ranging from business firms and governmental organisations to user groups, trade unions, and marginalised populations (ibid., p. 27).

Neither is business a monolithic single vested interest, and the outcomes sought by business may not be realised. Firms may fail to capture the benefits of their own innovations, for instance (Teece, 2006). Equally, changes in the regulatory framing of, for example, electricity generation and supply in many countries were largely undertaken to 'liberalise' the energy market, break up state monopolies, and reduce costs to consumers. One consequence, however, has been to open the space for alternative technology suppliers with innovative market propositions and business models.

Each individual moment of business model innovation is one tiny data point in the grand history of socio-technical transition, a bit of 'noise' in the signal. However, each moment of business model innovation is also potentially contributory to a transition pathway or, alternatively, to continuing inertia enabling incumbents to resist change (Wells & Nieuwenhuis, 2012). From a transitions perspective, it could be argued that transitions pathways help to create the 'space' for innovative business models. This space can be understood as the consequence of disruptive technological innovations that enable business model innovation, or as shifts in regulatory, governance, and market opportunities that then become accessible via business model innovation (Bolton & Hannon, 2016). Hence, transitions processes may underwrite business model innovation, and simultaneously be a product of that innovation, by virtue of the business model design space that they enable (Huijben et al., 2016; Wesseling et al., 2020). Considering the above discussed characteristic of business models as complex systems of (sub-)systems—which can interrelate in various ways with other business models, organisations, stakeholders, and further system elements—makes us realise that identifying, studying, and understanding how business model innovation, sustainability, and socio-technical transitions interrelate is anything but trivial.

It is a task of some urgency, therefore, to engage in research that helps in understanding whether and how business model innovation for sustainability is also contributory to the societal challenge of achieving sustainability transitions. A fundamentalist perspective is to see the entire episode of capitalist market expansion over more than 200 years as one 'deep' transition (Schot & Kanger, 2018). In this view, it is unlikely that business organisations embedded in neo-liberal market economies can possibly also be participants in the end state of a transition to a sustainable economy and society. However, it is possible that even if such a post-capitalist world was to emerge, business organisation transformations might still be a constituent part of the mechanisms by which that end state is achieved. Rare examples, such as the business experiment going on at Welsh car designer Riversimple, offer insights into how businesses can help to 'change the system from within.' In the case of Riversimple, this is attempted by combining an eco-designed product with a business model that promotes using instead of owning cars and that is governed by a radically stakeholder-inclusive system of stewards and management board (Wells, 2016).

Key to understanding the contribution of business model innovation then becomes an understanding of context within specific domains of production and consumption relations, as these are key to determining the design space available to business model innovation (Huijben et al., 2016; Wesseling et al., 2020). Extant research into business model innovation for sustainability has tended to emphasise the significance of issues beyond the narrow boundary of the firm, compared with neo-classical economic treatments (a pioneering and still up-to-date paper in this regard is Stubbs & Cocklin, 2008). This 'beyond the boundaries' understanding of the firm also extends to a 'beyond profit' understanding of the business logic. Hence the location of the firm in this sense is within a constellation of related participants, interest groups, and social actors that rather reflects the characterisation of a regime in socio-technical transitions—albeit on a micro scale. Here, again, the 'system of (sub-) system' characteristic of business models, which is typically neglected in business model studies, but can be very useful in combination with a sustainability transitions perspective, comes to the fore (Massa et al., 2018). There are intersections with concepts such as business networks, business ecosystems, extended producer responsibility, circular economies, and others. There is an almost fractal quality to the respective theorisations, even though the temporal and societal scales are widely different, and even though the epistemological foundations of the respective schools of thought are also widely distanced. Indeed, it is evident that many individual actors within business organisations have a distinct social vision of the alternative, more sustainable, future they are seeking to create.

The theoretical and empirical opportunity therefore is to envisage business model innovation for sustainability and sustainability transitions as two ends of a continuum in which there are multiple possible intermediary concepts that act to bridge between these extremes. From a business model innovation for sustainability perspective, those concepts might include aspects of boundary crossing or redefinition that relate to the business ecosystem, actor networks, supply chains, and other constellations of corporate activity that are greater than one individual business. From a sustainability transitions perspective, intermediate or related macro-societal and political economy concepts might include degrowth, the circular economy, deep transitions, or green growth.

The following 'spiral' analogy is a first conceptual attempt to illustrate the continuum between micro-level considerations and phenomena related to business models and business model innovation and meso- and macro-level issues of sustainability transitions.

5 The 'Spiral' of Business Models for Sustainability Transitions

The 'spiral' was motivated by several observations made while reviewing and discussing the chapters in this book as well as our reading of the current literature on business models for sustainability and sustainability transitions. These observations include the following:

- Authors typically struggle to consider, conceptualise, and investigate micro-, meso-, and macro-level phenomena simultaneously with sufficient depth and grounding in the respective bodies of literature. This may be due to the 'natural' limitations of their respective disciplinary backgrounds, including the epistemologies and ontologies they typically apply.
- The resulting studies are either weak in terms of business model theory and analysis, which is an admittedly very heterogeneous field, or they show weaknesses in terms of how they connect to major assumptions and insights from the field of sustainability transition studies, which is no less and maybe even more heterogeneous.
- The preceding two points lead to an interesting observation: Many authors tend to turn their attention to meso-level phenomena, including inter-organisational phenomena such as networks and collaboration, multi-stakeholder issues, or other phenomena that provide insights about how organisations connect to and interact with their environments.
- While contributing new approaches to the study of meso-level phenomena and of what is going on between organisations and their socio-technical environment, understanding business models for sustainability transitions requires embracing the duality of system structures and patterns of action—or, in other words, the boundary

conditions shaping business activities and how business is trying to influence and change these boundary conditions.
- Time is crucial in studying transitions. However, time is hardly considered. Influential transition studies typically take a historical point of view and *re*construct transitions, their causes, dynamics, and their consequences. But sustainability transition studies are to a large extent looking into the future, hence showing a tendency of *pre*constructing a sustainable future. Time must be considered in relation to the phenomena under investigation, but also in terms of its methodical, epistemological, and ontological consequences.
- Further, business model innovation is characteristically short term, while socio-technical transitions permeate society over decades, and yet the temporal dynamics must intersect.

The following 'spiral' framework includes several theoretical assumptions and conceptual components that, as we think, are important to consider when studying business models for sustainability transitions, that is, transformational and transformed business models. It is meant to be an initial framework responding to the aforementioned observations (Fig. 1).

The spiral represents how the scope, or sphere of influence, of business activities extends over time. It begins with a rather narrow focus on an existing or new business model, which is connected to networks, collaborating partners, and other meso-level entities. Finally, its influence (e.g., new ways of producing and consuming) reaches the system level. This is, of course, a theoretical ideal. Although companies may aim to come up with influential business models for sustainability transitions, their influence may be very limited, or even negative in the case of unintended consequences.

The duality of (current and anticipated) system structures and (current and planned) patterns of action requires considering the boundary conditions under which companies develop and implement their business models (e.g., current and anticipated regulations, consumption trends) and at the same time the business models themselves. The latter may be

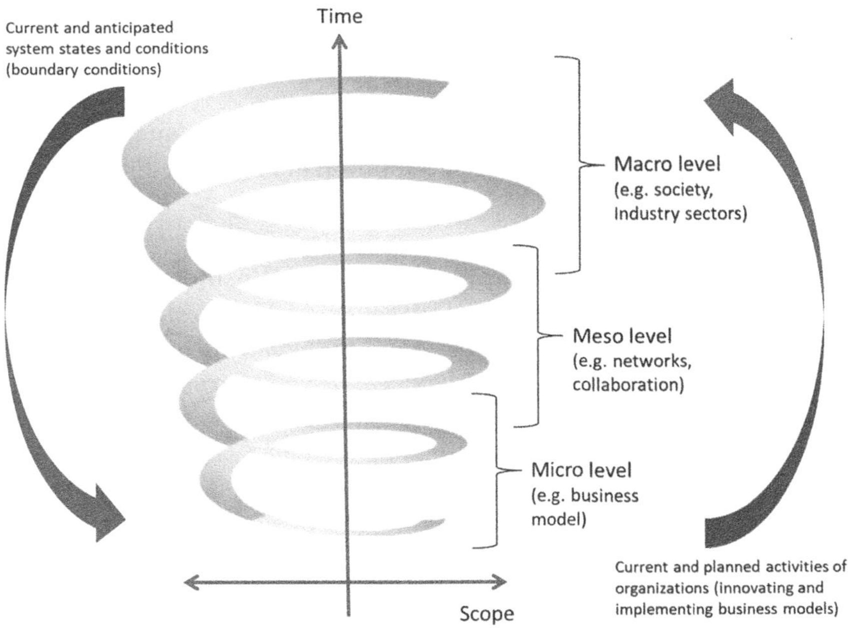

Fig. 1 The 'spiral'—Framework connecting business models to sustainability transitions

developed to both adapt to current boundary conditions and to try to influence and change these, which reminds of the different transition pathways defined by Geels and Schot (2007) discussed above.

While the spiral framework motivates thinking systematically about the scope of a transition phenomenon across time, as well as the dynamics between boundary conditions and business models, it also provides a structure in terms of micro-level phenomena and those to be located at meso and macro levels. This can help in providing clarity when it comes to studying phenomena on different levels simultaneously. Appropriate theories and methods of investigation can be systematically selected to fit with the respective framework elements and their interrelations.

6 Themes and Chapters Contained in This Book

In the following, the main themes and contributions contained in this book will be introduced and, where appropriate, connected to the spiral framework.

Part I: Crossing the Chasm: Integrating Business Model and Sustainability Transition Perspectives *Part I presents new frameworks that integrate micro-, meso-, and macro-level concepts and phenomena. New perspectives are offered that allow considering current and anticipated system states and conditions (boundary conditions such as given industrial practices) while at the same time using a business model perspective to discuss current and planned activities of organisations that are both transformative and transformed.*

Transformative Business and Sustainability Transitions: A Framework and an Empirical Illustration *by PJ Beers, Marjo Baeten, Erwin Bouwmans, Bram van Helvoirt, Jos Wesselink, Ruud Zanders* New business models have been widely touted for their promise of sustainability. However, conceptual approaches to new business models largely fail to connect to sustainability transitions. In this contribution, we draw upon sustainability transitions research to introduce a transformative business model framework. Given the radically incremental nature of sustainability transitions, we propose that the radicalism and potential of new business models should be assessed in relation to their capacity to influence wider institutional settings and to the transition to which they belong. We report on an exploratory study of six transformative business cases in the context of the Dutch agri-food transition. Our results suggest that, in order to be transformative, businesses need to co-evolve with specific wider institutional, discursive, practical, and relational developments.

The Networked Business Model for Systems Change: Integrating a Systems Perspective in Business Model Development for Sustainability Transitions *by Julia Planko, Jacqueline Cramer* To realise sustainability transitions, firms need to collaborate in networks and carry out system-changing activities. In this way, they pro-actively build a more sustainable system and change the environment in which they operate. This in turn will help them to market their own sustainable product or service. Partners in a network can co-develop a 'networked business model', which takes on a systemic perspective and helps them to align their sustainability efforts. This latter model comprises transition goals, system building activities, system resources, benefits created for stakeholders, and costs to the network. The networked business model feeds into each network member's individual firm-centric business model and vice versa. The business models at the firm level and the system level are interconnected and mutually influence one another.

Sustainable Value Creation for Advancing Sustainability Transition: An Approach to Integrate Company- and System-Level Sustainability *by Minttu Laukkanen, Kaisa Manninen, Janne Huiskonen, Nina Kinnunen* While a sustainable business model is recognized as providing a link between an individual company and the larger socio-technical system to which it belongs and as leveraging wider sustainability transition, relatively little integration between business and management research and system transition research has been done to explore how companies enable wider sustainability transition through their business models. Based on a review of the prior literature on sustainable business models and sustainability transition and a single in-depth case study, this study proposes sustainable value creation, which is a central part of any sustainable business model, as an approach to integrate company-level sustainability into broader system-level sustainability transition. This study contributes to the literature by describing how companies make their business sustainable, leverage wider sustainability transition, and advance system-level sustainability through sustainable value creation. For managers, this study offers five key recommendations, which highlight the most crucial points to be considered for adopting a sustainable value creation approach.

Building BOP Business Models for Sustainable Poverty Alleviation: System Tips and System Traps *by Jodi C. York, Krzysztof Dembek* Sustainable development requires both long-term and large-scale changes to production and consumption patterns and the eradication of extreme poverty. In this study, we argue that pursuing these goals independently can result in business models that tie poverty alleviation to increased environmental degradation, and thus work at cross purposes to sustainability transition. We explore how three types of business models for addressing poverty at the bottom of the pyramid (BOP)—delivering, sourcing, and reorganising models—can either impede or support sustainability transition in the global south by enacting different business model roles. We use examples from 17 business models from Indonesia and the Philippines to explore the sustainability misalignment risks each model type is prone to and distil key business model design features and enablers that support their alignment with sustainability transition by enabling them to avoid common system traps.

Part II: Beyond Business-as-Usual: Alternative Value Creation Logics Driving Sustainability Transitions *Sufficiency, sharing, and non-commercial approaches to creating value for stakeholders are discussed in Part II. The business model perspective offers a micro-level lens that helps in understanding the niche dynamics of these approaches and how actors try to change industries and society. Their potential to influence meso-level constellations (such as inter-organisational cooperation and networks) and even macro-level structures (*e.g., *consumption trends) is discussed.*

The Business Model of Enough: Value Creation for Sufficiency-Oriented Businesses *by Maren Ingrid Kropfeld, André Reichel* In this chapter we conceptualize a generic business model for a transition toward a sustainable economy and society as an ideal-type by (a) focusing on sufficiency in order to highlight a more radical perspective on sustainability transformations in line with the notion of strong sustainability, and its implications for changing business models and the environment of business, as well as (b) undertaking a reconstruction of the business model concept from the viewpoint of social practice theory, which will give us a much clearer theoretical framework to infer connections between business and consumer practices. We show how such a 'Business Model of Enough' can constitute the core for communities of sufficiency practice, thus enabling institutional change within the political-economic background of business, and we discuss which role sufficiency-based business models and consumers play in transition pathways, for example, by introducing and supporting boundary spanning practices and including the perspective of fundamental transformations in everyday consumer practices.

Collaborative Business Models and Platforms in Shared Mobility Transitions: The Case of Bikeshare Integration *by Brett John Mathew Petzer, Anna Wieczorek, Geert Verbong* Collaboration between organizations plays an increasingly fundamental role in a growing number of sectors, including Mobility-as-a-Service (MaaS), and has given rise to the Collaborative Business Model (CBM). A review of literature on CBMs provides an overview of CBM interpretations, and finds that tensions between collaboration and competition, and those related to the commons, are major emerging tensions. A further review of MaaS business model literature, and a case study of three platforms attempting to deliver bikeshare-inclusive MaaS, focuses on these tensions. The means by which common resources are made available to MaaS CBMs is found to be a significant determinant of how far these CBMs depart from conventional business model logic and morphology, in part because they determine the leverage that city governments can bring to bear on MaaS CBMs.

Upscaling Sustainable Niches: How a User Perspective of Organisational Value Logics Can Help Translate Between Niche and System *by Alexandra Palzkill, Karoline Augenstein* A great variety of business organisations, environmentally or socially motivated entrepreneurs, aim to contribute to the development of more sustainable societies. A key question is how these organisations can move beyond isolated, protected niches and increase their impact on the mainstream without compromising their sustainability-oriented core mission and values? In this chapter, this question is approached by focusing on the organisational value logics of sustainability-oriented entrepreneurs and how these are related to, translated, and defended against dominant regimes built around market and commercial logics. It will discuss how a user perspective of organisational value logics can shed light on the process of niche-regime interaction and the upscaling potential of sustainable niches or provide a way to manage different logics using an outside-in-perspective. This chapter presents a case study of a civil society initiative's entrepreneurial activities and reflects on the question of how organisations can contribute to sustainability transitions while confronted with different and often fundamentally incompatible niche and regime logics.

Part III: Being the Change: Transformative and Transformed Business Models in Selected Industries *The chapters contained in Part III present exemplary cases in industries such as textile services, clothing, energy services, and smart technologies for buildings. While new technologies are important drivers for change, boundary conditions such as regulation, stakeholder expectations, social acceptance, and also the limits of technology itself are critical drivers and barriers. The case studies presented in Part III provide insightful and fresh examples of how organisations try to be the change and to extend the scope and effects of their transformative and transformed business models.*

IoT-Driven Reuse Business Models: The Case of Salesianer Textile Rental Services *by Andres Alcayaga, Hanna Geyerlechner, Erik G. Hansen* Service business models such as rental, leasing, and performance contracting can contribute to a circular economy by keeping products, components, and materials longer in use and thereby preserving their value over time. These business models are, however, subject to higher complexity and information demand. Smart products and the Internet of Things facilitate the optimisation of such closed-loop value creation processes. We present an in-depth case study of a textile rental firm, in the business-to-business domain, that has recently become a front-runner in using textiles equipped with RFID chips. The firm has used smart textiles to improve the transparency of the product life cycle, raise awareness on textile losses, and improve procurement decisions. We show that combining smart textiles with a rental business model could accelerate the transition towards circularity and sustainability.

Business Models for Smart Sustainability: A Critical Perspective on Smart Homes and Sustainability Transitions *by Lara Anne Blasberg* This chapter examines the sustainability of smart technologies in the housing segment of the building sector critical perspective. It considers the prerequisites for digital technologies, business models, and user practices to support a sustainable trajectory of the housing segment. This research adopts socio-technical and practice-based perspectives to investigate the interrelated dynamics of individuals, organisations, and institutions for sustainable socio-technical transitions. It is based on an organisational ethnography of the VELUX Group and the Active House Alliance, as well as interviews across the building industry, centring on two demonstration projects in Brussels, Belgium, and Toronto, Canada. This chapter points towards the following prerequisites for a sustainability trajectory of smart homes: integrated building performance that can deliver measurable sustainability results; balancing personal data usage with the personal significance of digital technology uses; and considering housing sustainability as a joint responsibility between producers and consumers. Altogether, this chapter outlines both the basis of these prerequisites and how business models can interlink the changes needed on multiple levels for sustainable socio-technical transitions.

Business Models for Energy Efficiency Services: Four Archetypes Based on User-Centredness and Dynamic Capabilities *by Ruth Mourik, Carolina Castaldi, Boukje Huijben* Energy Efficiency Services (EES) represent a promising solution to increase energy efficiency and contribute to reducing emissions. Unfortunately, they are still underdeveloped and companies delivering them are struggling to remain viable. In this study, we study EES through the lens of business models. We propose that business models of companies delivering EES can be analysed along two conceptual dimensions: how user-centred they are and what dynamic capabilities they require. We use this framework to analyse 46 cases in five European countries and South Korea. Four business model archetypes emerge, with varying degrees (low, medium, high) of user-centredness and a focus on different dynamic capabilities. Based on the insights from our qualitative analysis, we discuss the opportunities and barriers for further market uptake of EES and possible policy interventions.

Reverse Logistics Process for Business Transition: An Example from the Clothing Industry *by Ignes A. Castro Contreiras de Carvalho, Pascale Schwab Castella, Marcos Queiroz* The negative environmental impact of clothing industry is well known and requires the effort for redesigning one of the world's most polluting industries. Its image is tied up with a strong production of textile waste and a large amount of use of chemicals, energy, water, and other essential resources. However, some actors are demonstrating opportunities for the development of sustainability transitions using new business models. This research focuses on the drivers of socio technical transitions integrating a life-cycle perspective and open innovation in the design of sustainable business models. The applications of conceptual frameworks reveal possibilities for the promotion of slow fashion practices through a case study.

7 Summary and Outlook

Research at the intersection of business models and socio-technical transitions towards sustainability is emerging as a new, yet nascent, research field. Over the last decades, sustainable development has become a priority in some parts of the world where it holds the potential to cause fundamental shifts in many industries, markets, and lifestyles. Thus, knowledge on how to drive transitions to sustainability and how to deal with them becomes critical. Consequently, this edited book attempts to answer how business models and business model innovation may contribute to sustainability transitions (i.e., fundamental change in socio-technical systems) and whether change at systems level can contribute to the emergence of fundamentally different business models.

The book offers exemplary studies of transformational and transformed business models, which we have presented as 'business models for sustainability transitions'. Thus, the aim is to explore how these two research strands might be combined to offer new knowledge of how business model innovation can be applied as a catalyst for system-wide sustainability transitions, and vice versa. The theoretical frameworks and case studies presented in this edited book provide new knowledge on both the socio-technological transitions and the unique role of business, networks, and collaborations in making sustainable transformations and transitions happen. We therefore hope that this book will (1) inspire academia in progressing research in the field of business models for sustainable transitions and (2) provide knowledge and models for businesses and society to pursue the necessary transformations in their domains and at large.

In referring back to Wells (2013), we conclude that the conceptual integration of business model and sustainability transition research can indeed contribute considerably to a 'more structured contextual explanation' of business models and complement transition theory with explanations of 'more detailed causal mechanisms (p. 42)'. This book integrates research on business models and sustainability transitions to acknowledge the interrelation between organisations and their wider environment, respectively, the systems in which they are embedded, while they try to contribute to sustainable development.

The chapters contained in this book touch upon a number of key areas in understanding and leveraging business models for sustainability transitions through three themes: Part I: Crossing the Chasm: Integrating Business Model and Sustainability Transition Perspectives; Part II: Beyond Business-as-Usual: Alternative Value Creation Logics Driving Sustainability Transitions; and Part III: Being the Change: Transformative and Transformed Business Models in Selected Industries.

The research gaps identified by discussing these themes point to several interesting questions for future research. For one, we need to explore the role of time for business models for sustainability transitions. Second, we need to explore how business models may assist in understanding the interaction patterns between organisations and society in transition processes. Third, how do the transition pathways, as described in the transition literature (e.g., Geels et al., 2016), impact business models, and vice versa? And finally, we have to open the black-box of public policy and its role for motivating business models for sustainability transitions and socio-technical system change.

References

Aagaard, A. (2019). *Sustainable business models: Innovation, implementation and success*. Palgrave Macmillan.

Aagaard, A., & Ritzén, S. (2019). The critical aspects of co-creating and co-capturing sustainable value in service business models. *Creativity and Innovation Management, 29*(2), 292–302.

Bansal, P. (2005). Evolving sustainability: A longitudinal study of corporate sustainable development. *Strategic Management Journal, 26*, 197–218.

Berkhout, F., Smith, A., & Stirling, A. (2004). Sociotechnical regimes and transition contexts. In B. Elzen, F. W. Geels, & K. Green (Eds.), *System innovation and the transition to sustainability: Theory, evidence and policy* (pp. 48–75). Edward Elgar.

Bidmon, C. M., & Knab, S. F. (2018). The three roles of business models in societal transitions: New linkages between business model and transition research. *Journal of Cleaner Production, 178*, 903–916.
Bolton, R., & Hannon, M. (2016). Governing sustainability transitions through business model innovation: Towards a systems understanding. *Research Policy, 45*(9), 1731–1742.
Boons, F., & Lüdeke-Freund, F. (2013). Business models for sustainable innovation: State-of-the-art and steps towards a research agenda. *Journal of Cleaner Production, 45*, 9–19.
Boons, F., Montalvo, C., Quist, J., & Wagner, M. (2013). Sustainable innovation, business models and economic performance: An overview. *Journal of Cleaner Production, 45*, 1–8.
Dryzek, J. S. (2005). *The politics of the earth: Environmental discourses*. Oxford University Press.
EEA Report. (2019). Sustainability transitions: Policy and practice. No 09. ISSN 1977-8449. Access online here: https://www.eea.europa.eu/publications/sustainability-transitions-policy-and-practice
Foss, N. J., & Saebi, T. (2017). Fifteen years of research on business model innovation: How far have we come, and where should we go? *Journal of Management, 43*, 200–227.
Foxon, T., Bale, C., Busch, J., Bush, R., Hall, S., & Roelich, K. (2015). Low carbon infrastructure investment: Extending business models for sustainability. *Infrastructure Complexity, 2*, 4.
Geels, F. W. (2005). *Technological transitions and system innovations: A co-evolutionary and socio-technical analysis*. Edward Elgar Publishing Ltd.
Geels, F. W., & Johnson, V. (2018). Towards a modular and temporal understanding of system diffusion: Adoption models and socio-technical theories applied to Austrian biomass district-heating (1979–2013). *Energy Research and Social Science, 38*, 138–153.
Geels, F. W., Kern, F., Fuchs, G., Hinderer, N., Kungl, G., Mylan, J., Neukirch, M., & Wassermann, S. (2016). The enactment of socio-technical transition pathways: A reformulated typology and a comparative multi-level analysis of the German and UK low-carbon electricity transitions (1990–2014). *Research Policy, 45*, 896–913.
Geels, F. W., & Schot, J. (2007). Typology of sociotechnical transition pathways. *Research Policy, 36*, 399–417.

Global Footprint Network. (2020). World footprint. Global Footprint Network website. http://www.footprintnetwork.org/en/index.php/GFN/page/world_footprint/. Accessed Mar 2020.

Grin, J., Rotmans, J., & Schot, J. W. (Eds.). (2010). *Transitions to sustainable development. New directions in the study of long term transformative change* (Routledge studies in sustainability transitions). ebrary, Inc. Routledge.

Hannon, M. (2012). *Co-evolution of innovative business models and sustainability transitions: The case of the Energy Service Company (ESCo) model and the UK energy system*. PhD thesis. School of Earth and Environment, University of Leeds.

Hannon, M. J., Foxon, T. J., & Gale, W. F. (2013). The co-evolutionary relationship between energy service companies and the UK energy system: Implications for a low-carbon transition. *Energy Policy, 61*, 1031–1045.

Huijben, J. C. C. M., Verbong, G. P. J., & Podoynitsyna, K. S. (2016). Mainstreaming solar: Stretching the regulatory regime through business model innovation. *Environmental Innovation and Societal Transitions, 20*, 1–15.

Köhler, J., Geels, F. W., Kern, F., Markard, J., Wieczorek, A., Alkemade, F., Avelino, F., Bergek, A., Boons, F., Fünfschilling, L., Hess, D., Holtz, G., Hyysalo, S., Jenkins, K., Kivimaa, P., Martiskainen, M., McMeekin, A., Mühlemeier, M. S., Nykvist, B., Onsongo, E., Pel, B., Raven, R., Rohracher, H., Sandén, B., Schot, J., Sovacool, B., Turnheim, B., Welch, D., & Wells, P. (2019). An agenda for sustainability transitions research: State of the art and future directions. *Environmental Innovation and Societal Transitions, 31*, 1–32.

Loorbach, D., Van Bakel, J. C., Whiteman, G., & Rotmans, J. (2010). Business strategies for transitions towards sustainable systems. *Business Strategy and the Environment, 19*, 133–146.

Lüdeke-Freund, F., Carroux, S., Joyce, A., Massa, L., & Breuer, H. (2018). The sustainable business model pattern taxonomy—45 patterns to support sustainability-oriented business model innovation. *Sustainable Production and Consumption, 15*, 145–162.

Lüdeke-Freund, F., & Dembek, K. (2017). Sustainable business model research and practice: Emerging field or passing fancy? *Journal of Cleaner Production, 168*, 1668–1678.

Lüdeke-Freund, F., Rauter, R., Pedersen, E. R. G., & Nielsen, C. (2020). Sustainable value creation through business models: The what, the who and the how. *Journal of Business Models, 8*, 62–90.

Markard, J., Geels, F. W., & Raven, R. (2020). Challenges in the acceleration of sustainability transitions. *Environmental Research Letters, 15*(8), 81001.

Markard, J., Raven, R., & Truffer, B. (2012). Sustainability transitions. An emerging field of research and its prospects. *Research Policy, 41*(6), 955–967.

Massa, L., Tucci, C., & Afuah, A. (2017). A critical assessment of business model research. *Academy of Management Annals, 11*(1), 73–104.

Massa, L., Viscusi, G., & Tucci, C. L. (2018). Business models and complexity. *Journal of Business Models, 6*, 59–71.

Remane, G., Hanelt, A., Tesch, J., & Kolbe, L. M. (2017). The business model pattern database — A tool for systematic business model innovation. *International Journal of Innovation Management, 21*(01), 1750004.

Schaltegger, S., Hansen, E. G., & Lüdeke-Freund, F. (2016). Business models for sustainability: Origins, present research, and future avenues. *Organization & Environment, 29*(1), 3–10.

Schaltegger, S., Lüdeke-Freund, F., & Hansen, E. G. (2016). Business models for sustainability: A co-evolutionary analysis of sustainable entrepreneurship, innovation, and transformation. *Organization & Environment, 29*(3), 264–289.

Schot, J., & Kanger, L. (2018). Deep transitions: Emergence, acceleration, stabilization and directionality. *Research Policy, 47*, 1045–1059.

Smith, A., Vos, J.-P., & Grin, J. (2010). Innovation studies and sustainability transitions: The allure of the multi-level perspective and its challenges. *Research Policy, 39*, 435–448.

Sovacool, B. K., Hess, D. J., Amir, S., Geels, F. W., Hirsh, R., Medina, L. R., Miller, C., Palavicino, C. A., Phadke, R., Ryghaug, M., & Schot, J. (2020). Sociotechnical agendas: Reviewing future directions for energy and climate research. *Energy Research & Social Science, 70*, 101617.

Starik, M., Stubbs, W., & Benn, S. (2016). Synthesising environmental and socio-economic sustainability models: A multi-level approach for advancing integrated sustainability research and practice. *Australasian Journal of Environmental Management, 23*(4), 402–425.

Stoknes, P., & Rockström, J. (2018). Redefining green growth within planetary boundaries. *Energy Research and Social Science, 44*, 41–49.

Stubbs, W., & Cocklin, C. (2008). Conceptualizing a sustainability business model. *Organization & Environment, 21*(2), 103–127.

Teece, D. J. (2006). Reflections on "Profiting from Innovation". *Research Policy, 35*(8), 1131–1146.

Teece, D. J. (2010). Business models, business strategy and innovation. *Long Range Planning, 45*(2–3), 172–194.
Turnheim, B., & Sovacool, B. K. (2020). Exploring the role of failure in socio-technical transitions research. *Environmental Innovation and Societal Transitions, 37*, 267–289.
Wells, P. (2013). *Business models for sustainability*. Edward Elgar.
Wells, P. (2016). Degrowth and techno-business model innovation: The case of Riversimple. *Journal of Cleaner Production*. https://doi.org/10.1016/j.jclepro.2016.06.186
Wells, P., & Nieuwenhuis, P. (2012). Transition failure: Understanding continuity in the automotive industry. *Technological Forecasting and Social Change, 79*, 1681–1692. https://doi.org/10.1016/j.techfore.2012.06.008
Wesseling, J. H., Bidmon, C., & Bohnsack, R. (2020). Business model design spaces in socio-technical transitions: The case of electric driving in the Netherlands. *Technological Forecasting and Social Change, 154*, 119950.
Wirtz, B., Göttel, V., & Daiser, P. (2016). Business model innovation: Development, concept and future research directions. *Journal of Business Models, 4*, 1–28.
Wirtz, B. W., Pistoia, A., Ullrich, S., & Göttel, V. (2016). Business models: Origin, development and future research perspectives. *Long Range Planning, 49*(1), 36–54.
Zott, C., Amit, R., & Massa, L. (2011). The business model: Recent developments and future research. *Journal of Management, 37*(4), 1019–1042.

Part I

Crossing the Chasm: Integrating Business Model and Sustainability Transition Perspectives

Transformative Business and Sustainability Transitions: A Framework and an Empirical Illustration

P. J. Beers, Marjo Baeten, Erwin Bouwmans, Bram van Helvoirt, Jos Wesselink, and Ruud Zanders

1 Introduction

New business models are increasingly recognised for their promise of sustainability. Indeed, various business model frameworks explicitly include sustainability considerations, with the assumption that sustainable business will increase societal sustainability (Schaltegger et al., 2016). However,

P. J. Beers (✉)
HAS University of Applied Sciences, 's-Hertogenbosch, The Netherlands

Dutch Research Institute for Transitions, Erasmus University Rotterdam, Rotterdam, The Netherlands
e-mail: beers@drift.eur.nl; p.beers@has.nl

M. Baeten • E. Bouwmans • B. van Helvoirt • J. Wesselink
HAS University of Applied Sciences, 's-Hertogenbosch, The Netherlands
e-mail: m.baeten@has.nl; e.bouwmans@has.nl; b.vanhelvoirt@has.nl

A. Aagaard et al. (eds.), *Business Models for Sustainability Transitions*,
https://doi.org/10.1007/978-3-030-77580-3_2

while sustainable business models may outperform conventional business models with regard to sustainability, it is not so clear whether they may also contribute to more sustainable societal systems, as we will argue. In this contribution, we propose that the sustainability of new business models should be assessed in relation to the performance of the wider societal systems they are part of. To that end, we introduce a framework to reflect on systemic sustainability effects of business models. This strikes at the heart of transition studies.

From a transition perspective, the sustainability of a societal system depends on its ability to adapt to wider "landscape" developments (e.g. demographic, climate, energy, geopolitical). A sustainability transition is necessary when certain sustainability challenges cannot be met through system optimisation but demand a reconfiguration of a societal system's structure, culture and practice (e.g. Geels, 2002; Loorbach et al., 2017; Rotmans et al., 2001). It follows that new business models should be *transformative* in order to contribute to sustainability transitions (cf. Bidmon & Knab, 2018; Bolton & Hannon, 2016; Schaltegger et al., 2016) in the sense that they should be seen as contextualised in a multifaceted, coevolutionary environment. However, while current frameworks for new business models do address sustainability in various different ways, and while more and more recent studies recognise the coevolutionary nature between business model development and societal change (Bolton & Hannon, 2016; Foxon, 2011; Schaltegger et al., 2016), such considerations have, to our knowledge, very rarely led to the explicit inclusion of the transformative character of a business model (see Hannon et al., 2013, for a notable exception).

We propose a transformative business model framework that builds on existing sustainable business model approaches and that adds a transition orientation through systemic considerations of discursive, relational, practical and institutional change. It explicitly distinguishes between the business per se and its wider societal systemic context. We use images of

R. Zanders
Kipster, Castenray, The Netherlands
e-mail: ruud@kipster.nl

future system states and the transition pathways that produce them as an explicit system reference for the business model.

We report the results of an empirical study in which we applied the transformative business model framework to six Dutch agri-food businesses, divided over two transition pathways. For each pathway, we then synthesise one generic, ideal-type business model. Our results show that, in different transition pathways, businesses need to coevolve with specific wider institutional, discursive, practical and relational developments. If successful, they may be both sustainable and transformative.

1.1 Sustainable Business Models

The Osterwalder canvas model (Osterwalder, 2004; Osterwalder & Pigneur, 2013) is probably the most popular description of business models in business theory literature. However, it has received much criticism from a sustainability perspective. Many scholars point out that conventional business model approaches treat value in terms of financial profit as the most important success criterion (Bocken et al., 2015; Miller et al., 2016; Upward & Jones, 2016). This view of value is criticised because it does not include other considerations such as environmental and societal value (People-Planet-Profit, or in other words, the triple bottom line; Elkington, 1997). Moreover, it only sees value as being something positive, whereas many businesses have negative impacts (negative externalities), produce something valuable for which they do not get paid (positive externalities) or produce value that cannot yet be monetised but will be in the future (Bocken et al., 2015).

Such criticisms have given rise to a broad range of recent contributions that more explicitly account for sustainability, under various monikers such as new business models (Jonker, 2014), sustainable business models (Schaltegger et al., 2016) and sufficiency-driven business models (Bocken & Short, 2016)—in short, new business models have a promise for fostering sustainability. The common thread running through these approaches is that they add normative requirements (Boons & Lüdeke-Freund, 2013) to the business model, centred around an inclusive value proposition and supported with sustainable value architecture and clear communication to consumers (Schaltegger et al., 2016). Schaltegger et al. give the following definition of business models for sustainability (p. 6):

> *A business model for sustainability helps describing, analyzing, managing, and communicating (i) a company's sustainable value proposition to its customers, and all other stakeholders, (ii) how it creates and delivers this value, (iii) and how it captures economic value while maintaining or regenerating natural, social, and economic capital beyond its organizational boundaries.*

Note the broad orientation to value in this definition, which concerns both the social, environmental and economic value proposition and social, environmental and economic system impacts over time (cf. Laasch, 2018).

Clearly, the approach focussing on the sustainability of business models adds a perspective that enables comparing different business models in terms of their sustainability performance. However, apart from accounting for business impact, most of the sustainable business model approaches leave the wider systemic context (largely) implicit. Indeed, a relatively more sustainable business model (take, for instance, a substantially more efficient coal-fired power plant) might in fact prolong an unsustainable system (in this case, an energy system based on fossil fuels).

Stubbs and Cocklin (2008) take a different view (also see Starik et al., 2016) and argue that aspects of a systemic setting such as infrastructures, institutions (rules and legislation) and cultural/discursive elements such as the dominant economic model should be included in a sustainable business model. With Stubbs and Cocklin, we argue that the impacts of sustainable business models can only be assessed when the wider systemic context is explicitly taken into account. In this contribution, we take their line of reasoning one step further by asking the question how new business models might have a role in *transforming* their systemic context: to what extent may new business models act as a catalyst of wider systemic change? Of *sustainability transitions*? How can we distinguish a new "business-as-usual" model from a "transformative" new business model?

Sometimes this question is approached from the perspective of radicalism—a "truly" new business model should provide a radical departure from incumbent business-as-usual (cf. Schaltegger et al., 2016). However, this line of reasoning is still problematic: various businesses are able to quite radically respond to sustainability challenges—take, for example, greenhouse growers that are able to fully decarbonise their production—without fundamentally changing their business model. This suggests that incrementally new (say—*conventional, new*) business models can make important contributions to sustainability transitions. Conversely, some business models do radically deviate from the current practice—take, for instance, a food forest—but have a very limited potential to enter mass markets. The promise might be there, but what about actual societal change?

We conclude that it is impossible to assess the transformative potential of a business model without consideration of its wider systemic environment.

1.2 Sustainability Transitions

Transition studies represents a fairly young, emerging interdisciplinary field of research that concerns itself with processes of radical societal change (see Markard et al., 2012, and Loorbach et al., 2017, for review). While societal systems are conceived in socio-technical, socio-institutional and socio-ecological terms within transition studies (Loorbach et al., 2017), for our purposes it is most important to sketch the common thread in these approaches: societal systems include both material (natural, technical) and non-tangible (cognitive, institutional) elements, across such domains as infrastructures, markets, discourses, politics, science, actors and practices.

In transition studies, societal systems are viewed as complex and adaptive (Rotmans & Loorbach, 2009). Societal systems feature histories of coevolutionary growth that lend them dynamic stability: as practices evolve over time, rules and physical structures are developed that enable further practice development (Schot & Geels, 2007). Over time, practices become entrenched in systemic structures—practice and structure co-stabilise each other (Geels et al., 2016). As a consequence, societal systems have a tendency towards optimisation—incumbent systemic structures favour dominant practices while providing barriers and obstacles to alternative practices. At the scale of the societal system, complexity, among other things, entails that uncertainty and controversy are inherent to transitions: societal actors by definition have limited knowledge and limited awareness of the effects produced by their actions.

While stability is usually seen as good, it becomes problematic when systems are confronted with external developments that cannot be adequately dealt with by optimising current practices (doing things better). According to one of the most influential conceptual frameworks in transition studies, the multi-level perspective (Geels, 2002), one might speak of a transition challenge when external (landscape) pressures necessitate radical systemic change.

A transition concerns the shift of a societal system from one state of dynamic equilibrium to another (Rotmans et al., 2001). Being an example of societal system development, transitions are coevolutionary processes, both internally (changes in one subsystem will affect the performance of another) and externally (a societal system evolves within a wider external environment, e.g. Loorbach et al., 2017; Loorbach & Rotmans, 2006; Markard et al., 2012; Geels et al., 2016). The dynamics of a transition are particular in the sense that they are characterised by a combination of systemic *destabilisation* (Turnheim & Geels, 2012) and non-linear growth (Rotmans et al., 2001), as a consequence of external developments that are at odds with incumbent systemic practices and structures. The result is a coevolutionary process of incremental change with a radical direction (Rotmans et al., 2001). For that reason, a transition-in-the-making essentially is a long-term incremental process that, in hindsight, looks like a revolution. We speak of a sustainability transition when an unsustainable system state is transformed into a more sustainable system state (Rotmans et al., 2001).

From a business model perspective, it is important to note that sustainability and transition are two distinct concepts. It is perfectly possible to make current business models more sustainable without moving towards a radically changed system state, just as it is possible to have a transition that might lead to a less sustainable future system state. Therefore, if we want to draw connections between new business models and sustainability transitions, *we should assess the extent to which a new business model is*

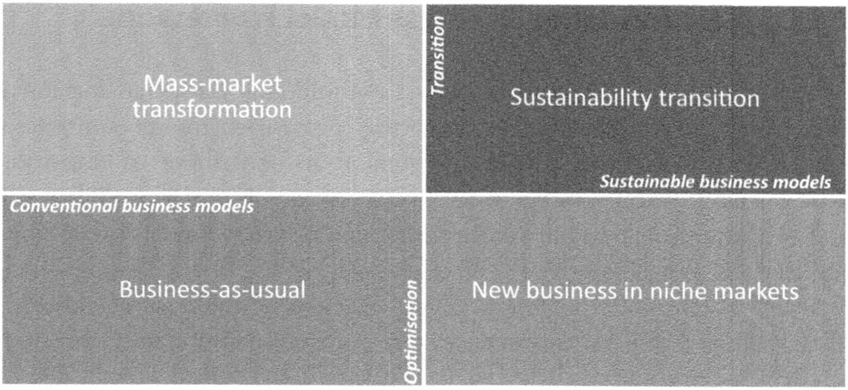

Fig. 1 Business model types and directions of systemic change. (Cf. Schaltegger et al., 2016)

transformative, *in the sense that it might contribute to sustainability transition.* This does not necessitate that the business model is radically different, nor does it require the business model itself to be radically sustainable. Rather, it means that the business model can play a role in fostering and accelerating wider, systemic processes of transformative change towards sustainability. In other words, the sustainability potential of new business models should be assessed at the level of the system and not at the level of the business itself (see Fig. 1 for a summarised depiction of potential combinations of "new" business models and societal transition).

It follows from the above that a sustainability transitions perspective requires a clear conceptual connection between societal change and business model. Current approaches to sustainable business models increasingly include consideration of businesses' wider systemic environment (e.g. Bocken et al., 2015; Schaltegger et al., 2016; Upward & Jones, 2016) but only rarely with reference to societal systems as featured in transition studies (rare exceptions include Bidmon & Knab, 2018; Stubbs & Cocklin, 2008; and Bolton & Hannon, 2016). From a transition perspective, the societal system itself features as the businesses' continuously moving context: changing laws and regulations; changing public opinion; as well as emerging new practices and movements, such as local-for-local and foodies. And a context in flux is continuously offering new opportunities and obstacles.

1.3 Transformative Business Model Framework

We draw upon the above to identify a twofold goal for a transformative business model framework. A transformative business model combines a sustainability orientation with a potential to contribute to transition (upper-right quadrant in Fig. 1). With regard to *sustainability*, we broadly follow the authors that have concentrated on business models for sustainability (e.g. Schaltegger et al., 2016; Laasch, 2018; Bocken et al., 2015; Upward & Jones, 2016; Jonker, 2014). The core of the business model is then captured by four aspects that can be used to characterise business models (green inner circle in Fig. 2; cf. Laasch, 2018; Proka et al., 2018).

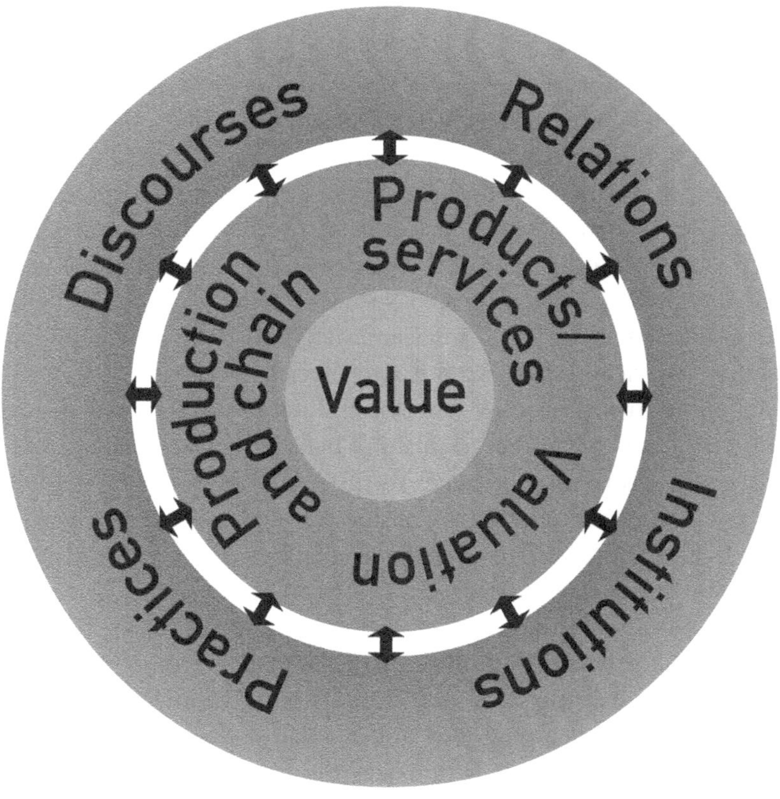

Fig. 2 Transformative business model framework

First, for *value* (core of Fig. 2), we adopt a broad orientation that goes beyond what can be described in monetary terms today, including people, planet and prosperity, that includes how value might change in the future and that accounts for both positive and negative values. This approach encompasses the value proposition to the customer and other stakeholders associated with the business model, as well as systemic impacts in general (Laasch, 2018). We add the business's products and services, the production processes and valuation:

- *Products/services:* in which products/services is this value evident (including the production process)?
- *Production and chain:* how can I create the product/service and deliver it to the client/consumer (including key parties/partners)?
- *Valuation*: what do I get back for the added value I provide, and how?

With regard to *transformative change*, the coevolutionary nature of transitions suggests that transformative business models should explicitly consider wider systemic contexts and dynamics—institutional change might affect value propositions, discursive changes about what is and is not sustainable might affect security of supply, and newcomers in the system might open up new market opportunities (cf. Hannon et al., 2013). Transitions are uncertain and unpredictable, which requires a *reflexive* orientation (cf. Beck et al., 2003; Voss & Kemp, 2006) in the business model. In other words, an awareness of, and attention to, how external developments might demand a change in course of action or might unexpectedly open up new opportunities and, ideally, a keen, strategic eye for influencing one's wider systemic development in order to pave the way for further business development (Beers & Van Mierlo, 2017).

For system innovation initiatives, Beers and Van Mierlo (2017) operationalise reflexivity in terms of changing external discourses, relations, practices and institutions (cf. Beck et al., 2003; Hendriks & Grin, 2007). And since transformative business models can be seen as business-oriented system innovation initiatives, it seems useful to adopt these aspects of reflexivity here. For a transformative business model in the food system, this could mean attention to increasing criticism of intensive livestock-farming (discourses), the Paris Agreement on climate change (institutions), new home delivery (practices) and changing relationships with relevant stakeholders (e.g. greenhouse cultivators talking to Greenpeace about climate issues). We add a reflexive orientation to our framework by drawing on Beers and Van Mierlo (2017; outer ring in Fig. 2):

- *Discourses:* changing ways of thinking in society, for example, when it comes to animal welfare, climate change, healthcare or mobility that can represent opportunities and threats for a business model.
- *Relations:* changing (potential) relationships with societal actors that can offer opportunities and threats in the form of new clients, new stakeholders and new co-producers.
- *Practices:* upcoming and disappearing practices that could create possibilities and limitations for new business models, such as with respect to logistics (home delivery), the "maker" movement (citizens creating more and more themselves), information and communication technology (production and supply chains are becoming more transparent) and energy supply (more and more citizens and farmers are producing and selling their own energy).
- *Institutions:* changes in laws and regulations that lead to changing access to the market. For example, Dutch supermarkets that no longer sell battery-cage eggs.

In sum, we contribute a *transformative business model* framework built on sustainable business model approaches and including a reflexive orientation (see Fig. 2) to explicitly model the business's changing environment. The core of the business model (the green circle in Fig. 2) is drawn from work on sustainable business models and can be seen as the part that is within the business's direct sphere of control. The reflexive orientation (Fig. 2's red ring) concerns the business's systemic context, beyond its sphere of control.

Every conceptual framework has a specific purpose, which can be recognised in what it conceptually conceals and reveals. The transformative business model framework that we propose conceals some detail of a business's core, in order to better reveal the reflexive relations between a business and its wider systemic context. In so doing, we offer a clear conceptual basis to make the framework useful for sustainability transitions, for example, to underpin the analysis of how transformative business models relate to sustainability transitions and to support the development of transition-oriented business models.

2 Methods

We explore the use of the transformative business model framework in the context of ongoing food system transition in the Netherlands. We studied six novel agri-food business cases as exemplars for two transition pathway scenarios in the Dutch agri-food system. From these analyses, we construct one ideal-typical business model for each of the pathways. Given the primarily conceptual nature of this contribution, we describe our methods in brief.

2.1 Transition Pathways for the Dutch Agri-Food System

In line with our argument that a transformative business model should be connected to its wider systemic context, we use the Dutch agri-food system as an analytical backdrop for the reflexive aspects of the business model. And since our case concerns a transition-in-the-making, we use two back-casting scenarios—the transition pathways—of the Dutch agri-food transition as placeholders for systemic context: (1) "Added value with and for the countryside" and (2) "More sustainable food production". These pathways were derived from a series of stakeholder workshops with a wide variety of participants from the Dutch food system.

2.2 Business Cases

For each transition pathway, we identified and studied three typical businesses in the Dutch context. By typical, we mean that core aspects of the business cases coincided with core aspects of the scenario. For the "added value" pathway, this meant that we included cases that focussed on a local-for-local sustainability narrative and a business strategy focussed on increasing the profit margin. For "sustainable production", this meant that we focussed on business cases that improved sustainability by changing the production processes and the value chain, while the business strategy was, to an important extent, still focussed on increasing cost efficiency.

For each business case, we conducted a series of semi-structured interviews with entrepreneurs and associated stakeholders. Interviews focussed on the business itself (value for people, planet and profit, the production and chain, products and services, valuation) and the business's wider systemic environment, in terms of obstacles and opportunities for the business. Interview data were either fully transcribed or summarised and offered for correction to the interviewee. Data collection was done by students as part of their bachelor thesis projects.

2.3 Analysis

Each business case was analysed qualitatively using the eight categories of the transformative business model as analytical categories (coding scheme): (1) value; (2) products and services; (3) production and chain; (4) valuation; (5) discourses; (6) relations; (7) practices; and (8) institutions. For each category, we used open coding to identify every structurally different way in which it conceptually applied to the data. We first produced an analysis for each business case separately. Then we used the two pathways to synthesise ideal-typical business models, based on the separate business cases. The synthesis was carried out by students and researchers of HAS University of Applied Sciences. The final analysis was conducted by the first and second authors of this chapter.

3 Results

We describe the results for the two transition pathways. For each pathway, we first shortly introduce the pathway itself and the associated business cases, then we describe the ideal-type transformative business model that we constructed from the business case analyses, and we round off with a few notes on its transformative potential.

3.1 Added Value with and for the Countryside

In the "added value with and for the countryside" (henceforth: "added value") pathway, new businesses focus on strengthening the connection between consumers and the origin of their food. As such, these businesses seek to respond to the growing number of (urban) Dutch consumers who want to know: "Where does my food come from?" And "How and by whom is it produced?" The extra added value in these types of business models is provided in various ways, such as transparency about the products' unique origins and production methods and the creation of direct market linkages between producers and consumers. It often concerns small volume flows of niche goods that run through short and highly localised supply chains.

3.1.1 Business Cases

Three different businesses have been analysed: Heideboerderij, mixed farming systems and permaculture systems.

Heideboerderij (heath farm) is a concept based on the traditional heath-farming system that has a historical presence in various parts of the Netherlands. Sheep play a pivotal role in this extensive production system, as sheep graze the heathlands (outfields) in order to produce manure for the crop fields (infields). As such, the heath-farming system seeks to combine agricultural production with nature conservation by connecting their nutrient cycles. The food products stemming from this system are destined for local markets.

Mixed farming systems are similar to heath-farming systems in their goal to optimise nutrient cycles by integrating cash crop and animal production systems. This is connected with lowering agrochemical production inputs, diversifying company revenue base and enhancing resilience to external shocks. Mixed farming systems have clear historical roots in the Netherlands, especially in regions with poor sandy soils but are rare in the current context.

Thirdly, **permaculture systems** seek to mimic natural ecosystems while producing food. They tend to be highly integrated systems with a rich diversity of plant species that are mostly perennial. In addition to food production, permaculture initiatives also engage in nature restoration and management, knowledge creation and sharing as well as social involvement which includes the local economy and community-building.

3.1.2 Transformative Business Model Ideal Type

Figure 3 visualises the "added value" business model.

Values: sustainability, fairness and transparency. The findings revealed that the values sustainability, fairness and transparency were at

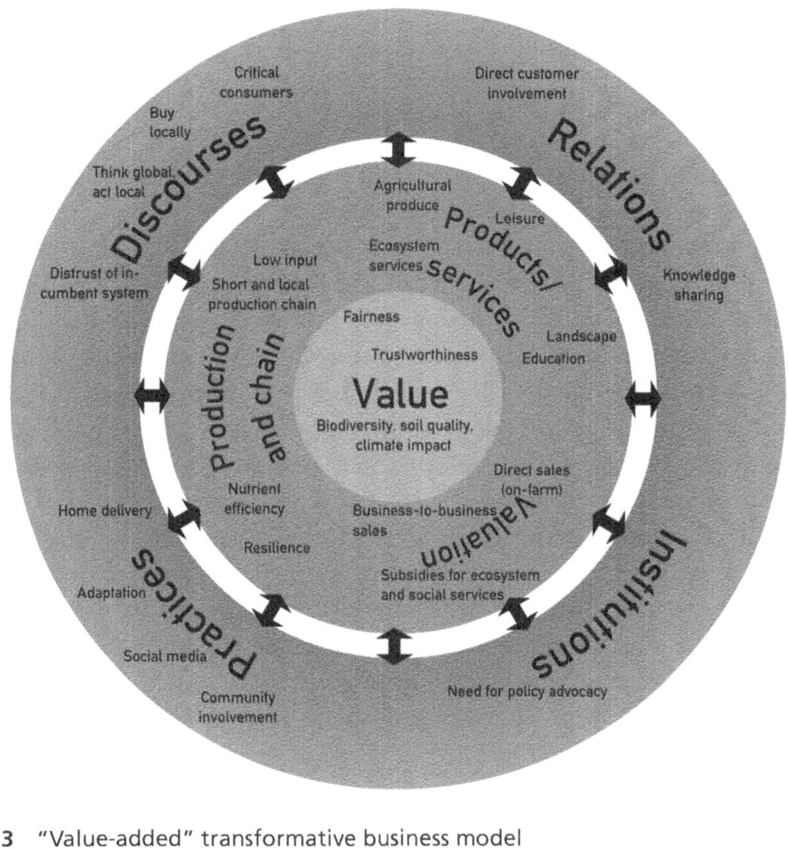

Fig. 3 "Value-added" transformative business model

the very centre of the transformative business cases heather farm, mixed farming systems and permaculture. With regard to sustainability, a key value of the three investigated production systems was to minimise environmental impacts. Examples of environmental considerations in the production methods are enhancing biodiversity, closing nutrient cycles, efficient natural resources use, improving soil quality and mitigation of CO_2 emissions. Fairness is a second value, which pertains to social aspects of agricultural production. This includes considerations about fair compensation for the farmer, taking into account the producer's efforts regarding environmental considerations.

Transparency is a third value and pertains to an openness about production practices: the producers enable the consumers to inform themselves about what is happening on-site and why. Transparency, in a sense, supports sustainability, because it enables the consumer to verify that the sustainability value offered by the producer is in fact produced. Furthermore, transparency helps the consumer to decide whether the added value on offer is indeed priced fairly.

The value considerations of sustainability, fairness and transparency resonate with the local-for-local values of a (predominantly urban) customer base that deliberately selects and purchases food products by assessing their origin and environmental impact.

Products and services: private and public goods. In addition to producing food, many businesses in this pathway offer commercial services connected to their production systems and natural environments, such as educational workshops and recreational activities. Furthermore, the interviewees expressed the importance of the (non-monetary) public services they offer with regard to the maintenance of cultural landscapes and the quality of ecosystems and their services to society (e.g. carbon sequestration and biodiversity).

Production and chain: consumer engagement in responsible businesses. Businesses seek to create a responsible production system. In the production process, environmental responsibility involves the usage of renewable resources and crop selection on nitrogen fixation and natural pest resistance. In practice, this results in a relatively extensive mode of agricultural production that uses little to no chemical inputs (such as chemical pest management or artificial fertiliser). Compared to their more conventional colleagues, producers seek to counter environmental problems usually associated with agricultural production, such as biodiversity loss and soil degradation.

A crucial aspect of the production and supply chain of the three business cases is that they are organised at a local level, allowing for face-to-face interactions between producers and consumers. In practice, this often means that consumers can purchase their products at the production site (farm shop), in addition to being able to buy produce online, through retail channels that relay the producer's transparency. Buying at the farm is considered a meaningful experience that supports trust-building between producer and consumer. This also holds for on-site catering services offered by the businesses. This way, new rural-urban market linkages are forged.

On-site purchasing enables customers to become personally familiar and engaged with producers and their production processes and produces the transparency value that is so important for these businesses. Such transparency, in turn, is key in producing consumer trust, with the associated benefit that there is no need for certification schemes to gain and retain customers' trust and loyalty. Customers can easily establish personal contact with producers and take stock of who they are and how they work. In sum, a high level of informal transparency and mutual accountability serve as crucial supportive pillars of the local marketing chains.

Valuation: beyond monetary gains. The main type of valuation of the three businesses is revenue from selling agricultural produce. A second revenue stream stems from services, both commercial and public. Regarding the latter, businesses may retrieve subsidies on the basis of their provisioning of public goods. These may relate to ecosystem services via ecologically friendly production processes (e.g. resource efficiency and natural pest management) or social benefits like rural community building.

Furthermore, the businesses expressed the importance of non-monetary returns resulting from their strong environmental and social orientation. This refers to ecological valuation expressed in terms of soil fertility and groundwater quality improvement. Finally, customer loyalty is considered an important social gain that stems from the close ties between the businesses and their customer base.

Discourses: conscious and critical consumption. Businesses in the emerging "value-added" pathway respond to, and also represent, (perceived) changes in the awareness, needs and concerns of Dutch citizens. These include a growing attention to health, food safety and food origin, as well as mounting distrust in globalised food systems and anonymous, distant corporate stakeholders (e.g. supermarkets) among certain customer groups. These discursive developments are perceived to be reflected in conscious and critical consumers in search of autonomy, authenticity and transparency.

The local-for-local principle that emphasises the value of regional products and short supply chains is further fuelled by the emergence of sustainability catchphrases such as "think global, act local". This view favours the local initiatives that offer an alternative to the dominant global system. In general, these initiatives emphasise the environmental and social aspects of their production processes, including animal welfare, and seek to reconnect primary producers and consumers via short supply chains.

Relations: building new local-for-local networks. In their attempt to offer a local alternative to the offerings from the global food system, the "value-added" businesses are faced with the challenge to create new local marketplaces. A key challenge resides in finding and aligning with local suppliers (of inputs, raw materials, equipment, etc.) that share the same business principles. The formation of, and participation in, local business support networks is often a decisive success factor. Through such multi-stakeholder networks, it is possible for individual businesses to pool resources, expand supply and marketing networks, engage in collective marketing, connect with local communities and exchange knowledge and experience. This leads to relatively diverse networks in which different links in the production chain and different types of producers are present.

Practices: adaptation, digitalisation and community involvement. When looking at the production practices of the "value-added" businesses we explored, a key guiding principle of their production systems is adaptation. This is considered the opposite of conventional agri-food production systems based upon the principle of control. The adaptation strategy, which is closely connected to the core business value of environmental sustainability and is geared towards resilience, is built on the premise that the production system should be "working with nature" instead of trying to control it via interventions such as chemical pest or weed control. The adaptation principle also serves a marketing purpose, as the businesses seek to engage in demand-driven production that caters to the growing consumer interest in sustainable, authentic local produce.

Digitalisation is used by the businesses to engage with local consumers and network partners. Social media and apps are used to share news updates, give insights into production processes, offer recipes and home delivery services and inform regarding the availability of in-stock products. Many of these activities and services tie in with the practice of community engagement of the businesses, as services and networks are firmly rooted in the local community.

Institutions: unknown niches in need of advocacy. Due to their relatively small number and size, as well as their fragmented organisation and local outreach, "value-added" businesses are not (yet) firmly represented publicly and politically, beyond the local level. As such, the (supra) national institutional context, which is decisive in shaping the agri-food landscape in terms of policies, subsidies and regulations in the Netherlands, is predominantly oriented towards conventional production of commodities and cost-price leadership. This is usually not in the interests of the "value-added" businesses: it creates institutional hurdles that hamper their ability to diversify or expand their activities. Hence, the need for policy advocacy is stressed by the businesses. One such policy could be fair pricing, the idea to add externalities to the product price. This would favour "added value" businesses over their conventional colleagues.

3.1.3 Transformative Potential of "Added Value" Businesses

The added value pathway appears rather far-reaching in terms of systemic reconfiguration, in the sense that it presupposes changes in logistical systems, food chains, as well as modes of production, diets and institutional change. Furthermore, the associated ideal-type business model involves a rather radically different role from the traditional farmer, with a very different orientation at value and a departure from incumbent food industries. In that sense, "added value" businesses can be seen as strongly transformative, because they presume substantial change throughout the food system.

Associated businesses already have some commercial success with specific consumer groups. The transformative challenge, however, resides in scaling up, since that would require market access to conventional consumers that do not share the same level of awareness and preferences as the current consumers. For them, the products should be at least as good as conventional products and cheaper as well. So, while the business models exist, the challenges for transition are far reaching and require further institutional change such as "fair pricing". Furthermore, the "added value" pathway entails substantial changes in dominant consumption patterns and in the channels through which consumers procure their food. In sum, while the business model presupposes and fosters a radically different food system, the question remains to what extent it can scale towards sustainability transition.

3.2 More Sustainable Food Production

Business models for "more sustainable production" seek to combine technological innovations and societal values, especially with regard to environmental impact. Examples include odour nuisance reduction, preventing mineral emissions, antibiotics use reduction and moving to fully renewable energy sources. Social considerations concern fair wages, labour conditions and improving animal welfare. Hence the pathway qualification "more sustainable production". However, associated businesses are traditional in the sense that they operate on mainstream (inter) national markets with (seemingly) conventional products.

3.2.1 Business Cases

We analysed three Dutch agri-food companies: Kipster, Verstegen Spices & Sauces and Token Coffee.

Kipster is a laying hen farm started by four entrepreneurs in 2017. Kipster built a new stable with 24.000 hens in Oirlo (province of Limburg, the Netherlands) according to high and innovative animal welfare and environmental standards (i.e. energy efficiency and fine dust emission). Kipster distinguishes itself in their creation of a circular food system (the company feeds the laying hens solely with waste streams (residues) from the food industry), in their production of meat from roosters (which are considered to be redundant in the egg-laying industry and therefore killed shortly after they hatch) and in being CO_2 neutral in terms of energy use.

Verstegen Spices & Sauces is a Rotterdam-based business involved in importing raw spices and herbs, packaging raw spices for retailers, production and packaging of sauces for retailers and production of premixes for the food industry. Verstegen distinguishes itself from other businesses in the industry by strongly striving for sustainability, in particular via direct sourcing. Verstegen employs direct linkages with primary producers of spices and herbs across the world, to build strong trade relationships, to offer technical assistance to producers, to empower local communities and to implement innovative production systems such as agroforestry.

Moyee Coffee is a Dutch-Ethiopian specialty coffee trading company engaged in sourcing, roasting, mixing, packaging and marketing specialty coffee beans. A distinctive feature of Moyee is that they carry out processing activities in the country of origin. In 2017, the company initiated a new specialty brand called Token FairChain coffee. The critical facilitator in this FairChain coffee concept is blockchain technology that enables a direct digital connection between consumers and producers for every coffee purchase. In addition, the technology enables the consumer to pay fees directly to the producer. In doing so, Moyee seeks to enhance local value addition in the country of origin, while simultaneously creating a transparent value chain that enables primary producers to connect with end consumers in a fair way.

3.2.2 Transformative Business Model Ideal Type

Figure 4 depicts the ideal-type "more sustainable production" business model.

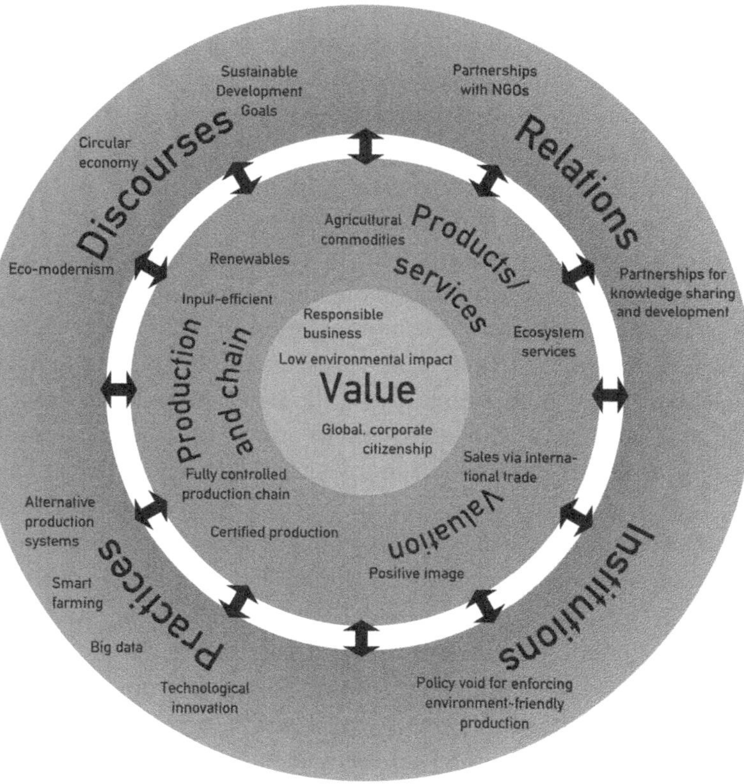

Fig. 4 "More sustainable production" transformative business model

Values: global corporate citizenship and responsible business. The businesses explored within the "more sustainable production" pathway are strongly committed to dealing with global sustainability issues associated with their industries, both in environmental (e.g. CO_2 emissions and pollution) and social terms (e.g. labour conditions and living wages). Importantly, they explore ways and means to internalise their global corporate citizenship in the heart of their operations, based on an awareness that this is the only way towards more sustainable business practices and products. These businesses have societal responsibility as a core value that infuses their product- and service-related value propositions.

Products and services: sustainability as a distinctive factor. In terms of physical characteristics, the products produced, sourced, processed and traded (i.e. chicken eggs, spices and herbs, and coffee) are by and large indistinguishable from their conventional counterparts. The sustainability value is not inherent in the product but in the production process. Hence the use of certifications such as "fair trade" or "organic" to offer the sustainability value on the market.

Production and chain: pivotal hubs in direct trade. In their quest to make their products more sustainable, the "more sustainable production" businesses strive for more vertical integration in their supply chains, both downstream and upstream. This focus on direct trade is considered a crucial (strategic) element because it allows for more transparency and a stronger relationship with suppliers. In addition, it helps in sourcing of raw materials that are deemed more sustainable (e.g. chicken feed from food industry waste streams and spices from agroforestry systems).

Initiating these new direct trade linkages and serving as a crucial linking pin between producers and consumers, the businesses feel the responsibility to create trust in the products they offer to their customers. This is done via public recognition by third parties (e.g. "better life" animal welfare standard for Kipster eggs) and the usage of innovative verification technologies such as blockchain (e.g. FairChain coffee). In addition to downstream marketing, the businesses are also involved in upstream services to their suppliers via the sharing of knowledge and expertise, technical assistance and introduction of new practices and technologies.

Valuation: financial returns and non-monetary gains. While the financial returns from the "more sustainable" products sold are expected to increase, businesses also indicate that they do see important non-monetary gains stemming from the marketing of more sustainable products. These gains are expressed in terms such as customer loyalty, brand recognition and trust. In addition, the companies foresee strategic upstream benefits, such as enhanced stability of sourcing via a more constant supply of raw materials.

Discourses: Sustainable Development Goals. The core values of the "more sustainable production" businesses can be partly seen as responses to leading global discourses on sustainable development. This discourse can be recognised in the Sustainable Development Goals (SDGs), the

United Nations' global action agenda towards sustainable development. Corporate recognition of, and commitment to, these goals is strongly present among the global business community. As such, the SDGs represent a shared agenda and common language for sustainability and how business can contribute. Specific SDGs related to "more sustainable production" include circularity (SDG 12), fairness (SDG 10) and climate action (SDG 13). In addition, the message to work together in partnerships (SDG 17) resonates strongly with these businesses.

Relations: knowledge partnerships and direct trade. Knowledge institutes (universities, research institutes) represent important partners for "more sustainable production" businesses. Both commercial service providers (consultants, engineering companies) and public research institutes are crucial for the technology-driven push towards more sustainable food production. Furthermore, the businesses seek to establish close ties upstream in the chain by partnering with primary producers in order to successfully introduce sustainable production practices. Finally, some businesses have forged relations with NGOs that share the same sustainability values. These NGOs may then champion their sustainable produce.

Practices: alternative production systems. The new practices that the businesses have introduced reach beyond the boundaries of the firm in the sense that they have a chain-wide orientation. This implies that some alternative production practices (e.g. waste stream valorisation, agroforestry, processing at origin) will affect downstream partners in the chain as well. The use of new technologies, for example, not only enables the businesses to effectively introduce these alternative production processes, it also allows them to build a sustainability value proposition for their products into their downstream marketing activities.

Institutions: policy void? Apart from the standards and processes that stem from private sector initiatives, the institutional context of the businesses is shaped by government organisations at various administrative levels. However, these governments tend to be perceived as rather passive by the "more sustainable production" businesses: they continue to respond to both commercial and societal incentives for sustainable production while rules, regulations and policies appear to be lagging. Hence, our analysis indicates a governmental void in the institutional context of these businesses and their sustainability transition processes.

3.2.3 Transformative Potential of "More Sustainable" Production Businesses

The more sustainable production scenario seems relatively straightforward in terms of business models. Businesses in this scenario deliver the same products as their conventional counterparts, and they have some advantage in that they can use existing logistical channels. Furthermore, the attitude of the producer towards the food industry and their role in the food system can remain largely the same: international collaboration on international markets with commodities. Even the role of technology remains to an important extent the same—that is, increasing efficiency. The most important difference resides in a broader scope of efficiency, including people and planet considerations and reflecting these considerations in substantial changes in the production process. Perhaps the essential driver in this scenario would be institutional change that enforces certain production methods.

In terms of transformative potential, the "more sustainable production" businesses benefit from their limited deviance from the incumbent system. They already fit quite well with dominant culture and practices in the food system. However, if a transition along this pathway would ensue, this also would mean that the actual systemic change would be limited. One might even question to what extent this scenario represents a transition from the business perspective.

4 Discussion

In this chapter, we've introduced a transformative business model framework that links recent research in the field of sustainable (new) business models to sustainability transitions. We've presented the results of an illustrative study to support our hypotheses that the innovative potential of business models is rooted in their transformative capacity, that is, influencing their wider systemic settings—systemic discourses, relations, practices and institutions—and that the radicalism of new business models can only be assessed in relation to the transition to which they might contribute. In this section, we further discuss the role of new business models in the Dutch agri-food transition, and then we draw some conclusions about the transformative business model framework.

With regard to transformative capacity, we want to highlight two differences between the pathways and their associated business models. First, they connect to very different wider discourses about sustainability. "Added value" links to sustainability in terms of local-for-local, personal contact and mutual fairness between consumer and producer. This can be seen as a small-scale, personalised discourse about sustainability. In contrast, the "more sustainable production" pathway links to sustainability using the rather abstract terms of the "global community": Sustainable Development Goals.

It comes as no surprise that we see this difference reflected in how the two business models breed trust: the former through (near-)personal contact, the latter through certification schemes, blockchain technology and NGO partnerships. This represents a second important difference between the two business models: they seek change and support in very different, wider (i.e. beyond the value chain) relational networks. Whereas the "added value" businesses require strong local communities of related business and citizens, the "more sustainable production" businesses seek partnerships with knowledge institutes and NGOs. This suggests that businesses need to coevolve with wider institutional, discursive, practical and relational developments associated to the specific transition pathway.

The above differences between the two transition pathways and associated business models indicate that our approach helps to understand the (potentially transformative) relations between business models and their wider systemic contexts. With regard to the transformative business model framework, this suggests that our contribution of adding a reflexive orientation—wider systemic (change in) discourses, institutions, relations and practices—enables us to explicitly account for relations between developing businesses and their wider systemic context. This means that the transformative business model framework helps uncover relations between businesses and wider systemic settings, which in turn can help identifying important barriers and enablers for scaling up/scaling out a business model in the context of a sustainability transition. Combined with a sustainability orientation, the transformative business model framework thus helps to understand the transformative potential of a sustainable business model and might also help understand how, for instance, policy advocacy can strengthen the contribution of sustainable business to sustainability transition.

Our transformative business model framework builds on the existing scholarly literature that addresses both sustainable business models and transitions. There are clear similarities between our reflexive approach and the works by Schaltegger et al. (2016), Bolton and Hannon (2016) and Foxon (2011), all of whom explicitly call attention to the evolutionary character of business model development and note that business models are subject to processes of systemic variation, selection and retention. Put slightly differently, this same point was brought forward by Boons (2020). We proceed with this work by explicitly including these notions in our transformative business model framework and by further delineating the relations between business models for sustainability and sustainability transitions.

Our work also is similar to other studies that connect transition studies to new business models. Both Bolton and Hannon (2016) and Bidmon and Knab (2018), for instance, use the multi-level perspective on socio-technical transitions to connect it to new business model frameworks. Similarly, Proka et al. (2018) use the socio-technical niche concept, as used in transition studies, to connect transformative business to transition studies. The approach presented here is slightly different in that we connect sustainable business models to sustainability transitions—be they socio-ecological, socio-technical or socio-institutional—in a more general way, informed by the coevolutionary, radically incremental character of sustainability transitions and operationalised with a reflexive orientation rather than through specific conceptual transition studies frameworks, such as the multi-level perspective (Geels, 2002) or technological innovation systems (Hekkert et al., 2007). In doing so, we hope that our contribution can be adopted across different research traditions within the field of transition studies.

The current study included six different business models. The empirical data was introduced primarily for illustrative purposes, and we did not elaborate much on our data collection. In that sense our results should be taken as mainly indicative for the usefulness of the transformative business model framework and of our transition-oriented approach to new business models in general. However, it does merit mention that we already applied the transformative business model framework in over 14 different studies, that we also used it in educational settings and that we see promise for using it in advisory contexts. In future publications, we hope to share more business model analyses to provide in-depth understanding of transformative business and specific pathways for sustainability transition.

Finally, we suggest that the transformative business model framework can be useful for entrepreneurs that hope to contribute to transition. The study implies that entrepreneurs should adopt a perspective on the type of sustainable future and transition pathway that they prefer, in order to reflexively find options to further develop their own new business models. And, conversely, for those who seek to foster sustainability transition, the results suggest that it helps to use the transformative business model framework to select promising new business models and to find ways to create the systemic circumstances that foster these business models. We hope that our work contributes to a better understanding of the relations between business and sustainability in general and of the success of transformative businesses in particular.

Acknowledgements This chapter is in part built on seven thesis projects at HAS University of Applied Sciences. We would like to thank Nigel Kennedy, Mark van Oijen, Thomas Pulles, Ruben Bots, Claire Wimmers, Matthé Wind, Koert van Bemmel, Sandra van der Maas, Katharina Grimm, Freek Braaksma, Talash Huijbers, Shanna de Groot, Joris van Lierop, Bart Millenaar, Sandra Kaiser, Janina Panning, Julia de Candido, Jocelyn van Reekum, Ana Maria Duursma, Razee Seyyed, Dominique Aarts, Elmar Adriaanssen, Aji Bajdan, Eveline Brouwers and Igor Gaina for all their empirical work and business model analyses.

The work presented here was made possible by a grant from the Netherlands Enterprise Agency to HAS University of Applied Science for the research chair in "New Business Models" and a grant from ACCEZ—Accelerating Circulair Economy Zuid-Holland—to the Dutch Research Institute for Transitions, for the project "A circular Green Heart."

References

Beck, U., Bonss, W., & Lau, C. (2003). The theory of reflexive modernization: Problematic, hypotheses and research programme. *Theory, Culture & Society, 20*(2), 1–33.

Beers, P. J., & Van Mierlo, B. (2017). Reflexivity and learning in system innovation processes. *Sociologia Ruralis, 57*(3), 415–436.

Bidmon, C., & Knab, S. F. (2018). The three roles of business models in societal transitions: New linkages between business model and transition research. *Journal of Cleaner Production, 178*, 903–916.

Bocken, N. M. P., Rana, P., & Short, S. W. (2015). Value mapping for sustainable business thinking. *Journal of Industrial and Production Engineering, 32*(1), 67–81.

Bocken, N. M. P., & Short, S. W. (2016). Towards a sufficiency-driven business model: Experiences and opportunities. *Environmental Innovation and Societal Transitions, 18*, 41–61.

Bolton, R., & Hannon, M. (2016). Governing sustainability transitions through business model innovation: Towards a systems understanding. *Research Policy, 45*, 1731–1742.

Boons, F. (2020). From sustainable business models to sustainable provision: How to get beyond SBM rhetorics. Online presentation at the New Business Models 2020 conference. https://vimeopro.com/user57999492/nbm2020-keynotes/video/429548599

Boons, F., & Lüdeke-Freund, F. (2013). Business models for sustainable innovation: State of the art and steps towards a research agenda. *Journal of Cleaner Production, 45*, 9–19.

Elkington, J. (1997). *Cannibals with forks: The triple bottom line of 21st century business*. Capstone.

Foxon, T. J. (2011). A coevolutionary framework for analysing a transition to a sustainable low carbon economy. *Ecological Economics, 70*, 2258–2267.

Geels, F. W. (2002). Technological transitions as evolutionary reconfiguration processes: A multi-level perspective and a case-study. *Research Policy, 31*, 1257–1274.

Geels, F. W., Kern, F., Fuchs, G., Hinderer, N., Kungl, G., Mylan, J., Neukirch, M., & Wassermann, S. (2016). The enactment of socio-technical transition pathways: A reformulated typology and a comparative multi-level analysis of the German and UK low-carbon electricity transitions (1990–2014). *Research Policy, 45*, 896–913.

Hannon, M., Foxon, T. J., & Gale, W. F. (2013). The co-evolutionary relationship between energy service companies and the UK energy system: Implications for low-carbon transition. *Energy Policy, 61*, 1031–1045.

Hekkert, M. P., Suurs, R. A. A., Negro, S. O., Kuhlmann, S., & Smits, R. E. H. M. (2007). Functions of innovation systems: A new approach for analysing technological change. *Technological Forecasting and Social Change, 74*(4), 413–432.

Hendriks, C. M., & Grin, J. (2007). Contextualizing reflexive governance: The politics of Dutch transitions to sustainability. *Journal of Environmental Policy & Planning, 9*(3–4), 333–350.

Jonker, J. (Ed.). (2014). *Nieuwe Business Modellen*. Stichting Our Common Future 2.0/Academic Service.

Laasch, O. (2018). Beyond the purely commercial business model: Organizational value logics and the heterogeneity of sustainability business models. *Long Range Planning, 51*, 158–183.

Loorbach, D., Frantzeskaki, N., & Avelino, F. (2017). Sustainability transitions research: Transforming science and practice for societal change. *Annual Review of Environment and Resources, 42*, 599–626.

Loorbach, D., & Rotmans, J. (2006). Managing transitions for sustainable development. In X. Olsthoorn & A. J. Wieczorek (Eds.), *Understanding industrial transformation: Views from different disciplines* (pp. 187–206). Springer.

Markard, J., Raven, R., & Truffer, B. (2012). Sustainability transitions: An emerging field of research and its prospects. *Research Policy, 41*, 955–967.

Miller, K., Park, C., Evans, S., Bamford, I., & Bocken, N. (2016, June). *Critique of the canvas: A new honeycomb approach to business model innovation*. Paper presented at the New Business Models Conference.

Osterwalder, A. (2004). *The business model ontology – A proposition in a design science approach*. Université de Lausanne.

Osterwalder, A., & Pigneur, Y. (2013). Designing business models and similar strategic objects: The contribution of IS. *Journal of the Association for Information Systems, 14*(5), 237–244.

Proka, A., Beers, P. J., & Loorbach, D. (2018). Transformative business models for sustainability transitions. In L. Moratis, F. Melissen, & S. O. Idowu (Eds.), *Sustainable business models* (pp. 19–29). Springer.

Rotmans, J., Kemp, R., & Van Asselt, M. (2001). More evolution than revolution: Transition management in public policy. *Foresight/the Journal of Future Studies, Strategic Thinking and Policy, 03*(01), 1–17.

Rotmans, J., & Loorbach, D. (2009). Complexity and transition management. *Journal of Industrial Ecology, 13*(2), 184–196.

Schaltegger, S., Hansen, E. G., & Lüdeke-Freund, F. (2016). Business models for sustainability: Origins, present research, and future avenues. *Organization & Environment, 29*(1), 3–10.

Schot, J., & Geels, F. W. (2007). Niches in evolutionary theories of technical change. A critical survey of the literature. *Journal of Evolutionary Economics, 17*, 605–622.

Starik, M., Stubbs, W., & Benn, S. (2016). Synthesising environmental and socio-economic sustainability models: A multi-level approach for advancing integrated sustainability research and practice. *Australasian Journal of Environmental Management, 23*(4), 402–425.

Stubbs, W., & Cocklin, C. (2008). Conceptualizing a "sustainability business model". *Organization & Environment, 21*(2), 103–127.

Turnheim, B., & Geels, F. W. (2012). Regime destabilisation as the flipside of energy transitions: Lessons from the history of the British coal industry (1913–1997). *Energy Policy, 50*, 35–49.

Upward, A., & Jones, P. (2016). An ontology for strongly sustainable business models: Defining an enterprise framework compatible with natural and social science. *Organization & Environment, 29*(1), 97–123.

Voss, J.-P., & Kemp, R. (2006). Sustainability and reflexive governance: Introduction. In J.-P. Voss, D. Bauknecht, & R. Kemp (Eds.), *Reflexive governance for sustainable development*. Edward Elgar.

The Networked Business Model for Systems Change: Integrating a Systems Perspective in Business Model Development for Sustainability Transitions

Julia Planko and Jacqueline Cramer

1 Introduction

To enable the world population to satisfy its needs within the limits of our planet's finite resources, and to mitigate the societal challenges we face, sustainability transitions are necessary. These have been defined as 'long-term, multi-dimensional, and fundamental transformation processes through which established socio-technical systems[1] shift to more sustainable modes of production and consumption' (Markard et al., 2012, p. 956). Systemic

[1] Socio-technical systems consist of networks of actors, societal norms, technical standards, regulations and material artifacts (Geels, 2005; Musiolik & Markard, 2011).

J. Planko (✉)
University of Applied Sciences Leiden, Leiden, The Netherlands

J. Cramer
Utrecht University, Utrecht, The Netherlands

A. Aagaard et al. (eds.), *Business Models for Sustainability Transitions*,
https://doi.org/10.1007/978-3-030-77580-3_3

change is necessary to set this shift in motion. It has become clear from research on fundamental sustainability transitions that government incentives can promote socio-technical system change via regulatory and economic measures (Foxon et al., 2004; Kemp et al., 2001; Verbong et al., 2013).

However, the entrepreneurial activities of businesses are also key to sustainability transitions (Hall et al., 2010; Vogel & Fischler-Strasak, 2014). Businesses invent technologies and create new products, services and business models that can stimulate sustainable behaviour (Farla et al., 2012; Hall et al., 2010; Hockerts & Wüstenhagen, 2010; Musiolik, 2012). Moreover, business actors can pro-actively shape the operational environment to increase the market success of their sustainability innovation.

Still, business actors cannot build a new socio-technical system on their own. Together with other actors such as business partners, the government, NGOs, financial institutions, research institutions and user groups, they can shape the system[2] in which they operate, thereby fostering sustainability transitions. In different constellations of actors, they can engage in system-building activities, in other words in activities that firms can undertake in networks in order to collectively create a favourable environment for their sustainability innovation (Planko et al., 2016). Engaging in strategic system-building not only helps them to market their own product or service but also stimulates system change and accelerates the sustainability transition (Planko et al., 2016).

While most studies addressing system-building in sustainability transitions take a policy perspective (Farla et al., 2012; Jacobsson & Bergek, 2011b), a few adopt a business perspective (Loorbach & Wijsman, 2013; Planko et al., 2016, 2017, 2019). However, the role of business models in these latter studies is still underexposed (Köhler et al., 2019). The business models literature itself does not address the linkage with fostering

[2] In transition studies, the term 'system' is often used in various ways, even in the same publication. It usually refers to the system whose change is being studied, depending on the unit of analysis, the perspective adopted, and the boundaries drawn. For example, it can vary from a socio-technical system, technological innovation system, innovation ecosystem, national innovation system, regional innovation system, social, economic and technological system, production and consumption system to a societal system (see for example Köhler et al., 2019). Here, we use the term 'system' mostly in the sense of business ecosystem when we describe the actors that collaborate, and the term 'socio-technical system' to refer to the system these actors are trying to build or change. We ultimately refer to the same system – the system in which networks of actors operate and which they are trying to change, as a business ecosystem is part of a socio-technical system.

sustainability transitions either. Much attention has been paid to sustainable business models from a firm-centric viewpoint (Neumeyer & Santos, 2018). Several business model scholars have shown the need to adopt a systems perspective and develop business models from a perspective beyond the single organisation (Breuer & Lüdeke-Freund, 2017; Rohrbeck et al., 2013; Starik et al., 2016; Stubbs & Cocklin, 2008; Upward & Jones, 2016). However, the overall systemic change, which is needed for a sustainability transition, has not yet been integrated (Diepenmaat et al., 2020). Our contribution aims to bridge this knowledge gap. Our research question is: how can firms co-develop networked business models that help them to integrate systemic change towards sustainability into their individual business models?

Below, we connect the sustainability transition literature with the business model literature. Based on the transition literature, we argue that companies do not have to wait for favourable sustainability conditions. Instead, they can pro-actively create these conditions by undertaking specific combinations of system-building activities in collaborative networks. By combining this perspective with the business models literature, we have designed a theoretical model which we call the 'networked business model' approach. Conceptually, it is positioned between the corporate level of a single business and the socio-technical systems level. Therefore, the networked business model is a representation to theorise corporate agency in socio-technical transitions. It is then used for analytical (ex post) purposes to study two illustrative cases. The main findings are summarised and reflected upon in the discussion section.

2 Importance of a Systems Perspective in Business Model Design for Sustainability Transitions

2.1 Business Models for Sustainability

A business model is a representation of the way in which businesses create value for their customers. It 'describes how a company creates, delivers and captures value for its customers and itself' (Breuer & Lüdeke-Freund,

2017, p. 6). In addition, business models for sustainability ideally 'incorporate pro-active multi-stakeholder management, the creation of monetary and non-monetary value for a broad range of stakeholders, and hold a long-term perspective' (Geissdoerfer et al., 2018, p. 403). Financial value is created for the business, and simultaneously social, environmental and economic value is created for various stakeholders (Roome & Louche, 2016; Schaltegger et al., 2016). As a consequence, firms aim to optimise value for the system in which they are embedded (Bocken et al., 2019).

To achieve a sustainability transition, firms must base their business models on collaborative networks, often referred to as multi-actor collaboration (Rossignoli & Lionzo, 2018; Zander et al., 2016). Sustainability challenges are best addressed when actors collaborate in value networks, which enable their participants to collectively use their power (Freudenreich et al., 2020; Hörisch et al., 2014). Therefore, companies need to collaborate with a variety of actors (Neumeyer & Santos, 2018; Velter et al., 2020). Beyond creating sustainable products and services, multi-actor networks need to create enabling conditions and must shape their own business environment or 'business ecosystem'[3] (Diepenmaat et al., 2020; Lupova-Henry & Dotti, 2019; Veleva & Bodkin, 2018). Understanding the dynamics of such business ecosystems is important for making representations of sustainable business models (Galvão et al., 2020).

2.2 Transition Studies, System-Building and Business Models

The link between business ecosystems and the micro-dynamics at firm level, and particularly the use of business models, has hardly been addressed yet in sustainability transitions literature (Bidmon & Knab, 2018). On the other hand, the business models for sustainability literature do not yet

[3] A business ecosystem is a business network that goes beyond the supply chain of the focal company. It consists of all the individuals with whom a business interacts, including suppliers, technology producers, customers, competitors, producers of complementary assets, sellers, financial actors, governmental actors, media and regulatory agencies. It further comprises the economic and social landscape in which an individual business evolves together with other business. The health of the ecosystem determines the success and survival of the individual firm (Diepenmaat et al., 2020; Iansiti & Levien, 2004; Moore, 1996).

theorise the governance of sustainability transitions via multi-actor networks and multi-value creation (Diepenmaat et al., 2020). Diepenmaat et al. (2020) have started filling this gap by connecting the 'collective system-building framework', which originates from the transitions literature, with the business models literature.

'Collective system building' comprises the strategic activities of network actors—usually driven by firms that want to launch a sustainability innovation—who aim to build a supportive environment in which their innovation will flourish. Firms cannot do this on their own. They combine their forces to trigger systemic changes in society that will contribute to sustainable development. Successful collective system building can lead to larger markets and more widespread implementation in society of the firms' products or services. These networks consist of a variety of actors, such as technology producers, policymakers, municipalities, research institutions, user groups, education institutions, service providers, retailers, complimentary technology producers, suppliers, branch organisations, financial institutions and NGOs. Figure 1 gives an

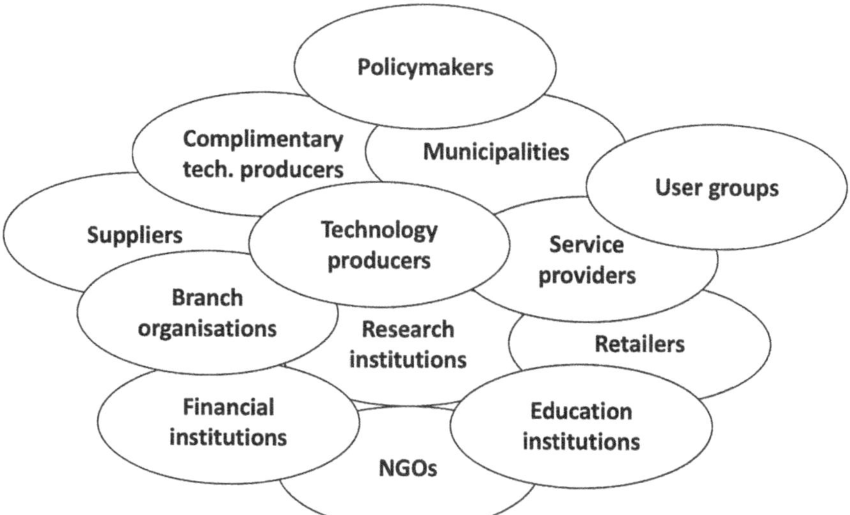

Fig. 1 Overview of types of actors in innovation ecosystems. (Figure produced by the authors, based on Planko et al., 2016)

overview of these actors. Depending on the system-building goal they want to achieve, firms will choose different constellations of actors and networks (Planko et al., 2016).

For networks of actors who want to collaborate on building a supportive ecosystem for a sustainability transition, Planko et al. (2016) created the 'strategy framework for collective system building', an overview of system-building activities that networks of firms can undertake to achieve system-level changes. It is based on an in-depth study of the transition literature (e.g. Farla et al., 2012; Geels et al., 2008; Hekkert et al., 2007; Jacobsson & Bergek, 2011a), combined with the strategic management literature on business ecosystems (e.g. Astley, 1984; Iansiti & Levien, 2004; Moore, 1993; Pitelis, 2012; Van de Ven, 1993). This strategy framework consists of four key areas for collective strategy-making at the network level: product development and optimisation, market creation, socio-cultural changes and coordination. Each of these key strategic areas consists of a set of system-building activities. The categories 'product development and optimisation', 'market creation' and 'socio-cultural changes' are system-building goals which actors strive for collectively. The category 'coordination' comprises all the activities that manage and align system-building efforts, and thus lead to combining forces and resources, and consequently accelerate the system-building processes (Planko et al., 2016). An overview of the categories and system-building activities is presented in Fig. 2. The activities are carried out collectively by networks of actors. For example, when they collaborate on pilot projects or demonstration activities, they develop knowledge, co-create products and test these with user groups. While companies could also undertake innovation activities on their own, when they combine their forces, they are more likely to succeed in building a prosperous ecosystem and in achieving macro-level changes to the system in which they operate. Triggering socio-cultural changes is usually such a long-term and resource-intensive process that it can only be achieved through collaboration in quadruple-helix networks.

The strategy framework for system-building can help innovating firms to determine and coordinate collective action, which is necessary for societal innovation and systemic change (Diepenmaat et al., 2020).

Coordination

- System orchestration
- Creating a shared vision
- Defining a common goal
- Standardisation of the new technology
- Providing a platform for open innovation
- Thinking in system-building roles
- Creating transparency of all activities going on in the field

Technology development & optimisation	Market creation	Socio-cultural changes
• Testing new technologies and applications • Knowledge development • Knowledge exchange • Co-creation of products and services • Development of commercially viable products • Feedback loops with user groups	• Generate new business models • Collaboration with government for enabling legislation • Creation of temporarily protected niche market • Collaborative marketing to raise user awareness • Shared infrastructure	• Changing user behaviour • Changing perception of the new technology • Changing the education system • Generating a pool of skilled labour • Creating new facilitating organisations • Establishing collaboration-prone organisational cultures

Fig. 2 Overview of collective system-building activities for sustainability transitions. (Figure designed by the authors, based on Planko et al., 2016)

2.3 'Networked Business Models' Essential for System Change

Firms need to collaborate in networks to carry out system-building activities. They do so in various constellations of actors, depending on the different system-building goals they strive for. Each system-building network carries out one or usually a combination of system-building activities, and actors are usually part of several system-building networks. For example, a firm can be part of a standardisation network as well as of a network lobbying for enabling legislation (Planko et al., 2017). For this, actors need resources, and in the transition literature, these are called 'system resources' (Musiolik et al., 2012). System resources can be provided by individual companies, and they can take various forms, including in-kind contributions, provision of machines or technology for pilot projects, or financial contributions. Furthermore, some system resources cannot easily be provided, but need to be developed, such as technology standards or a shared infrastructure. To represent how these networks create value for their stakeholders, we suggest designing a 'networked business model' for system-building networks. Just as firm-centred business models are used to describe how a firm captures value, a networked business model can be used to develop and communicate how the collective efforts of the stakeholder network lead to value creation and to achieving sustainability goals. The networked business model helps these firms to connect their individual business models.

3 Interconnected Business Models Needed at Company and Network Level

Although we emphasised the need for a 'networked business model' above, the firm-centred business model also remains important. Each actor in the system-building network needs to have his own business model, because each contributes to the transition process in a different way. Different individuals have different needs and hold different values; as a result, each actor has a different understanding of what constitutes value (Freudenreich et al., 2020). At the same time, actors depend on each other to realise their own needs and wishes (Diepenmaat et al., 2020). However, it is the firm-centred business model that helps actors to realise their own vision and to tailor their activities to their specific customer group and stakeholder needs. While designing their firm-centric business model, actors should adopt a systems perspective on sustainable development that values the environment and society as stakeholders (Rossignoli & Lionzo, 2018; Upward & Jones, 2016). Moreover, they should integrate the resources that they need for system-building into the costs part of their firm-centric business model. Their individual business model is interconnected with the networked business model. Therefore, actors also need to consider the consequences of their network participation on their individual business model design (Rossignoli & Lionzo, 2018). Firms need to align their business rationale with other network actors (Lahti et al., 2018). Moreover, changes in the business model of one firm may require changes in the business models of other firms (Velter et al., 2020).

In addition to their own firm-centric business models, the actors of the network working on systems change for sustainability need to design a 'networked business model' together. In the following section, we discuss elements of a business model, and the way in which they can be translated into a 'networked business model' for sustainability transitions.

3.1 Networked Business Model for System-Building

Business models are representations of how businesses create value for their customers. Business models for sustainability also incorporate value creation for diverse stakeholders and include value creation for the environment and society. There are many different variations of business models, but they usually contain the following elements:

1. Value proposition (benefits for the customers and in business models for sustainability also for other stakeholders)
2. Customer interface/value delivery (including customer segments, customer relationships and channels)
3. Infrastructure/value creation (including key partners, resources and key activities)
4. Financial structure/value capture (including costs and revenue streams) (Bocken et al., 2014; Chesbrough, 2010; Dijkstra et al., 2020; Lüdeke-Freund et al., 2019; Osterwalder & Pigneur, 2010; Teece, 2010; Zott et al., 2011)

For multi-actor networks that create value by building a system that stimulates the sustainability transition, we suggest adjusting these business model elements to generate a 'networked business model'. Figure 3 displays the elements of the focal-firm business model in the upper box and the elements of the suggested networked business model in the lower box. Each private actor should generate their own focal-firm business model, and the network of actors should collectively draw up the networked business model for system-building. The business models of several individual firms—one per network actor—feed into the networked business model and vice versa, as illustrated by Fig. 4.

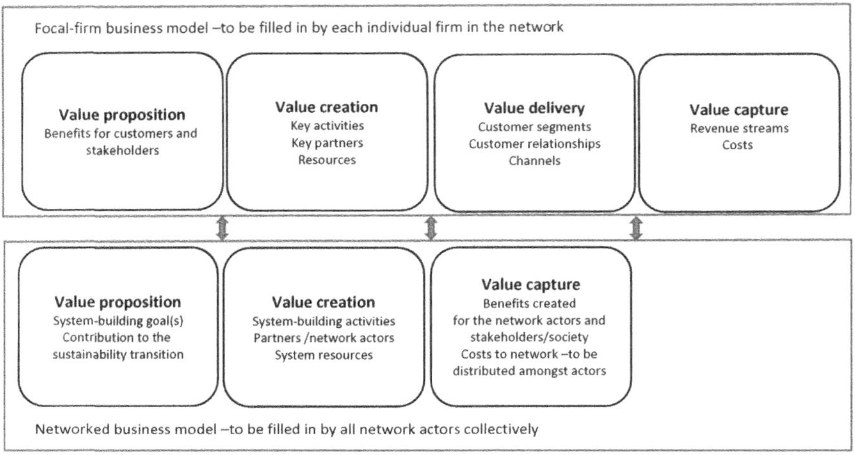

Fig. 3 Networked business model and the way it feeds into the business models of the individual firms. (Figure created by the authors)

Below, we explain the elements of the networked business model and discuss arguments identified in the business models for sustainability literature that are in line with the suggested elements of the networked business model.

Value Proposition → System-Building Goal The value proposition describes which benefits the business creates for its customer. It is the reason why the customer should buy the product or service. In the networked business model for system-building, the benefit being generated through the network's activities is a contribution to a new, more sustainable production and consumption system. Just like a business that defines which benefit it exactly strives to create, the network defines what its **system-building goal(s)** are. For example, these may be the creation of a standard for compatible technology development, changes in legislation or mind-shifts of users or potential users. Depending on the system-building goal(s) selected, the constellation of necessary network partners is likely to change. It is possible that several overlapping networks need to be created to cover the different aspects of system-building necessary for the sustainability transition. In the business model literature, the following five arguments are put forward that underline the need for system-

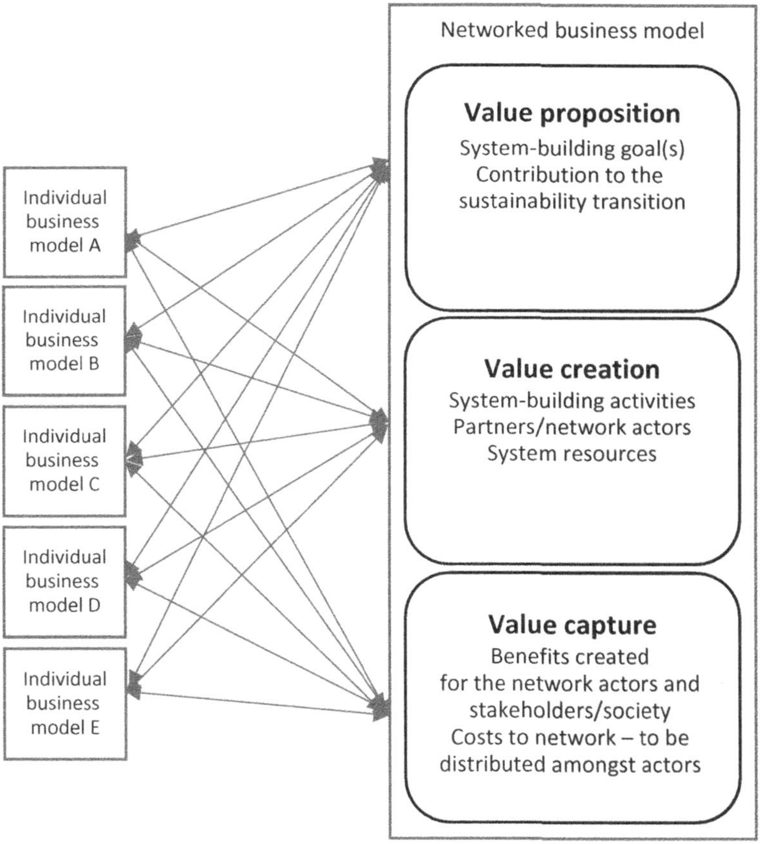

Fig. 4 The business models of the individual firms influence the networked business model and vice versa. (Figure created by the authors)

building goals. First, networks help to achieve sustainability goals (Rossignoli & Lionzo, 2018). Second, the collective efforts of stakeholder networks are at the core of value creation (Freudenreich et al., 2020). Third, multiple actors are needed to align their efforts towards shared goals (Vazquez-Brust et al., 2020). Fourth, it is important to identify development paths and develop networks around them (Mårtensson & Westerberg, 2016). Fifth, network participation patterns evolve over time, according to the network goals (Rossignoli & Lionzo, 2018).

Value Creation ***Key activities → system-building activities*** Key activities describe the activities that firms have to undertake in order to create value for their customers or stakeholders. For the networked business model, these are the system-building activities that the network actors need to undertake in order to achieve their system-building goal. An overview of system-building activities is presented in Fig. 2. In the business model literature, several scholars describe the need for a systems perspective in which networks or partnerships need to collaborate to achieve their goals related to sustainable development (Breuer & Lüdeke-Freund, 2017; Rohrbeck et al., 2013; Starik et al., 2016; Stubbs & Cocklin, 2008; Upward & Jones, 2016). In terms of specific system-building activities, Lewandowski (2016) states that to achieve the socio-technical changes necessary, for example, changes in customer habits and public opinion, or a predictable demand for future products, actors can engage in activities such as lobbying for incentivising legislation or building organisational capabilities. Galvão et al. (2020) argue that consumer education is fundamental for circular business models. In addition, Lahti et al. (2018) discuss the importance of forming new markets for implementing circular business models. The strategic system-building framework can help networks of firms and other ecosystem actors to develop these activities in a more structured way.

Key resources → system resources

Key resources describe the main resources necessary for value creation activities. For the networked business model, these are the necessary 'system resources' (Musiolik et al., 2012), that is, the resources needed to build the new system or change the old one. These could be resources already available in the individual organisations (e.g. a technology or labour) or 'system resources' that have to be built collaboratively, such as knowledge development for a new technology, or larger pilot projects to test innovative product-service combinations. This means that resources can either be provided by network actors or need to be created together and made available to the system. In line with this, business model scholars state that multi-actor networks provide resources and influence their business environment (Freudenreich et al., 2020), and that a networked firm can acquire and develop external resources made available by the partners and the network for sustainability (Rossignoli & Lionzo, 2018).

Key partners → network actors

Key partners in a focal-firm business model are the actors—often other firms—which are necessary for a business to produce or market its product. In a networked business model, the key partners are the network actors which are necessary to achieve the system-building goal. These can be other firms, policymakers, user groups or any other type of ecosystem actor as displayed in Fig. 1. After having identified the system-building goals and the necessary system-building activities, actors can determine which additional network partners they need for carrying out these activities. Business model scholars argue that firms must develop networks because they cannot perform all tasks independently, and that partner selection is important in this process (Reim et al., 2015). Moreover, it is argued that networks and partnerships strongly influence value creation (Wirtz et al., 2016).

Value Capture ***Revenue streams → benefits for the system*** In a focal-firm business model, the revenue streams show the financial benefit of conducting the business activity and selling its product. In the networked business model, instead of revenue streams, the benefits for the business ecosystem are stated. Usually, there are different types of benefits for different stakeholder groups. In system-building, it is difficult to express the achieved values in monetary value. However, the collectively created benefits can often be indirectly turned into monetary value by companies. For example, a company creating environmental benefits can project a positive image, which can increase sales volume or attract a talented workforce. The individual value for businesses differs per firm and should be part of their individual, firm-focused business model. In the networked business model, the benefits created for the stakeholders are listed here, as are the benefits for the system as a whole, in other words the positive contribution to the sustainability transition. As in multi-stakeholder business models, a range of different system actors can benefit, and not only the actors who are actively involved in this network.

In the business model literature, several arguments can be identified in support of these ideas. Rossignoli and Lionzo (2018) refer to a network as a new approach of capturing value, and this takes place in interaction with other players in the ecosystem (Galvão et al., 2020). Stakeholder relationships form the basis of joint value creation. A business model may have various outcomes, including monetary and non-monetary benefits, for a variety of different stakeholders, such as the firm, society and environment (Freudenreich et al., 2020). Benefits are created 'for a broad range of actors', and they consist 'of immediate values such as cost reduction, unburdening and convenience (core benefits) as well as rather diffuse benefits such as long-term health, local production or environmental improvements (co-benefits)' (Velter et al., 2020).

Cost-structure → system-building costs
The item cost-structure in a focal-firm business model translates into 'system-building costs' in the networked business model. The network actors should consider what costs are involved in developing the more sustainable system, or, more specifically, what costs are involved in this specific part of system building. For example, this may include in-kind contributions by managers, the provision of an innovative technology, a common infrastructure and access to a consumer database. It is often not evident to whom these costs can be allocated. Network actors have to share these collective costs as well as determine who pays for what. Their individual share of the system-building costs feeds into the cost-structure of their focal-firm business model.

In line with these ideas, business model scholars state that it is required that there is mutual alignment of and agreement about a proper distribution of the costs and benefits of collaboration for a transition (Diepenmaat et al., 2020). In business models for sustainability, an equal distribution of economic costs and benefits among all the actors involved is necessary (Boons & Lüdeke-Freund, 2013). Innovating for sustainability involves a wide range of actors splitting the risk of business model innovation among several participants connected through a business model that enables each member to capture economic profit from a network (Rossignoli & Lionzo, 2018).

Value Delivery ***Customer relationships/channels/customer segments → only in individual business model*** The value delivery part of the focal-firm business model does not translate into the networked business model for system-building, as each of the network actors involved is likely to develop their unique value proposition and target a different customer segment with their product or service. Network actors often collaborate upstream or in the pre-competition stage, but downstream, when the process comes closer to the consumers, they prefer to compete, and they develop their own products or services for their specific target group (Bengtsson & Kock, 1999, 2000; Bouncken et al., 2018).

3.2 Interrelatedness of Firm-Centred Business Models and the Networked Business Model

The individual business model and the networked business model are interlinked and strongly influence each other. Several individual firms' business models—one per network actor—feed into the networked business model and vice versa. Usually, business models of individual firms exist before there is a networked business model. Firms make resources available to the network, and their individual goals influence the networked business model. However, if network actors together strategically generate a networked business model to achieve their respective system-building goals (or sustainability transition sub-goals), this is likely to influence their individual business models and will lead to adjustment to these models. Figure 4 shows how each networked business model is connected to and influenced by several individual business models—one per network member. The value created by the individual firms, but also their positive and negative externalities and spill-overs, feeds into the networked business model. Moreover, the firms' resources will be used as network resources, and firms and their key partners will also constitute network actors. In Fig. 4, this interdependency is indicated by bi-directional arrows.

The network creates benefits at the system level, by collective network action. These benefits may be advantageous to all network actors, such as a shared infrastructure or collective marketing, or to society as a whole, such as cleaner air or higher biodiversity. The benefits flow back into the value proposition of the individual firms' business model, as benefits to the stakeholders. These benefits could also be used by firms to enhance their marketing communication and build better customer relationships. In a similar manner, the sustainability benefits are likely to influence the individual firms' value creation processes. For example, if the network develops knowledge on more sustainable or circular production techniques, then the participating companies are likely to implement these techniques in their production processes. System resources created by the network will be accessible to the individual firms and will thus flow back into their business models.

The costs that the network incurs when engaging in system-building activities—with the aim of contributing to the sustainability transition—need to be paid by the participating organisations, through in-kind contributions or funding. Therefore, they flow back into the individual firms' business models as costs. As all elements of the individual firm's business model influence the networked business model, the two models are highly interconnected.

Some network actors, in particular firms, are actively involved in creating a networked business model, while other actors are more indirectly involved, by being supportive of building the system. This holds, for instance, for the government in its function as guardian of the common goods, aiming to minimise negative externalities. The government will contribute resources, perhaps in the form of funding the network, thus hoping to generate sustainability benefits. However, as contracting entity the government acts as a market actor and therefore has a direct interest in actively developing a networked business model, particularly as a means of sharing the costs and benefits in a balanced manner. While non-firm actors usually do not have a fully developed individual business model, they, too, need to consider how to spend their resources on system-building for sustainability transitions, and they need to have expectations about the benefits of the networked endeavour. That is why it is important for all types of stakeholders—firms and other actors—to collectively generate the networked business model.

4 Illustrative Cases

In this section, we use the networked business model for sustainability transitions ex post as an analytical tool to study two empirical examples to illustrate its application. The cases focus on two Dutch value chains: baby nappies and mattresses. Actors in these value chains have jointly taken the initiative to make their value chains more circular, meaning that they aimed to move away from the linear approach of make, take and discard the product. Instead they attempted to cycle the product, including its parts and materials, to improve resource efficiency in the use and end-of-life phases. To create, capture and deliver value in view of improving the resource efficiency over the whole value chain, networked business models are adopted. In both cases, one of the authors of this chapter acted as intermediary (called 'transition broker'). By participating in this role, knowledge was gained about the collaboration process, the partners involved and the system-building activities to be created. Moreover, each author acted as a reflective scientist to analyse her case (Wittmayer & Schäpke, 2014). Both case studies were conducted in the context of the regional programme on circular economy in the Amsterdam Metropolitan Area, which has been run by the Amsterdam Economic Board since 2015 (Cramer, 2020). The following data were used for the analysis. Case 1 (Baby nappies): minutes of six interviews, one brainstorming session with representatives of the value chain and eight follow-up meetings. Case 2 (Mattresses): minutes and video recording of a Circular Economy Lab on Mattresses (see www.usi.nl), minutes of three meetings with representatives of the value chain, six informal meetings and a final report.

For each case we will show which actors are involved, which combination of system-building activities they engage in, and which networked business model is created. After describing the cases, we illustrate the networked business model elements of both cases in Table 1.

Case 1: Baby Nappies Each year, people in the Amsterdam Metropolitan Area throw away a total of about 29 metric tons of baby nappies (which constitute 142 million nappies). Only 1% of these is collected and pro-

Table 1 Empirical evidence and illustration of the networked business model elements

Networked business model elements		Empirical findings: Case 1: Baby nappies	Case 2: Mattresses
Value proposition	System-building goals	Network goal: To recycle and reuse (at the regional level) high-value nappy components	Network goal: To redesign new mattresses and recycle discarded mattresses of high value at the national level
		Transition goals: Reduction of environmental impact (i.e. reduction of virgin materials and resource use; CO_2 reduction; reduction of incineration fumes); creation of employment and promotion of innovation	Transition goals: Reduction of environmental impact (i.e. increase of resource efficiency; reuse of resources; reduction of environmental hazards); creation of employment and promotion of innovation
		System-building goals: Testing technologies and applications; knowledge development; co-creation of services; feedback loops with user groups; shared infrastructure; changing user behaviour	System-building goals: Testing technologies; knowledge development; co-creation of products and services; development of commercially viable products; feedback loops with user groups; shared infrastructure; generating new business models; changing user behaviour; collaborative marketing

(*continued*)

Table 1 (continued)

Networked business model elements		Empirical findings: Case 1: Baby nappies	Case 2: Mattresses
Value creation	System-building activities	1. Market creation of nappy components for second use (including independent quality control) 2. Research and technology development 3. Socio-cultural changes, particularly in collection and logistics of nappies 4. Orchestration by transition brokers	1. Market creation of mattress components for second use (including independent quality control) and of new, more circular mattresses via redesign 2. Research and technology development, particularly in redesign for circularity and better recycling techniques 3. Socio-cultural changes, particularly in collection and logistics of mattresses 4. Orchestration by transition brokers
	System resources	Innovative and tested technology; large-scale experimental setting; provision of developable plot of land (e.g. for factory); shared infrastructure for nappy disposal bins as well as for collection and logistics	Research and technology; infrastructure for shared collection system and logistics; network of nationally dispersed (decentralised) recycling facilities
	Network actors	Innovative recycler, business partner or landowner, municipalities, day care centres, customers of the recyclates and transition brokers	Mattress producers and their suppliers, recyclers, waste incineration companies, waste management departments of municipalities and their branch organisation, transition brokers, Parliament and the national government

(*continued*)

Table 1 (continued)

Networked business model elements		Empirical findings: Case 1: Baby nappies	Case 2: Mattresses
Value capture	Benefits for the system	Viable business case for all value chain partners, increased resource efficiency and more jobs	Viable business case for all value chain partners, increased resource efficiency and more jobs
	System-building costs	Costs and benefits divided proportionally among the partners with the intention of no cost increase for citizens	Costs and benefits divided proportionally among the partners, which has been made possible through a small price increase for each mattress sold (voluntary extended producer responsibility)

cessed for composting; the rest is incinerated. In 2016, the Amsterdam Economic Board wanted to create a closed loop of the baby nappies being discarded, and to this end it called for the reclamation of resources from recycled nappies in order to produce new products. Having investigated the most promising options available in the market by means of a brainstorming session and informal meetings, the Board approached the Amsterdam waste incineration company. The company expressed an interest to join the consortium, as nappy recycling was appropriate to the diversification of its portfolio (e.g. selling its residual heat). Moreover, the company could host the new business on its own land. For this reason, it was willing to co-invest in demonstration and commercial scale facilities. The next step was to select the most appropriate recycler, which happened to be a spin-off of a nappy manufacturer. Together with this company, the Board and the waste incineration company built a consortium with various municipalities and day care centres, which could organise the collection and logistics of the nappies on a substantial scale. Subsequently, the demand for the recyclates had to be created. So far, the intention has been to produce bottle caps out of the R-plastics that are recovered from the nappies, for example, for cleaning fluids and washing liquids. Furthermore, the sterilised super absorbent polymers can be reused in nappies. Research on applications for the recovered sterilised cellulose is still ongoing. The final step was an agreement on the networked business model balancing the costs and benefits in a just manner throughout the value chain. However, when the financial deal was almost closed, the waste incineration company withdrew, as it had changed its strategy due to financial and organisational issues. Awaiting the creation of a new consortium, the initiative is currently on hold. Nevertheless, after solving this problem, the initiative will be a first and important step on the road towards a more circular product chain of nappies. The baby nappies case shows that a large variety of actors had to be found in order to create a viable circular business case. Besides the innovative recycler, the waste incineration company, the municipalities and the day care centres, customers of the recyclates were also asked to join the consortium. In order to distribute the costs and benefits proportionally among the partners, a networked business model had to be developed. The main obstacle to agreement on a fair deal was transparency about the financial implications for each partner in the consortium. As some activities cost relatively more (e.g. the collection and logistics), the actors responsible for these activities needed to be compensated. This was true in particular for the municipalities, which did not want to raise the cost of waste management for their citizens. This negotiation process in the network of consortium partners differs from the regular procedure, in which each partner bears their own costs. The elements of the networked business model for this case are presented in Table 1.

Case 2: Mattresses Yearly, about 1.2 million old mattresses are discarded in the Netherlands. Until recently, most mattresses were incinerated at a relatively high cost. Waste incineration companies were averse to incineration due to the technical problems that waste incineration facilities encounter when storing and processing mattresses; consequently, the call for redesign and recycling of mattresses became more pronounced. However, the existing alternative pathway—mattress recycling—is exceedingly expensive, which implies that it is barely possible for the two Dutch scale-up mattress recyclers to survive and optimise their recycling technologies. To break this stalemate, a Circular Economy Lab was set up, which consisted of representatives of the whole value chain, including recyclers and local governments. The aim was to develop a strategy to organise the redesign and recycling of mattresses. In the end, a national initiative was launched to set up a voluntary scheme for extended producer responsibility. This scheme includes a small price increase for each mattress sold in order to finance collection and recycling as well as to promote the redesign of mattresses for reuse and recycling through innovation. To put pressure on the mattress value chain, the Dutch Parliament asked the Secretary of State for the Environment to introduce obligatory extended producer responsibility if the mattress value chain did not respond adequately. This process was orchestrated by a transition broker. It led to an agreement on voluntary extended producer responsibility among the partners in the value chain. Mattress manufacturers are now taking the lead in the execution of this plan. In anticipation of the introduction of the initiative, an innovative manufacturer has already managed to redesign and sell a 'circular' mattress that sets an example to the entire sector. The mattresses case illustrates that a large number of partners are needed to develop an alternative strategy which promotes redesign and recycling. Besides the mattress producers and their suppliers, the recyclers and the waste incineration companies, this also involved waste management departments of municipalities and their branch organisation, Parliament and the national government. As this initiative could not be solved on a regional scale, the Economic Board took the lead to help launch a national initiative. Preconditions were an effective collection and logistics system, a guaranteed volume of waste, an articulated demand for the recycled material and a quality standard for the recyclates accepted. However, the most important obstacle was how to finance the redesign and recycling of mattresses. Although mattress companies had different views on this issue, they ultimately agreed upon a voluntary scheme for extended producer responsibility to which all companies should conform. This successful result represents a meaningful step towards closing the loop of mattresses, even though there is still a long way to go before mattresses are fully circular. The elements of the networked business model for this case are described in Table 1.

Table 1 illustrates the networked business model of both cases, showing that each network of actors has a common value proposition. In addition, the table shows which activities are necessary to reach that goal, which resources are needed and which network actors need to be included. Moreover, the system-level costs and benefits are displayed. These feed into the business models of the individual firms. For example, the small price increase for each mattress was acceptable to individual mattress producers as it was to become obligatory for the whole sector. The recyclers' business became more profitable as a result of the financial contribution generated via the price increase. It goes beyond the scope of this paper to display the business models of the individual firms in detail here, which is why only the networked business model part is illustrated.

5 Conclusion

To make sustainability transitions happen, a systemic perspective of business models is needed. Instead of merely embedding sustainability in a focal-firm business model, a business model should also be embedded in the sustainability transition. To accommodate this systemic part and transition in the external environment, we developed a networked business model. This model can help networks of actors to structure and align their efforts in shaping a more sustainable system, which in turn will help them to market their own sustainable product or service. However, a networked business model is not sufficient: it needs to be linked to the individual business models of the firms in the network. Therefore, we argued that two interconnected business models are necessary—one at the firm level and one at the system level. Each firm in the network needs to design its own business model, which feeds into the networked business model. In turn, the networked business model feeds into the firm-centred business model, too. Through the interconnected networked business model, firms can integrate the systemic change to more sustainable modes of production and consumption into their business model.

We have added to the business model literature the concept of the 'networked business model' for system change, which is interconnected with the individual business models of the firms in the network. We have not only added the systems perspective and the need for networked collaboration, which has already been addressed by business model scholars.

We go further as we also illustrate how firms can integrate the collective activities necessary to achieve a sustainability transition into their focal-firm business model.

We used the networked business model for analytical (ex post) purposes to study two illustrative Dutch cases. It would be valuable to study additional cases in other cultural and economic contexts, so that general conclusions can be drawn on how networked business models are operationalised. The cases presented here indicate that the networked business model may also be useful for practitioners, particularly firms. It would be interesting to develop a practical tool for designing networked business models for system-building and to test it with industry actors in different settings.

To conclude, actors who want to market sustainable products or services need to consider the ecosystem in which they operate, and the sustainability transition to which they want to contribute. To embed their firm-centric business model in this transition, they need to adopt a systems perspective, and identify the ways in which they can pro-actively influence the emergence of a more sustainable production and consumption system that can help their product or service to flourish. Together with other network actors, they can develop a networked business model which feeds into their own firm-centric business model and vice versa. Both business models will then be interconnected and mutually influence one another.

Acknowledgements We would like to thank Hanna Dijkstra for her useful ideas on the visualisation of the networked business model (Fig. 3). In addition, we thank her and the editors of this book for their constructive feedback on this chapter.

References

Astley, W. G. (1984). Toward an appreciation of collective strategy. *The Academy of Management Review, 9*(3), 526–535.

Bengtsson, M., & Kock, S. (1999). Cooperation and competition in relationships between competitors in business networks. *Journal of Business &*

Industrial Marketing, 14(3), 178–194. https://doi.org/10.1108/08858629910272184
Bengtsson, M., & Kock, S. (2000). "Coopetition" in business networks—To cooperate and compete simultaneously. *Industrial Marketing Management, 29*(5), 411–426. https://doi.org/10.1016/S0019-8501(99)00067-X
Bidmon, C. M., & Knab, S. F. (2018). The three roles of business models in societal transitions: New linkages between business model and transition research. *Journal of Cleaner Production, 178*, 903–916. https://doi.org/10.1016/j.jclepro.2017.12.198
Bocken, N. M. P., Boons, F., & Baldassarre, B. (2019). Sustainable business model experimentation by understanding ecologies of business models. *Journal of Cleaner Production, 208*, 1498–1512. https://doi.org/10.1016/j.jclepro.2018.10.159
Bocken, N. M. P., Short, S. W., Rana, P., & Evans, S. (2014). A literature and practice review to develop sustainable business model archetypes. *Journal of Cleaner Production, 65*, 42–56. https://doi.org/10.1016/j.jclepro.2013.11.039
Boons, F., & Lüdeke-Freund, F. (2013). Business models for sustainable innovation: State-of-the-art and steps towards a research agenda. *Journal of Cleaner Production, 45*, 9–19. https://doi.org/10.1016/j.jclepro.2012.07.007
Bouncken, R. B., Fredrich, V., Ritala, P., & Kraus, S. (2018). Coopetition in new product development alliances: Advantages and tensions for incremental and radical innovation. *British Journal of Management, 29*(3), 391–410. https://doi.org/10.1111/1467-8551.12213
Breuer, H., & Lüdeke-Freund, F. (2017). Values-based network and business model innovation. *International Journal of Innovation Management, 21*(3), 1–35. https://doi.org/10.1142/S1363919617500281
Chesbrough, H. (2010). Business model innovation: Opportunities and barriers. *Long Range Planning, 43*(2–3), 354–363. https://doi.org/10.1016/j.lrp.2009.07.010
Cramer, J. M. (2020). The function of transition brokers in the regional governance of implementing circular economy – A comparative case study of six Dutch regions. *Sustainability, 12*(12), 5015. https://doi.org/10.3390/su12125015
Diepenmaat, H., Kemp, R., & Velter, M. (2020). Why sustainable development requires societal innovation and cannot be achieved without this. *Sustainability (Switzerland), 12*(3), 1–26. https://doi.org/10.3390/su12031270
Dijkstra, H., van Beukering, P., & Brouwer, R. (2020). Business models and sustainable plastic management: A systematic review of the literature. *Journal*

of Cleaner Production, 258, 120967. https://doi.org/10.1016/j.jclepro.2020.120967
Farla, J., Markard, J., Raven, R., & Coenen, L. (2012). Sustainability transitions in the making: A closer look at actors, strategies and resources. *Technological Forecasting and Social Change, 79*(6), 991–998. https://doi.org/10.1016/j.techfore.2012.02.001
Foxon, T., Makuch, Z., Mata, M., & Pearson, P. (2004). Innovation systems and policy-making processes for the transition to sustainability. In K. Jacob, M. Binder, & A. Wieczorek (Eds.), *Governance for industrial transformation. Proceedings of the 2003 Berlin conference on the human dimensions of global environmental change* (pp. 96–112). Environmental Policy Research Centre.
Freudenreich, B., Lüdeke-Freund, F., & Schaltegger, S. (2020). A Stakeholder theory perspective on business models: Value creation for sustainability. *Journal of Business Ethics, 166*(1), 3–18. https://doi.org/10.1007/s10551-019-04112-z
Galvão, G. D. A., Homrich, A. S., Geissdoerfer, M., Evans, S., scoleze Ferrer, P. S., & Carvalho, M. M. (2020). Towards a value stream perspective of circular business models. *Resources, Conservation and Recycling, 162*, 105060. https://doi.org/10.1016/j.resconrec.2020.105060
Geels, F. W. (2005). Processes and patterns in transitions and system innovations: Refining the co-evolutionary multi-level perspective. *Transitions Towards Sustainability Through System Innovation, 72*(6), 681–696. https://doi.org/10.1016/j.techfore.2004.08.014
Geels, F. W., Hekkert, M. P., & Jacobsson, S. (2008). The dynamics of sustainable innovation journeys. *Technology Analysis & Strategic Management, 20*(5), 521–536. https://doi.org/10.1080/09537320802292982
Geissdoerfer, M., Vladimirova, D., & Evans, S. (2018). Sustainable business model innovation: A review. *Journal of Cleaner Production, 198*, 401–416. https://doi.org/10.1016/j.jclepro.2018.06.240
Hall, J., Daneke, G., & Lenox, M. (2010). Sustainable development and entrepreneurship: Past contributions and future directions. *Journal of Business Venturing, 25*(5), 439–448. https://doi.org/10.1016/j.jbusvent.2010.01.002
Hekkert, M. P., Suurs, R. A. A., Negro, S. O., Kuhlmann, S., & Smits, R. E. H. M. (2007). Functions of innovation systems: A new approach for analysing technological change. *Technological Forecasting and Social Change, 74*(4), 413–432. https://doi.org/10.1016/j.techfore.2006.03.002
Hockerts, K., & Wüstenhagen, R. (2010). Greening Goliaths versus emerging Davids – Theorizing about the role of incumbents and new entrants in sus-

tainable entrepreneurship. *Journal of Business Venturing, 25*, 481–492. https://doi.org/10.1016/j.jbusvent.2009.07.005

Hörisch, J., Freeman, R. E., & Schaltegger, S. (2014). Applying Stakeholder theory in sustainability management: Links, similarities, dissimilarities, and a conceptual framework. *Organization and Environment, 27*(4), 328–346. https://doi.org/10.1177/1086026614535786

Iansiti, M., & Levien, R. (2004). Strategy as ecology. *Harvard Business Review, 82*(3), 68–81.

Jacobsson, S., & Bergek, A. (2011a). Innovation system analyses and sustainability transitions: Contributions and suggestions for research. *Environmental Innovation and Societal Transitions, 1*(1), 41–57. https://doi.org/10.1016/j.eist.2011.04.006

Jacobsson, S., & Bergek, A. (2011b). Innovation system analyses and sustainability transitions: Contributions and suggestions for research. *Environmental Innovation and Societal Transitions, 1*(1), 41–57. https://doi.org/10.1016/j.eist.2011.04.006

Kemp, R., Rip, A., & Schot, J. W. (2001). Constructing transition paths through the management of niches. In R. Garud & P. Karnoe (Eds.), *Path dependence and creation* (pp. 269–299). Lawrence Earlbaum.

Köhler, J., Geels, F. W., Kern, F., Markard, J., Onsongo, E., Wieczorek, A., Alkemade, F., Avelino, F., Bergek, A., Boons, F., Fünfschilling, L., Hess, D., Holtz, G., Hyysalo, S., Jenkins, K., Kivimaa, P., Martiskainen, M., McMeekin, A., Mühlemeier, M. S., … Wells, P. (2019). An agenda for sustainability transitions research: State of the art and future directions. *Environmental Innovation and Societal Transitions, 31*(December 2018), 1–32. https://doi.org/10.1016/j.eist.2019.01.004

Lahti, T., Wincent, J., & Parida, V. (2018). A definition and theoretical review of the circular economy, value creation, and sustainable business models: Where are we now and where should research move in the future? *Sustainability, 10*(8), 2799. https://doi.org/10.3390/su10082799

Lewandowski, M. (2016). Designing the business models for circular economy—Towards the conceptual framework. *Sustainability, 8*(1), 43.

Loorbach, D., & Wijsman, K. (2013). Business transition management: Exploring a new role for business in sustainability transitions. *Journal of Cleaner Production, 45*, 20–28. https://doi.org/10.1016/j.jclepro.2012.11.002

Lüdeke-Freund, F., Gold, S., & Bocken, N. M. P. (2019). A review and typology of circular economy business model patterns. *Journal of Industrial Ecology, 23*(1), 36–61. https://doi.org/10.1111/jiec.12763

Lupova-Henry, E., & Dotti, N. F. (2019). Governance of sustainable innovation: Moving beyond the hierarchy-market-network trichotomy? A systematic literature review using the 'who-how-what' framework. *Journal of Cleaner Production, 210*, 738–748. https://doi.org/10.1016/j.jclepro.2018.11.068

Markard, J., Raven, R., & Truffer, B. (2012). Sustainability transitions: An emerging field of research and its prospects. *Research Policy, 41*(6), 955–967. https://doi.org/10.1016/j.respol.2012.02.013

Mårtensson, K., & Westerberg, K. (2016). Corporate environmental strategies towards sustainable development. *Business Strategy and the Environment, 25*(1), 1–9. https://doi.org/10.1002/bse.1852

Moore, J. F. (1993). Predators and prey: A new ecology of competition. *Harvard Business Review, 71*(3), 75–86.

Moore, J. F. (1996). *The death of competition: Leadership and strategy in the age of business ecosystems*. HarperBusiness. http://www.worldcat.org/title/death-of-competition-leadership-and-strategy-in-the-age-of-business-ecosystems/oclc/34079071?lang=nl

Musiolik, J. (2012). *Innovation system-building: On the role of actors, networks and resources*. Universiteit Utrecht. http://www.eawag.ch/forschung/ess/publikationen/pdf/PhD_thesis_Musiolik_2012.pdf

Musiolik, J., & Markard, J. (2011). Creating and shaping innovation systems: Formal networks in the innovation system for stationary fuel cells in Germany. *Energy Policy, 39*, 1909–1922.

Musiolik, J., Markard, J., & Hekkert, M. P. (2012). Networks and network resources in technological innovation systems: Towards a conceptual framework for system building. *Technological Forecasting and Social Change, 79*(6), 1032–1048. https://doi.org/10.1016/j.techfore.2012.01.003

Neumeyer, X., & Santos, S. C. (2018). Sustainable business models, venture typologies, and entrepreneurial ecosystems: A social network perspective. *Journal of Cleaner Production, 172*, 4565–4579. https://doi.org/10.1016/j.jclepro.2017.08.216

Osterwalder, A., & Pigneur, Y. (2010). *Business model generation: A handbook for visionaries, game changers, and challengers*. Wiley. www.businessmodelgeneration.com

Pitelis, C. (2012). Clusters, entrepreneurial ecosystem co-creation, and appropriability: A conceptual framework. *Industrial and Corporate Change, 21*(6), 1359–1388. https://doi.org/10.1093/icc/dts008

Planko, J., Chappin, M. M. H., Cramer, J. M., & Hekkert, M. P. (2017). Managing strategic system-building networks in emerging business fields: A case study of the Dutch smart grid sector. *Industrial Marketing Management, 67*, 37–51. https://doi.org/10.1016/j.indmarman.2017.06.010

Planko, J., Chappin, M. M. H., Cramer, J., & Hekkert, M. P. (2019). Coping with coopetition – Facing dilemmas in cooperation for sustainable development: The case of the Dutch smart grid industry. *Business Strategy and the Environment, November 2018*, 1–10. https://doi.org/10.1002/bse.2271

Planko, J., Cramer, J. M., Chappin, M. M. H., & Hekkert, M. P. (2016). Strategic collective system building to commercialize sustainability innovations. *Journal of Cleaner Production, 112*, 2328–2341. https://doi.org/10.1016/j.jclepro.2015.09.108

Reim, W., Parida, V., & Örtqvist, D. (2015). Product-Service Systems (PSS) business models and tactics – A systematic literature review. *Journal of Cleaner Production, 97*, 61–75. https://doi.org/10.1016/j.jclepro.2014.07.003

Rohrbeck, R., Konnertz, L., & Knab, S. (2013). Collaborative business modelling for systemic and sustainability innovations. *International Journal of Technology Management, 63*(1/2), 4. https://doi.org/10.1504/IJTM.2013.055577

Roome, N., & Louche, C. (2016). Journeying toward business models for sustainability: A conceptual model found inside the black box of organisational transformation. *Organization and Environment, 29*(1). https://doi.org/10.1177/1086026615595084

Rossignoli, F., & Lionzo, A. (2018). Network impact on business models for sustainability: Case study in the energy sector. *Journal of Cleaner Production, 182*, 694–704. https://doi.org/10.1016/j.jclepro.2018.02.015

Schaltegger, S., Hansen, E. G., & Lüdeke-Freund, F. (2016). Business models for sustainability: Origins, present research, and future avenues. *Organization and Environment, 29*(1), 3–10. https://doi.org/10.1177/1086026615599806

Starik, M., Stubbs, W., & Benn, S. (2016). Synthesising environmental and socio-economic sustainability models: A multi-level approach for advancing integrated sustainability research and practice. *Australasian Journal of Environmental Management, 23*(4), 402–425. https://doi.org/10.1080/14486563.2016.1188425

Stubbs, W., & Cocklin, C. (2008). Conceptualizing a "sustainability business model". *Organization and Environment, 21*(2), 103–127. https://doi.org/10.1177/1086026608318042

Teece, D. J. (2010). Business models, business strategy and innovation. *Long Range Planning, 43*(2–3), 172–194. https://doi.org/10.1016/j.lrp.2009.07.003

Upward, A., & Jones, P. (2016). An ontology for strongly sustainable business models: Defining an enterprise framework compatible with natural and social science. *Organization and Environment, 29*(1), 97–123. https://doi.org/10.1177/1086026615592933

Van de Ven, A. H. (1993). The development of an infrastructure for entrepreneurship. *Journal of Business Venturing, 8*(3), 212–230.

Vazquez-Brust, D., Piao, R. S., de Melo, M. F. D. S., Yaryd, R. T., & Carvalho, M. M. (2020). The governance of collaboration for sustainable development: Exploring the "black box". *Journal of Cleaner Production, 256*, 120260. https://doi.org/10.1016/j.jclepro.2020.120260

Veleva, V., & Bodkin, G. (2018). Corporate-entrepreneur collaborations to advance a circular economy. *Journal of Cleaner Production, 188*, 20–37. https://doi.org/10.1016/j.jclepro.2018.03.196

Velter, M. G. E., Bitzer, V., Bocken, N. M. P., & Kemp, R. (2020). Sustainable business model innovation: The role of boundary work for multi-stakeholder alignment. *Journal of Cleaner Production, 247*, 119497. https://doi.org/10.1016/j.jclepro.2019.119497

Verbong, G. P. J., Beemsterboer, S., & Sengers, F. (2013). Smart grids or smart users? Involving users in developing a low carbon electricity economy. *Energy Policy, 52*, 117–125. https://doi.org/10.1016/j.enpol.2012.05.003

Vogel, P., & Fischler-Strasak, U. (2014). Fostering sustainable innovation within organizations. In C. Weidinger, F. Fischler, & R. Schmidpeter (Eds.), *Sustainable entrepreneurship* (pp. 191–205). Springer Berlin Heidelberg. https://doi.org/10.1007/978-3-642-38753-1

Wirtz, B. W., Pistoia, A., Ullrich, S., & Göttel, V. (2016). Business models: Origin, development and future research perspectives. *Long Range Planning, 49*(1), 36–54. https://doi.org/10.1016/j.lrp.2015.04.001

Wittmayer, J. M., & Schäpke, N. (2014). Action, research and participation: Roles of researchers in sustainability transitions. *Sustainability Science, 9*(4), 483–496. https://doi.org/10.1007/s11625-014-0258-4

Zander, S., Trang, S., & Kolbe, L. M. (2016). Drivers of network governance: A multitheoretic perspective with insights from case studies in the German wood industry. *Journal of Cleaner Production, 110*, 109–120. https://doi.org/10.1016/j.jclepro.2015.03.010

Zott, C., Amit, R., & Massa, L. (2011). The business model: Recent developments and future research. *Journal of Management, 37*(4), 1019–1042. https://doi.org/10.1177/0149206311406265

Sustainable Value Creation for Advancing Sustainability Transition: An Approach to Integrate Company- and System-Level Sustainability

Minttu Laukkanen, Kaisa Manninen, Janne Huiskonen, and Nina Kinnunen

1 Introduction

Companies can act as important agents in sustainability transitions (Farla et al., 2012; Markard et al., 2012) if they successfully implement ambitious sustainability strategies through new sustainable business models (SBMs) (Bolton & Hannon, 2016). Business models are part of and interact with established socio-technical systems, being a bridge between the company and the economic and social systems (Lüdeke-Freund & Dembek, 2017; Roome & Louche, 2016). Further, SBMs are recognised

M. Laukkanen (✉) • K. Manninen • J. Huiskonen
LUT University, Lappeenranta, Finland
e-mail: Minttu.Laukkanen@lut.fi; Kaisa.Manninen@lut.fi; Janne.Huiskonen@lut.fi

N. Kinnunen
Kekkilä-BVB, Vantaa, Finland
e-mail: nina.kinnunen@kekkila-bvb.com

A. Aagaard et al. (eds.), *Business Models for Sustainability Transitions*,
https://doi.org/10.1007/978-3-030-77580-3_4

as a key to the creation of sustainable business and to leverage wider sustainability transition, that is, a process through which established socio-technical systems shift to more sustainable modes of production and consumption (Loorbach et al., 2017; Markard et al., 2012). However, the interaction between companies and the larger socio-technical system in which they operate and impact on is still a less-researched area (Bidmon & Knab, 2018; Bocken et al., 2019). Company-level actions only make a marginal contribution to sustainability transition if the link between the micro-level concept of corporate sustainability and the global macro-level concept of sustainable development is not comprehensively understood (Dyllick & Muff, 2016). In this chapter, the terms "system" and "macro" level or the "societal" level of society are used interchangeably.

Sustainable business models incorporate the three pillars of sustainability: economic, environmental, and social, as an integral part of the company's value proposition and value creation logic (Stubbs & Cocklin, 2008). SBMs are seen as vehicles for responding to the world's increasing ecological and social problems and to assist all types of companies to make their business sustainable (Lüdeke-Freund & Dembek, 2017). For example, many traditional manufacturing companies have changed their business models from selling products to selling services, which have the potential to increase sustainability, for example, by improving utilisation of resources and products or extending product life (Yang & Evans, 2019). Today, there is great interest in SBMs based on circularity, saving resources, and eliminating waste (Pieroni et al., 2019), and interest in new forms of consumption, for example, through sharing economy business models (Laukkanen & Tura, 2020). These represent radical changes in the existing business logics and wholly new ways of doing business, leveraging sustainability transition.

Thus far, only a few studies have integrated business and management research with system transition research (Köhler et al., 2019). The business model literature remains largely dominated by company-, industry-, or business network-level analyses and examples, and only few studies have considered the link with macro developments at the systemic level (Abdelkafi & Täuscher, 2016; Bidmon & Knab, 2018). Transition research, which considers systems (e.g., energy transition), has neglected the micro-level dynamics and the role of single companies (Köhler et al.,

2019; Markard et al., 2012). Consequently, further research is needed on how sustainability strategies of companies impact the outcome of sustainability transitions (Farla et al., 2012), and the rationale of how individual companies can enhance sustainability transitions through their SBMs (Iñigo & Albareda, 2016). In conclusion, there is a strong call for an integration of business research with transition research to better understand the interrelations between SBMs and sustainability transitions (Bocken et al., 2019; Köhler et al., 2019; Sarasini & Linder, 2018).

The main objective of this study is to bridge the research gap between the company-level SBMs and system-level sustainability transitions. The research question guiding the research is: How can individual companies contribute to and enable wider sustainability transition through their business models?

This study presents a company-driven approach by proposing sustainable value creation (SVC) as an approach to integrate company-level sustainability into broader system-level sustainability transition. Sustainable value creation is a central part of any SBM, and it can be understood as a core process that mediates the impacts of an individual SBM to different system levels by contributing to wider value networks (Hellström et al., 2015) and creating value with and for various stakeholders (Freudenreich et al., 2020). The proposed approach is based on an extensive literature review and analysis of SBMs and sustainability transitions and the empirical case example of Europe's leading horticultural company, Kekkilä-BVB.

This study offers initial guidelines for business managers aiming to adopt SBMs that contribute to sustainability transition through SVC. Contributing conceptually to the existing SBM and sustainability transition literatures, this study explains how the concept of SVC can be interpreted as a bridge between a company and economic and social systems, and further as a component of the larger system-level transition to sustainability. As the emerging SBM research field has its roots in multiple disciplines—the natural sciences (e.g., sustainability), management sciences (e.g., business models, corporate sustainability), and social sciences (e.g., transition)—this study summarises the key concepts (related to SBMs and SVC as contributing to sustainability transition) aiming to narrow the gap between different disciplines.

The chapter is structured as follows. The second section presents the theoretical background and builds an integration between company- and system-level sustainability by integrating views from the corporate sustainability, traditional business model, and sustainability transition literature. The third section presents the research design. The fourth section discusses the concept of SVC for advancing sustainability transition and uses the case study company to present the key steps in adopting an SVC approach. The chapter concludes with a discussion of implications and avenues for future research.

2 Theoretical Foundation

2.1 Integrating Company- and System-Level Sustainability Through Sustainable Business Model Research

Sustainable business model research is an emerging research field that integrates different disciplines (Lüdeke-Freund & Dembek, 2017). This study adopts such an integrative approach to SBMs by combining views of corporate sustainability, traditional business model, and system transition from their respective literatures (Fig. 1).

A corporate sustainability literature has emerged in the twenty-first century that considers how the macro-level concept of sustainable development can be applied to the company level (Baumgartner & Ebner, 2010). Corporate sustainability refers to translating the general principles of system-level sustainability (Robèrt et al., 2012) and sustainable development into a corporate context, referring to activities to incorporate environmental and social concerns in company's strategy and business operations (Montiel, 2008). The concept of sustainable development, which is formally defined as the ability to meet the needs of the present without compromising the ability of future generations to meet their own needs (WCED, 1987), was introduced about thirty years ago, and the consideration of sustainability in the management literature has grown quickly since the 1990s (Zemigala, 2019). Although the terms

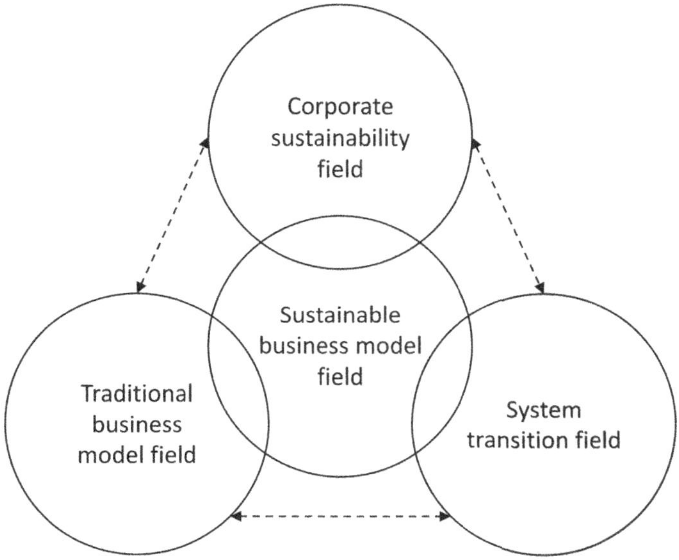

Fig. 1 Sustainable business model research as an integrative field. (Adapted from Lüdeke-Freund & Dembek, 2017)

"sustainable development" and "sustainability" are often used interchangeably (Williams & Millington, 2004), sustainability can be understood as the target goal and sustainable development as a holistic process for achieving sustainability over time (Shaker, 2015). The concept of sustainable business has also been adopted to emphasise a business-centred approach to sustainability. "Sustainable business" refers to translating macro-level sustainability challenges into business opportunities that make "business sense" of societal and environmental issues and creating a significant positive impact in critical and relevant areas for society and the planet while easing conflicts between financial demands and societal needs. Moreover, it refers to engaging on a sectorial or cross-sectorial level aiming to change the common practices, rules, and standards shared by all members in an industry and along supply chains towards approaches that advance system-level sustainability. Changing current approaches requires collaboration with all stakeholders involved, as big sustainability challenges like climate change, availability of fresh water, and loss of biodiversity cannot be solved by business alone (Dyllick & Muff, 2016).

Likewise, traditional business model research has flourished in the management literature since the end of the 1990s, especially with the emergence of the Internet and rapid advances in information and communication technologies (Demil & Lecocq, 2010). The term "business model" has been used in various ways over the years. For example, it is confused with other popular terms in the management literature such as "strategy," "business concept," "revenue model," and "economic model" (DaSilva & Trkman, 2014). Today, the common understanding of the business model is that it describes the rationale of how an organisation creates, delivers, and captures value (Biloslavo et al., 2018; Osterwalder & Pigneur, 2010; Teece, 2010). Such a value-based approach provides a broader definition of a business model. As a business model is applied to various purposes, business model research covers various themes at a general level, including the static approach, which describes the core business model components and their coherence, and a more transformational approach, using the concept as a tool for addressing change and innovation (Demil & Lecocq, 2010). In this study, the business model is adopted to provide a link between an individual company and the larger production and consumption system to which it belongs (Boons et al., 2013).

The system transition literature studies systemic change (i.e., transition), a concept applied in many scientific disciplines that refers to a non-linear shift from one dynamic equilibrium to another. Transition is the result of actions and an interplay of a variety of changes, at different levels and in different domains, which somehow interact with and reinforce each other to produce a fundamental change in a societal system (Clarke & Crane, 2018; Loorbach et al., 2017). In the system transition literature, businesses are typically perceived as agents that can challenge the status quo of the current economy by contributing to it through radical and holistic changes in the existing business logics and business models (Köhler et al., 2019). The literature on sustainability transitions has been developed to address the large-scale societal changes aimed at solving the global challenge of sustainability (Loorbach et al., 2017; Smith et al., 2010). Sustainability transition is a long-term, multidimensional, and fundamental transformation process through which established socio-technical systems shift to more sustainable modes of production and consumption (Markard et al., 2012). Transitions are coevolutionary processes entailing multiple interdependent developments and involving changes in a range of elements: technologies, markets, user practices, cultural meanings, infrastructures, policies, industry structures, business models, and supply chains (Köhler et al., 2019; Markard et al., 2012). Companies act as important agents in sustainability transition by developing novel technologies, products, services, and business models; creating new value networks; lobbying for specific policies; influencing customer behaviour; and shaping entire industries (Köhler et al., 2019).

Sustainable business model research has emerged from flaws in existing research fields (Lüdeke-Freund & Dembek, 2017). The corporate sustainability literature has traditionally focused on business-level activities such as sustainable supply chain management (Wolf, 2014), sustainability performance measurement (Goyal et al., 2013), or sustainability strategies (Baumgartner & Ebner, 2010), but omitted the strategic link between the company and economic and societal system levels. The traditional business model literature has focused on how companies create value for customers, capture value itself, and enhance competitiveness (Zott et al., 2011) lacking sustainability and multi-stakeholder perspectives. On the other hand, transition research has traditionally focused on single systems, for example, energy transition, but not the rationale of how individual companies can enhance sustainability transitions. Recently, the first studies focusing on the interplay between business models and sustainability transitions have emerged in both the management and transition literature (Bidmon & Knab, 2018; Sarasini & Linder, 2018). Through integrating the views from the research fields of corporate sustainability, traditional business models, and system transitions, SBM research considers the role of individual companies contributing and enabling wider sustainability transitions. Sustainable business models provide a link between company- and system-level sustainability, leveraging wider sustainability transition by integrating science-based sustainability principles (Robèrt et al., 2012) into the company's value proposition and value creation logic, and providing value to the various stakeholders and to the natural environment and/or society (Abdelkafi & Täuscher, 2016; Lüdeke-Freund & Dembek, 2017).

2.2 Key Concepts in Sustainable Business Model Research

In the following, company- and system-level sustainability are integrated through the key concepts discussed in the previous section: system-level sustainability, sustainability transition, sustainable business, and sustainable business model. Figure 2 provides the link from company-level SBM to system-level sustainability: Through SBM, an individual company integrates sustainability principles into its core business, delivers the shift towards sustainable business, and accelerates the broader transition towards system-level sustainability (Bidmon & Knab, 2018). Further, Table 1 summarises the key concepts in the SBM literature, reflecting that SBM research has its roots in multiple disciplines: the natural sciences (e.g., sustainability), management sciences (e.g., business model, corporate sustainability), and social sciences and technology studies (e.g., transition).

Integrating macro-level sustainability targets with the company-level strategy and the business model requires that companies clearly understand the meaning and relevance of the sustainability concept (Rauter et al., 2017). Increasing environmental, social, and economic problems require systemic solutions through which companies create sustainability benefits and solve macro-level sustainability challenges, not just minimise negative impacts at the company level. The term "system-level sustainability" is therefore used in this study to describe the final goal of a company. Following the definition of strong sustainability (Neumayer, 2013), system-level sustainability refers to conditions that enable a good quality of life and welfare of current and future generations within ecological limits. Companies aiming to advance system-level sustainability create economic and social value while protecting the natural environment and reducing environmental pollution.

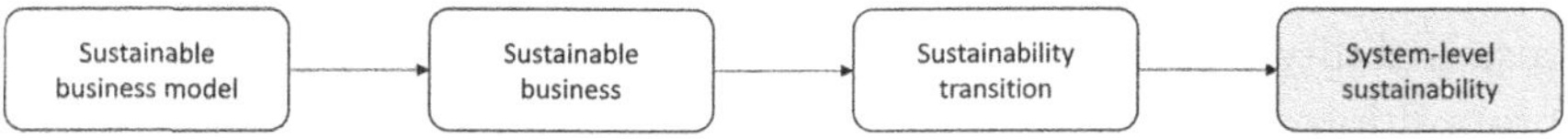

Fig. 2 Key concepts as integrating company- and system-level sustainability

Table 1 Key concepts

Concept	Definition
System-level sustainability	System-level sustainability refers to conditions that enable a good quality of life and welfare of current and future generations within ecological limits.
Sustainable development	Sustainable development refers to a process for advancing system-level sustainability over time.
Corporate sustainability	Corporate sustainability is about translating the general principles of system-level sustainability and sustainable development to the company level, referring to activities to incorporate environmental and social concerns in company's strategy and business operations (Montiel, 2008).
Sustainable business	Sustainable business refers to translating macro-level sustainability challenges into business opportunities making "business sense" of societal and environmental issues and creating a significant positive impact in critical and relevant areas for society and the planet while easing conflicts between financial demands and societal needs. It also refers to engaging on a sectorial or cross-sectorial level aiming to change the common practices, rules, and standards shared by all members in an industry and along supply chains towards approaches that advance system-level sustainability (Dyllick & Muff, 2016).
Transition	Transition (i.e., systemic change) refers to a non-linear shift from one dynamic equilibrium to another; it is the result of actions and an interplay of a variety of changes, at different levels and in different domains, that somehow interact with and reinforce each other to produce a fundamental change in a societal system (Clarke & Crane, 2018; Loorbach et al., 2017).
Sustainability transition	Sustainability transition is a long-term, multidimensional, and fundamental transformation process through which established socio-technical systems shift to more sustainable modes of production and consumption (Markard et al., 2012).
Business model	A business model describes the rationale of how a company creates, delivers, and captures value (Osterwalder & Pigneur, 2010), and provides a link between an individual company and the larger production and consumption system to which it belongs (Boons et al., 2013).

(*continued*)

Table 1 (continued)

Concept	Definition
Sustainable business model	A sustainable business model provides a link between company- and system-level sustainability, leveraging wider sustainability transition by integrating sustainability principles (Robèrt et al., 2012) into the company's value proposition and value creation logic, and providing value to the various stakeholders and to the natural environment and/or society (Abdelkafi & Täuscher, 2016; Lüdeke-Freund & Dembek, 2017).
Sustainable business model innovation	Sustainable business model innovation refers to the conceptualisation and implementation of new business models, or changes in existing business models aiming to advance system-level sustainability.
Value creation	Value creation consists of value creation processes, which refer to expected value or a company's attempt to increase value (including the activities and resources involved in the value creation process), and value outcomes, which consider how value is actually perceived by the beneficiaries.
Sustainable value creation	Sustainable value creation refers to positive environmental, social, and economic impacts (co)created by a company and its value network and perceived by a company and different stakeholders.

To contribute to system-level sustainability, businesses need to implement new business models or make changes to existing business models (i.e., SBM innovations). SBM innovations vary with the scope and degree of change and with the level of innovation (Adams et al., 2016). The innovations required for leveraging sustainability transition and for contributing to system-level sustainability are linked to higher levels of business model innovation and more radical business model changes (Boons et al., 2013). The focus has recently shifted to more systemic, non-technological, and people-centred innovations in which sustainability is treated as a socio-technical challenge (Adams et al., 2016). From this perspective, SBM's role is important but is not an end in itself. Therefore, the proposed approach considers sustainable value creation (SVC), which can be understood as a core SBM process that mediates the impact of individual SBMs.

2.3 Sustainable Value Creation for Advancing Sustainability Transition

Sustainable business models are commonly considered combinations of the general value concepts of value proposition, value creation and delivery, and value capture (e.g., Abdelkafi & Täuscher, 2016; Evans et al., 2017) (Fig. 3). Besides new business models, sustainability calls for a redefinition of value concepts (Roome & Louche, 2016). While a traditional business model aims mainly to create value for customers, an SBM aims to align business goals with the needs of an ecosystem and society translated into multiple value concepts (Kristensen & Remmen, 2019) such as increased happiness for customers, increased eco-effectiveness for supply chain partners, and increased prosperity and wellbeing at the societal level (den Ouden, 2012). The focus has recently shifted increasingly towards larger systems of stakeholders and various economic, environmental, social, and psychological perspectives of value building on an

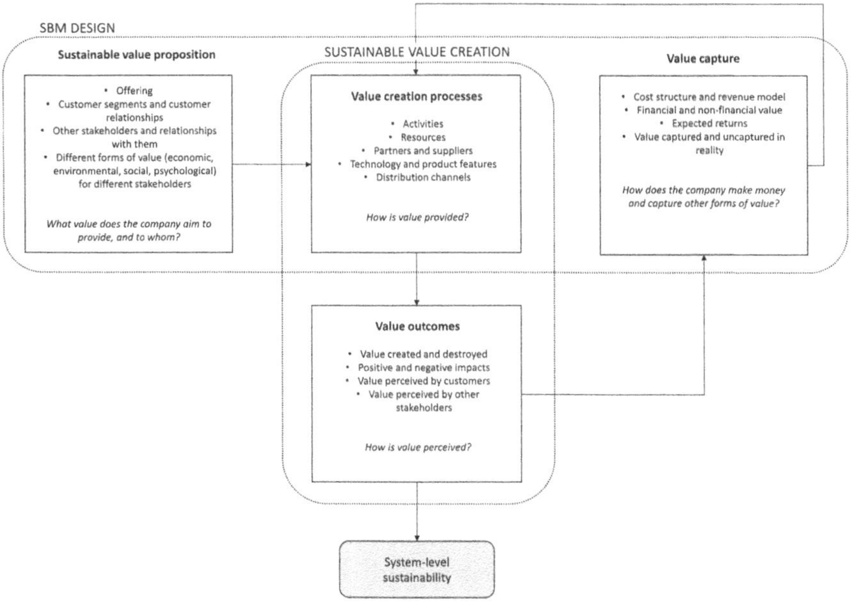

Fig. 3 Different value concepts related to SBM

integrated view of sustainable value (den Ouden, 2012; Evans et al., 2017; Freudenreich et al., 2020), which refers to positive environmental, social, and economic impacts. Economic value relates to factors such as increased profit and financial resilience. Social value includes elements that individuals or society in general consider valuable, such as health and safety and happiness and belonging, which are often also linked to psychological value elements. Environmental value refers to businesses' positive impacts on the natural environment and environmental capital (Stubbs & Cocklin, 2008), for example, through increased biodiversity. In sum, the multi-stakeholder perspective on value is central to an SBM, where the aim is to create value for a larger group of stakeholders, including the natural environment and human beings with whom the company will probably never engage (Upward & Jones, 2016).

In this study, SVC refers to positive environmental, social, and economic impacts (co)created by a company and its value network and perceived by a company and different stakeholders. SBMs propose sustainable value, although in practice such value can be either created and captured or destroyed (Roome & Louche, 2016; Yang et al., 2017). What is profitable for one company, benefits one stakeholder or increases value in one dimension of sustainability may not be profitable for another company or may destroy value from another stakeholder's perspective or in another dimension of sustainability (Van Bommel, 2018; Yang et al., 2017). Therefore, eliminating or reducing the negative consequences of value creation (Van Bommel, 2018; Roome & Louche, 2016; Yang et al., 2017) is a prerequisite for advancing system-level sustainability. Value destruction includes the negative outcomes of the business, that is, damage to the planet, people, and profits, such as rebound effects, greenhouse gas emissions, resource scarcity, biodiversity loss, unemployment, neglect of health and safety, unfair competition, and inequality and job losses (Bocken et al., 2019; Yang et al., 2017). Thus far, most research on SBM innovations and SVC has focused on designing sustainable value propositions (Kristensen & Remmen, 2019) and how business models create ecological and social benefits, but much less attention has been paid to the possible negative consequences and conflicts that business models may cause among multiple stakeholders and perceived value outcomes (Biloslavo et al., 2018). In the corporate sustainability literature, there has been growing interest in tensions in sustainability (Van der Byl & Slawinski, 2015), in which economic, environmental, and social values cannot be achieved simultaneously and increased value in one dimension of sustainability can cause decreased value in another. Thus, the success of SBMs depends on a company's ability to consider, resolve, and manage tensions and conflicting sustainability values (Van Bommel, 2018).

Research on SVC can be divided into two streams: (1) SVC processes that consider the activities, resources, and value network involved; and (2) sustainable value outcomes that consider how the value is perceived by the beneficiaries and what the actual impacts on the environment and society are (Bocken et al., 2014; Upward & Jones, 2016). SVC is concerned with value co-creation, in which multiple value forms are created for but also with multiple stakeholders (Freudenreich et al., 2020). As SVC incorporates a multi-stakeholder perspective, companies play a broader strategic role in affecting system-level sustainability (Sulkowski et al., 2018). Furthermore, value creation and value capture should be viewed as distinct processes. Value capture represents the value that the company generates for itself from its value proposition and value creation activities (Abdelkafi & Täuscher, 2016), such as decreased costs or increased profits, brand value, and social and environmental responsibility (Schaltegger et al., 2012). If the value creation process does not lead to desired outcomes (related to system-level sustainability and value captured by the company), changes in the business model will be necessary. No company is able to achieve system-level goals (such as system-level sustainability) on its own, but it is possible within a wider ecosystem in which companies operate (Hellström et al., 2015). An individual company's business model can reflect only part of the overall value creation, but it can be seen as a unit that serves a certain function in the broader system, thereby enabling system-level value creation (Koistinen et al., 2018).

3 Research Design

This paper considers how companies can contribute to and enable sustainability transition through their business models. To address the research objective, this study combined the previous literature and findings from a case company, Kekkilä-BVB. The single in-depth case study approach (Eriksson & Kovalainen, 2016) was applied, and the case was used for both inspirational and illustrative purposes (Siggelkow, 2007).

The selected case company, Kekkilä-BVB, is a Finnish-Dutch horticultural company that provides products and services for professional growers and home gardeners, landscapers, horticultural raw material customers, and bedding peat customers to over 100 countries worldwide. Kekkilä-BVB is the European leader in growing media (materials in which plants are grown) and offers high-quality substrates, peat products, fertilisers, garden products, and landscaping soils and mulches.

Kekkilä-BVB was chosen because it represents a company that has already taken considerable steps towards sustainability, and sustainable growth has always been at the core of Kekkilä-BVB's business. The company has an ambitious goal of moving from being a market-driven company to one that shapes the future by being part of a larger food system and solving the global food challenge. They focus on sustainability challenges and possibilities such as CO_2 reduction, water management, and wellbeing through greener homes and cities, as well as enabling plant-based food for the growing population of the world.

Both secondary data collection, that is, the broad range of written material related to Kekkilä-BVB's sustainability strategy development process, and semi-structured interviews were applied in empirical data collection. Data was collected between 2018 and 2020. Overall, data collection and analysis were iterative and circular processes in which literature reviews on corporate sustainability, business models and system transitions, and empirical data collection considering Kekkilä-BVB, as well as data collection and qualitative data analysis, were alternated (Eriksson & Kovalainen, 2016).

Data collection and analysis were conducted through the following main steps. First, to gain an initial understanding of the topic, written material concerning the case company's sustainability focus areas, that is strategic goals, indicators, stakeholder maps, action plans, and so on, was reviewed and analysed. The analysis was based on the inductive reasoning and grounded theory method (Silverman, 2014). Second, to obtain answers to open questions, the case company's sustainability manager and the sustainability, brand, and communications director were interviewed. The semi-structured interview covered the motivation to create sustainable value, sustainable value creation for multiple stakeholders, the value destruction perspective, and net positive impacts. Third, to deepen understanding and build an initial framework, a review of the scientific literature was conducted. The findings were analysed using the thematic content analysis method (Myers, 2013), resulting in the initial framework of an SVC approach for advancing sustainability transition and system-level sustainability. Fourth, the initial framework was illustrated and developed further, based on the semi-structured interviews and open discussions with company representatives.

4 Adopting a Sustainable Value Creation Approach

In the following, we offer an SVC approach (Fig. 4) for business managers coping with the designing, developing, and implementing of SBMs. The approach describes how individual companies make their business sustainable, leverage wider sustainability transition, and advance system-level sustainability through SVC. The SVC approach is explained below in the form of key recommendations and illustrated through the case company, Kekkilä-BVB.

4.1 Place Your Business into a System-Level Context and Define System Boundaries

First, for contributing to broader sustainability transition, individual businesses should be considered as part of the larger macro-level system. According to a boundary setting, if there are no frames or an

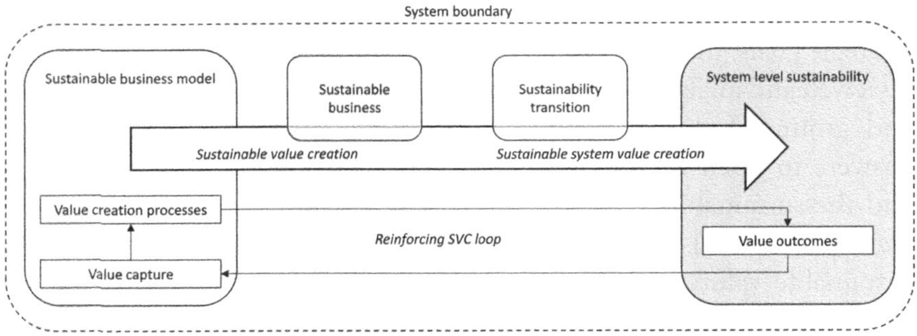

Fig. 4 The SVC approach for advancing sustainability transition and system-level sustainability

understanding of the overall system where the business model operates, it is extremely difficult to assess the sustainable value created (Bocken et al., 2019). The direct and indirect impacts resulting from a business model vary depending on how boundaries are traced around the system of analysis. In practice, Kekkilä-BVB has used the Framework for Strategic Sustainable Development (FSSD) (Broman & Robèrt, 2017), which aids organisations in putting themselves in the context of global sustainability challenges in their sustainability strategy development process. Kekkilä-BVB started to build their sustainability strategy by creating an understanding of several megatrends that have an impact on their business, but also global socio-economic and Earth system trends or challenges that Kekkilä-BVB could have an impact on through their business model and SVC, such as population growth, urbanisation, climate change mitigation, and food safety. Through its horticultural business, Kekkilä-BVB sees its broader strategic role as being a part of a macro-level food production system and solving a global food challenge, for example, relating to reducing food production's environmental impact and feeding an exploding population.

Although growing media has not been a central topic within discussions about sustainable food production, Kekkilä-BVB sees itself as having an important role in the food production value chain. Kekkilä-BVB enables both food production globally and wellbeing in homes and cities, for example, by producing specialised, high-quality substrates and fertilisers for professional growers and the global horticultural industry and by creating opportunity for local gardening and offering information about sustainable food production and giving growing tips for home gardeners. The COVID-19 crisis increased people's enthusiasm for gardening and private food production. The crisis also affected the self-sufficiency of countries. These trends forced Kekkilä-BVB to reconsider its system boundaries and how to operate globally when the international movement of products becomes difficult, as well as locally and near consumers.

4.2 Define What System-Level Sustainability Means to Your Business and Set a Final Goal

The second recommendation highlights the need to internalise the concept of system-level sustainability, which refers to operate within planetary and social boundaries, and conditions that enable a good quality of life (Raworth, 2017; Whiteman et al., 2013), and set the final goal. Defining a goal requires the internalising of the concept of sustainability, and further goal-setting is a requirement for the assessment of SVC. If sustainability goals are based on the benchmarks, such as comparisons relative to a baseline year, relative to current best practice or relative to a company's own short-term targets, there is a risk that incremental and, in absolute terms, even ineffective improvements are seen as progress towards sustainability (Dyllick & Rost, 2017). Recent studies on SVC have proposed that the assessment should be scientifically based, using, for example, the four sustainability principles related to natural cycles and the root causes of unsustainability (Broman & Robèrt, 2017), planetary boundaries, or laws of thermodynamics. A scientifically defined final sustainability goal that operates within ecological and social boundaries that are expressed in terms of company-specific thresholds and allocations (McElroy & Thomas, 2016) is the best way to ensure a company's journey towards system-level sustainability. However, these currently represent a paradigm shift rather than established practice.

Kekkilä-BVB has an ambition to develop their business based on research. Before undertaking concrete actions, they built a common understanding about the most important sustainability areas to which they contribute and can advance with their business. The strategic planning procedures of the FSSD, science-based sustainability principles, and the Sustainable Development Goals (United Nations, 2020), such as zero hunger, reduced inequalities, and sustainable cities and communities, have guided its strategy development process and further SBM development and SVC towards system-level sustainability. Kekkilä-BVB has identified four key focus areas where they consider they can truly make a difference: helping people to flourish, sustainable food and living, green growth and recycling, and biodiversity and restoration. These four strategic focus areas aim at covering the whole scope of nature's cycles, from sourcing raw materials to nature's restoration, society's operations, and food production. They also meet several UN Sustainable Development Goals, helping Kekkilä-BVB achieve their main goal: becoming a net positive company (putting back more into the global economy, society, and the environment than taking out). Today, global responsibility is fully integrated into Kekkilä-BVB's business strategy, which has replaced the separate sustainability strategy. Kekkilä-BVB's commitment is not just about causing as little harm as possible but is about being a change agent, a proactive player, and a significant force in improving system-level sustainability by creating sustainable value with and for multiple stakeholders. Kekkilä-BVB entitles its own existence by giving more than taking. However, this only represents goal-setting and ensures that Kekkilä-BVB focuses on essential actions, which are prerequisites for further actions and defining the KPIs (key performance indicators).

4.3 Create a Common Understanding of a Sustainable Future Through the Concrete Targets and Build Your Own Value Creation Processes Sustainably

Sustainable value creation begins with outlining the big picture through organisational values (Manninen & Huiskonen, 2019), mission, vision, and final sustainability goals as described above, and creating a common understanding of a sustainable future within a company. This is followed by building a company's own value creation processes, that is, concrete actions towards the goals, sustainably. In Kekkilä-BVB, all employees were involved in the strategy development process, as the implementation of SVC initiatives requires a lot of effort and expertise and collaboration between different departments. All employees are committed to work towards common goals that are agreed on together, and employees are trained continuously to take sustainability into consideration in their work.

Kekkilä-BVB's business is guided by a sustainability roadmap including eight concrete targets aiming to ensure SVC in the whole value chain during the coming years. Table 2 presents these eight targets and links them to the SVC processes. In general, collaboration and co-creation with value chain partners and other stakeholders, innovativeness, and a systemic perspective are prerequisites to achieve the sustainability targets. For example, replacing a packaging system that uses virgin plastics with one that uses recycled plastic or alternative packaging methods is not possible without chain partners' co-operation. Although sustainability is integrated into Kekkilä-BVB's strategy, it is not yet fully integrated into its value creation processes and daily operations. Therefore, separate sustainability projects, in which people at different positions work together, were needed. The aim of these projects is, for example, to ensure that new products or solutions designed to launch truly improve sustainability.

4.4 Focus on Sustainable Value Outcomes and Pay Attention to the Negative Consequences of Value Creation

Once value creation processes are sustainable, it is time to focus on value outcomes, that is, how value is perceived by customers and other stakeholders. As sustainable value is a multifaceted concept, including economic, social, and environmental dimensions of sustainability and perspectives of multiple stakeholders, various indicators are needed. Further, considering the negative consequences of value creation is at least as important as considering positive value outcomes; it is a prerequisite for advancing system-level sustainability. Assessing net positivity, which is the main target of Kekkilä-BVB, requires considering how much

Table 2 Kekkilä-BVB's main targets related to SVC processes

Target	Examples of SVC processes
1. We enhance the wellbeing of our employees, customers, and partners in the value chain.	Improving the wellbeing of personnel through concrete actions with bi-lateral communication defined in a wellbeing year clock. Introducing a supplier code of conduct where suppliers commit to the highest social and environmental standards according to local, Finnish, or UN law, whichever is stricter.
2. In 2020, our sustainability impact is understood and transparent and we have set up measurement to ensure that we reach our main goal: net positivity.	Providing an E-learning platform for employees, customers, partners, and other stakeholders, and offering training on the sustainability targets. Participating in sector organisation to establish a common way of measuring and communicating the sustainability impact. Creating transparency through the set-up of a sustainability dashboard.
3. We will co-create and pilot three new smart service concepts per year related to food and living, which significantly increase our own and our partners' positive sustainability impact.	Reducing environmental impacts of inbound logistics by changing from trucks to trains. Introducing concepts in various segments working with high-tech equipment enabling a shift to measured, controlled actions based on data.
4. By 2022, we will have innovative new products and services that optimise water management.	Providing soil products in urban environments that reduce the unwanted impacts from excess rainfall. Providing covering mulch materials that reduce evaporation of water to consumers as well as professional growers.
5. From 2020, all of our innovations promote sustainability.	Providing new sustainable raw materials, for example, Accretio, which has high water retention rates and ensures a quick absorption of water.

(*continued*)

Table 2 (continued)

Target	Examples of SVC processes
6. By 2024, we will replace 80% of single-use plastics in our packaging with recycled plastic or alternative packaging methods. 100% of our packaging will be recyclable.	80% recycled content in 50% of the packaging used for retail sector in the Netherlands and Germany. 97% of packaging is recyclable and 3% is biodegradable.
7. Together with stakeholders, we will develop sustainable harvesting and an afterlife concept for peat bogs.	Focusing on new ways of harvesting peat that reduce the harvesting cycle. Increasing the amount of RPP (Responsibly Produced Peat) certified peat used.
8. Our actions will significantly increase biodiversity in urban areas.	Providing urban roof and balcony gardens, parks, and green parking spots to help to purify the air, reduce the concentration of fine particles, reduce heat build-up, and create water buffers in the city.

sustainable value is created and refers to the total contribution, which is the difference between positive and negative impacts. While a business model can never have a zero footprint (negative impacts), a company can still create net positive impacts if its handprint (positive impacts) is bigger than its footprint (Dyllick & Rost, 2017). The goal of being a net positive company forces Kekkilä-BVB to determine what their business model gives to and what it takes from society and the environment. The net positivity approach also forces Kekkilä-BVB to see their role in society from a systemic perspective, as they cannot concentrate only on internal processes and improvements.

Kekkilä-BVB aims to make their sustainability work as measurably as possible and assesses the sustainability impact that their work has on a regular basis. According to the literature (Dyllick & Rost, 2017) and Kekkilä-BVB's knowledge, there are no simple methods available yet for measuring net positive (or net negative) impacts. As an example, consider the matter of how to measure the impacts of growing media offered by Kekkilä-BVB when it gives life to new trees that absorb carbon that is further harvested and utilised somewhere else. The development of specific guidelines and measures takes time. So far, different one-dimensional indicators can be useful for making overall quantifications or comparisons, but Kekkilä-BVB already has preliminary proofs of their net positive sustainability impacts. The estimations are based on the Upright Project's Upright net impact model (Upright Project, 2020), which is an automated way to quantify companies' net impact. The main idea of the artificial intelligence-based model is to show what resources companies use and what they achieve by using them. The Upright net impact model utilises scientific papers and machine learning to summarise how companies impact the environment, the health of people, and society at large, and further to create a net impact profile of the company. Although based on Upright's model Kekkilä-BVB is already a net positive company, they do not trust the results literally, as the model is still developing. Based on the results, Kekkilä-BVB trusts that it is doing good things, but that its net positivity can always be higher.

Kekkilä-BVB is aware of negative impacts that their sustainability actions might cause. For example, the use of peat causes negative impacts even if peat is produced as sustainably as possible. One main concern related to peat is its categorisation as a fossil resource. So far, Kekkilä-BVB has identified different concepts that represent both positive and negative impacts, such as eco-effectiveness or ecological damages, and the actions that lead to those impacts, such as carbon sinks and compensation models or the heavy use of fossil fuels in road transportation. Further, Kekkilä-BVB has started to do Strategic LCAs (Life Cycle Assessments) on its products to define, assess, and communicate products' sustainability. In addition to insights from the Upright Project and LCA calculation, Kekkilä-BVB assesses how their sustainability initiatives advance SDGs. Through a materiality analysis Kekkilä-BVB ensures that it prioritises the economic, social, and environmental issues that matter most to its stakeholders. Further, by utilising consumer surveys, Kekkilä-BVB ensures that its goals are aligned with consumers' and stakeholders' needs. Finally, Kekkilä-BVB is building a monthly updated dashboard that assesses progress towards their eight sustainability targets through KPIs.

4.5 Commit to System-Level Sustainability Targets and Identify the Value Capturing Potential to Enhancing Virtuous Circles

Identifying value capturing potential drives companies to commit to SVC, and captured value motivates companies to create even more sustainable value, leading to virtuous circles (Casadesus-Masanell & Ricart, 2011). Companies are primarily interested in creating sustainable value if it brings economic benefit (Yang & Evans, 2019), that is, increased profit or decreased costs, so it is not truly realistic to expect commercially oriented businesses to wholly refocus on sustainability challenges and value creation for the common good (Dyllick & Muff, 2016). Previous studies have identified several direct and indirect links between SVC activities and a company's economic performance, for example, through increased resource efficiency, reputation, or customer satisfaction (Saeidi et al., 2015; Schaltegger et al., 2012). Further, a broader perspective on SVC raises the value capture potential of companies (Laukkanen, 2019). However, the value capture of SVC activities is a multidimensional and complex process. It explains how companies can translate sustainable value created for multiple stakeholders into monetary terms and other intangible benefits for a company. Additionally, a company has to be aware of the facts that value capturing might require a long time period to be realised, that some actions have more certain value capturing potential than others, and that with some actions value capturing depends on factors that a company cannot influence beforehand.

Although the value capture potential of planned SVC activities is unclear, Kekkilä-BVB is committed to their sustainability targets. They trust that sustainability investments will pay back in the long term. Kekkilä-BVB identifies the value capture potential through different methods, such as input-output analysis, where the required resources and expected impacts are listed, or ROI-template, where expected financial, social, and environmental returns on investments in both the short and long term are evaluated. As Kekkilä-BVB has an ambitious sustainability strategy, most of their SVC activities are not linked to direct financial value capture potential but to benefits such as increased attractiveness as an employer or value chain partner, increased innovation capabilities, increased reputation and brand value, better risk management, or simply increased social and environmental responsibility for its own sake. Kekkilä-BVB aims to create positive reinforcement loops between SVC and value capture through transparent communication and continuous collaboration with customers and stakeholders. Further, the increasing trend has been that investors invest in sustainability projects, which is another driver for Kekkilä-BVB to act increasingly responsibly.

5 Discussion and Conclusion

In this study, the aim was to understand how individual companies can contribute to broader sustainability transition through their SBMs. By combining views of corporate sustainability, traditional business model, and system transition from their respective literatures, the study proposed the SVC approach to advance sustainability transition and system-level sustainability.

First, it addresses the need to place individual businesses within their system-level contexts, which is a prerequisite for SVC, as the terms "sustainable development" and "sustainability" are macro-level concepts and the SBM of an individual company may reflect only part of the overall SVC. Second, it highlights the need to set sustainability goals and business objectives based on science-based sustainability principles to ensure progress towards system-level sustainability and enable sustainability transition through SVC. Third, it instructs on how to build up value creation processes (i.e., the company's and its value network's activities and resources for creating value outcomes) sustainably, for example, through close collaboration or value co-creation with employees and other stakeholders. Fourth, the approach guides one to consider sustainable value outcomes (i.e., how the value is perceived by various stakeholders), and especially to pay attention to negative consequences of value creation, such as rebound effects or conflicting interests between different stakeholders, which is a prerequisite for advancing system-level sustainability. Fifth, it emphasises the identification of value capturing potential of SVC, which motivates individual companies to commit to system-level sustainability targets and contribute to system-level SVC and create even more sustainable value.

The SVC approach is proposed to narrow the current research gap between the SBM literature and sustainability transition literature, and integrate company-level sustainability into wider socio-technical transition to sustainability. In the previous literature, SBMs are noted as vehicles for advancing sustainability (Lüdeke-Freund & Dembek, 2017). This study specifies that SVC is a core SBM process that mediates the impact of individual SBMs. Through SVC, companies have the potential to advance sustainable business towards system-level sustainability, therefore acting as agents of sustainability transitions. The SVC links the concepts of SBM, sustainable business, sustainability transition, and system-level sustainability, building the bridge between micro-level corporate sustainability and macro-level sustainable development, as well as between different disciplines.

From a business model perspective, the SVC approach broadens the company-centred perspective and the traditional view of value creation, considering wider system-level sustainability targets and an integrative view on value. From a system transition perspective, SVC represents the concept through which the coevolutionary processes entailing multiple actions and changes in a range of elements (e.g., technologies, user practices, infrastructures, policies, industry structures, supply chains, and business models) can be approached. Through SVC, companies can play multiple roles in advancing system-level sustainability. First, by adopting an integrative view of value companies contribute to sustainability by creating economic, environmental, and/or social value for multiple stakeholders. Second, by placing individual businesses into a broader system-level context and setting business targets based on system-level sustainability goals, companies enable system-level SVC, which refers to overall value creation executed by multiple companies and other societal actors. Third, by adopting an SVC approach companies challenge the current regime and act as agents in sustainability transitions.

5.1 Managerial and Policy Implications

From a managerial perspective, this study proposes five key recommendations for adopting an SVC approach. These recommendations highlight the most crucial points to be considered and serve as a starting point for implementing SVC. Although the key recommendations presented in this study are directly aimed at managerial audiences, contributing to sustainability transitions and advancing system-level sustainability through SVC requires the involvement of and collaboration between all societal actors (including government representatives, policymakers, interest groups, educators, and consumers).

For example, the public sector can provide businesses with a favourable environment and regulatory framework to encourage SBM innovations and SVC. Effective regulations guide companies to adopt SVC by creating limits to and costs of negative environmental and social impacts related to, for example, waste charges or environmental protection taxes. However, as the main target—sustainability—is a macro-level concept, and individual companies reflect only part of the overall SVC, regulations cannot be too specific. Further, as the wider sustainability transition calls comprehensive transformations of business models and value creation logics, structural changes in policy are also needed. Finding a balance between different policies and creating a favourable environment for system-level SVC is not an easy task. It may require the integration of national and international regulation and courage to lead the way (e.g., Germany's Energiewende) guided by system-level sustainability targets. Favourable regulation is flexible and it supports different options for solving sustainability issues through SVC.

5.2 Limitations and Future Research

Naturally, this study has several limitations, which point to interesting avenues for future research. First, there are limitations related to methodological choices as the study followed the single case study approach, which sets some limitations for generalising results. However, the aim of this study was not to test or build theory but to explore a relatively new research area and provide a basis for its further development. Future research might explore the proposed SVC approach across other companies and contexts.

The focus of this study is both a strength and a limitation. The focus was broad: The aim was to explore how to integrate company-level sustainability into wider socio-technical transitions to sustainability through SBMs. The proposed SVC approach covers five general recommendations, and hence each of them should be studied more in depth. For example, more research is needed on how to assess SVC, including negative consequences of value creation and how to translate created sustainable value into economic value for the company, and further, how sustainable value created for stakeholders and value captured by the company can reinforce each other. Further, closer integration with the natural sciences is also needed to advance system-level sustainability within the limits of planetary boundaries and to understand the roots of (un)sustainability and ecological resilience. Systems thinking offers a more holistic lens through which to examine the role of SVC by companies within socio-ecological systems (Williams et al., 2017).

At the same time, the focus of this study was narrow: It represents only one aspect of sustainability transition by integrating company-level sustainability into system-level sustainability transition through SVC. The literature on sustainability transitions covers multiple themes that are connected with others (Köhler et al., 2019); for example, research on individual businesses in sustainability transitions is connected with industries, politics, or social movements. From the company perspective, understanding system transitions covers, for example, the companies' and other actors' actions that lead to system transition, the system transition and the role of companies and other actors in that transition, or the institutional environment and how it relates to the companies' and other actors' actions as well as the roles in that transition (Clarke & Crane, 2018). These highlight the bidirectional interaction between company and system levels (Geels, 2014). Therefore, more interaction and synergies between the company and system level are required. For example, since the current regime strongly pressurises companies' operations, for example, via legislation, a sustainable regime would assist companies in adopting SVC. Studies focusing on both business models and system transitions for increasing sustainability are just emerging. Thus, there are plenty of research opportunities to develop more comprehensive and formal models of the interaction between the company and system levels. More knowledge is needed on companies' key barriers and drivers in adopting SVC, for example, how different actors enhance the adoption of SVC. More research is also needed on how individual business models contribute to the overall system-level SVC. It is fruitful to apply the theories and frameworks used in system transition studies, for example, a technological innovation system approach or a multi-level perspective, to management research. In contrast, management frameworks and design research, which are adopted quite widely in business model research but not in transition research, can build the bridge between these fields.

References

Abdelkafi, N., & Täuscher, K. (2016). Business models for sustainability from a system dynamics perspective. *Organization and Environment, 29*(1), 74–96.

Adams, R., Jeanrenaud, S., Bessant, J., Denyer, D., & Overy, P. (2016). Sustainability-oriented innovation: A systematic review. *International Journal of Management Reviews, 18*(2), 180–205.

Baumgartner, R. J., & Ebner, D. (2010). Corporate sustainability strategies: Sustainability profiles and maturity levels. *Sustainable Development, 18*(2), 76–89.

Bidmon, C. M., & Knab, S. F. (2018). The three roles of business models in societal transitions: New linkages between business model and transition research. *Journal of Cleaner Production, 178*, 903–916.

Biloslavo, R., Bagnoli, C., & Edgar, D. (2018). An eco-critical perspective on business models: The value triangle as an approach to closing the sustainability gap. *Journal of Cleaner Production, 174*, 746–762.

Bocken, N. M. P., Short, S. W., Rana, P., & Evans, S. (2014). A literature and practice review to develop sustainable business model archetypes. *Journal of Cleaner Production, 65*, 42–56.

Bocken, N., Boons, F., & Baldassarre, B. (2019). Sustainable business model experimentation by understanding ecologies of business models. *Journal of Cleaner Production, 208*, 1498–1512.

Bolton, R., & Hannon, M. (2016). Governing sustainability transitions through business model innovation: Towards a systems understanding. *Research Policy, 45*(9), 1731–1717.
Boons, F., Montalvo, C., Quist, J., & Wagner, M. (2013). Sustainable innovation, business models and economic performance: An overview. *Journal of Cleaner Production, 45*, 1–8.
Broman, G. I., & Robèrt, K. (2017). A framework for strategic sustainable development. *Journal of Cleaner Production, 140*, 17–31.
Casadesus-Masanell, R., & Ricart, J. E. (2011). How to design a winning business model. *Harvard Business Review, 89*(1/2), 100–107.
Clarke, A., & Crane, A. (2018). Cross-sector partnerships for systemic change: Systematized literature review and agenda for further research. *Journal of Business Ethics, 150*(2), 303–313.
DaSilva, C. M., & Trkman, P. (2014). Business model: What it is and what it is not. *Long Range Planning, 47*(6), 379–389.
Demil, B., & Lecocq, X. (2010). Business model evolution: In search of dynamic consistency. *Long Range Planning, 43*(2–3), 227–246.
Den Ouden, E. (2012). *Innovation design: Creating value for people, organizations and society*. Springer.
Dyllick, T., & Muff, K. (2016). Clarifying the meaning of sustainable business: Introducing a typology from business-as-usual to true business sustainability. *Organization and Environment, 29*, 156–174.
Dyllick, T., & Rost, Z. (2017). Towards true product sustainability. *Journal of Cleaner Production, 162*, 346–360.
Eriksson, P., & Kovalainen, A. (2016). *Qualitative methods in business research* (2nd ed.). Sage.
Evans, S., Vladimirova, D., Holgado, M., Van Fossen, K., Yang, M., Silva, E. A., & Barlow, C. Y. (2017). Business model innovation for sustainability: Towards a unified perspective for creation of sustainable business models. *Business Strategy and the Environment, 26*, 597–608.
Farla, J., Markard, J., Raven, R., & Coenen, L. (2012). Sustainability transitions in the making: A closer look at actors, strategies and resources. *Technological Forecasting and Social Change, 79*(6), 991–998.
Freudenreich, B., Lüdeke-Freund, F., & Schaltegger, S. (2020). A stakeholder theory perspective on business models: Value creation for sustainability. *Journal of Business Ethics, 166*(1), 3–18.

Geels, F. (2014). Reconceptualising the co-evolution of firms-in-industries and their environments: Developing an inter-disciplinary Triple Embeddedness Framework. *Research Policy, 43*, 261–277.

Goyal, P., Rahman, Z., & Kazmi, A. A. (2013). Corporate sustainability performance and firm performance research: Literature review and future research agenda. *Management Decision, 51*(2), 361–379.

Hellström, M., Tsvetkova, A., Gustafsson, M., & Wikström, K. (2015). Collaboration mechanisms for business models in distributed energy ecosystems. *Journal of Cleaner Production, 102*, 226–236.

Iñigo, E. A., & Albareda, L. (2016). Understanding sustainable innovation as a complex adaptive system: A systemic approach to the firm. *Journal of Cleaner Production, 126*, 1–20.

Köhler, J., Geels, F. W., Kern, F., Markard, J., Onsongo, E., Wieczorek, A., Alkemade, F., Avelino, F., Bergek, A., Boons, F., Fünfschilling, L., Hess, D., Holtz, G., Hyysalo, S., Jenkins, K., Kivimaa, P., Martiskainen, M., McMeekin, A., Mühlemeier, M. S., … Wells, P. (2019). An agenda for sustainability transitions research: State of the art and future directions. *Environmental Innovation and Societal Transitions, 31*, 1–32.

Koistinen, K., Laukkanen, M., Mikkilä, M., Huiskonen, J., & Linnanen, L. (2018). Sustainable system value creation: Development of preliminary frameworks for a business model change within a systemic transition process. In L. Moratis, F. Melissen, & S. Idowu (Eds.), *Sustainable business models: Principles, promise, and practice* (pp. 105–127). Springer International Publishing.

Kristensen, H. S., & Remmen, A. (2019). A framework for sustainable value propositions in product-service systems. *Journal of Cleaner Production, 223*, 25–35.

Laukkanen, M. (2019). Sustainable business models for advancing system-level sustainability. Retrieved from https://lutpub.lut.fi/handle/10024/160340

Laukkanen, M., & Tura, N. (2020). The potential of sharing economy business models for sustainable value creation. *Journal of Cleaner Production, 253*. https://doi.org/10.1016/j.jclepro.2020.120004

Loorbach, D., Frantzeskaki, N., & Avelino, F. (2017). Sustainability transitions research: Transforming science and practice for societal change. *Annual Review of Environment and Resources, 42*, 599–626.

Lüdeke-Freund, F., & Dembek, K. (2017). Research and practice on sustainable business models: Emerging field or passing fancy? *Journal of Cleaner Production, 168*, 1668–1678.

Manninen, K., & Huiskonen, J. (2019). Sustainability goal setting with a value-focused thinking approach. In A. Aagaard (Ed.), *Sustainable business models: Innovation, implementation and success* (pp. 89–118). Palgrave Macmillan.

Markard, J., Raven, R., & Truffer, B. (2012). Sustainability transitions: An emerging field of research and its prospects. *Research Policy, 41*(6), 955–967.

McElroy, M. W., & Thomas, M. P. (2016). *The multicapital scorecard.* Chelsea Green Publishing.

Montiel, I. (2008). Corporate social responsibility and corporate sustainability: Separate pasts, common futures. *Organization and Environment, 21*(3), 245–269.

Myers, M. D. (2013). *Qualitative research in business & management* (2nd ed.). Sage.

Neumayer, E. (2013). *Weak versus strong sustainability: Exploring the limits of two opposing paradigms* (4th ed.). Edward Elgar.

Osterwalder, A., & Pigneur, Y. (2010). *Business model generation. A handbook for visionaries, game changers, and challengers.* Wiley.

Pieroni, M. P. P., McAloone, T. C., & Pigosso, D. C. A. (2019). Business model innovation for circular economy and sustainability: A review of approaches. *Journal of Cleaner Production, 215*, 198–216.

Rauter, R., Jonker, J., & Baumgartner, R. J. (2017). Going one's own way: Drivers in developing business models for sustainability. *Journal of Cleaner Production, 140*, 144–154.

Raworth, K. (2017). *Doughnut economics: Seven ways to think like a 21st-century economist.* Chelsea Green Publishing.

Robèrt, K., Broman, G., Waldron, D., Ny, H., Byggeth, S., Cook, D., Johansson, L., Oldmark, J., Basile, G., Haraldsson, H., MacDonald, J., Moore, B., Connell, T., & Missimer, M. (2012). *Sustainability handbook. Planning strategically towards sustainability.* Studentlitteratur AB.

Roome, N., & Louche, C. (2016). Journeying toward business models for sustainability. *Organization and Environment, 29*, 11–35.

Saeidi, S. P., Sofian, S., Saeidi, P., Saeidi, S. P., & Saaeidi, S. A. (2015). How does corporate social responsibility contribute to firm financial performance? The mediating role of competitive advantage, reputation, and customer satisfaction. *Journal of Business Research, 68*(2), 341–350.

Sarasini, S., & Linder, M. (2018). Integrating a business model perspective into transition theory: The example of new mobility services. *Environmental Innovation and Societal Transitions, 27*, 16–31.

Schaltegger, S., Lüdeke-Freund, F., & Hansen, E. G. (2012). Business cases for sustainability: The role of business model innovation for corporate sustainability. *International Journal of Innovation and Sustainable Development, 6*(2), 95–119.

Shaker, R. R. (2015). The spatial distribution of development in Europe and its underlying sustainability correlations. *Applied Geography, 63*, 304–314.

Siggelkow, N. (2007). Persuasion with case studies. *Academy of Management Journal, 50*(1), 20–24.

Silverman, D. (2014). *Interpreting qualitative data* (5th ed.). Sage.

Smith, A., Voß, J.-P., & Grin, J. (2010). Innovation studies and sustainability transitions: The allure of the multi-level perspective and its challenges. *Research Policy, 39*(4), 435–448.

Stubbs, W., & Cocklin, C. (2008). Conceptualizing a "sustainability business model". *Organization and Environment, 21*, 103–127.

Sulkowski, A. J., Edwards, M., & Freeman, R. E. (2018). Shake your stakeholder: Firms leading engagement to cocreate sustainable value. *Organization and Environment, 31*, 223–241.

Teece, D. J. (2010). Business models, business strategy and innovation. *Long range planning, 43*, 172–194.

United Nations. (2020). About the sustainable development goals. Retrieved from https://www.un.org/sustainabledevelopment/sustainable-development-goals/

Upright Project. (2020). Upright model. Retrieved from https://www.upright-project.com/

Upward, A., & Jones, P. (2016). An ontology for strongly sustainable business models: Defining an enterprise framework compatible with natural and social science. *Organization and Environment, 29*(1), 97–123.

Van Bommel, K. (2018). Managing tensions in sustainable business models: Exploring instrumental and integrative strategies. *Journal of Cleaner Production, 196*, 829–841.

Van der Byl, C. A., & Slawinski, N. (2015). Embrasing tensions in corporate sustainability: A review of research from win-wins and trade-offs to paradoxes and beyond. *Organization and Environment, 28*, 54–79.

WCED World Commission on Environment and Development. (1987). *Our common future*. Oxford University Press.

Whiteman, G., Walker, B., & Perego, P. (2013). Planetary boundaries: Ecological foundations for corporate sustainability. *Journal of Management Studies, 50*(2), 307–336.

Williams, C., & Millington, A. (2004). The diverse and contested meanings of sustainable development. *The Geographical Journal, 170*(2), 99–104.

Williams, A., Kennedy, S., Philipp, F., & Whiteman, G. (2017). Systems thinking: A review of sustainability management research. *Journal of Cleaner Production, 148*, 866–881.

Wolf, J. (2014). The relationship between sustainable supply chain management, stakeholder pressure and corporate sustainability performance. *Journal of Business Ethics, 119*(3), 317–328.

Yang, M., & Evans, S. (2019). Product-service system business model archetypes and sustainability. *Journal of Cleaner Production, 220*, 1156–1166.

Yang, M., Evans, S., Vladimirova, D., & Rana, P. (2017). Value uncaptured perspective for sustainable business model innovation. *Journal of Cleaner Production, 140*, 1794–1804.

Zemigala, M. (2019). Tendencies in research on sustainable development in management sciences. *Journal of Cleaner Production, 218*, 796–809.

Zott, C., Amit, R., & Massa, L. (2011). The business model: Recent developments and future research. *Journal of Management, 37*(4), 1019–1042.

Building BoP Business Models for Sustainable Poverty Alleviation: System Tips and System Traps

Jodi C. York and Krzysztof Dembek

1 Introduction

It has been established with relative certainty since the 1980s that humanity collectively needs to make a rapid and profound shift toward sustainable development, involving both long-term and large-scale changes to production and consumption patterns, and the eradication of extreme poverty (WCED, 1987). While this has been known for more than a generation, the visible acceleration of climate change impacts over the last decade has underscored the need for urgent action if we are to avert environmental disaster (e.g. IPCC, 2014, 2018). Although the unsustainable production and consumption patterns in question are overwhelmingly

J. C. York (✉)
Department of Management and Marketing, University of Melbourne, Parkville, VIC, Australia
e-mail: jodi.york@unimelb.edu.au

K. Dembek
Centre for Social Impact, Swinburne University, Hawthorn, VIC, Australia
e-mail: krzysztof.dembek@unimelb.edu.au

A. Aagaard et al. (eds.), *Business Models for Sustainability Transitions*,
https://doi.org/10.1007/978-3-030-77580-3_5

associated with wealthy countries, these patterns are propped up by extreme poverty at the base of the global economic pyramid (BoP). Extreme poverty forces people to make short-term survival-based decisions with profoundly negative long-term environmental consequences to meet their basic needs, whether for their own direct subsistence like clearing forest to plant crops, or to satisfy unsustainable global supply chains like those destroying reefs with cyanide fishing (Clark, 2007).

The continued existence of extreme poverty is a key element enabling unsustainable supply chains, which are able to engage those with no better income options as suppliers or employees in precarious conditions. Despite this mutually constitutive relationship, poverty alleviation and sustainability agendas have been pursued in isolation and with little regard for the other until relatively recent efforts to reinforce their integration, for instance, through the UN Sustainable Development Goals and the UN Poverty Environment Initiative (now succeeded by Poverty Environment Action) (Clark, 2007). Key poverty and development metrics have largely been silent on environmental sustainability,[1] and schemes to conserve natural resources as both natural environments and inputs to production have excluded and displaced poor communities and exacerbated environmental degradation (e.g. Alao, 2007; Barrett et al., 2011; Peluso & Watts, 2001; York, 2002). While coordinated global efforts to eradicate the extreme poverty have been celebrated as one of the great success stories of the early twenty-first century (World Bank, 2018), many approaches to poverty alleviation have also contributed to strengthening and stabilising the patterns of unsustainable production and consumption we need to replace.

The profound and rapid shift of our socio-technical systems toward more sustainable modes of production and consumption, termed a 'sustainability transition', has been the topic of considerable research interest across a range of disciplines (Markard et al., 2012). To date, sustainability transition agendas and research have centred largely on the role played by technological innovation in the developed world, with relatively less

[1] For instance, environmental considerations are largely absent from Gross Domestic Product (GDP), the UN's Human Development Index, the World Bank's 'Dollar-a-day' definition of poverty, and the two main academic approaches to the measurement of relative poverty: Townsend's idea of relative deprivation (Townsend, 1979) and Sen's Capabilities Approach (Sen, 1999).

space in the field given to the developing world (Ramos-Mejía et al., 2018; Romijn et al., 2010). Those studies that are beginning to fill in more evidence from the global south (e.g. Raven et al., 2017; Truffer et al., 2015; van Welie et al., 2018; Verbong et al., 2010; Wieczorek et al., 2015) largely do so with the presumption that technology transfer from richer countries will allow less developed countries to catch up and converge with wealthier ones (Jolly et al., 2012; Wieczorek, 2018).

The intensification of environmental degradation is progressing more quickly than society and policy are responding, and more quickly than innovations developed in richer countries can reach the global south through technology transfer. If we are to maintain and increase the planet's capacity to absorb the products of environmentally unsustainable living while we transition away from those patterns, it is critical to recognise that sustainable alleviation of extreme poverty in the global south is necessarily part of sustainability transition. That is why it is so important to extend the focus of sustainability transitions research, currently concentrated on shifting unsustainable production and consumption patterns largely in the developed world, to include the transition to sustainable livelihood in the global south as suggested by Köhler et al. (2019) and Ramos-Mejía et al. (2018).

Business models are critical tools for building sustainable livelihoods in the global south, especially those for BoP communities carving out a livelihood at the intersection of extreme poverty and livelihood-threatening environmental degradation. However, Bidmon and Knab (2018) show that while business models are an important tool for achieving systemic change, they can both impede and support sustainability transition. Hence, this chapter asks: *what roles can business models addressing BoP poverty play in sustainability transition, and what determines their success?* We explore this question by applying the framework from Bidmon and Knab (2018) to 17 of the 55 BoP business models from Dembek et al. (2018) to explore the potential roles in sustainability transition for three different types of business models seeking to alleviate poverty at the BoP: delivering models, sourcing models, and reorganising models. We find that each type of BoP business model has the potential to alleviate poverty in ways that align to the goals of sustainability transition.

In order to understand and explain what determines sustainable poverty alleviation outcomes and how to guide BoP business models toward sustainability, we draw on the concept of 'system traps' (Meadows & Wright, 2008). System traps are archetypes of system structures that produce widely observed, problematic behaviour that can occur within complex systems of all kinds (Meadows & Wright, 2008). The problematic outcomes caused by system traps emerge over time from the ways in which different elements of the system interact, such as feedback loops, feedback delays, or separation between those who can observe the causes and those who experience the effects. Once a particular system trap is identified, it can either be avoided entirely, or escaped by altering the structure of system to counter the problematic dynamic. BoP business models can achieve this by embedding key sustainability enablers and processes into the business model, which we illustrate using examples from Dembek et al. (2018).

In the next section, we review the role of BoP business models in addressing poverty and environmental degradation. We then introduce the data and analysis method used in this research, using examples from Dembek et al. (2018) to illustrate how different BoP business model types can adopt the roles described by Bidmon and Knab (2018). This is followed by a distillation of key design features and suggested enablers for avoiding common system traps that can be used by those seeking to undertake or guide similar work. The chapter concludes with consideration of the contributions of this work and directions for future research.

2 Business Models at the Bottom of the Pyramid

The business model is a long-established strategic tool for designing and describing how an organisation will create, deliver, and capture value for its stakeholders within a given set of market conditions (Teece, 2010; Zott et al., 2011). Business models can rapidly disrupt and reshape existing systems of production and consumption precisely because they 'connect multiple actors, mediate between the production and the consumption side of business and support the introduction of novel technologies into the market' (Bidmon & Knab, 2018: 903). As such, business models are a critical tool for poverty alleviation and play a critical role in determining whether the livelihood opportunities developed for and with BoP communities of the global south are aligned to sustainability transition or set up at cross-purposes to that goal.

The concept of a BoP-specific business model was originally expressed in top-down terms as a way for multinational corporations to target the poor as customers, thereby 'helping them improve their lives by producing and distributing products and services in culturally sensitive, environmentally sustainable, and economically profitable ways' (Prahalad & Hart, 2002: 1). The concept has since evolved to include business models engaging the BoP in a range of ways including as clients, entrepreneurs, and employees (Dembek et al., 2020). More recently, BoP business models have been specifically identified within the field of so-called 'sustainable business models', where they are considered a subset of the 're-purpose the business for society/environment' archetype (Bocken et al., 2014). However, not all BoP business models should be considered 'sustainable business models', nor do they necessarily align to the goals of sustainability transition. Depending on their relationship to environmental and economic outcomes, BoP business models can be a vehicle for sustainability transition, or they can work against sustainability transition by entrenching impoverishment and/or environmental degradation (see Fig. 1).

BoP business models nominally attempt to help the poor and make their lives better in some way through inclusion in the market economy. Those that focus solely on income generation, rather than engaging with poverty as a complex problem, do nothing to understand and address the underlying causes of poverty. Those that focus solely on enabling the poor to consume without consideration of actual needs or environmental impact are equally problematic and cannot serve sustainability transition. These are unsustainable business models, represented by the bottom oval in Fig. 1. These models risk destroying more value than they create at best, and at worst exploit the poor and do damage to their communities (Hall et al., 2012).

Economic development that increases BoP income in ways that are tied to environmental degradation (often without addressing the underlying causes or considering impact on other wellbeing needs) works against sustainability transition. While it may appear effective in poverty

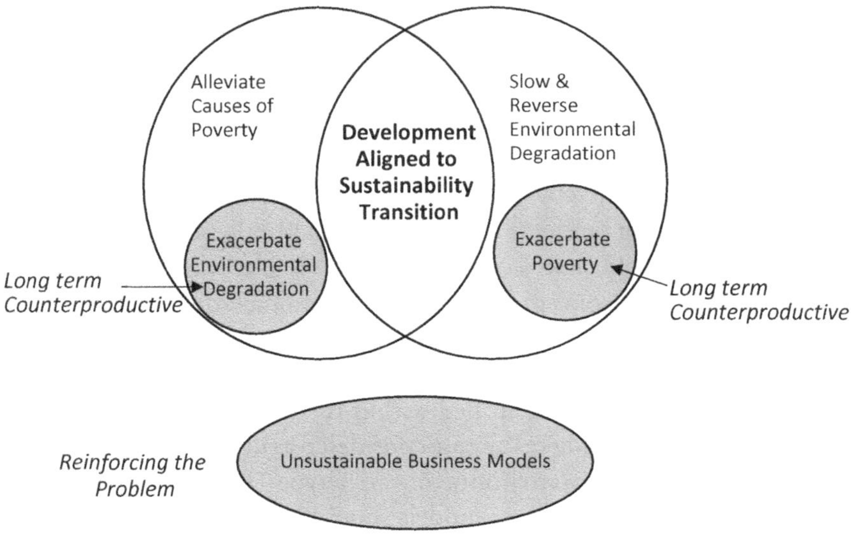

Fig. 1 How BoP business models can contribute to sustainability transition

alleviation for a decade or more, this is at best a damaging short-term approach that displaces the problem in time without solving it. Over time, the feedback loop of increased income and environmental degradation compromises the ability to pursue the livelihood. Examples of this category include unsustainable primary production and polluting sweatshops.

Environmental protection efforts that destroy livelihoods are similarly counterproductive. These efforts often displace the poor to a different location, where their pursuit of livelihood may be just as environmentally destructive, for instance, when forest-based farmers are displaced in the creation of conservation zones (e.g. Peluso & Watts, 2001; York, 2002), or when certain production activities are criminalised for environmental reasons without consideration of the underlying market drivers and lack of alternative income sources (e.g. Dembek & York, 2020). These long-term counterproductive approaches are represented by the small dark circles on the left and right of the Venn diagram in Fig. 1, respectively.

In this chapter, we focus only on those BoP business models that actively seek to address poverty (denoted by the left-hand circle of the

Venn diagram) to understand how they can contribute to sustainability transition. Which is to say, how those in the counterproductive dark circle of addressing the causes of poverty while exacerbating environmental degradation can be minimised, and how business models that address the causes of poverty can be aligned with sustainability transition.

In their in-depth exploration of 55 organisations directly seeking to address BoP poverty in Indonesia and the Philippines, Dembek et al. (2018) identified three distinct types of BoP business models, which could be delivered as stand-alone entities, platforms, or networks.

1. *Delivering models* are those that develop and deliver technologies, services, and solutions to meet BoP needs. Globally, these consumption-focused approaches seek to adapt existing or develop new products for improved accessibility to cash- and space-constrained BoP consumers living in informal communities through innovation in product or service design, packaging, outbound logistics, and/or revenue collection. This includes but is not limited to smaller packages (e.g. single-dose medicines or single-use shampoo sachets designed to be used with cold water), lower price points, and targeted distribution networks like Unilever India's Shakti model of using local women as door-to-door rural sales agents (Mahajan, 2016). The innovation involved in tailoring products for BoP consumers may also be valued outside of the BoP, for instance, inexpensive cataract surgery techniques (Prahalad, 2011).
2. *Sourcing models* source materials, products, and/or services from BoP communities, usually for sale to non-BoP markets. In doing so they create income opportunities for BoP communities engaged in these models by creating entirely new markets or connecting them with markets that were previously inaccessible. Dembek et al. (2018) found that sourcing models are often accompanied by social support or capacity development programmes of various sorts, without which they may not succeed in the longer term.
3. *Reorganising models* remodel or replace systems and ways of life to be more beneficial to BoP communities. Rather than meeting pre-defined needs, these models address an evolving set of issues contributing to a community's problems. The business model is driven by an iterative

experimentation process that identifies and combines different solution ideas. While reorganising models include the production of one or more products and services, their key purpose is to take on large systemic problems in a particular location through multiple interconnected activities. These activities address the problem in a comprehensive way and go far beyond focusing on providing a product or service. Examples include eradicating illegal logging, or creating more sustainable and formalised transport systems.

3 Applying Multi-Level Perspective at the Bottom of the Pyramid

Sustainability transitions studies commonly adopt a multi-level perspective (MLP) as a framework for understanding transition in socio-technical systems (Geels, 2002; Markard et al., 2012; Schot & Geels, 2008), analysing such change in terms of three different levels: regime, landscape, and niche. The socio-technical regime is 'the network of actors such as users, producers, suppliers, public authorities, financiers as well as the respective infrastructures, patterns of behaviour, cultural values and policies that link them', the rules and structures of which are continuously stabilised through use and reproduction (Bidmon & Knab, 2018: 904). The landscape represents deep structural trends, while niches are spaces that are protected from the selection pressures of the market, and therefore can generate radical innovation (Geels, 2002). Given the fundamental stability that defines the socio-technical regime, transition is most often a response to forces outside of the regime, such as (macro) landscape changes or (micro) innovation that emerges from nascent and therefore unstable niches and becomes more stable as the network of actors and resources around it develops.

Niches are protected spaces where novelty or innovation can emerge, and the thus of particular interest as a target of intentional and collaborative strategic niche management (SNM) by such actors as 'state policymakers, a regulatory agency, local authorities (e.g. a development agency), non-governmental organizations, a citizen group, a private company, an industry organization, a special interest group or an independent individual' (Kemp et al., 1998: 188). The innovation produced within niches has largely been presumed within sustainability transitions research to be technological, though the subset dedicated to non-technological innovation is growing (e.g. Černe et al., 2016; Edwards-Schachter, 2018; Hansen et al., 2009; Heredia Pérez et al., 2019; Hyard, 2013; Korhonen & Seager, 2008; Pino et al., 2016), and researchers have recently observed non-technological innovation is a significantly more studied form of innovation in a recent meta-analysis of 153 empirical cases (Hoogstraaten et al., 2020).

Relative to European countries, the institutional context of developing countries is a dynamic patchwork of formal and informal institutions with contested legitimacy that is sometimes personalised in the hands of the elite to the detriment of the masses (see Ramos-Mejía et al., 2018, for an exploration of the empirical literature exploring this). Because of this, the MLP lens is valuable but must be applied somewhat loosely. Understanding the socio-technical regimes in these locations is not straightforward and requires 'embracing high levels of social complexity' (Ramos-Mejía et al., 2018: 219).

Within this context, BoP communities are generally considered 'informal' spaces, characterised by low levels of capital, technology, and skills (Harriss-White, 2010), and recognisable by their illegal housing, street vendors, and unregulated labour markets (Porter, 2011). Informality exists as 'an organising logic, a system of norms that governs the process of urban transformation itself' (Roy, 2005: 148). This means they are highly agentic spaces unto themselves that exist alongside of, but often as an exception to, the formal orders of urbanisation, legislation, routinisation associated with socio-technical regimes (see Banks et al., 2020, for a review of the informality literature). To the extent that they are 'protected or insulated from 'normal' market selection in the regime' (Geels, 2002: 1261), BoP communities are niches by virtue of their exclusion. They are what Smith and Raven (2012) term 'initial niches' in that they are naturally occurring (rather than advocate-mobilised) passive protective spaces 'where the selection pressures are felt less keenly for contingent rather than strategic reasons' (Smith & Raven, 2012: 1027). Similar to the way that sites of grassroots innovation in the developed world are often eclipsed by innovation in more conventional business settings (Seyfang

& Smith, 2007), BoP communities have so far been neglected within sustainability transition studies as potential sites of sustainable innovation.

By virtue of increasing a BoP community's integration into the dominant market economy, BoP business models alter the degree to which they are insulated from the regime—some will remain isolated enough to remain niches with their own prevailing logic of informality, some will not. For those communities that are incorporated into the dominant socio-technical regime, BoP business models determine in part how and on what terms that happens, with significant implications for sustainability transition alignment.

3.1 Potential Roles of Business Models in Sustainability Transitions

In seeking to understand the mechanisms by which business models impact sustainability transitions, Bidmon and Knab (2018) identified three roles that business models can play: supporting sustainability transition as an intermediate between niche and socio-technical regime, supporting sustainability transition as a form of non-technological niche innovation, and hindering sustainability transition as part of the socio-technical regime.

As an *intermediate* between niche and regime (Bidmon & Knab, 2018), a business model helps stabilise a niche through (1) articulation of expectations, (2) knowledge transfer, and (3) linking it to actors and resources. These are three of the structuration processes identified by Kemp et al. (1998) as supporting the potential breakthrough of innovation from niche to regime level.

As form of *non-technological niche innovation* unto themselves (Bidmon & Knab, 2018), a business model challenges past ways of working with a novel cognitive frame that creates a value network (Stabell & Fjeldstad, 1998) bringing multiple actors together in an orchestrated fashion to change their own business models. Because they create networks with a critical mass of actors by definition, these non-technological innovations emerge at a higher level of stability or structuration than a novel technology does. These novel business models are able to stabilise by virtue of having expectations and visions that are robust (i.e. shared by more actors), specific (i.e. able to provide guidance for the coordination of actors), and high quality (i.e. substantiated by ongoing projects), having learning processes that 'allow for second-order learning (i.e. enable changes of cognitive frames and assumptions)' and social networks that are both broad (i.e. involve different stakeholders) and deep (i.e. able to mobilise commitment and resources) (Bidmon & Knab, 2018: 910). In this role, business models have significant potential to drive transitions and 'lay the foundation for what can become industry recipes in a new regime (i.e. build up a substantial part of a new regime)' (Bidmon & Knab, 2018: 911).

Barring these sustainability-aligned roles, business models hamper sustainability transition by serving as part of the dominant regime. As *part of the dominant socio-technical regime*, a business model reinforces the stability of existing systems of unsustainable production and consumption by playing out roles in 'industry recipes', or the conventional wisdom within a system that determines what innovation is selected and retained (Bidmon & Knab, 2018). In this role, the business model 'connects various interrelated industries and other regime actors', and 'interacts with complementary industry recipes and other actors' working logics', as well as a 'dominant regime logic' shared by all regime actors (Bidmon & Knab, 2018: 907). The business model itself forms the link between the rules and structures between actors that determine how the larger system works, and the lower-level rules and structures that determine how business works on a local level, including the working logic of non-business actors such as consumers, financiers, or public authorities.

3.2 Methods and Data

To better understand what roles these three types of business models addressing BoP poverty can play in sustainability transition, and what determines their success, we revisited the analysis of qualitative data that formed the basis of the Dembek et al. typology (see Dembek et al., 2018, for a detailed methodological information). We identified a subset of 17 of the original 55 organisations, shown in Table 1, that purposefully

Table 1 Business models from Dembek et al. (2018) designed to address poverty while avoiding or relieving environmental degradation

Enterprise name	Description	Sustainability focus	Business model type
Bambike	Builds bamboo bicycles with fair-trade labour and sustainable building practices	Sustainable production and transport	Delivering
Ibeka	Establishes community-owned hydro- or wind electrical microgrids	Renewable energy	Delivering
Kopernik	Distributes products tailored for BoP communities (e.g. solar lanterns)	Renewable energy	Delivering
Kophi	Climate change-resilient infrastructure interventions in BoP communities	Sustainable Infrastructure	Delivering
Stiftung Solarenergie	Provides solar energy solutions in rural and marginalised areas	Renewable energy	Delivering
Apikri	Empowers micro and small handicraft producers	Sustainable handicrafts	Sourcing
Habi	Makes sustainable upcycled footwear	Upcycling	Sourcing
Sidlakpinoy	Makes reinforced fire bricks from farm wastes	Upcycling	Sourcing
Bali recycle	Collects waste and sells waste-based products	Upcycling	Reorganising
Coffee for peace	Uses coffee production as a transition tool for conflict-affected communities	Sustainable agriculture	Reorganising
Danone Ecosysteme	Uses sustainable agriculture to develop inclusive economies	Sustainable agriculture	Reorganising
EVEEI	Provides electric vehicle public transport solutions	Sustainable transport	Reorganising
Garbage Insurance	Uses recyclable waste as a financial resource to provide micro-health insurance programme	Waste recovery	Reorganising

(continued)

Table 1 (continued)

Enterprise name	Description	Sustainability focus	Business model type
Getevee	Provides electric vehicle public transport solutions	Sustainable transport	Reorganising
Health in Harmony	Implements community-led programmes to combat tropical deforestation	Illegal logging	Reorganising
Koperasi Desa Mina	Community development via fisheries community cooperative	Overfishing	Reorganising
Trees 4 trees	Develops community forestry	Illegal logging	Reorganising

address some aspect of environmental sustainability alongside a focus on poverty alleviation. The original analysis of these 17 was reviewed to identify distinguishing themes and characteristics.

We found cases pursuing both sustainability and poverty alleviation distributed across all three types of models.

- Five of the original 16 delivering models in the study focused on both sustainability and poverty alleviation, supporting BoP communities through small-scale sustainability transition by enabling them to convert infrastructure and transportation to more sustainable alternatives.
- Only 3 of the original 19 sourcing models pursued both sustainability and poverty alleviation goals, all by incorporating sustainable and/or recycled inputs in their products. This type had the lowest representation amongst organisations pursing both types of goals.
- Nine of the original 19 reorganising models pursued both sustainability and poverty alleviation goals, by replacing environmentally unsustainable livelihood activities with more sustainable alternatives. A much larger proportion of reorganising models had both sustainability and poverty alleviation objectives than either of the other types.

The business model attributes of these 17 organisations explicitly addressing both BoP poverty and sustainability, clustered by type, were analysed using the Bidmon and Knab framework on roles of business models in sustainability transitions (described above) to better understand their potential role in sustainability transitions.

Whether a BoP business model lives up to its sustainable poverty alleviation intent and its potential in supporting sustainability transition is determined in part by whether the model is designed and implemented in ways that enable it to navigate around particular pitfalls that can be represented and understood through the lens of system traps. In the next section, we draw on the concept of system traps (Meadows & Wright, 2008) to understand the systemic factors that influence whether the different types of BoP business models live up to their potential in supporting sustainability transition, and how they can be structured for more sustainable outcomes.

4 System Traps as Sources of Sustainability Misalignment for BoP Business Models

System traps are identified archetypes of problem-generating structures within systems across fields ranging from software to politics to development. These traps result in unintended outcomes which can be difficult to trace. Because system traps are dynamics that emerge from the system structure rather than being a result of bad actors or events, they can be addressed in the design and implementation of the business models. These system traps are summarised in Table 2.

In the first common system trap, known as *shifting the burden*, quick fixes with negative long-term consequences create a downward spiral in the larger system (Meadows & Wright, 2008). For instance, in the short term, soil nutrients can be boosted with fertiliser, political goodwill can be purchased with targeted spending, shrinking catches can be boosted with more intensive fishing, resistant bacteria or weeds can be met with stronger antibiotics and herbicides. Rather than addressing the underlying problem, these approaches temporarily mask the symptoms of the real problem, interfering with actions that could solve the real problem. Over time, this approach deteriorates the ability to solve the bigger problem. *Shifting the burden* can be seen within particular product or value

Table 2 System traps faced by BoP business models aligning to sustainability

System trap	Description	Solution
Shifting the burden	Repeated application of 'quick fixes' (1) divert attention away from the underlying causes of the problem and (2) undermine the ability to address the true causes in the long term	Avoid if possible, otherwise remain alert to symptom-relieving approaches that mask the underlying problem
Wrong goal	Targeting the wrong success indicators sets the entire system to create accurate but unintended results	Correct goal identification
Drift to low performance	Downward spiral of performance and standards over time because standards are influenced by past performance	Absolute, rather than relative, performance standards
Tragedy of the commons	Misalignment of feedback in the system means that every user benefits directly from using commonly shared resource, but the costs of its abuse are distributed across all users, leading over time to destruction of the commonly shared resource	Strengthen the missing feedback link from the system or regulate the access of all users
Success to the successful	Winners are systematically rewarded with the means to win again, leading to growing inequality between winners and losers	Diversification allowing those who are losing to get out of that game and start another one

offerings (discussed in the next section), and in the longer-term dynamics affecting BoP communities, where it in MLP terms is best thought of as a commonly occurring driver of landscape pressure.

The remaining system traps are things that happen within the business models themselves, rather than in the landscape. In the system trap of seeking the *wrong goal*, targeting the wrong success indicators sets the entire system to create accurate but unintended results, causing misalignment of BoP business with sustainability transition. In the *tragedy of the commons* system trap, all users of a collective resource benefit individually from using the resource, but the cost of overusing the resource are shared across the group, thus reducing any disincentive for abusing the resource for individual benefit. For instance, if some boats overfish by a small amount, eventually everyone suffers from the collapse of the fishery resource. In the *success to the successful* system trap, the structure of a system consistently rewards winners with the means to win again. For instance, a fisher with a larger boat is able to catch more fish, enabling them to afford more boats, widening the gap between them and the other fishers.

5 Potential Roles for Different Types of BoP Business Models in Sustainability Transition

The reminder of this chapter examines the three types of BoP business models in terms of the potential and risk they have to take the three sustainability transition roles identified by Bidmon and Knab (2018) (i.e. to stabilise existing socio-technical regimes, to intermediate between a niche and socio-technical regime and advance a non-technological niche innovation). In doing so we discuss the system traps each type of business model faces, and what can be done in order to make these business models work for rather than against sustainability transition. Table 3 matches each business model type with potential roles presented by Bidmon and Knab (2018). It summarises the risks it can pose to sustainability transition as part of the existing socio-technical regime, and the opportunities for advancing sustainability transition as an intermediate or as a form of non-technological innovation. Real examples of each model from Dembek et al. (2018) are offered in sidebars toward the end of the chapter.

5.1 Delivering Models

Delivering models develop and deliver technologies, services, and solutions to meet BoP needs. Delivering models can intermediate between niche and regime and advance sustainability transition by introducing innovation from the dominant socio-technical regime and enabling BoP communities to consume more sustainably.

Table 3 Sustainability transition opportunities and risks for BoP business model types

	Potential role in sustainability transition (Bidmon & Knab, 2018)		
BoP business model type	Part of existing socio-technical regime (risks for hindering ST)	Intermediate between niche and socio-technical regime (opportunities for advancing ST)	Non-technological niche innovation (opportunities for advancing ST)
Delivering Provide access to products or services to the BoP communities Address single needs within BoP community (e.g. lighting)	Promote BoP overconsumption Create dependency on unsustainable production Shift focus away from genuine and unmet needs to those that are most economically exploitable Contribute to unmanaged solid waste, especially plastic	Introduce innovation to BoP communities Sustainably meet genuine and previously unmet BoP community needs May transmit innovations developed for BoP to be used in other locations	Finance and revenue collection innovations developed for BoP accessibility may be used elsewhere, for example, pay finance from revenue generated by product (e.g. Ibeka) or pay per use rather than purchase products (Kopernik)
Sourcing Source materials, products, and services from BoP communities for sale to non-BoP customers Address a defined set of needs within the BoP community (e.g. skills development, income, and access to market)	Create economic dependency on unsustainable production (e.g. agriculture) practices or overproduction of low-value goods in exploitative conditions Observed potential to cause conflict and disruption in BoP communities	Introduce innovation to BoP communities Develop BoP capacities, ability to meet basic needs, and economic resilience Can also transmit non-technological innovation from BoP community to regime	*Not observed*

(*continued*)

Table 3 (continued)

	Potential role in sustainability transition (Bidmon & Knab, 2018)		
BoP business model type	Part of existing socio-technical regime (risks for hindering ST)	Intermediate between niche and socio-technical regime (opportunities for advancing ST)	Non-technological niche innovation (opportunities for advancing ST)
Reorganising Create new or modify existing systems and ways of life to benefit BoP communities Community wellbeing comprised of interconnected needs that change over time	Attach livelihood to environmentally unsustainable production and consumption or to exploitative social relations	Introduce innovation to BoP communities Develop BoP capacities, ability to meet basic needs, and economic resilience Can also transmit non-technological innovation from BoP community to regime	Create novel, bottom-up, sustainable poverty alleviation solutions that become increasingly resilient with growth

As an ideal type, delivering models connect the BoP community with sustainably-made, low-waste products or services that meet genuine unsatisfied needs without creating negative social or environmental externalities. This enables some degree of sustainable economic and human development, as well as climate adaptation, without necessarily altering the levels of informality or insulation from the dominant regime that makes the BoP community a niche.

Delivering models may become misaligned with sustainability by the *shifting the burden* trap (1) when the models promote overconsumption of goods like skin lightening creams that don't fill a genuine BoP community need, (2) when they create dependency on the products of unsustainable supply chains like palm oil or cacao, and (3) when BoP products are designed without consideration for negative social and environmental consequences of the consumption. For instance, the same single-use packaging that enables consumption by space- and capital-constrained BoP consumers can increase environmental degradation by reinforcing unsustainable supply chains and generating unmanaged plastic waste at the point of consumption (Nulkar, 2016; Prahalad & Hart, 2002).

Models that deliver unneeded goods or socially destructive goods and services can shift focus and resources away from genuine and unmet needs to those that are merely profitable to satisfy (e.g. tobacco, cosmetics, and disposable nappies), forcing BoP communities to make a long-term counterproductive trade-off between satisfaction of a consumption need and environmental degradation that directly affects their communities (Jaiswal & Gupta, 2015). This is especially damaging when a product or service displaces existing ways of meeting a need that are sustainable and low cost, such as replacing banana leaves and cloth wrapping with plastic bags, or replacing breastfeeding with infant formula.

Delivering models may also become misaligned with sustainability by the *wrong goal* trap when they optimise for maximising only producer profit, rather than profitably maximising the satisfaction of genuine BoP community needs for essentials like food, housing, clothing, basic health-care, education, and employment, that improve the consumer's quality of life and help them realise their full potential (Jaiswal & Gupta, 2015). Focusing on delivering the most profitable goods and services also opens the door to environmentally unsustainable overconsumption.

5.2 Sourcing Models

Sourcing models source materials, products, and/or services from BoP communities. Sourcing models can intermediate between niche and regime and advance sustainability transition by introducing innovation to and from the dominant socio-technical regime and enabling BoP communities to produce and consume more sustainably.

As an ideal type, sourcing models as intermediates equitably engage BoP communities in the creation of durable, sustainably made, and low-waste products or services without creating negative social or environmental externalities. Through this arrangement, sourcing models empower BoP communities, developing their capacities, ability to meet basic needs, and economic resilience. All else being equal, sourcing models can be expected to strengthen ties to the socio-technical regime, decreasing a BoP community's informality and therefore insulation and protection from the dominant regime.

Sourcing models can become misaligned with sustainability by the *shifting the burden* system trap when the models create economic dependency (through employment) on environmentally unsustainable production practices of all kinds, and overproduction of unnecessary goods that are low quality, have short product lives before ending up in landfill, and/or are produced in exploitative conditions like sweatshops (e.g. Gold et al., 2015; Kumar, 2020). This includes most mass-produced, low-end items like handicrafts, toys, fast fashion, candy, or electronics. This is particularly problematic when the overproduced goods are of low value, since high production volume is required to meet basic income needs for the BoP communities involved.

Sourcing models can also become misaligned with sustainability by the *wrong goal* trap in two different ways. First, they can become misaligned in terms of BoP community outcomes if it optimises strictly for satisfying the BoP community's instrumental need for income, without consideration of social and environmental outcomes of production. Increasing a BoP community's disposable income does not necessarily increase wellbeing in terms of access to food, housing, clothing, basic healthcare, or education. Abruptly increasing income may also have negative unintended consequences like increasing alcohol consumption, gambling, or family violence. Sourcing models have been observed to destroy existing social capital and wellbeing with conflict and community disruption (Dembek et al., 2018; Dembek & York, 2020). The second way they can become misaligned is by optimising for making low-cost products that require environmentally unsustainable high production volume to meet basic needs, rather than setting their sites on higher value add and more sustainable products that are actually needed in the market and generate more value for the BoP communities involved in the model. This can trigger a secondary system trap, known as *drift to low performance*, in which standards and performance erode over time because standards are influenced by past performance, locking the community into unambitious and uncritical production of substandard goods that are not valued in the market.

5.3 Reorganising Models

Reorganising models remodel or replace systems and ways of life to be more beneficial to BoP communities.

As an ideal type, reorganising models are a form of *non-technological niche innovation* that iteratively unpicks parts of a local socio-technical system that are holding problems in place, replacing them with options that are more aligned with overall community wellbeing. Over a relatively short period of a few years of deliberate and ongoing strategic niche management, reorganising models can diminish many connections to the dominant regime through which the BoP community was stabilising patterns of unsustainable production and consumption, replacing them with connections to sustainable activities within an expanding business model centred on advancing the wellbeing of BoP community itself. This process enables sustainable economic and human development while increasing the degree to which the BoP community is insulated and protected from the dynamics and selection pressures of the broader socio-technical system.

While reorganising models generally lack the direct involvement of institutional actors such as development agencies and industry bodies expected by Kemp et al. (1998), they have much in common with those seen in strategic niche management studies within sustainability transitions research. They represent local experiments supported by local networks and generating locally applicable lessons (Smith & Raven, 2012) that can be deliberately mobilised by advocates to shift BoP communities away from environmentally damaging economic pursuits to economically sustainable ones. Where the actors exist to do so, these localised lessons can be carried to other localities, with the potential to create novel, bottom-up, sustainable poverty alleviation solutions. Through this process of co-innovation between actors, and the development or incorporation of more enterprises, the reorganising model can stabilise and become an increasingly resilient socio-technical space or proto-regime that co-exists alongside the dominant regime. While not achieving socio-technical regime status, the results could be described in the language of Fuenfschilling and Binz (2018: 736) as niches that 'consist of multi-scalar actor networks and discourses that get implemented in many places at once'. Developed world parallels of this model can be found in grassroots innovations such as the UK's Transition Towns (e.g. Hargreaves et al., 2013; Seyfang & Haxeltine, 2012).

Reorganising models can become misaligned with sustainability by the *wrong goal* trap in the same ways as those described above for sourcing models—optimising for income rather than wellbeing, or producing goods at a price point that necessitates unsustainable production volumes and processes.

Additionally, the degree to which reorganising models depend on careful coordination and timing of activities to reorient the complex systems that hold social and environmental problems in place introduces other vulnerabilities. Reorganising models risk falling into the *tragedy of the commons* system trap if, through insufficient oversight or stakeholder buy-in, component activities of the business model overgrow at the expense of developing the system as a whole. Reorganising models can also become misaligned to sustainability by the *success to the successful* system trap if coordination is captured by powerful members of the community seeking to reorganise systems to their benefit, to the detriment of those less successful and the long-term interests of the community as a whole.

5.3.1 Designing BoP Business Models to Avoid System Traps and Align to Sustainability Transitions

Table 4 summarises the findings discussed above and takes the analysis further to provide indications of what is needed to align BoP business models and to support sustainability transition rather than stabilising and strengthening unsustainable socio-technical regimes. It matches each business model type with its potential role in aligning to transition, the misalignment risks of the business model type as described above, the system traps that lead to each risk, and the design and implementation of sustainability enablers that can be embedded into the BoP business model to avoid the system trap and fulfil that type of business model's potential in advancing sustainability transition.

As Table 4 indicates, all of the sustainability misalignment risks associated with particular BoP business model types can be mitigated through more considered business model design and implementation, thus enhancing the likelihood that BoP business models will align to or drive sustainability transition through their operation.

Summarising, we can identify three universal systemic design considerations that should help any of the three types of BoP business models to avoid common system traps and fulfil its potential as a driver of sustainability transition, and three universal enablers that were effective in helping BoP business models address both poverty and environmental degradation to fulfil their potential in supporting sustainability transition. We now discuss these universal design considerations and enablers in more detail.

5.4 Business Model Design Principles to Address Specific System Traps

First and foremost, BoP business model design for sustainability transition should involve commitment to identifying, understanding, and addressing root causes of poverty and environmental degradation in a particular location. This is to navigate around the shifting the burden system trap and mitigate the very real risk of long-term harm to the BoP community and the environment.

Table 4 Sustainability alignment enablers for different BoP business model types

BoP business model type	Key enablers for fulfilling potential in advancing transition
All types	Embedded, inclusive process to identify BoP community needs and monitor impact
Delivering Provide access to products or services to the BoP communities Address single needs within BoP community (e.g. lighting)	Network of aligned stakeholders collaborating to maintain ongoing sustainability focus Deep consideration of long-term social and environmental consequences of goods sold
Sourcing Source materials, products, and services from BoP communities for sale to non-BoP markets Address a defined set of needs within the BoP community (e.g. skills development, income, and access to market	Network of aligned stakeholders collaborating to inspire and support performance improvement while maintaining ongoing sustainability focus Deep consideration of long-term, net environmental footprint and social consequences of production
Reorganising Create new or modify existing systems and ways of life to benefit BoP communities Community wellbeing composed of interconnected needs that change over time	Network of aligned stakeholders collaboratively guiding the timing of business model activities to be reinforcing while maintaining the ongoing sustainability focus Deep consideration of long-term, net environmental footprint and social consequences of production Continued iteration to include diversified business model activities

(*continued*)

Table 4 (continued)

How system traps are addressed
At outset, identifies genuine BoP community needs, helps avoid *wrong goal* trap
As ongoing monitoring, enables early identification and mitigation of emerging challenges such as entry into *shifting the burden*, *success to the successful*, or *tragedy of the commons* traps
Ongoing and focused attention on ways to address genuine BoP needs with sustainably produced products and services helps avoid the *shifting the burden* trap, which deteriorates the ability to solve problems while reinforcing them
Explicit consideration helps avoid the *wrong goal* trap in which the business model delivers producer profits without meeting genuine BoP needs, and helps avoid unintended environmental consequences like unmanaged plastic waste
Ongoing and focused attention on ways to improve performance, and improve product quality and sustainability helps avoid the *shifting the burden* trap, in BoP community is increasingly dependent on income, but deteriorating product quality or BoP community issues deteriorates the ability to bring in that income. Stakeholder input helps address problems identified by BoP community
Explicit consideration helps avoid two versions of the *wrong goal* trap: (1) Addressing the instrumental need for BoP income, rather than the underlying inherent needs, and (2) Optimising for lowest cost rather than high value creation, leading to *drift to low performance* through unambitious and uncritical production
Explicit consideration also helps avoid the *shifting the burden* trap by unwittingly creating economic dependency on unsustainable production practices (e.g. palm oil production) or overproduction of low-value goods in exploitative conditions
This helps avoid falling into the *shifting the burden* trap by unwittingly attaching livelihood to environmentally unsustainable production and consumption or to exploitative social relations
Ensuring that no component activities of the business model to overgrow at the expense of the system as a whole due to weak coordination and institutions helps avoid a *tragedy of commons* trap
Explicit consideration helps avoid two versions of the *wrong goal* trap: (1) Addressing the instrumental need for BoP income, rather than the underlying inherent needs, and (2) Optimising for lowest cost rather than high-value creation, leading to *drift to low performance* through unambitious and uncritical production
Explicit consideration also helps avoid the *shifting the burden* trap by unwittingly creating economic dependency on unsustainable production practices (e.g. palm oil production) or overproduction of low-value goods in exploitative conditions
If a *success to the successful* or *tragedy of the commons* trap emerges, diversification ensures that opportunities still exist rather than allowing the process to be captured by powerful community members to their benefit or to exhaust shared resources

Delivering Model as *Intermediate* connecting BoP niche to dominant regime

- Transmits innovation and capacity
- Enables sustainable BoP production and consumption

Example: IBEKA is a non-profit organisation supporting rural electrification by installing small-scale hydro- or wind mini grids (both off-grid and grid-connected) and setting up village-based organisations to own and operate the systems. This provides lighting, electricity for charging phones, and supports BoP agriculture processes like drying and roasting coffee or producing lemon grass oil. Income from electricity sales is used for village development funds such as scholarships, healthcare, seed capital for business, village infrastructure such as road construction, clean water supply, and sanitation (IBEKA, 2012; Cannon et al. 2020).

Sustainability misalignment risks:

- Spreading and stabilising unsustainable consumption patterns, with potential to and create dependency
- Creating unmanaged waste, for example, from packaging

Sustainability alignment enablers:

- Develops renewable energy programmes that prioritise the benefit of the community and positively impact its self-reliance, as well as its socio-economic and environmental issues
- Uses a mix of adapted technology and social awareness to empower BoP communities
- Partners with regional and international sustainability advisors and collaborators, including Stanford University Engineers for a Sustainable World (ESW)

The second essential principle that must underpin BoP business model design for sustainability transition is a careful identification of the goal it is designing toward and alignment of system incentives toward that goal. This helps sidestep the risks of the wrong goal system trap.

Third, the design and implementation of reorganising models addressing poverty and environmental degradation must steer a middle path between too little coordination leading to a tragedy of the commons system trap on the one hand, and capture of coordination by powerful interests leading to a success to the successful system trap on the other hand. The goal is to keep coordination aligned with the long-term interests of both the BoP community and the environment. Ongoing coordination and convening are particularly critical to reorganising models, as the addition of activities must be carefully sequenced to target high leverage opportunities, and interconnected so that they reinforce each other to create novel, bottom-up, sustainable poverty alleviation solutions. In the developed world, the state and interested incumbents are logical convenors and coordinators of sustainability transitions; in communities with weak institutions, a dedicated convener aligned with the long-term interests of the community must take on this this role.

5.5 Universal Sustainability Enablers for BoP Business Models

In addition to the systemic design considerations, our study identified three universal enablers that were effective in helping BoP business models addressing both poverty and environmental degradation to fulfil their potential in supporting sustainability transition, either as an intermediate or as a non-technological niche expanding into a novel, bottom-up, sustainable poverty alleviation solution. These are the addition of an iterative community problem identification and resolution process to support the business model, a network of aligned stakeholders, and deep consideration of long-term, net environmental footprint and social consequences of business model activities and goods sold, accompanied by ongoing impact monitoring.

Sourcing Model as *Intermediate* connecting BoP niche to dominant regime

- Transmits innovation and capacity
- Enables sustainable BoP production and consumption

Example: Habi Footwear leverages the existing weaving skills of its BoP suppliers to create durable and fashionable shoes from recycled materials. Its business model incorporates a process to identify and address emerging community concerns and enable BoP suppliers to meet other community-identified needs such as enhanced education for their children (Dembek & York, 2020).

Sustainability misalignment risks:

- Stabilising and creating dependency on existing unsustainable production
- Creating unmanaged waste through overproduction of low-value goods
- Introducing community conflict and disruption

Sustainability alignment enablers:

- Network of aligned stakeholders inspiring and supporting performance improvement and maintaining the ongoing focus on sustainability transition, including Ateneo de Manila University Institute of Sustainability and sustainability-aligned capital providers
- Upcycled materials
- Manufacturing approaches that build on existing capacities of its BoP supplier communities
- BoP suppliers have autonomy in how they organise their work and diverse and proactive community support

The universally needed design elements of correct goal identification and commitment to identifying, understanding, and addressing root causes of poverty and environmental degradation in a particular location seemed to be met most successfully by including in the model design an iterative and community-inclusive process of listening, learning, and adapting. This was an intentional process of understanding how the problem exists for and affects different stakeholders, identifying feedback loops reinforcing the problem, identifying potential leverage points, designing interventions able to shift behaviour at those leverage points, implementing changes, monitoring change and emergence in collaboration with BoP community members. This process can be embedded within the main entity or provided by a partner entity working in tandem. This process can be used to great effect when it precedes the commencement of other business model activities, and is used first to identify real and unmet (or underserved) BoP needs in their own terms in the first instance, and then on an ongoing basis to identify and mitigate emerging challenges. This business model activity can also be introduced once the business model is running. This was the case for footwear company Habi [see sidebar], where the process was introduced in response to unmanaged conflict within the BoP community caused by changing economic power dynamics with the introduction of additional income, which created a crisis that threatened to destabilise the entire organisation (Dembek & York, 2020).

A second valuable universal enabler was the cultivation of a network of aligned advisors and stakeholders made up of actors seeking the solution, those who can enable the solution (e.g. through provision of capital or access to market), those whose livelihood needs support or benefit from the problem as it currently exists. This network can reinforce the business model's ongoing focus on sustainability transition, inspire and support performance improvement in sourcing models, and guide the selection and timing of reorganising model activities to ensure that they are both mutually reinforcing and high leverage in terms of the desired system change. In-depth knowledge of the system is necessary to decide which activities should be implemented first. For example, Health in Harmony [see sidebar] spent significant time gathering diverse community perspectives before identifying a non-obvious starting intervention point that had little to do with the illegal logging it sought to end: excessive cash expenditure travelling to a distant hospital. If the organisation had implemented ranger services before introducing organic farming training and healthcare provision, it would not have created the desired effect of stopping illegal logging because there would have been no alternative means of meeting needs if logging remained the only available source of needed cash income.

Reorganising model as *non-technological niche innovation*

- Multi-actor co-innovation process
- Lays foundations of multi-scalar actor networks and discourses that can be implemented in many places at once

Example: Health in Harmony reorganised a regional economy in West Kalimantan away from illegal logging to organic farming and reforestation through an iterative process of identifying leverage points and replacing system components with more sustainable livelihood options. This involved identifying immediate income needs that could be satisfied in other ways, developing new capacities, setting up alternative income generation activities, and iteratively adding additional components that increased the strength and resilience of the new system in various ways—rangers providing technical assistance, a tree nursery, an ambulance and medical clinic, a manure-based payment system to build up fertiliser supply, and so on.

Sustainability misalignment risks:

- Stabilising and creating dependency on unsustainable production patterns
- Inadequate coordination of model resulting in divergent and non-reinforcing activities, or capture of the process by powerful community interests

Sustainability alignment enablers

- Network of aligned stakeholders collaboratively coordinating development of business model
- Focus on identifying high-impact leverage points within system
- Continued iteration to include diversified value creation activities interconnected with behaviour-changing incentives

Finally, business models underpinned by deep consideration of long-term, net environmental footprint and social consequences of the activities and goods sold, and accompanied by ongoing impact monitoring, were more able to anticipate and avoid common pitfalls. Embedding this consideration of potential consequences into the business model design process increased the likelihood that the model delivered lasting benefits for multiple stakeholders, that income streams were not attached to sources of environmental degradation, and that the business model would be aligned to sustainability transition rather than an obstacle to it. As an illustration, many organisations provide microgrids for access to cleaner electricity, which enables access to lighting, power, and connectivity for BoP communities. By pairing this with a financing mechanism, Ibeka [see sidebar] ensures that over time the microgrid is wholly owned by the BoP community and creates an income stream that feeds a village development fund for scholarships, seed funding, and the like. This generates significantly more empowerment for the BoP community than the electricity alone would do.

6 Conclusion

The problems of poverty and environmental degradation are closely entwined for world's poorest people in the global south, and every effort to alleviate poverty that expands and reinscribes the currently unsustainable modes of production and consumption is long-term counterproductive to sustainability transition. Despite this, BoP business models have not previously been seen as significant in sustainability transitions research (Jolly et al., 2012; Köhler et al., 2019). This study used empirical data from the global south to illuminate the ways in which BoP business models can reinforce or break down currently unsustainable models of production and consumption that are edging the planet toward environmental disaster. It also demonstrates the strong potential of BoP business models addressing both poverty and environmental degradation to advance sustainability transition, either as intermediates between the technological niche and the socio-technical regime or as non-technological niche innovations that create novel, bottom-up, sustainable poverty alleviation solutions.

In addition to highlighting the relevance of poverty alleviation and BoP business models to sustainability transitions research and practice, our key contribution is to show specific systemic design considerations and enablers that help BoP business models avoid the system traps that lead them to stabilise unsustainable socio-technical regimes. These findings are directly relevant to national and subnational policy-makers (regime actors), and the managers of regime and niche organisations seeking to promote undertake the development of similar business models.

This work presents opportunities for a research agenda in both business models and sustainability transitions studies. Sustainability transition is a system-based process. Future studies, both those focused on the role of business models in sustainability transition and those looking at this process more broadly, could explore the risks of falling into system traps and potentially develop a set of problem-solution patterns (Lüdeke-Freund et al., 2018) for avoiding and mitigating the risk. Another useful perspective for future research is identification of systemic leverage points. Leverage points could help explore how we should design business models and sustainability transition initiatives to maximise their potential for swift change to more sustainable production and consumption patterns.

References

Alao, A. (2007). *Natural resources and conflict in Africa: The tragedy of endowment*. University of Rochester Press.

Banks, N., Lombard, M., & Mitlin, D. (2020). Urban informality as a site of critical analysis. *The Journal of Development Studies, 56*(2), 223–238.

Barrett, C. B., Travis, A. J., & Dasgupta, P. (2011). On biodiversity conservation and poverty traps. *PNAS, 108*(34), 13907–13912.

Bidmon, C., & Knab, S. (2018). The three roles of business models in societal transitions: New linkages between business model and transition research. *Journal of Cleaner Production, 178*, 903–916.

Bocken, N., Short, S., Rana, P., & Evans, S. (2014). A literature and practice review to develop sustainable business model archetypes. *Journal of Cleaner Production, 65*, 42–56.

Cannon, M., Thorpe, J., & Emili, S. (2020). IBEKA: Community-owned and managed mini grids in Indonesia. *Institute for Development Studies*. https://s3.amazonaws.com/participedia.prod/440f2e5c-df02-45d1-a244-449ab428fa63. Accessed on 30 June 2020.

Černe, M., Kašea, R., & Škerlavaj, M. (2016). Non-technological innovation research: Evaluating the intellectual structure and prospects of an emerging field. *Scandinavian Journal of Management, 32*(2), 69–85.

Clark, G. (2007). Evolution of the global sustainable consumption and production policy and the United Nations Environment Programme's (UNEP) supporting activities. *Journal of Cleaner Production, 15*(6), 492–498.

Dembek, K., Sivasubramaniam, N., & Chmielewski, D. A. (2020). A systematic review of the bottom/base of the pyramid literature: Cumulative evidence and future directions. *Journal of Business Ethics, 165*, 365–382.

Dembek, K., & York, J. (2020). Applying a sustainable business model lens to mutual value creation with base of the pyramid suppliers. *Business & Society*. https://doi.org/10.1177/0007650320973450

Dembek, K., York, J., & Singh, P. J. (2018). Creating value for multiple stakeholders: Sustainable business models at the base of the pyramid. *Journal of Cleaner Production, 196*, 1600–1612.

Edwards-Schachter, M. (2018). The nature and variety of innovation. *The International Journal of Innovation Studies, 2*(2), 65–79.

Fuenfschilling, L., & Binz, C. (2018). Global socio-technical regimes. *Research Policy, 47*, 735–749.

Geels, F. W. (2002). Technological transitions as evolutionary reconfiguration processes: a multi-level perspective and a case-study. *Research Policy, 31*(8/9), 1257–1274.

Gold, S., Trautrims, A., & Trodd, Z. (2015). Modern slavery challenges to supply chain management. *Supply Chain Management, 20*(5), 485–494.

Hall, J., Matos, S., Sheehan, L., & Silvestre, B. S. (2012). Entrepreneurship and innovation at the base of the pyramid: A recipe for inclusive growth or social exclusion? *Journal of Management Studies, 49*, 785–812.

Hansen, E. G., Grosse-Dunker, F., & Reichwald, R. (2009). Sustainability innovation cube: A framework to evaluate sustainability-oriented innovations. *International Journal of Innovation Management, 13*(4), 683–713.

Hargreaves, T., Hielscher, S., Seyfang, G., & Smith, A. (2013). Grassroots innovations in community energy: The role of intermediaries in niche development. *Global Environmental Change, 23*(5), 868–880.

Harriss-White, B. (2010). Work and wellbeing in informal economies: The regulative roles of institutions of identity and the state. *World Development, 38*(2), 170–183.

Heredia Pérez, J. A., Geldes, C., Kunc, M. H., & Floresa, A. (2019). New approach to the innovation process in emerging economies: The manufacturing sector case in Chile and Peru. *Technovation, 79*, 35–55.

Hoogstraaten, M. J., Frenken, K., & Boon, W. P. C. (2020). The study of institutional entrepreneurship and its implications for transition studies. *Environmental Innovation and Societal Transitions, 36*, 114–136.

Hyard, A. (2013). Non-technological innovations for sustainable transport. *Technological Forecasting and Social Change, 80*(7), 1375–1386.

IBEKA. (2012, March 16). IBEKA/Community-owned micro hydro. *Ashden*. https://www.ashden.org/winners/ibeka. Accessed 30 June 2020.

IPCC. (2014). Part A: Global and sectoral aspects. In C. B. Field, V. R. Barros, D. J. Dokken, K. J. Mach, M. D. Mastrandrea, T. E. Bilir, M. Chatterjee, K. L. Ebi, Y. O. Estrada, R. C. Genova, B. Girma, E. S. Kissel, A. N. Levy, S. MacCracken, P. R. Mastrandrea, & L. L. White (Eds.), *Contribution of working group II to the fifth assessment report of the intergovernmental panel on climate change*. Cambridge University Press. Accessed 30 June 2020.

IPCC. (2018). Global warming of 1.5°C. In V. Masson-Delmotte, P. Zhai, H. O. Pörtner, D. Roberts, J. Skea, P. R. Shukla, A. Pirani, W. Moufouma-Okia, C. Péan, R. Pidcock, S. Connors, J. B. R. Matthews, Y. Chen, X. Zhou, M. I. Gomis, E. Lonnoy, T. Maycock, M. Tignor, & T. Waterfield (Eds.), *An IPCC special report on the impacts of global warming of 1.5°C above pre-industrial levels and related global greenhouse gas emission pathways, in the context of strengthening the global response to the threat of climate change, sustainable development, and efforts to eradicate poverty*. Cambridge University Press. Accessed 30 June 2020.

Jaiswal, A. K., & Gupta, S. (2015). The influence of marketing on consumption behavior at the bottom of the pyramid. *Journal of Consumer Marketing, 32*(2), 113–124.

Jolly, S., Raven, R., & Romijn, H. (2012). Upscaling of business model experiments in off-grid PV solar energy in India. *Sustainability Science, 7*(2), 199–212.

Kemp, R., Schot, J., & Hoogma, R. (1998). Regime shifts to sustainability through processes of niche formation: The approach of strategic niche management. *Technology Analysis and Strategic Management, 10*, 175–196.

Köhler, J., Geels, F. W., Kern, F., Markard, J., Onsongo, E., Wieczorek, A., Alkemade, F., Avelino, F., Bergek, A., Boons, F., Fünfschilling, L., Hess, D., Holtz, G., Hyysalo, S., Jenkins, K., Kivimaa, P., Martiskainen, M., McMeekin, A., Mühlemeier, M. S., Nykvist, B., Pel, B., Raven, R., Rohracher, H., Sandén, B., Schot, J., Sovacool, B., Turnheim, B., Welch, D., & Wells, P. (2019). An agenda for sustainability transitions research: State of the art and future directions. *Environmental Innovation and Societal Transitions, 31*, 1–32.

Korhonen, J., & Seager, T. P. (2008). Beyond eco-efficiency: A resilience perspective. *Business Strategy and the Environment, 17*(7), 411–419.

Kumar, A. (2020). *Monopsony capitalism: Power and production in the twilight of the sweatshop age*. Cambridge University Press.

Lüdeke-Freund, F., Carroux, S., Joyce, A., Massa, L., & Breuer, H. (2018). The sustainable business model pattern taxonomy – 45 patterns to support sustainability-oriented business model innovation. *Sustainable Production and Consumption, 15*, 145–162.

Mahajan, V. (2016). How unilever reaches rural consumers in emerging markets. *Harvard Business Review*. Accessed 30 June 2020.

Markard, J., Raven, R., & Truffer, B. (2012). Sustainability transitions: An emerging field of research and its prospects. *Research Policy, 41*, 955–967.

Meadows, D. H., & Wright, D. (2008). *Thinking in systems: A primer*. Chelsea Green Pub.

Nulkar, G. (2016). The environmental costs of serving the bottom of the pyramid. *Sustainability: The Journal of Record, 9*(1), 31–38.

Peluso, N. L., & Watts, M. (Eds.). (2001). *Violent environments*. Cornell University Press.

Pino, C., Felzensztein, C., Zwerg-Villegas, A. M., & Arias-Bolzmann, L. (2016). Non-technological innovations: Market performance of exporting firms in South America. *Journal of Business Research, 69*(10), 4385–4393.

Porter, L. (2011). Informality, the commons and the paradoxes for planning: Concepts and debates for informality and planning. *Planning Theory and Practice, 12*(1), 115–153.

Prahalad, C. K. (2011). Bottom of the pyramid as a source of breakthrough innovations. *Journal of Product Innovation Management, 29*(1), 6–12.

Prahalad, C. K., & Hart, S. L. (2002). The fortune at the bottom of the pyramid. *Strategy + Business, 26*, 1–15.

Ramos-Mejía, M., Franco-Garcia, M.-L., & Jauregui-Becker, J. M. (2018). Sustainability transitions in the developing world: Challenges of socio-technical transformations unfolding in contexts of poverty. *Environmental Science & Policy, 84*, 217–223.

Raven, R., Ghosh, B., Wieczorek, A., Stirling, A., Ghosh, D., Jolly, S., Karjangtimapron, E., Prabudhanitisarn, S., Roy, J., Sangawongse, S., & Sengers, F. (2017). Unpacking sustainabilities in diverse transition contexts: Solar photovoltaic and urban mobility experiments in India and Thailand. *Sustainability Science, 12*, 579–596.

Romijn, H., Raven, R., & de Visser, I. (2010). Biomass energy experiments in rural India: Insights from learning-based development approaches and lessons for strategic niche management. *Environmental Science Policy, 13*, 326–338.

Roy, A. (2005). Urban informality: Toward an epistemology of planning. *Journal of the American Planning Association, 71*(2), 147–158.

Schot, J., & Geels, F. W. (2008). Strategic niche management and sustainable innovation journeys: Theory, findings, research agenda, and policy. *Technology Analysis & Strategic Management, 20*(5), 537–554.

Sen, A. (1999). *Development as freedom*. Oxford University Press.

Seyfang, G., & Haxeltine, A. (2012). Growing grassroots innovations: Exploring the role of community-based initiatives in governing sustainable energy transitions. *Environment and Planning C: Government and Policy, 30*(3), 381–400.

Seyfang, G., & Smith, A. (2007). Grassroots innovations for sustainable development: Towards a new research and policy agenda. *Environmental Policy, 16*(4), 584–603.

Smith, A., & Raven, R. (2012). What is protective space? Reconsidering niches in transitions to sustainability. *Research Policy, 41*, 1025–1036.

Stabell, C. B., & Fjeldstad, O. D. (1998). Configuring value for competitive advantage: On chains, shops, and networks. *Strategic Management Journal, 19*, 413–437.

Teece, D. J. (2010). Business models, business strategy and innovation. *Long Range Planning, 43*, 172–194.

Townsend, P. (1979). *Poverty in the United Kingdom*. Penguin Books Ltd.

Truffer, B., Murphy, J. T., & Raven, R. (2015). The geography of sustainability transitions: Contours of an emerging theme. *Environmental Innovation and Societal Transitions, 17*, 63–72.

van Welie, M. J., Cherunya, P. C., Truffer, B., & Murphy, J. T. (2018). Analysing transition pathways in developing cities: The case of Nairobi's splintered sanitation regime. *Technological Forecasting and Social Change, 138*, 259–271.

Verbong, G., Christiaens, W., Raven, R., & Balkema, A. (2010). Strategic niche management in an unstable regime: Biomass gasification in India. *Environmental Science and Policy, 13*(4), 272–281.

WCED. (1987). *Report of the world commission on environment and development: Our common future*. United Nations General Assembly document A/42/427.

Wieczorek, A. J. (2018). Sustainability transitions in developing countries: Major insights and their implications for research and policy. *Environmental Science & Policy, 84*, 204–216.

Wieczorek, A. J., Raven, R., & Berkhout, F. (2015). Transnational linkages in sustainability experiments: A typology and the case of solar photovoltaic energy in India. *Environmental Innovation and Societal Transitions, 17*, 149–165.

World Bank. (2018). *Poverty and shared prosperity 2018: Piecing together the poverty puzzle*. World Bank.

York, J. (2002). Forests for whom? Ethnic politics of conservation in northern Thailand 1996–2001. *Berkeley Journal of Sociology, 46*, 132–154.

Zott, C., Amit, R., & Massa, L. (2011). The business model: Recent developments and future research. *Journal of Management, 37*(4), 1019–1042.

Part II

Beyond Business-as-Usual: Alternative Value Creation Logics Driving Sustainability Transitions

The Business Model of Enough: Value Creation for Sufficiency-Oriented Businesses

Maren Ingrid Kropfeld and André Reichel

1 Introduction

We live in an era of unsustainability. Our political-economic systems are producing massive economic wealth on the back of large-scale ecological degradation. Regardless what measure we are looking at, be it the concept of planetary boundaries (Rockström et al., 2009; Steffen et al., 2015) or the ecological footprint (Lin et al., 2018; Wackernagel & Beyers, 2019) or the annual IPCC reports on climate change (IPCC, 2018), the political economy of humankind is not fit for its available ecological space. When we use the term "political economy", we refer to the classical understanding of the subject of any economic theory: the interrelationships of

M. I. Kropfeld (✉)
University of Oldenburg, Oldenburg, Germany
e-mail: maren.ingrid.kropfeld@uni-oldenburg.de

A. Reichel
International School of Management (ISM), Stuttgart, Germany
e-mail: andre.reichel@ism.de

A. Aagaard et al. (eds.), *Business Models for Sustainability Transitions*,
https://doi.org/10.1007/978-3-030-77580-3_6

political and social processes driving and shaping economic activities and decisions. Businesses and their business models are important economic value creators and drivers of innovation in any political-economic framework. Business models in particular are answering questions of what kind of value is produced and for whom, why this particular value is produced (and not something else), and how this value is produced. Thus, the challenge to transform society, and our political economy, towards sustainability cannot be sufficiently conceptualized without charting the transformation potentials, possibilities and barriers of businesses and their business models (Boons & Lüdeke-Freund, 2013; Wells, 2008).

In this chapter we conceptualize a generic business model for a transition towards a sustainable economy and society as an ideal-type by (a) focusing on sufficiency in order to highlight a more radical perspective on sustainability transformations in line with the notion of strong sustainability (Heikkurinen et al., 2019; Neumayer, 2003), assuming that economic and natural capital (also: social capital) is not substitutable, and its implications for changing business models and the environment of business, as well as (b) undertaking a reconstruction of the business model concept from the viewpoint of social practice theory, which will give us a much clearer theoretical framework to infer connections between business and consumer practices. At the same time, this approach will provide a bridge between changes within the business model and the immediate business environment (especially the new role of consumers as active prosumers). We show how a "Business Model of Enough" can constitute the core for communities of sufficiency practice, enabling institutional change within the political-economic background of business. Finally, this chapter contributes to the body of literature pointing out how business models act as intermediaries between niches and socio-technical regimes and thus drive transitions (Bidmon & Knab, 2018). Applying social practice theory to the business model concept allows for a deeper understanding of which role sufficiency-based business models and consumers play in transition pathways, for example, by introducing and supporting boundary spanning practices and including the perspective of fundamental transformations in everyday consumer practices (Shove & Walker, 2007; Velter et al., 2020).

2 Sufficiency for Sustainability

Traditional strategies towards more sustainability are predominantly focused on increasing efficiency via technological means: more energy and resource efficiency, less energy and resource use. However, efficiency gains are even more often offset by rebound, scaling and growth effects: higher efficiency leads to lower costs in resource or energy use, which consequently increases the potential for further production and consumption (Alcott, 2008; Bocken & Short, 2016; Daly, 1991; Jackson, 2009; Kallis et al., 2018; Lorek & Fuchs, 2013; Sachs, 1993; Santarius, 2016). These efficiency increases can trigger rebound effects. Rebound effects can be direct, increasing demand for the more resource- or energy-efficient good or service; they can be indirect, enabling increased demands in other goods and service because of more free income; and they can be macroeconomic, which are longer-term rebound effects, when overall increased demand leads to an increase of production capacities within an economy. Empirically we can see, on average and across a variety of goods and services, rebound effects of around 30 to 50 percent, that is, up to half of the efficiency increase is "destroyed" by induced higher demand (Breakthrough Institute, 2011). Unless we want to advocate a global regime of efficiency taxation, implying a permanently increasing tax on efficiency gains in order to counter rebound effects, a singular focus on efficiency will never be able to deliver true sustainability transformation (Alfredsson et al., 2018; Griese et al., 2015; Princen, 2005).

Even a consistency approach, in which economic processes mimic natural ecosystems and materials are continually recycled and reused to limit demand for new materials, can lead to increased resource consumption if the total consumption of products and services is not moderated (Allwood, 2014; Bocken & Short, 2016). Closed-loop models do not work for all kinds of materials, either because they cannot be recycled (e.g. cement), or degrade with recycling, or because the economic costs so far outweigh the benefits of recycling (Allwood, 2014). A successful circular economy could then only be achieved if the total global demand for products and resources is stabilized, which—in a world of growing population and rising living standards—would require an economic system beyond the economic growth paradigm (Allwood, 2014; Bocken & Short, 2020; Boulding, 1966; Princen, 2005).

The good news is that efficiency and consistency are not the only strategies available. There is also sufficiency (Huber, 2000; Princen, 2005; von Winterfeld, 2007). Sufficiency is not predominantly focused on technological innovations but on social and behavioral change. Sometimes it is narrowed down to the notion of consuming differently and consuming less. However, sufficiency is a much broader perspective than just changing your consumption patterns. It is about the question: What is enough? While everyone will have different understandings what is enough for themselves personally, under the perspective of a new political-economic framework and the role businesses play within it, sufficiency not only becomes a political issue, especially one of distribution and social equity, but also a business issue (Diekmann, 1999; Ott & Voget, 2008; Spangenberg & Lorek, 2019; Wilts & von Gries, 2015). For politics, sufficiency could be translated into the principles for a human right of not being conditioned to want more (e.g. by marketing, by advertising, by social pressures and peer groups) than you personally need. For businesses, sufficiency is the strategy to enable its customers to exercise that right through products and services.

Sufficiency-oriented business models can support sufficiency-oriented consumption by offering alternative practices that moderate consumption and support consumers in doing more with less (Bocken & Short, 2016; Gossen & Schrader, 2018; Profijt, 2018; Reichel, 2013). Their offers help consumers to reduce their absolute material and energy use while avoiding sufficiency-related rebound effects (Reichel, 2018). In our current market economy, sufficiency-oriented business models are acting within a corridor of minimum financial stability and a maximum of ecological impact (Reichel, 2013; Reichel & Seeberg, 2011). This corridor is based on the same idea as Kate Raworth's Doughnut Economics (2017), who defines social and planetary boundaries for our future economy. The social, and for businesses also financial, foundation demarks the Doughnut's (or corridor's) inner boundary, while the ecological ceiling demarks the outer boundary. Beyond this outer boundary, humanity's and thus also a businesses' pressure on our planet's life-giving systems is in dangerous overshoot. Table 1 shows an overview of some of the main

Table 1 Sufficiency-oriented business model literature (own illustration)

Price and Joseph (2000), Bocken and Short (2016)	Sachs (2015), Schneidewind and Palzkill-Vorbeck (2011)	Reichel (2018)	Bocken et al. (2020)
Avoid over-consumption & planned obsolescence	Regionalization		Offering quality local products incl. premium pricing
	De-cluttering	Dematerialization & tertiarization	Educating & engaging consumers
			Creating new revenue models incl. demand reduction services
		Non-marketing	Applying conscious sales & marketing/ under-selling
			Implementing choice architecture
			Choice editing
			Setting default options
Reduce material and resource use	Slowing down	Ensuring repairability & efficient resource use	Reducing material input
			Designing products for sustainable consumption
		Extending product life	Developing lasting products
	De-commercialization/ commons economy	Dematerialization & tertiarization	Selling inconvenience for a better price
			Changing conventional consumer perception
Reuse products over time or across multiple people		Encouraging reuse	Repurposing products/items
			Providing reusable product components

sufficiency-related business approaches in the research literature. Our starting points are the three top levels of the waste hierarchy—avoid, reduce, reuse—as defined by Price and Joseph (2000) and applied to business strategies by Bocken and Short (2016). We then matched these three levels with the four main sufficiency strategies—regionalization, de-cluttering, slowing down, de-commercialization—as defined by Sachs (2015, see also Schneidewind & Palzkill-Vorbeck, 2011). These strategies are intersectoral (politics, business, civil society) as well as cutting across the macro (political economy), meso (organizations) and micro level (individuals). Additionally, we used sufficiency-oriented business strategies by Reichel (2018) and the most recent work by Bocken et al. (2020), who defined 14 different sufficiency-oriented business strategies, in order to complement our overview.

The overview shows some crucial elements of viable business models for sufficiency, for example, educating and engaging consumers, offering quality local products, applying conscious sales and marketing techniques, sharing and contracting models, open-source initiatives, slow streaming, dematerialization (or product-service-systems) and changing conventional consumer perception. It also highlights some initiatives of the circular economy that can already be considered good sufficiency initiatives such as longevity, repair and reuse (Bocken & Short, 2020).

Apart from changing the general focus of a business and its strategy, sufficiency is also about transforming the building blocks and understanding of business models (Bocken & Short, 2016; Figge et al., 2014; Reichel, 2018). The proposed value becomes one of being able to live a sufficient lifestyle, a lifestyle of enough, and entails not just economic or instrumental value but also social and ecological value. In Ivan Illich's (1973) terms: enabling you to realize your autonomy in interdependence with your human and non-human others. Value creation then has to take into account the customer, their needs and desires, their hopes and fears, their full human creativity. It demands a much stronger connection, a much closer interdependence between producers and consumers, thus making this barrier more fluid and transforming passive consumers into active prosumers (Ritzer et al., 2012; Toffler, 1980). The value that is captured also differs. It is not just monetized economic value, a revenue stream, but also more social cohesion between all value creators and more ecological equity. Value capture under a sufficiency perspective also transforms the profit motive from profit maximization to profit sufficiency: what profit is needed in order to sustain our business and support our mission in the long run—and not making profit for the sole sake of profit maximization.

Looking beyond businesses, sufficiency also offers a valuable approach for the wider sustainability transition. It has been criticized that current management literature has too narrow a focus, is limited by its dominant research paradigm and focused on creating shareholder value (Markard, 2017). A sufficiency approach addresses those issues by widening the focus of study, allowing more factors to play a role in the business model design and by taking into account natural and moral issues. By extending the scope beyond the business itself and including consumption behavior change, sufficiency-oriented business models can play an important role in sustainability transitions.

3 Introducing Social Practice Theory

One of the central questions in the social sciences is what constitutes the social, that is, what the building blocks of social life are. Often the debate revolves around the dualism between structure and agency, between the workings of more abstract social systems and the more directly observable behavior of people. With the notion of structuration and the duality of structure and agency, Anthony Giddens (1984) proposed a third way by placing a recursive relationship between the two as the central process constituting social reality. Along this line, and also taking in ideas from Pierre Bourdieu, Judith Butler, Michel Foucault, Bruno Latour, Charles Taylor, Theodore Schatzki and others, the field of social practice theory has been established within social sciences, signifying the so-called practice turn (Reckwitz, 2002). According to this perspective, everyday social practices are the basic building blocks of social life, re-creating a stable social order and the large-scale patterns we can observe in society. Therefore, everyday practices are also an important type and agent of sustainability transitions (Shove & Walker, 2007). As Andreas Reckwitz (2002, 249) argues, a social practice is "a routinized type of behavior which consists of several elements, interconnected to one other: forms of bodily activities, forms of mental activities, 'things' and their use, a background knowledge in the form of understanding, know-how, states of emotion and motivational knowledge." In a more simplified and easier to operationalize view, we follow Shove et al. (2015) by understanding a social practice consisting of (i) *ideas, meanings and understandings* (the "why" and "what" of practice), (ii) *personal skills for carrying out a practice* and (iii) the *materialities of a practice* (tools, machines, physical infrastructure). While ideas, meanings and understandings refer more to social structures and intersubjective knowledge and values of a practice, skills are anchored within the biographies and experiences of people, while the focus on materialities retraces the material turn (Latour, 2005) and provides a link to issues of ecological sustainability (Fig. 1).

Social practice theory also allows for the analysis of linked practices and the dynamics between the three elements constituting a practice, making it useful for sustainability transitions research (Spotswood et al., 2015). Moreover, social practice theory recognizes different degrees of stability within practices, which allows for a distinction between

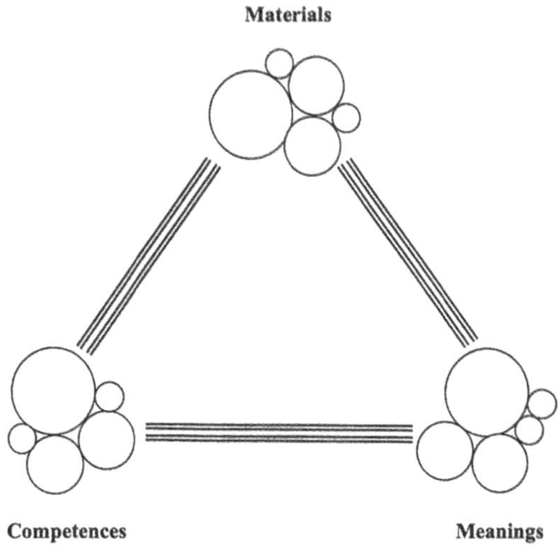

Fig. 1 Elements of a social practice. (Own illustration based on Pantzar & Shove, 2010)

routinized "mainstream" practices and new, emerging ones (Geels, 2011; Hargreaves et al., 2013). In terms of consumption practices, Røpke (2009) points out that consumption per se is seldomly meaningful. Rather than being a purpose in itself, consumption is part of our everyday practices. Changing unsustainable consumption behavior thus happens not by educating and persuading consumers to consume more sustainably, but when elements of a practice are changed, and enable practices as a composite whole to develop (Warde, 2005), for example, by providing customers with care and repair guides or repairing equipment to enable them to engage in repairing practices. Practices can emerge, change, stabilize and also die out as the links between their elements are created, reconstructed or broken (Pantzar & Shove, 2006). Transitioning to more sustainable practices therefore requires "the links and elements of existing, unsustainable practices to be challenged and broken before being replaced and re-made in more sustainable ways" (Hargreaves, 2011, 83). This shifts the focus away from individual attitudes and behaviors towards an understanding of how social practices form, persevere, how they are reproduced, challenged and changed, and how consumers are adapting more sustainable practices.

This practice-based approach also offers an alternative view on value creation and business models as a whole. Value or meaning is not created by one party alone but formed within practices (Korkman et al., 2010; Schatzki, 2001). The value lies within the offering of a business to enhance their customers' practices: "Value is created as the practice is improved" (Korkman et al., 2010, 239). An improvement of practice can mean enhancing skills and changing ideas or understandings (social aspects), while at the same time material use undergoes changes, for example, by consuming less material or different materials (ecological aspects). Such practice improvements would thereby create more sustainable value. Turning this into a more normative statement it means in order to deliver truly sustainable value, social practices have to be changed and improved accordingly. Any solution that enables customers to continue their (unsustainable) practices unchanged cannot be a sustainable or value-creating solution. In developing sufficiency practices for their customers, businesses become active agents within these new practices (Korkman et al., 2010; Toffler, 1980). Value co-creation does then not just imply that consumers become prosumers and are integrated into the value chain but rather that businesses and consumers are actors within the same shared practices. This perspective implies an inclusion of ecological, environmental and social aspects beyond the traditional boundaries of the firm. However, it also demands a businesses' management to balance other, potentially more powerful, stakeholder interests that might endanger their sustainability objectives (Hörisch et al., 2014). Furthermore, applying practice theory allows a holistic view on communication, change, resource integration and the interaction of structure, rules, people and skills within an organization (Korkman et al., 2010; Korkman & Araujo, 2018; Wilz, 2015). Instead of defining businesses as structures with clear boundaries, a sufficiency orientation offers a new understanding of businesses as fluid networks of routinized, interlinked and collaborative practices (Bocken et al., 2020; Breuer et al., 2018; Hernes & Maitlis, 2010; Hörning, 2004; Schaltegger, Hansen, & Lüdeke-Freund, 2016; Vargo & Lusch, 2016; Wilz, 2015).

4 An Ideal-Type Business Model for Sufficiency

4.1 A Practice-Theoretical View on Business Models

When we look at business models, we can reconstruct their basic building blocks from the perspective of social practice theory, creating a richer understanding of their reproduction and change. We focus on the three basic building blocks of a business model, namely, (i) what kind of value is created and for whom (value proposition), (ii) how this value is created and with whom (value creation), as well as (iii) how the value is captured and distributed among the value creators (value capture) (Schaltegger, Hansen, & Lüdeke-Freund, 2016). These building blocks each form a set of social practices, while they also constitute a larger social practice.

The *value proposition*, on the one hand, consists of ideas, meanings and understandings of what value is actually created by a business and who the recipients of that value are, that is, who the customers are. Value is not just economical, not just a result of a utility function, but also social and ecological, while the value recipients are not just those who buy the product or service but also those who either benefit or suffer from its externalities, that is, all stakeholders who perceive either positive or negative outcomes from a given value proposition. On the other hand, we have the personal skills of management and employees of a business to innovate, maintain and market its value proposition. This is intricately linked with R&D and marketing activities and forces us to focus on skills within those departments. Finally, any value proposition understood as a social practice, or consisting of interconnected social practices, is also a material proposition. It is either a product itself or it needs tools, machines and physical infrastructure to work as a service. As pointed out above, from a practice-theoretical point of view, a value proposition is a proposal for an improvement of a social practice. Whether a value proposition is actually of value for a specific recipient lies in the eye of the beholder, respectively, customer or other stakeholders. Only if this is the case, value is actually created.

Turning our attention to the prerequisites of *value creation*, questions concerning insourcing, outsourcing and networking are part of the ideas, meanings and understandings of value creation as a social practice. But also, the role of the customer in the value creation process as either passive consumer or active prosumer falls in this category (Ritzer et al., 2012; Toffler, 1980). Skills and competences for value creation are especially focused on interaction, communication and collaboration with a company's value creation partners; these might be suppliers or—according to the idea of prosumption introduced above—their customers, as it is ultimately them who determine which product or service improves their practice, thus is valuable to them. Furthermore, value creation typically involves various more active and passive value (co-)creators, which leads to a conceptualization of value creation as occurring in various stakeholder relationships and networks (Freudenreich et al., 2020). Materials are an important aspect of sociality and social practices, as they can be essential enablers of certain practices (Korkman & Araujo, 2018, 461, based on Korkman et al., 2010): "value is created when actors engage in practices and resource integration is a central element of practices." The materiality of value creation consists, on the one hand, of IT-based management systems like ERP systems, but on the other hand comprises of the entire physical supply chain with trucks, trains, planes, ships for freight as well as office and factory buildings for employees. Depending on the kind of work regime in place, commuting infrastructure or broadband internet access is also part of the materiality of value creation.

The social practice of *value capture* in a business model is reflecting the understanding, ideas and meanings of its value proposition. We need to understand the differences between economic, social and ecological value added in order to capture those multiple values accordingly. Along those lines, it is best to distinguish between monetary value capture and non-monetary value capture. Monetary value capture focuses on shared understandings of product versus solution or ownership versus access, thus paying a price upfront or having a fee-based value capture system in place. Non-monetary value capture focuses on loyalty of and reputation among customers, employees and other value chain partners, as well as legitimacy from societal stakeholders. The nexus of value capture, in our view, is the immediate network of practices between companies and their customers, rather than more systemic or political-economic levels of practices. However, there is some spillover embedded into the fabric of our generic business model: if there are changes to practices within this close network, it might have spillover effects to other parts of customers' lives, thereby influencing other practices and decisions they make. If those wider changes to practices proliferate, there is a possibility for change on a systemic level: new ideas, new managerial and organizational skills, as well as new products and services emerge and all of those can be copied and reproduced by others, thus creating a different kind of marketplace. Connected to these ideas is the business logic of profit itself and if it is about maximization and optimization or if it is about sufficiency, that is, making enough profit to maintain the business model and pursue its mission—and not profit for profit's sake. The skill sets and competencies necessary revolve around the design of the value capture system itself when it comes to different payment and reward models, but also the design of a value distribution system among value creators. Here, negotiation and mediation capabilities are important to ensure acceptance and satisfaction within the value chain, respectively, stakeholder network. The material aspects of value capture, its materiality as a practice, are then all physical and virtual payment systems in place, be it cash-based or online-based via credit cards, online payments or cryptocurrencies. This also includes the possibility of creating alternative currencies like corporate currencies or performance-based currencies like in local exchange trading systems.

4.2 A Practice-Theoretical Framework for Sufficiency-Oriented Business Models

In the following section, we will synthesize the ideas developed in the two previous sections to develop an ideal-type sufficiency-oriented business model from a social practice theoretical perspective. We will build this framework (cf. Table 2) on the business models for sufficiency identified by previous literature (cf. Table 1) and reconstruct it from a practice-theoretical point of view to identify the central practices of sufficiency-oriented business models, which elements are critical for their success, and which of them are shared with the customer.

The framework reveals that in terms of materials (and people), high-quality materials that are long-lived and repairable and highly skilled people as well as an up-to-date IT infrastructure are the basis for a sufficiency-oriented business model. For value capture, this suggests an orientation towards premium pricing and/or a competitive advantage as the business is better able to react to consumer demands, changes in the market or crisis that might impact the supply chain. An example might be slow vs. fast fashion businesses, the latter being more susceptible to market and consumer volatility than those businesses that focus on smaller collections, short and local supply chains and durable as well as repairable products that are made on-demand. Especially from a materials perspective, sufficiency-oriented business models show parallels to and overlap with ideas of the circular economy, which in itself can be understood as a different set of practices (Bocken & Short, 2020). It thereby also has an impact on the company's revenue model as product maintenance, and repairing can be understood as circular economy business model patterns (Lüdeke-Freund et al., 2019; Tunn et al., 2019).

Table 2 Generic framework for a sufficiency-oriented business model (own illustration)

	Materials	Competences	Meanings
Value proposition	Focusing on longevity, reparability and modular expandability of products	Promise of developing necessary/new competences for enhanced practices in collaborative process	Social & ecological values formed by consumers & business within practices
Examples	*High-quality garments, furniture leasing*	*Developing ideas for waste avoidance*	*Ecological concern, sociality/community*
Value creation	Lowering resources and energy use for production Long lasting, intuitive product design Regionalization of supply-chain Dematerialization by offering services instead of products Providing space, platforms, & tools	Providing sufficiency-related know-how & skills Supporting adaptation & creativity of consumers by sharing user stories Facilitating exchange of experiences among consumers Engaging in collaborative innovation	Framing marketing around sufficiency-related meanings Focusing on ecological concern, incl. resource & energy use, waste avoidance and re-use Creating sense of community among customers Jointly defining the meaning of 'enough'
Examples	*Repairing tools, sharing platforms, co-housing facilitations*	*Repairing skills, communication skills, planning skills*	*Reducing emissions, saving money, being part of a community*
Value capture	Higher prices & market shares Cheaper fees for continued product use Contracting models	Highly skilled employees Social value through consumer education	Positive image of business, products and services Long-term customer loyalty
Examples	*Waste contracting*	*Sharing services*	*Product reviews*

Looking at the competences and skills that are related to sufficiency-oriented business practices, this interaction between the business and the customer becomes even more obvious. Rather than engaging in a one-way-directed communication, such as traditional marketing, the business will have to enter into a dialogue with the customer. Choice editing requires a shared understanding of both parties about how improved practices can look like and which role both sides play in them. Consumer education is a vital point here as well as including the consumer in the value creation process. The customer of a sufficiency-oriented business is no longer a mere receiver and consumer of value—but takes an active part in the creation of this value. The passive consumer turns into an active prosumer (Ritzer et al., 2012; Toffler, 1980). Engaging in collaborative innovation, transferring skills necessary for the new and enhanced sufficiency practices and thus creating not only economic, but also social and environmental value, are key features of the 'Business Model of Enough'.

The meanings across the whole value creation process are constantly negotiated between the business and its customers. They do not necessarily have to share the meanings attached to the practices, but for a business to be authentic and gain the long-term loyalty of its customers, it is necessary that it shares some of the values and meanings behind the practices with its customers.

5 Impacts of the Business Model of Enough

The practice-theoretical approach to sufficiency-oriented business models offers several novel insights, three of which we will discuss in this chapter. Firstly, the understanding and role of communities of sufficiency practices. Secondly, how the practice-theoretical approach explains change and development of sufficiency practices. Thirdly, and finally, we will look at spillover effects into other industries and their contribution to wider sustainability transitions.

5.1 Communities of Sufficiency Practices

As shown above, customers take an active and participatory role in sufficiency-oriented business models. Customer and business representatives are both members of the same practices through which a behavior change towards sufficiency is negotiated and developed. The integration of the customer into the value creation process, his change of role from consumer to prosumer and the shared practices between business and customer lead away from the traditional understanding of the boundaries of a business. In line with the boundary work framework for sustainable business model innovation by Velter et al. (2020), we find that in order to achieve sustainable value creation, mutual boundary changes are necessary in the process of multi-stakeholder engagement and alignment. Prosumers are an inherent part of sufficiency-oriented business models. Without the active involvement and integration of the customer, there will be no sufficiency-oriented prosumptive practices changing and shaping the business model and consumer practices. We therefore conceptualize a business model as a bundle of practices (Boons & Laasch, 2019). This concept has already been introduced for businesses by Wenger (1998) and can be observed within and across organizations. It also supports the idea of Velter et al. (2020) that boundary work activities lead to multi-stakeholder networks that are based on shared meanings. According to this perspective, communities of practices are not some kind of organizational unit, but a different perspective on the structure, processes and boundaries of an organization. Such an understanding is not only useful in discussing the dissemination of knowledge throughout an organization; it can also explain how competencies are stewarded to keep the organization up to date. In a sufficiency context, this is of course vital as the organization develops, teaches and shares competencies that are necessary for sufficiency-oriented consumer practices, such as repairing. This open business model approach fosters value co-creation within the shared practices and helps the organization to stay on top of their customers' needs and desires and to steer a sufficiency-oriented behavior change (Coombes & Nicholson, 2013). By incentivizing this behavior change in their network or community of sufficiency practices, they can act as niche innovators or incumbent change agents within sustainability transitions.

A sufficiency-oriented business model is of course not based on one practice alone. Rather, it consists of many different practices, some within the organization, and some shared with its customers. As Mele (2011) points out, these are 'multilateral relationships amongst all actors of a network'. Based on this view, we expand the idea of a business model to be a network of various social practices. These networks of social practices can be conceptualized as business model patterns, as introduced by Lüdeke-Freund et al. (2018). Examples for sustainable business model patterns that summarize different sufficiency-oriented business practices are supply chain patterns (shorter supply chains), service and performance patterns, eco-design patterns, giving and access provision patterns, social mission patterns and cooperative and community platform patterns (Lüdeke-Freund et al., 2018).

5.2 Practice-Based Institutional Change

Conceptualizing business models as communities of practices also gives opportunity to explain institutional change. According to a process-oriented perspective, persistence of any practice, and thus ultimately the business model itself, requires continued enactment and enrollment (Boons & Laasch, 2019). Coming back to Geels' (2011) idea of varying degrees of stability within practices, this opens up opportunities for change, such as subtle changes in the reenactment of the practice by various organizational members, or the recruitment of members inside and outside of the organization into the communities of sufficiency practices. The latter may be achieved by active boundary leadership, which connects communities among each other (Wenger, 1998), and by boundary work activities as proposed by Velter et al. (2020), which lead to novel multi-stakeholder networks that are based on shared understandings of value (rather than traditional sectors or industries). Apart from personal inspiration or leadership (meanings), practices may change, or co-evolve (Schaltegger, Lüdeke-Freund, & Hansen, 2016), due to changes in the materials, such as a new extremely durable and sustainable fabric or know-how such as repairing skills brought into practice by new members of the community (competences). In terms of the business model, communities of practices may change their practices by variation of existing practices, a selection of more sufficiency-oriented ones or retention of valuable innovations (Schaltegger, Lüdeke-Freund, & Hansen, 2016).

In the 'Business Model of Enough', there needs to be a shift in terms of material quality towards more durable, repairable and high-quality materials, which will not only change the product and supply chain but also the way the customer interacts with the product and the business itself. Repairing services might be expected, for example, or ownership stays with the company and the product is merely leased to the customer. Furthermore, developing specific competences and sharing joint meanings are crucial for a sufficiency-oriented business model. An authentic awareness-raising marketing campaign, for instance, requires new strategies and channels of communication as well as a company-wide vision and orientation towards sufficiency. These changes towards more sufficiency-oriented (business) practices might be inspired by changes in technology or materiality, such as various transition theories suggest (Markard, 2017). But they might also stem from new members to a practice, who can introduce new competences and direct the focus towards new meanings, such as a change in leadership would incentivize.

5.3 Spillover Effects for Sustainability Transitions

Businesses and other market actors play critical roles in sustainability transitions (Köhler et al., 2019). Communities of sufficiency practices can have an impact on sustainability transitions beyond the internal transformations of their business model. Firstly, practices may be shared across company boundaries, for example, using the same fabrics or engaging in a joint anti-Black-Friday-campaign. This not only fosters development within the community of practices but might also inspire others to 'join the club' by providing a competitive advantage or setting new standards within an industry. According to Bohnsack et al. (2020), first movers, seeing sustainable product innovation as a long-term competitive advantage or following altruistic motives, create normative and mimetic pressures within their industry that others will want to or even have to follow. Secondly, the business can grow and recruit new members, here especially customers, for their practices. This is especially true for business models of small entrepreneurial companies growing in and co-shaping their market. This idea is in line with the work of Kemp et al. (1998), who point out that a successful niche development may require the formation of new actor networks. But also established players may be part of a wider sufficiency transformation, if they mimic the offers of other sufficiency-oriented business models or acquire and integrate them into their business model (Schaltegger, Lüdeke-Freund, & Hansen, 2016). Theory suggests that transformative narratives can serve as a tool for changes within incumbent firms by simultaneously preserving the core of the existent business model and including new elements (Augenstein & Palzkill, 2015). In social practice theoretical terms, this would mean that incumbent firms become part of a community of practices that goes beyond organizational boundaries or recruit new members (e.g. a successful niche player via merger and acquisition activities) to their own community of practices, adding new know-how and skills. And thirdly, this adoption and co-evolution of practices is also true across industries. A practice in the clothing industry, such as the provision of repairing services, might well inspire other business to adapt their models to these practices as well, for example, a 100-year guarantee and life-long repairing service such as the company 'seit1832' offers for their bed sheets. This would then start to influence the political-economic make-up of society and push it towards more sustainability.

Social change towards more sufficiency-oriented lifestyles happens through transfers of materials, competences and meanings from one life area to another and by recruitment of new members for a practice. This understanding is in line with transition theories such as socio-technical transitions (Geels, 2002; Geels & Schot, 2007). Social practice theory allows for a micro-level perspective on macro-level transitions and account for transitions being multi-dimensional, co-evolutionary, multi-actor processes as well as the relation between stability and change (Köhler et al., 2019).

6 Conclusion

The 'Business Model of Enough' represents a novel approach to business models for sustainability transformations. Its practice-theoretical foundation enables research to tackle questions of sufficiency and the strong sustainability paradigm on the one hand and also allows us to make sense of increasing prosumer activities within the economy and their implications on new communities of sufficiency practices. In other fields of sustainability research, social practice theory has already been applied successfully. We believe this theoretical perspective will yield many benefits for the field of business model research, especially in the case of sustainable companies. The ideal-type sufficiency-oriented business model presented here may also inspire practitioners on how they can adapt their own business model to support sufficiency-oriented lifestyles. The future discourse on sufficiency-oriented business models will have to continue the discussion on controverse topics such as profit sufficiency, value co-creation for sustainability and stakeholder management, which could only be briefly touched upon in this chapter. Further steps in this line of research are drawing connections with adjacent fields like institutional and transformational entrepreneurship and leadership for sustainability studies. For empirical research, but also for informing business practice and consulting, we see the construction of case studies with, and measurement of, actual impacts of communities of sufficiency practices as the most promising avenue.

References

Alcott, B. (2008). Historical overview of the Jevons paradox in the literature. In J. M. Polimeni, K. Mayumi, M. Giampietro, & B. Alcott (Eds.), *The Jevons paradox and the myth of resource efficiency improvements* (pp. 7–79). Earthscan. https://doi.org/10.4324/9781849773102

Alfredsson, E., Bengtsson, M., Brown, H. S., Isenhour, C., Lorek, S., Stevis, D., & Vergragt, P. J. (2018). Why achieving the Paris agreement requires reduced overall consumption and production. *Sustainability: Science, Practice and Policy, 14*(1), 1–5. https://doi.org/10.1080/15487733.2018.1458815

Allwood, J. M. (2014). Squaring the circular economy. In *Handbook of recycling* (pp. 445–477). Elsevier. https://doi.org/10.1016/B978-0-12-396459-5.00030-1

Augenstein, K., & Palzkill, A. (2015). The dilemma of incumbents in sustainability transitions: A narrative approach. *Administrative Sciences, 6*(1), 1. https://doi.org/10.3390/admsci6010001

Bidmon, C. M., & Knab, S. F. (2018). The three roles of business models in societal transitions: New linkages between business model and transition research. *Journal of Cleaner Production, 178*(March), 903–916. https://doi.org/10.1016/j.jclepro.2017.12.198

Bocken, N. M. P., Morales, L. S., & Lehner, M. (2020). Sufficiency business strategies in the food industry—The case of Oatly. *Sustainability, 12*(3), 824. https://doi.org/10.3390/su12030824

Bocken, N. M. P., & Short, S. W. (2016). Towards a sufficiency-driven business model: Experiences and opportunities. *Environmental Innovation and Societal Transitions, 18*, 41–61. https://doi.org/10.1016/j.eist.2015.07.010

Bocken, N. M. P., & Short, S. W. (2020). Transforming business models: Towards a sufficiency-based circular economy. In M. Brandão, D. Lazarevic, & G. Finnveden (Eds.), *Handbook of the circular economy* (pp. 250–265). Edward Elgar Publishing. https://doi.org/10.4337/9781788972727.00028

Bohnsack, R., Kolk, A., Pinkse, J., & Bidmon, C. M. (2020). Driving the electric bandwagon: The dynamics of incumbents' sustainable innovation. *Business Strategy and the Environment, 29*(2), 727–743. https://doi.org/10.1002/bse.2430

Boons, F., & Laasch, O. (2019). Business models for sustainable development: A process perspective. *Journal of Business Models, 7*(1), 1–4.

Boons, F., & Lüdeke-Freund, F. (2013). Business models for sustainable innovation: State-of-the-art and steps towards a research agenda. *Journal of Cleaner Production, 45*, 9–19. https://doi.org/10.1016/j.jclepro.2012.07.007

Boulding, K. E. (1966). The Economics of the Coming Spaceship Earth. In Jarret, Henry (Ed.), *Environmental Quality in a Growing Economy* (pp. 3–14). Baltimore: Johns Hopkins University Press.

Breakthrough Institute. (2011). Energy emergence: Rebound & backfire as emergent phenomena.

Breuer, H., Fichter, K., Lüdeke-Freund, F., Tiemann, I., Freund, F. L., Tiemann, I., Lüdeke-Freund, F., & Tiemann, I. (2018). Sustainability-oriented business model development: Principles, criteria and tools. *International Journal of Entrepreneurial Venturing, 10*(2), 256–286. https://doi.org/10.1504/IJEV.2018.092715

Coombes, P. H., & Nicholson, J. D. (2013). Business models and their relationship with marketing: A systematic literature review. *Industrial Marketing Management, 42*(5), 656–664. https://doi.org/10.1016/j.indmarman.2013.05.005

Daly, H. E. (1991). *Steady-state economics* (2nd ed.). Island Press.

Diekmann, J. (1999). Zwischen Effizienz Und Suffizienz. *Ökologisches Wirtschaften.*

Figge, F., Young, W., & Barkemeyer, R. (2014). Sufficiency or efficiency to achieve lower resource consumption and emissions? The role of the rebound effect. *Journal of Cleaner Production, 69*, 216–224.

Freudenreich, B., Lüdeke-Freund, F., & Schaltegger, S. (2020). A stakeholder theory perspective on business models: Value creation for sustainability. *Journal of Business Ethics, 166*(1), 3–18. https://doi.org/10.1007/s10551-019-04112-z

Geels, F. W. (2002). Technological transitions as evolutionary reconfiguration processes: A multi-level perspective and a case-study. *Research Policy, 31*, 1257–1274. https://doi.org/10.1016/S0048-7333(02)00062-8

Geels, F. W. (2011). The multi-level perspective on sustainability transitions: Responses to seven criticisms. *Environmental Innovation and Societal Transitions, 1*(1), 24–40. https://doi.org/10.1016/j.eist.2011.02.002

Geels, F. W., & Schot, J. (2007). Typology of sociotechnical transition pathways. *Research Policy, 36*, 399–417. https://doi.org/10.1016/j.respol.2007.01.003

Giddens, A. (1984). The constitution of society: Outline of the theory of structuration. *Cognitive Therapy and Research, 12*, 448. https://doi.org/10.1007/BF01173303

Gossen, M., & Schrader, U. (2018). Welche Potenziale Die Digitalisierung Für Ein Suffizienzförderndes Marketing Bringt. *Ökologisches Wirtschaften, 1*(33), 8–9. https://doi.org/10.14512/oew330108

Griese, K.-M., Kumbruck, C., & Schlichting, A. (2015). Promotion of sufficient living to reduce CO2 emissions: The example of the tourism industry: An interdisciplinary analysis. *Uwf UmweltWirtschaftsForum, 23*(1–2), 23–31. https://doi.org/10.1007/s00550-015-0347-6

Hargreaves, T. (2011). Practice-ing behaviour change: Applying social practice theory to pro-environmental behaviour change. *Journal of Consumer Culture, 11*(1), 79–99. https://doi.org/10.1177/1469540510390500

Hargreaves, T., Longhurst, N., & Seyfang, G. (2013). Up, down, round and round: Connecting regimes and practices in innovation for sustainability. *Environment and Planning A, 45*, 402–420. https://doi.org/10.1068/a45124

Heikkurinen, P., Young, C. W., & Morgan, E. (2019). Business for sustainable change: Extending eco-efficiency and eco-sufficiency strategies to consumers. *Journal of Cleaner Production, 218*, 656–664. https://doi.org/10.1016/j.jclepro.2019.02.053

Hernes, T., & Maitlis, S. (2010). *Process, sensemaking, & organizing*. Oxford University Press.

Hörisch, J., Freeman, R. E., & Schaltegger, S. (2014). Applying stakeholder theory in sustainability management: Links, similarities, dissimilarities, and a conceptual framework. *Organization and Environment, 27*(4), 328–346. https://doi.org/10.1177/1086026614535786

Hörning, K. H. (2004). Soziale Praxis Zwischen Beharrung Und Neuschöpfung. Ein Erkenntnis- Und Theorieproblem. In K. H. Hörning & J. Reuter (Eds.), *Doing culture*. transcript Verlag. https://doi.org/10.14361/9783839402436-002

Huber, J. (2000). Towards industrial ecology: Sustainable development as a concept of ecological modernization. *Journal of Environmental Policy & Planning, 2*(4), 269–285. https://doi.org/10.1080/714038561

Illich, I. (1973). In R. N. Anshen (Ed.), *Tools for conviviality*. Hayday Books.

IPCC. (2018). Summary for policymakers. In V. Masson-Delmotte, P. Zhai, H.-O. Pörtner, D. Roberts, J. Skea, P. R. Shukla, A. Pirani, et al. (Eds.), *Global warming of 1.5°C. an IPCC special report on the impacts of global warming of 1.5°C above pre-industrial levels and related global greenhouse gas emission pathways, in the context of strengthening the global response to the threat of climate change*. World Meteorological Organization. https://doi.org/10.1016/j.oneear.2019.10.025

Jackson, T. (2009). Beyond the growth economy. *Journal of Industrial Ecology, 13*(4), 487–490. https://doi.org/10.1111/j.1530-9290.2009.00151.x

Kallis, G., Kostakis, V., Lange, S., Muraca, B., Paulson, S., & Schmelzer, M. (2018). Research on degrowth. *Annual Review of Environment and Resources, 43*, 4.1–4.26. https://doi.org/10.1146/annurev-environ-102017-025941

Kemp, R., Schot, J., & Hoogma, R. (1998). Regime shifts to sustainability through processes of niche formation: The approach of strategic niche management. *Technology Analysis & Strategic Management, 10*(2), 175–195. https://doi.org/10.1080/09537329808524310

Köhler, J., Geels, F. W., Kern, F., Markard, J., Onsongo, E., Wieczorek, A., Alkemade, F., et al. (2019). An agenda for sustainability transitions research: State of the art and future directions. *Environmental Innovation and Societal Transitions, 31*(December 2018), 1–32. https://doi.org/10.1016/j.eist.2019.01.004

Korkman, O., & Araujo, L. (2018). Using practice theory for understanding resource integration in S-D logic: A multinational study of leading-edge consumers. In S. L. Vargo & R. F. Lusch (Eds.), *The SAGE handbook of service-dominant logic* (pp. 449–465). SAGE.

Korkman, O., Storbacka, K., & Harald, B. (2010). Practices as markets: Value co-creation in e-invoicing. *Australasian Marketing Journal (AMJ), 18*(4), 236–247. https://doi.org/10.1016/j.ausmj.2010.07.006

Latour, B. (2005). *Reassembling the social – An introduction to actor-network-theory*. Oxford University Press. https://doi.org/10.1163/156913308X336453

Lin, D., Hanscom, L., Murthy, A., Galli, A., Evans, M., Neill, E., Mancini, M., et al. (2018). Ecological footprint accounting for countries: Updates and results of the National Footprint Accounts, 2012–2018. *Resources, 7*(3), 58. https://doi.org/10.3390/resources7030058

Lorek, S., & Fuchs, D. (2013). Strong sustainable consumption governance – Precondition for a degrowth path? *Journal of Cleaner Production, 38*, 36–43. https://doi.org/10.1016/j.jclepro.2011.08.008

Lüdeke-Freund, F., Carroux, S., Joyce, A., Massa, L., & Breuer, H. (2018). The sustainable business model pattern taxonomy – 45 patterns to support sustainability-oriented business model innovation. *Sustainable Production and Consumption, 15*, 145–162. https://doi.org/10.1016/j.spc.2018.06.004

Lüdeke-Freund, F., Gold, S., & Bocken, N. M. P. (2019). A review and typology of circular economy business model patterns. *Journal of Industrial Ecology, 23*(1), 36–61. https://doi.org/10.1111/jiec.12763

Markard, J. (2017). Sustainability transitions: Exploring the emerging field and its relations to management studies. *Academy of Management Proceedings, 2017*(1), 14100. https://doi.org/10.5465/ambpp.2017.14100abstract

Mele, C. (2011). Conflicts and value co-creation in project networks. *Industrial Marketing Management, 40*(8), 1377–1385. https://doi.org/10.1016/j.indmarman.2011.06.033

Neumayer, E. (2003). *Weak versus strong sustainability. Exploring the limits of two opposing paradigms* (2nd ed.). Edward Elgar.

Ott, K., & Voget, L. (2008). Suffizienz: Umweltethik Und Lebensstilfragen. *Vordenken in Ökologie Und Gesellschaft*.

Pantzar, M., & Shove, E. (2006). Circuits of reproduction and the dynamics of practice in everyday life. In *Paper for the second organization studies summer workshop on re-turn to practice: Understanding organization as it happens*, 15–16.

Pantzar, M., & Shove, E. (2010). Understanding innovation in practice: A discussion of the production and re-production of Nordic walking. *Technology Analysis and Strategic Management, 22*(4), 447–461. https://doi.org/10.1080/09537321003714402

Price, J. L., & Joseph, J. B. (2000). Demand management – A basis for waste policy: A critical review of the applicability of the waste hierarchy in terms of achieving sustainable waste management. *Sustainable Development, 8*(2), 96–105. https://doi.org/10.1002/(SICI)1099-1719(200005)8:2<96::AID-SD133>3.0.CO;2-J

Princen, T. (2005). *The logic of sufficiency*. MIT Press. https://doi.org/10.1080/00213624.2007.11507104

Profijt, M. (2018). Mobilitätssuffizienz Als Lösungsbeitrag Zur Treibhausgasreduktion. *Ökologisches Wirtschaften, 3*, 35–39. https://doi.org/10.14512/OEW330335

Raworth, K. (2017). *Doughnut economics: Seven ways to think like a 21st century economist*. Penguin Random House.

Reckwitz, A. (2002). Toward a theory of social practices: A development in culturalist theorizing. *European Journal of Social Theory, 5*, 243–263. https://doi.org/10.1177/13684310222225432

Reichel, A. (2013). Das Geschäftsmodell Des Weniger. *Politische Ökologie, 135*, 92–98.

Reichel, A. (2018). Sufficiency in business strategies. In J. Potocnik, J. Spangenberg, B. Alcott, V. Kiss, A. Coote, A. Reichel, S. Lorek, & M. V. Mathai (Eds.), *Sufficiency: Moving beyond the gospel of eco-efficiency* (pp. 22–25). Friends of the Earth Europe. http://www.foeeurope.org/sites/default/files/resource_use/2018/foee_sufficiency_booklet.pdf

Reichel, A., & Seeberg, B. (2011). The ecological allowance of enterprise: An absolute measure of corporate environmental performance, its implications for strategy, and a small case. *Journal of Environmental Sustainability, 1*(1), 1–15. https://doi.org/10.14448/jes.01.0006

Ritzer, G., Dean, P., & Jurgenson, N. (2012). The coming of age of the prosumer. *American Behavioral Scientist, 56*(4), 379–398. https://doi.org/10.1177/0002764211429368

Rockström, J., Steffen, W., Noone, K., Åsa, P., Stuart Chapin, F., Lambin, E. F., Lenton, T. M., et al. (2009). A safe operating environment for humanity. *Nature, 461*(September), 472–475. https://doi.org/10.5751/ES-03180-140232

Røpke, I. (2009). Theories of practice – New inspiration for ecological economic studies on consumption. *Ecological Economics, 68*(10), 2490–2497. https://doi.org/10.1016/j.ecolecon.2009.05.015

Sachs, W. (1993). Die Vier E's: Merkposten Für Einen Massvollen Wirtschaftsstil. *Politische Ökologie, 11*(33), 69–72. https://nbn-resolving.org/urn:nbn:de:bsz:wup4-opus-668

Sachs, W. (2015). Suffizienz. Umrisse Einer Ökonomie Des Genug. *Uwf UmweltWirtschaftsForum, 23*(1–2), 3–9. https://doi.org/10.1007/s00550-015-0350-y

Santarius, T. (2016). Investigating meso-economic rebound effects: Production-side effects and feedback loops between the micro and macro level. *Journal of Cleaner Production, 134*, 406–413. https://doi.org/10.1016/j.jclepro.2015.09.055

Schaltegger, S., Hansen, E. G., & Lüdeke-Freund, F. (2016). Business models for sustainability: Origins, present research, and future avenues. *Organization and Environment, 29*(1), 3–10. https://doi.org/10.1177/1086026615599806

Schaltegger, S., Lüdeke-Freund, F., & Hansen, E. G. (2016). Business models for sustainability: A co-evolutionary analysis of sustainable entrepreneurship, innovation, and transformation. *Organization & Environment, 29*(3), 264–289. https://doi.org/10.1177/1086026616633272

Schatzki, T. R. (2001). Subject, body, place. *Annals of the Association of American Geographers, 91*, 698–702. Blackwell Publishers.

Schneidewind, U., & Palzkill-Vorbeck, A. (2011). Suffizienz Als Business Case. In *Impulse Zur WachstumsWende, Umwelt Und Energie* (Vol. 2). Wuppertal. https://epub.wupperinst.org/files/3955/ImpW2.pdf

Shove, E., & Walker, G. (2007). Caution! Transition ahead: Policies, practice, and sustainable transition management. *Environment and Planning A, 39*, 763–770. https://doi.org/10.1068/a39310

Shove, E., Watson, M., & Spurling, N. (2015). Conceptualizing connections: Energy demand, infrastructures and social practices. *European Journal of Social Theory, 18*(3), 1–14. https://doi.org/10.1177/1368431015579964

Spangenberg, J. H., & Lorek, S. (2019). Sufficiency and consumer behaviour: From theory to policy. *Energy Policy, 129*(March), 1070–1079. https://doi.org/10.1016/J.ENPOL.2019.03.013

Spotswood, F., Chatterton, T., Tapp, A., & Williams, D. (2015). Analysing cycling as a social practice: An empirical grounding for behaviour change. *Transportation Research Part F: Traffic Psychology and Behaviour, 29*, 22–33. https://doi.org/10.1016/j.trf.2014.12.001

Steffen, W., Richardson, K., Rockström, J., Cornell, S. E., Fetzer, I., Bennett, E. M., Biggs, R., et al. (2015). Planetary boundaries: Guiding human development on a changing planet. *Science, 347*(6223). https://doi.org/10.1126/science.1259855

Toffler, A. (1980). *The third wave*. William Morrow.

Tunn, V. S. C., Bocken, N. M. P., van den Hende, E. A., & Schoormans, J. P. L. (2019). Business models for sustainable consumption in the circular economy: An expert study. *Journal of Cleaner Production, 212*(March), 324–333. https://doi.org/10.1016/j.jclepro.2018.11.290

Vargo, S. L., & Lusch, R. F. (2016). Institutions and axioms: An extension and update of service-dominant logic. *Journal of the Academy of Marketing Science, 44*(1), 5–23. https://doi.org/10.1007/s11747-015-0456-3

Velter, M. G. E., Bitzer, V., Bocken, N. M. P., & Kemp, R. (2020). Sustainable business model innovation: The role of boundary work for multi-stakeholder alignment. *Journal of Cleaner Production, 247*(February), 119497. https://doi.org/10.1016/j.jclepro.2019.119497

von Winterfeld, U. (2007). Keine Nachhaltigkeit Ohne Suffizienz. *Vorgänge, 3*, 46–54. https://epub.wupperinst.org/files/2740/2740_Winterfeld.pdf

Wackernagel, M., & Beyers, B. (2019). *Ecological footprint: Managing our biocapacity budget*. New Society Publishers.

Warde, A. (2005). Consumption and theories of practice. *Journal of Consumer Culture, 5*(2), 131–153. https://doi.org/10.1177/1469540505053090

Wells, P. (2008). Alternative business models for a sustainable automotive industry. In T. Arnold, M. Charter, C. Vezzoli, E. Stø, & M. M. Andersen (Eds.), *Perspectives on radical changes to sustainable consumption and production 1. System innovation for sustainability* (pp. 80–98). Greenleaf.

Wenger, E. (1998). *Communities of practice: Learning, meaning, and identity*. Cambridge University Press. https://doi.org/10.1017/CBO9780511803932

Wilts, H., & von Gries, N. (2015). Suffizienz Als Geschäftsfeld Der Kreislaufwirtschaft. *Uwf UmweltWirtschaftsForum, 23*(1), 41–47. https://doi.org/10.1007/s00550-015-0351-x

Wilz, S. M. (2015). Skizze Zur Praxistheoretischen Debatte Um Organisation. In M. Apelt & U. Wilkesmann (Eds.), *Zur Zukunft Der Organisationssoziologie* (pp. 253–270). Springer. isbn:978-3-658-07329-9.

Collaborative Business Models and Platforms in Shared Mobility Transitions: The Case of Bikeshare Integration

Brett John Mathew Petzer, Anna Wieczorek, and Geert Verbong

1 Introduction

Advances in smartphone penetration, geolocation and remote locking, online payment and battery performance have rapidly expanded the technological possibilities of shared access to vehicles in the past decade. These advances have also improved the commercial prospects for shared mobility, especially for smaller, lighter and cheaper vehicles, such as bicycles and micromobility modes (Boyd Cohen & Kietzmann, 2014). Services that provide shared access to these modes offer cities a relatively rapid means of increasing their mobility offering to residents and combatting car dependency. Ultimately, their success could produce a shift from a global status quo dominated by mass private ownership of

B. J. M. Petzer (✉) • A. Wieczorek • G. Verbong
Eindhoven University of Technology, Eindhoven, The Netherlands
e-mail: B.J.M.Petzer@tue.nl; A.J.Wieczorek@tue.nl; G.P.J.Verbong@tue.nl

A. Aagaard et al. (eds.), *Business Models for Sustainability Transitions*,
https://doi.org/10.1007/978-3-030-77580-3_7

passenger vehicles towards an Internet-enabled, integrated system that meets residents' mobility needs without the need for private ownership, especially of motorised vehicles (Machado et al., 2018). Such a shift is considered essential to realising the vision of mobility-as-a-service (MaaS) (Hensher et al., 2020). However, this transition will entail a profound transformation of aspects such as the business models through which mobility services are provided (Heikkilä, 2014; Yanying Li & Voege, 2017; Hensher et al., 2020) and the platforms or interfaces through which these services reach users. Promising innovations such as web-based platforms have already come to play an essential role in connecting users to the multiplicity of (new) mobility service providers. In particular, platforms that accommodate multiple providers merit closer study as they continue to proliferate. These platforms may constitute a distinct kind of business model in themselves, based on a degree of internal collaboration coupled with outward competition between providers. Their potential has also generated interest from the public sector, as local governments seek to harness platforms of this kind to deliver everyday urban mobility services that were formerly provided by the state. This chapter offers an exploratory review of how business models based on collaboration have been defined in various literatures and applies the results to a case study of three mobility services platforms shaped by public-sector actors.

Recently, the concept of the Collaborative Business Model (CBM) has emerged as a means of describing entities or practices that are characterised by very deep, sustained and technologically mediated integration between actors. In contrast to currently dominant frameworks in business model research, such as Osterwalder's Business Model Canvas (BMC) (2004), some proponents argue that CBMs are characterised (inter alia) by value propositions that cannot be satisfactorily analysed in terms of a focal firm and its partners, but depend intrinsically on collaboration between multiple actors (de Man & Luvison, 2019).

CBMs are an emergent stream of business model research, although business and management scholars have long attended to the theme of collaboration between firms. In the field of transport/mobility studies alone, scholars have explored collaboration between actors through frameworks such as business ecosystems (Kamargianni & Matyas, 2017), business alliances (de Man & Luvison, 2019) and agency theory (Boyd Cohen & Kietzmann, 2014). However, CBMs may offer a more powerful means of describing and analysing the advanced degree of integration and coordination between actors that will necessarily underpin the mature MaaS systems of the future. They may capture transformative features of collaborative entities and practices that are marginal in current business model research but which may occupy a central role in a future in which interoperability across entire sectors is the norm.

For this reason, CBMs may be particularly productive as an organising framework applied to contemporary urban mobility systems, in which progress towards MaaS has been slow and uneven (Mulley, 2017). Some scholars have explicitly attributed this lag to unresolved regulatory and institutional barriers that remain long after purely technological ones have been resolved (Ambrosino et al., 2016; Berger et al., 2014). More specifically, research into current empirical attempts to achieve MaaS has often pointed to a conflict between the assumptions of mainstream business model research (e.g. the assumption of competition between firms with similar offerings) and the requirements of an integrated mobility system, such as the non-duplication of services (Boyd Cohen & Kietzmann, 2014). This difference is especially marked given the norm of significant public ownership of 'natural monopolies' in transport (especially rail, trams and buses) in Europe, which created stable conditions for their development and maturation through the twentieth century[1] (Amaral, 2008; EC DG MOVE, 2019). Insofar as they potentially depart from these assumptions, CBMs may therefore offer novel insights into the limited progress that cities have made towards MaaS.

The analysis of MaaS also offers benefits to current understandings of CBMs, which differ very widely among scholars. The term 'collaborative', in particular, is used to refer to a broad set of meanings both within and beyond CBM literature, some of which are potentially contradictory. For example, Gyimóthy distinguishes between corporatized extractive models and altruistic communitarian or commons models of collaboration within the term *collaborative economy*. Botsman and Rogers (2011) introduce *collaborative consumption* to refer to Internet-enabled

[1] In 2001, the EU First Railway Package began the process of creating a single passenger rail market.

marketplaces as distinct from the more solidarity-minded and mutualist principles of peer-to-peer sharing platforms (especially in the early phase of platform development). In contrast, the term *collaborative* has a smaller range of meanings in the context of MaaS, because of the constraints imposed by the nature of the space required for storing and operating vehicles on public or semi-public[2] land. This space, which is fundamental to MaaS, is typically conceived of and governed as a commons, or common pool resource, and access to it is usually highly institutionalised. This institutionalisation has, in European cities, developed over centuries to produce distinct outcomes and mechanisms for domains such as outdoor restaurant seating, public markets, mass gatherings and tourist flows (Brandajs & Russo, 2019; de Magalhães & Freire Trigo, 2017). Furthermore, the means of access to this resource within MaaS differs widely between different modes: the space required by automobiles is generally highly commoditised (as parking space), while that required for modes such as bicycles is usually governed more informally or non-commercially (Petzer et al., 2019, 2021).

For this reason, the study of MaaS platforms that incorporate bicycles (most often in the form of docked or dockless public bikeshare) highlights a potentially productive tension within the term *collaborative* (and related terms, such as *cooperative* and *coordinated*) into CBM research. Additionally, considering MaaS platforms that include bikeshare[3] through the lens of the CBM brings to this new field a long empirical record of collaboration around a limited resource (space). This resource constraints, and is constrained by, the incentive for firms to compete, as this has been a constant feature of urban mobility governance for centuries (Akyelken et al., 2018; Gössling et al., 2016). The effects of this constraint are most pronounced in the case of platforms that already include, or make provision for, multiple providers of services based on the bicycle. This

[2] 'Public land' here refers to land owned by the state and intended for public use, such as roadways, sidewalks and squares. Semi-public here refers to space that is generally perceived as public and operates much like public land, but is owned or operated by a private firm, such as parking space at railway stations or what Carmona (2015) terms 'pseudo-public' spaces, such as London's privatised public squares.

[3] Following Fishman (2016) we define 'bikeshare' as shared cycling-based mobility systems providing temporary access to any form of bicycle and variations thereof, that is available to the public.

difference constitutes an essential distinction between MaaS and other parts of the 'collaborative economy', where commons resources may well be significant but are seldom fundamental to day-to-day operations[4] (Karppanen, 2017; Nieuwland & van Melik, 2018).

The meaning of *collaboration* in the empirical field of MaaS platforms that include bikeshare may therefore depart in significant ways from its meanings (which are themselves diffuse) in business model research.[5] By the same token, the forms of de facto collaboration, cooperation or coordination that can be empirically observed in these MaaS platforms could produce a more nuanced understanding of the nature of collaborative business models in general, and the diversity contained within this term. For this reason, we propose to further develop and critically assess the concept of CBMs that offer consumers access to bikeshare as a service (both on its own and as part of wider MaaS platforms), to answer our research question:

What are the existing challenges in creating MaaS platforms that integrate multiple bikeshare providers, and how could CBMs contribute to overcoming these?

In this chapter, we discuss how CBM can be defined in relation to MaaS, identify current efforts to integrate bikeshare into MaaS platforms and assess the challenges in these efforts. We address these questions by conducting a systematic literature review into conceptualisations of CBMs across various subject areas in Sect. 3.1. We supplement this with a thematic analysis of a systematic review of literature on the business models of MaaS platforms in Sect. 3.2. To underpin our theoretical findings, we analyse three cases—the Netherlands, Antwerp (BE) and Helsinki (FI)—in light of these organising concepts by drawing on interviews and grey and academic sources in Sect. 3.3. In particular, we will investigate, in greater detail than previous studies, the extent to which MaaS platform formation and bikeshare integration in these cases

[4] For example, research has shown that Airbnb has significant impacts on the 'commons' of neighbourhood liveability and affordability in certain contexts, but these effects are not yet well quantified or legally defined (Nieuwland & van Melik, 2018). In contrast, public space is explicitly governed by regulations around its permanent and temporary use.

[5] These definitions range from a mechanism requiring a dynamic of mutual trust between partners (Aagaard, 2019, 215) to the coordination of outward-facing actions (such as resource acquisition) between organisations (Dreyer et al., 2017).

is the result of voluntary 'collaboration', or a response to conditions imposed by government, and the consequences of these distinctions for the balance of risk and alignment between organisations (Yanwei Li et al., 2018). We discuss how the CBM concept could contribute to the success of bikeshare-inclusive MaaS platforms in Sect. 4 and provide conclusions and recommendations for further study in Sect. 5.

2 Methods

The systematic literature review method has been developed in the social sciences to synthesise findings from large bodies of information, especially where key concepts remain undefined or contested (Petticrew & Roberts, 2006, 21). We employed a 7-part systematic (literature) review approach to establish how CBMs are currently conceptualised across academic literatures. To ensure consistent quality and peer-reviewed status, we limited our search to Scopus, using the search term *TITLE-ABS-KEY* ('collaborative business model*') to retrieve 92 initial results, which were screened for relevance.[6] This process yielded 50 results which were coded using NVivo® software in an iterative process until saturation was reached. The rationale for coding was to establish the heterogeneity of interpretations or definitions of CBMs (see Addenda for sample lists and code tables).

The systematic review succeeded in providing an overview of heterogeneity in the meaning of CBMs, as well as a survey of related terms and their respective similarities and differences relative to CBMs. However, none of these sources addressed the field of MaaS, and only one addressed the question of commons or common pool resources to any extent (B. Cohen & Muñoz, 2015). We therefore conducted a second literature review to establish how and which business model terms were used to describe existing MaaS platforms, with an emphasis on the role of dominant business model frameworks (like the BMC) versus novel or niche frameworks. This survey was informed by the findings of the first,[7]

[6] Exclusion criteria: sources that mentioned but did not discuss CBMs; that focused solely on operational technical aspects of CBMs (e.g. business process engineering).

[7] For example, our inclusion of 'business ecosystem' and 'alliance formation' as alternatives to *business model* was prompted by highly relevant sources in the first survey that employed this term.

resulting in the Scopus search term TITLE-ABS-KEY ('business model*' OR 'business ecosystem*' OR 'alliance formation') AND TITLE-ABS-KEY (bikeshar* OR 'maas' OR 'mobility as a service' OR 'shared mobility'), which returned 45 initial results. This comprehensive sample was refined to 26 sources[8] for further thematic coding using NVivo® until saturation was reached.

We supplemented the generic and theoretical findings of two sets of surveys of peer-reviewed journal articles with the particular and embedded findings of multi-site case studies of MaaS platforms that included bikeshare. Multi-site case studies are effective means of testing theoretical assumptions against empirical data, revealing variations among ostensibly similar cases and defining new areas for research by exposing unanticipated findings (Yin, 2014). We selected three Northwestern European MaaS platforms for further study by means of semi-structured interviews with MaaS platform designers or project initiators, supported by web searches for grey literature published by these same platforms, as well as selected academic sources mentioned in grey literature or in interviews. The choice of platform designer or initiator as research participant allowed us to focus on the MaaS platform itself as an example of a potential CBM, and the design choices and constraints that shaped these platforms. Our interview questions aimed to inform limited organisational case studies focusing on a parameter of interest (MaaS platform design and structure), rather than the business ecosystem of each MaaS case as a whole, or the business models of participants in the platform. Our interview questions therefore asked platform designers to describe their platforms in terms of BMC categories (viz. Key Partners, Key Activities, Key Resources, Value Propositions, Customer Relationships, Channels, Customer Segments, Cost Structure and Revenue Streams) to aid comparison with the results of our literature surveys. These questions were supplemented by more open-ended questions regarding the aims and objectives of the platform, and the challenges encountered in operationalising it, to capture aspects of each case that may diverge from, or not be easily expressible within,

[8] Exclusion criteria: sources that explicitly excluded bikeshare or any form of micromobility (due to the modally distinct nature of open space allocation discussed above), or that focused on developing-world contexts (as our study cases were limited to high-income European contexts).

the parameters of the BMC (see Addenda for interview protocols, a list of interviews and a list of grey literature sources).

Three cases were selected for contrast in scale, in degree of initial success in achieving bikeshare-inclusive MaaS integration, and for consistency as relatively wealthy Northern European urban contexts. The first case is the CROW Deelfietsdashboard, a Dutch multi-city proto-platform for interoperable bikeshare that is currently in its pilot phase and which is intended to serve as the basis for a public-facing app. The second is the Antwerp Marketplace for Mobility, which already includes a public-facing app. In both the Dutch and Belgian cases, the platforms are limited to the provision of wayfinding and information services, and cycling modal share is very high by global standards. The third case, Helsinki's Whim app, is one of the very few current examples of a MaaS platform that provides public-facing services beyond wayfinding and information; here, cycling modal share is much lower than in the Dutch and Belgian cases. The three cases vary widely in terms of platform design, in terms of regulatory context and their relationship with institutional gatekeepers of common resources, and in terms of the services they offer. By means of interviews and a review of grey and selected academic literature related to these cases, we contrast theoretical claims made in academic literature about CBMs and MaaS, respectively, with the challenges arising from real-world attempts to operationalise bikeshare-inclusive MaaS.

3 Results

Our analysis of the CBM literature sampled reveals three distinct interpretations of the word 'collaborative' (see Table 1), as well as two characteristic tensions within CBMs: namely, that between collaboration and competition and that surrounding the role of place and the commons in CBMs. We find that only a small minority of sources (see group 3 in Systematic review of CBM literature in Table 1) explicitly describes CBMs as analytically distinct from other existing BM frameworks, especially Osterwalder's BMC (2004). In all other sources, CBMs serve

Table 1 Coding frequency and data for CBMs

Group of sources derived from coding	Coding: Files	Coding: References	Would exist without collaboration	Can be expressed in conventional BM terms	Focus
Group 1: CBMs as practice	29	34	Yes	Yes	B2B
Group 2: CBMs as activity or sector	13	14	No	Yes	B2B, B2C, for-profit P2P
Group 3: CBMs as analytically distinct	5	5	No	No	B2C, B2G, non-profit P2P

either as a means of describing the practice of collaboration between organisations (group 1), or as a reference to sectors deemed to belong to the sharing (or 'collaborative') economy (group 2). These three sets of interpretations provide a valuable overview of the theoretical and empirical uses to which the term CBM has been put.

3.1 Systematic Review of CBM Literature

3.1.1 Group 1: Collaboration Refers to Practices That Occur Between Organisations

In the great majority of sources, CBMs are deployed as a descriptor for collaborative practices that take place between organisations (B2B). These practices vary widely within the sample, from structured and contractual to informal and sporadic, but all are essentially activities undertaken by organisations that are or could be described in conventional BM terms. For this group, 29 out of 50 sources, the term 'CBM' is thus a descriptor of collaborative *practices*, not of a distinct type of BM. These practices vary widely in scale (some connect entire value chains, others only consist of regular coordination between two firms) and are found across many sectors (including manufacturing, the service sector and product-service firms). In general, within this group, the impetus or rationale for undertaking collaborative practices is provided by anticipated competition from rivals due to technological advances, market forces or established practices within a particular sector, but the decision to initiate collaborative practices is voluntary and strategic; further, the collaboration practised here is most commonly business-to-business (B2B), although consumers feature in some collaborations as significant and influential actors.

3.1.2 Group 2: Collaboration Refers to One Organisation's Key Activity or Sector

In a smaller group of sources, CBMs are used as a descriptor for single organisations whose business it is to facilitate collaboration, or who operate within a sector that the source considers to belong to the *collaborative* or *sharing economy*. As with group 1, these sources deploy the term CBM to refer to organisations with conventional BMs; in this case, these organisations profit financially from providing the means for others to collaborate, whether on a B2B, business-to-consumer (B2C), or for-profit peer-to-peer (P2P) basis. Group 2 includes many platform-based organisations, whose BM centres on the management of a platform as infrastructure for collaboration, as well as many project-based consortia. The 'collaboration' referenced in this use of CBM broadly serves as a synonym for activities that have traditionally been provided on a commercial basis (such as coordination activities, matching and networking), for which the advent of new communications technologies such as the Internet and smartphones represents an opportunity in terms of lower transaction costs, expanded potential markets or more efficient matching and coordination. Unlike group 1, organisations in this group depend on collaboration as a primary activity; within this group, a number of organisations have been set up explicitly as joint ventures or project-based consortia, while others have been founded in order to exploit perceived opportunities within the collaborative sector (such as Airbnb).

3.1.3 Group 3: Collaboration Refers to a Kind of BM That Is Analytically Distinct from the BMC

The smallest and final groups are presented in five sources as analytically distinct from conventional BMs on a number of grounds. Bleja et al. (2018, 2019) present a CBM as a *collaborative system business model* (CSBM) that is identical to the BMC in structure, but exists above the level of the individual BMCs of partner organisations, coordinating and consolidating their activities. For Grossman et al. (2017), the distinctiveness of a CBM from the BMC resides in its value proposition, which is irreducible to the value propositions of partner organisations, even if that value proposition is delivered or realised by the activities of individual partner organisations. As such, these sources argue that the organisations concerned could not exist except on the basis of collaboration and also cannot be adequately articulated in BMC terms. These organisations serve a range of markets including B2C, business to government (B2G) and not-for-profit P2P, as in the case below.

3.1.4 CBMs, Commons and the City

Three further sources within group 3 consider CBMs as analytically distinct due to their relationship with the commons in general (Gyimóthy, 2017), and on place, or the physical commons of the city (B. Cohen & Muñoz, 2015; Muñoz & Cohen, 2016), respectively. Gyimóthy (2017) introduces a distinction between two types of BMs within the sector of the collaborative economy, arguing that the term CBM has been widely but erroneously attributed to a particular archetype of 'corporatized extractive model' (such as Airbnb) that in fact represents a very conventional BM applied to the collaborative sector. Airbnb is an example of this model, in which individual private assets are exploited and the 'commons' of residential neighbourhoods monetised without an efficient mechanism by which the community can limit or demand compensation for the externalities of that monetisation (Nieuwland & van Melik, 2018). In opposition to this type of BM, Gyimóthy discusses the 'communitarian or commons' model of the collaborative economy, which differs intrinsically from the BMC in a number of ways. This Commons CBM is premised on solidarity, mutuality and co-ownership. Value is created through non-monetary exchange on a basis of reciprocity, mediated by a strong commitment to a physical or digital commons (such as a place, a natural resource or a virtual community). The role played by the commons in Gyimóthy's commons CBM differs substantively from the assumptions of the BMC in areas such as key resources (which are shared in perpetuity between stakeholders) and revenue streams (which are non-financial).

Cohen and Muñoz (2015) and Muñoz and Cohen (2016) argue that one kind of CBM is that created in practice through the work of purpose-driven urban entrepreneurs. This is a response to the limitations of conventional business models in the face of complex, interconnected urban challenges, which tend to be strongly mediated by various urban commons (such as urban space). Purpose-driven urban entrepreneurship, and the CBMs it gives rise to, have a number of characteristics that are unique in our sample. Firstly, Cohen and Muñoz situate CBMs explicitly in the city, for which CBMs are both locus and focus, using an approach to urban entrepreneurship that draws on the related concept of the *place-based enterprise* (PBE) (Shrivastava & Kennelly, 2013). Secondly, while other sources have treated the impetus or incentive to collaborate as voluntary and strategic, the complexity and physical constraints of cities mean that collaboration is not optional for urban entrepreneurs, but a requirement imposed by place. Lastly, through their engagement with place, urban entrepreneurs are obliged to collaborate with the public-sector actors tasked with the stewardship of public goods or the commons, or what Poderi (2019, 244) terms *gatekeepers*, making the articulation of the commons an essential component of CBMs for urban entrepreneurship. The urban entrepreneur is 'embedded in place' and aims to resolve 'unique, interconnected city challenges' (B. Cohen & Muñoz, 2015, 2) in close collaboration with public and private-sector actors. This requires that the entrepreneur respond not only to a local 'market' but to the tangible, physical and geospatial circumstances of the city and its 'place-specific anomalies', including deeply embedded social, cultural and political conditions (B. Cohen & Muñoz, 2015, 2; Shrivastava & Kennelly, 2013).

3.1.5 Balancing Competition and Collaboration: CBMs and Platform Competition

Within our sample, the term *collaboration* is used with much of the same variation as the term *CBM*: as a descriptor for both formal and informal interaction between organisations, as a sectoral designation for organisations in the *sharing* or *collaborative economy*, and additionally as a method for BM design. In this study, we therefore employ the term *collaboration* to refer to purposeful interaction between organisations in the broadest sense, without connotations of altruism or an assumption of common purpose or alignment of interests between collaborating partners. The most specific interpretation of collaboration in our sample is that of Salazar (2015), who presents it as the antithesis of classical competition. On this basis, Salazar argues that CBMs exhibit *platform competition*, a kind of behaviour that is distinct from the assumption of rational competition between organisations embedded in the BMC (Osterwalder, 2004), because it imposes value co-creation and shared appropriation as a collective project for all platform participants. As such, it resembles the *keiretsu* phenomenon of interfirm co-specialisation in manufacturing (Dyer, 1996), although service or product-service platforms are less often tied to a focal firm or dominant design. Platform capitalism therefore departs from elements of the BMC such as the assumed relationships between the firm and key partners, as competition *within* platforms is balanced by the mutual interest that platform participants have in competition *between* their platform and others, and positive network externalities are an essential factor for the success of the platform.

These three conceptions of CBMs differ substantially in their implicit or explicit definition of what CBMs are (see systematic review of CBM literature Table 1), but share a common emphasis on interdependence between the focal firm and other entities or actors that is not an inherent feature of the BMC. This interdependence, which serves as an impetus for collaboration, takes two forms in our analysis. Firstly, the majority of CBMs across our sample are subject to tensions between collaboration and competition, which in BMC terms can be expressed as a departure from the assumptions that underpin the category of Key Partners. Secondly, the CBMs presented as analytically distinct (group 3) are subject to significant tensions surrounding the commons. These themes of collaboration versus competition, and of engaging with the commons, are also prominent in MaaS and bikeshare literature, and will therefore be developed as common points of reference between these two literatures. They are discussed in the following sub-sections.

3.2 MaaS Platforms: Competition, Collaboration and the Commons

A discussion of business models across the scientific literature on MaaS is beyond the scope of this study. For our purposes, we limit ourselves to a discussion of key terms within the MaaS literature that describe elements of MaaS business models (see Table 2). We follow Smith and Hensher et al. (2020) in considering MaaS to be composed essentially of a single digital platform which grants users access to mobility services across multiple modes. This *mobility services* or *MaaS platform* (alternatively, a mobility *broker* or *aggregator*) integrates *mobility services* to connect *mobility service providers* (MSPs)—those who operate the physical means of transport, such as vehicles—with the users who demand mobility services. The data generated by the mobility system—such as route and timetable information for public transport, or trip data for bikeshare—constitutes a *data commons*, when it is (potentially) accessible as a common resource, and is often given form through *APIs*. The data commons has a finite and tangible analogue in what Petzer et al. (2019) term the *physical commons*, or the finite stock of urban open space that is available for the movement and storage of vehicles; Meurs et al. (2020) refer to a similar concept when they describe *complementary network resources* as the supporting physical infrastructure that enables mobility services. Access to the physical commons is highly institutionalised and regulated, as well as modally distinct, and is governed by the *city government* acting as a commons gatekeeper or steward. This gatekeeper role can sometimes take the form of a *spatial monopoly* operated either by a government, or a public transport authority with exclusive right to operate certain mobility services within a geographic area.

Table 2 MaaS terms used in this study

Term used in this study (*with alternatives*)	Role or description
MaaS platform *Mobility broker or aggregator* (Meurs et al., 2020; Pangbourne et al., 2020; Wong & Hensher, 2020)*; aggregator* (Jittrapirom et al., 2017)*; MaaS operator* (Polydoropoulou et al., 2020)	Integrates mobility services to connect demanders and suppliers of mobility services using an Internet-enabled platform
Mobility service provider (MSP) *MaaS partner* (Polydoropoulou et al., 2020)*; transport provider* (Meurs et al., 2020)	Operates the physical means of transport—vehicles, with and without drivers
Data commons (Pangbourne et al., 2020)	A description of a state in which public data useful in mobility service provision is commonly accessible
API (Audouin & Finger, 2018, 5)	An application programming interface provides a feed of data about transport, such as route and time information for public transport
Physical commons (Petzer et al., 2019) 'physical resources' (Polydoropoulou et al., 2020, 158)*, Complementary Network Resources* (Meurs et al., 2020)	The physical stock of open public space available for the storage and movement of vehicles, especially informal parking space
City government (Polydoropoulou et al., 2020)	Oversees and safeguards urban commons
Spatial monopoly (Meurs et al., 2020, 4)	An MSP provider holding a monopoly on transport within a geographic area

These terms are drawn from sources that vary considerably in focus and in their approach to MaaS, from studies of private-sector MaaS business alliances (G. Smith et al., 2018; Meurs et al., 2020) to a focus on public-sector MaaS policies (Göran Smith & Hensher, 2020), and using methods ranging from MaaS business model prototyping (Polydoropoulou et al., 2020) to econometric modelling of business models (Wong & Hensher, 2020).

The points of agreement across our sample touch on a set of interconnected problems.

Firstly, sources attribute the small number of full-service MaaS platforms operational today to the challenge of the complex and novel partnerships that MaaS requires between multiple private- and public-sector actors in a rapidly evolving sector (Mulley, 2017).

Secondly, the degree of integration and interoperability that MaaS will demand at scale from platform participants remains a technical and organisational challenge within current regulations, even when this level of collaboration is entirely voluntary (Meurs et al., 2020).

Thirdly, a number of sources acknowledge that the fixed-route, high-volume public transport modes (rail, buses) and active modes (bikeshare) which are viewed as the backbone of MaaS, and the core of its sustainability and accessibility promise, also offer very low profit margins and have traditionally been supported by public subsidy as a result (Göran Smith & Hensher, 2020). In contrast, the private mobility services offered on MaaS platforms seek to maximise private profits for their owners. Further, the interests of private mobility services may align closely with those of the incumbent, ownership-based regime, such that the former could potentially stabilise (rather than disrupt) the latter, as Wells et al. (2020) demonstrate with respect to 'automobility-as-a-service'. Combining these kinds of services within a single organisation is a key concern in the design and operation of MaaS platforms.

The tensions identified in the CBM literature are also present in studies of MaaS. These factors are presented in Fig. 1, in which the diagram at the top right represents a MaaS firm's business model using the conventional elements of the BMC (Osterwalder, 2004),[9] while the infinity symbols represent the open-endedness of the composition of the set of platform partners. The problem of a lack of control over platform partners, and that of deep dependence on reliable access to the contested key resource of the physical commons, is a key concern for MaaS firms. It is represented here by the extension of the physical mobility commons of the city (in grey) into the business model of the MaaS firm at the top right (as a key resource, labelled KR) and also into the business models (labelled BMs) of other MSPs. The physical mobility commons is therefore outside of the focal firm's control, but also simultaneously in demand by an unlimited number of other claimants of space (represented

[9] Where KP = Key Partners, KA = Key Activities, KR = Key Resources, VP = Value Propositions, CR = Customer Relationships, CH = Channels, CS = Cost Structure, and RS = Revenue Streams.

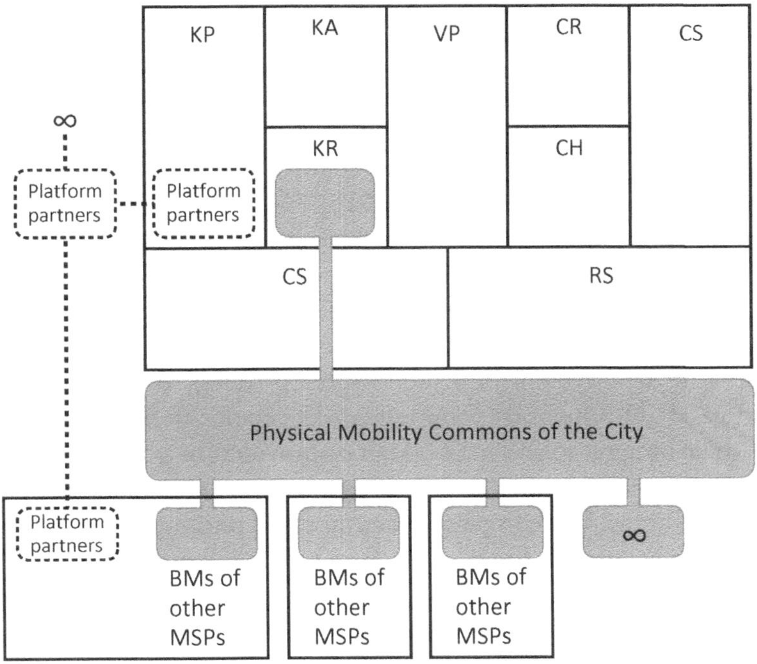

Fig. 1 The physical mobility commons in relation to the business models of a focal MSP and other MSPs

by the infinity sign at the bottom left), both within and beyond the mobility sector. Platform partners may also be added to or reduced against the wishes or the interests of the focal firm, especially in cases where local governments play a strong role in regulating platforms or require platforms to be created.

3.3 Case Studies

3.3.1 The Deelfietsdashboard (Rotterdam and Other Cities, NL)

In the Netherlands, bikeshare has long been integrated into public transport through the highly successful OV-Fiets system, a 24-hr bike hire system operated across the country's railway stations by the national railways. Following the rapid arrival of dockless bikeshare providers in Dutch cities in 2017–2018 and ensuing regulatory backlash in major jurisdictions (Petzer et al., 2019), the Netherlands' five largest cities[10] signalled in 2018 that they would henceforth allow dockless bikeshare providers to operate only through a single, interoperable platform, after the model of the OV-fiets (Slütter, 2018).[11] This platform would support governance of the physical and data commons by cities (through data sharing) and, more significantly, allow any user access to the services of every bikeshare provider present on the platform (Fietsberaad, 2018). This leveraging of access to some of the world's largest cycling markets against the achievement of a high degree of integration prompted the creation of the Openbike[12] initiative (de Haan, 2018; Slütter, 2018). Openbike brought together 12 bikeshare providers in a collective attempt to satisfy these requirements by developing a common technical standard in partnership with the five city governments. Funding for a pilot project to set up a test platform came from the Netherlands Ministry of Infrastructure & Water, which culminated in the Deelfiets ('bikeshare') Dashboard. In this phase, the function of the Dashboard was to relay real-time operations and geolocation data from MSPs to city governments for monitoring and enforcement of the activity in the physical commons. This phase was explicitly intended to lay the groundwork for a public-facing full-service platform (Boor & Vincent, 2019) by March 2019, structured around the GBFS+ data-sharing standard. At the time of writing (September 2020), progress towards this goal has stalled (Boor interview, 13/05/2020 and 16/07/2020), due to the challenges MSPs encounter in attempting to modify their business models to prepare for interoperability of services with other MSPs.

The first of these is the variation in value propositions and size between these individual MSPs, which range from multimillion-dollar

[10] Amsterdam, Rotterdam, The Hague, Utrecht and Eindhoven.

[11] 'Evenals de gemeenten Amsterdam, Rotterdam, Utrecht, Den Haag en Eindhoven die interoperabiliteit als voorwaarde stellen voor het toelaten van deelfietsen in de stad' (Slütter, 2018, 27).

[12] Participating providers are BimBimBikes, Cykl, Donkey Republic, Du Nord/Haagsche Stadsfiets, Emotion sustainable mobility, FlickBike, Hello-bike, Mobike, Nextbike, Urbee, Luud Schimmelpennink and Gobike. The national giant, OV-Fiets, is noticeably absent.

multinationals to one-person startups (Petzer et al., 2019), as well as major differences in the duties and deposits they require users to perform and pay (Boor interview, 13/05/2020). A second fundamental challenge lies in the aggregation of users acquired by each provider into a common pool accessible to all, especially in light of the cost to firms of acquiring a user. Third, the access to their respective commons that cities have promised, and the specific performance, enforcement and rebalancing requirements that major jurisdictions such as Amsterdam and Rotterdam have already signalled in new, dedicated policies (Gemeente Amsterdam, 2017, 2018), combined to impose high minimum operational costs on providers, against no guaranteed minimum in profits (Boor interview, 16/07/2020). Lastly, the public interface of any potential platform would have to resolve design issues rich in potential conflicts, such as the prominence given to each provider for a potential user request or query (Slütter, 2018).

The Deelfietsdashboard therefore develops out of what might be called coerced collaboration: dockless bikeshare MSPs initiated this collaboration in response to a decision by the Netherlands' largest cities to exclude dockless bikeshare from the physical commons (i.e. to refuse these MSPs permission to operate on public land and use public bicycle parking) absent an interoperable platform. In BMC terms, this could be articulated as a loss of control over the Key Partners that individual MSPs, as well as the mobility platform itself, must collaborate with to deliver interoperable services. Indeed, the challenge of combining direct competitors on a single platform has, to date, proven overwhelming, and more recent developments in Amsterdam indicate that the city has abandoned its support for an interoperable platform in favour of local concessions in which three MSPs will be invited to operate a fixed fleet size for a fixed term (Gemeente Amsterdam, 2019). The commons aspects of the Dashboard affect the Key Activities and Key Resources elements of the BMC. In its current pilot phase, a key activity of MSPs is to contribute to the data commons through APIs that allow participating local governments to see all authorised dockless bikeshare activity in real time. This contribution is an interim step to the original vision of the five cities, which is that access to their physical commons would be conditional on success in creating an interoperable platform for all (dockless) bikeshare MSPs. This case is conceptually illustrated in Fig. 2, which represents

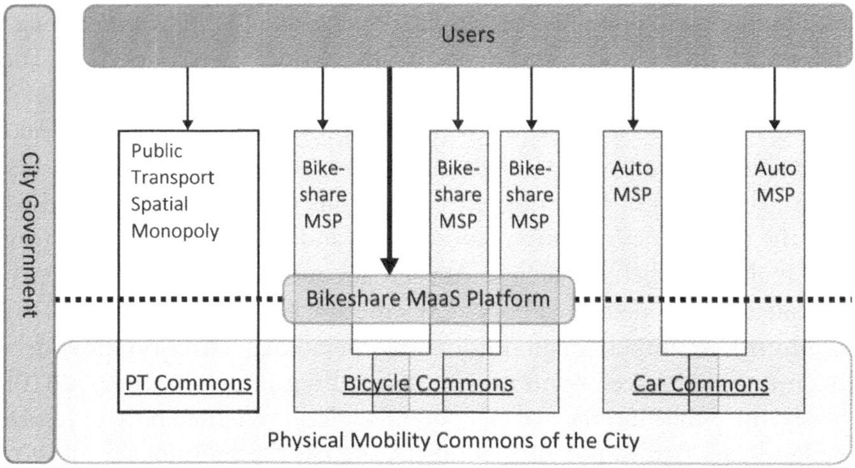

Fig. 2 A conceptual model of the physical mobility commons of the city in relation to compulsory bikeshare MaaS platforms, users, government and other MSPs

users (in darker grey at top) connected by arrows to the MSPs whose services they consume. These public transport, bikeshare and automobility MSPs each make claims on the physical mobility commons of the city (in light grey at bottom); these claims overlap for different MSPs belonging to the same mode, creating a distinct public transport ('PT'), bicycle and car commons. City government (at left) is adjacent to the commons and creates regulations (a dotted line) that restrict commercial access to the physical commons in Dutch cities. These regulations affect other MSPs but are suspended for bikeshare MSPs included in the 'Bikeshare MaaS Platform' (medium grey, where the dotted line is suspended). This platform thus offers an enhanced service to users (represented by a thicker arrow) as a result of its wide range of MSPs.

3.3.2 Antwerp Marketplace for Mobility (Antwerp, BE)

In Antwerp, a city of 520,000 and home to Europe's second-busiest port, imminent major roadworks required for freight movement required a concerted approach to the city's mobility as a whole, in order to preserve accessibility for residents. In 2016 this broad agenda prompted the creation by the City of Antwerp and its partners[13] of the Marketplace for Mobility (MfM), which is described as a 'cooperation framework' including three forms of commercial partnership, rather than a market platform (Kishchenko et al., 2019). The MfM could be described as a proto-platform, in that all formal relationships are between the city and individual service providers. The city retains full control of the physical commons of Antwerp by structuring MfM interactions on a clearly defined project basis on 'no fix, no pay' terms, meaning that no measurable impact means no financial support from the city (Kishchenko et al., 2019; Vernaillen, 2020). Furthermore, in commons terms, the city makes it mandatory for all mobility service providers to limit their fleet size, to share data with the city and to be integrated, at least on a data-sharing level, with at least two MaaS platforms. This leveraging of access to the city's physical commons against a requirement for contribution to the data commons has produced striking results: Antwerp is the only global market in which Bird, a last-mile electric scooter provider operated by the powerful rideshare giant Uber, shares data in this way (Vernaillen, 2020). Antwerp also offers its own wayfinding and information platform, which will soon offer full MaaS services: direct access to multiple service providers, payment, tax and payroll integration (Vernaillen, 2020), all built around an open-data, open-source platform standard with no vendor lock-in (Kishchenko et al., 2019; Maroey, 2019).

As with the Deelfietsdashboard, the set of Key Partners with which any individual MSP must necessarily partner is outside of its control, since collaboration in the city's official platform is a requirement for any MSP that seeks access to Antwerp's physical commons. Figure 3 represents the Antwerp case conceptually. In contrast to the previous case in Table 2, it shows a multimodal MaaS platform that also incorporates all of the MSPs within each mode. The pair of horizontal dotted and solid lines interrupted by the platform represent the various modally specific regulations that limit access to the physical commons; the city-backed platform ('MaaS Platform') partially shields participating MSPs from these.

[13] The Antwerp Port Authority, the Province of Antwerp, the Belgian federal railways (NMBS), the Flemish transport authority (De Lijn), the Antwerp mobility authority (beheersmaatschappij antwerpen mobiel) and a mobility consultancy (Traject).

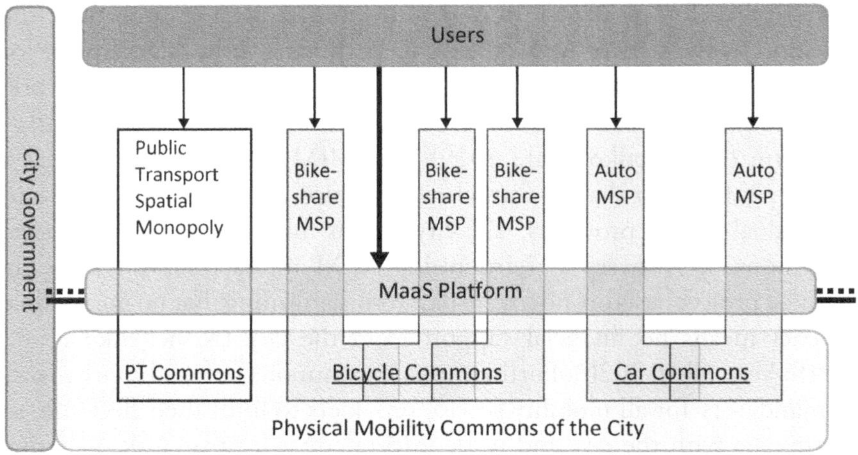

Fig. 3 A conceptual model of the physical mobility commons of the city in relation to a compulsory multimodal platform, users, government and other MSPs

3.3.3 Whim Helsinki (Helsinki, FI)

Helsinki is home to Whim, the world's first platform to provide full MaaS services (wayfinding, information, booking, un/locking and payment). Whim, launched by the firm MaaS Global in 2016, is the outcome of more than a decade of purposeful state planning, starting with Finland's world-first Intelligent Transport Strategy in 2009 and culminating in the 2017 Transport Service Act, the world's first comprehensive national legislation for the regulation of MaaS (Kivimaa interview, 30/06/2020). The Transport Service Act (TSA), for example, abolished quotas on mobility service fleet sizes; required all transport service providers to make essential data such as route, timetable and fare information publicly available; and established a framework for full interoperability of ticketing by requiring mobility service providers to open their ticket APIs (Audouin & Finger, 2018).[14] The TSA therefore created a publicly accessible and legally defined and enforced data commons for the kinds of information that MaaS platforms depend

[14]Taxi, ride-hailing and ride-sharing services are largely excluded from these requirements (including the surge pricing mechanism pioneered by Uber), although in October 2020 the Finnish Government tabled specific amendments to the Act that require greater price transparency for this sector (Finnish Government, 2020).

on. These requirements were informed by close but informal cooperation between the City of Helsinki and the founder of MaaS dating from 2013, in which an agenda of regulatory changes required for a successful MaaS platform was established (Audouin & Finger, 2018; Heikkilä, 2014). This cooperation continued as the City of Helsinki positioned itself as an international champion of MaaS, leading in 2015 to an open call for the creation of a private-sector MaaS firm. Out of 200 interested parties, 23 went on to collaborate through a new organisation, MaaS.fi, which went on to release Whim (as MaaS Global) in 2016.

The Whim platform business model is therefore an example of voluntary collaboration between competing firms to create a new organisation. The resulting joint venture operates a MaaS platform that acts much like a profit-making private-sector firm, as it integrates the mobility services of both public and private-sector MSPs into a platform that presents the public with full access to all modes, according to various subscription models (Ramboll and MaaS Global, 2019; Hietanen interview, 13/12/2017).

Figure 4 presents the case of MaaS in Finland in conceptual terms. In the Finnish case, the mandatory creation and maintenance of a data

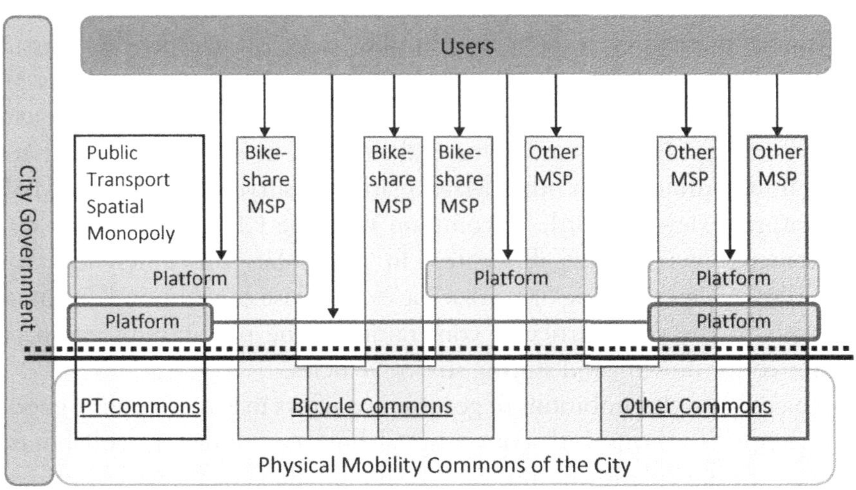

Fig. 4 A conceptual model of the physical mobility commons of the city in relation to multiple platforms, users and government

commons of basic information that can support MaaS platforms allows for the possibility of many MaaS platforms that offer different combinations of modes. Some, such as a rival platform pioneered by a public transport operator (white box), may attract a significant user base in their own right and produce a different form of competition between service providers. The pair of dotted and thick solid lines emanating from 'City Government' represent modally mediated regulations that limit or constrain access to the physical commons; these remain in operation and apply to the various MaaS platforms. However, unlike in Antwerp (29%) (Broer, 2016) and in Dutch cities, the bicycle has a small modal share in Helsinki (6% in 2012) (Ramboll and MaaS Global, 2019), meaning that the 'Bicycle Commons'—referring to the sum of the infrastructure and space required for bicycle movement and storage on public land—is relatively less saturated and contested by users.

4 Discussion

The cases of an interoperable bikeshare platform in the Netherlands, a multimodal proto-platform and 'cooperation framework' in Antwerp and a true MaaS platform in Helsinki that originated as a collaborative business present clear contrasts in the areas of competition versus collaboration, and that of coding and valuing the commons (see Table 3).

In theoretical terms, the forms of collaboration that exist de facto between organisations and other stakeholders in our three cases have much in common with other MaaS platforms surveyed in our snowball literature review, but little in common with the CBM examples in our systematic review. This illustrates, in particular, the difference that mobility makes, in tying firms that have otherwise conventional business models to the very particular constraints of the public outdoor space required for moving and storing shared vehicles.

In contrast, the ambitions of governance actors to achieve public goods by compelling firms with conventional business models to collaborate deeply through platforms illustrate the potential of collaborative business models to deliver on these social agendas. This is especially marked in the case of purpose-driven urban entrepreneurship (Muñoz & Cohen, 2016).

Table 3 Key characteristics of MaaS platforms per case

Case country	Conditions for MSP collaboration	Data commons conditions	Conditions for MSP access to physical commons	Services offered by platform
NL	Mandatory	MSPs must share with cities	(Initially) Strictly conditional on platform participation	Pilot: To city governments—trip and fleet information
BE	Mandatory	MSPs must share with city	Identical to those for private citizens	To public: Information and wayfinding (further services planned)
Fi	Optional	Both cities and MSPs must share data publicly by law	Identical to those for private citizens	To public: Information, wayfinding, plus full services—booking, un/locking, payment

In the Dutch case, these aims have not been met, and progress towards an interoperable national bikeshare platform is arguably moribund. The objectives that have justified five Dutch cities' demand for such a platform also appear difficult to achieve within the limitations of conventional business models and classical competition. However, these factors suggest that more support, more mitigation of risk and more efforts to level the playing field are required from governance actors, especially at the national level, where Finland's interventions have proven so decisive.

However, the risk involved for individual participants in such a platform is high, and the requirement that service providers (rather than, for example, intermediaries operating in a deregulated market) expose customers to the offerings of direct competitors runs counter to classical notions of competition that underpin Osterwalder's Business Model Canvas (2004), and which remain implicit across groups 1 and 2 in our CBM sample. This risk has not been managed or mitigated, as in the Finnish case, by the creation of an overarching regulatory framework that imposes a level playing field for all mobility service providers across all modes, at least in terms of information and ticketing functions. This is striking, considering that the Netherlands was the first country in the world to require open data sharing between all public transport operators in 2008 (Boor interview, 13/05/2020). The designer of the Deelfiets Dashboard proto-platform expressed regret that publicly available open data sharing had not been built into this system from the outset to address this competition problem (Boor interview, 16/07/2020), due to opposition from pilot funders.

In Antwerp, a collaborative business model may be said to exist in a loose sense in the form of the Marketplace for Mobility and its public-facing wayfinding and information app. Taken together, these MaaS proto-platforms facilitate the simultaneous provision of (sometimes competing) services by multiple providers to the City of Antwerp and its MfM partners. Risk is limited by the creation of non-overlapping and explicit project parameters for firms, which have formal relationships with the MfM (as client or *opdrachtgever*) rather than with each other. Antwerp's unilateral imposition of the requirement that service providers share their data with the city, and integrate their services with a minimum of two MaaS apps, has been successful in leveraging access to the city's commons to attract firms, even where this requires fundamental changes to their business models, as in the case of Bird scooters.

However, the development of a MaaS app that goes beyond wayfinding and information services is likely to require the development of a distinctively collaborative business model (as per group 3 in our CBM sample) rather than modifications of service providers' own business models, which is likely to pose a significant challenge. For example, the City of Antwerp has set a precedent by manipulating wayfinding services in order to achieve certain public goods, such as minimising city-centre automobile traffic and reducing automobile congestion to facilitate the movement of passengers and port freight. Providers of services such as taxis and automobiles may find that they become less visible to users requesting trips along particular routes or at particular times. Secondly, the principle of *no fix, no pay* represents a high risk for current MfM participants, especially since the current logic of the MfM is focused on the replacement of peak-hour automobile trips as the primary assessment criterion. Thirdly, the degree of integration between major mobility governance stakeholders at the federal, language community, provincial and urban levels is currently very minimal in comparison with the Netherlands (Vernaillen, 2020). This general fragmentation is reflected in the lack of a standard data sharing protocol between the national railways and local urban transport, or the fact that the federal Belgian mobility planning document expired in 2014–5 and has not been renewed. This lack of structured cooperation through official channels has, paradoxically, fostered an entrepreneurial culture of direct, informal contact between stakeholders.[15] For Antwerp, this has produced a high degree of flexibility and autonomy in defining the parameters of the MfM. It may also have potentially reduced the arenas in which powerful mobility operators, such as Uber, are able to (cost-)effectively lobby for favourable regulations. By the same token, the city's own requirements and policies do not have the force of law and may therefore run counter to the duties and imperatives that commercial law imposes on firms with conventional business models. Antwerp's experiment, while it thus benefits from a regulatory vacuum at some levels, may lock out organisations that would benefit from modifying their own business models to accommodate the demands of a MaaS platform, but are prevented from doing so on fiduciary grounds.

Regarding the success of Whim, however, closer examination of its first-in-the-world offering suggests that such prodigious success may have a price for Finland's urban commons, since the platform faces few demands from the city, such as for the limitation of shared vehicle fleets to prevent saturation of the physical commons. This factor may not yet be readily apparent as cycling mode share in Helsinki is low, but it is unclear that MaaS, in the particular instance of Whim, can be harnessed as an instrument to raise it, or to deliver on the City of Helsinki's current and future policy goals. Similarly, in Antwerp, automobile modal share is high, cycling rates are low compared to the Netherlands, and public transport use is falling (Vernaillen interview, 29/05/2020). The pressure on public open space, outside of car parking, is correspondingly lower than in Dutch cities, and the policy goals of the MfM are overwhelmingly framed in terms of managing automobile congestion and safeguarding

[15] For example, one of the initial challenges in setting up the SWtA project was simply gaining access to existing data streams regarding programmed and real-time route data from De Lijn, the Flemish public transport authority (Vernaillen, 2020).

the accessibility (by automobile) of the port and freeway system.[16] In the Netherlands, where the public urban space required for vehicle storage is highly contested due to the strength of cycling as a rival to automobility, the barriers against MaaS, and bikeshare, are higher. In the Dutch context, therefore, the achievement of MaaS (as in Helsinki) may be less beneficial than the achievement of a CBM for bikeshare (as per the objectives of Openbike), and the greater challenge of achieving MaaS via CBM (rather than MaaS at any cost) may be well worth the wait.

5 Conclusions and Recommendations for Future Research

The three cases of bikeshare integration into MaaS platforms reveal that MaaS platforms and the MSPs that partner with them still face significant challenges in achieving the integration, in commercial terms, that is already possible in strictly technological terms (i.e. integration of booking, un/locking and payments). The CBM sources we have analysed largely retain the assumptions of the BMC, such as that of classical competition between focal firms, a high degree of control over prospective key partners and key resources, and a value proposition that can be largely attributed to a single focal firm. In our cases, these conditions do not obtain. This chapter thus contributes a first attempt at a systematic review of the Collaborative Business Model across various literatures. It clarifies the meaning of collaboration and of the CBM within that sample according to three major interpretations. Of these, the most common is a 'narrow' interpretation of collaboration as a practice voluntarily undertaken by one or more organisations for an indefinite period, on a formal or informal basis. In the second-commonest interpretation, collaboration is a sectoral designation for organisations considered to form part of the sharing economy. Only a small minority of studies ascribe a 'broader' interpretation to collaboration and to CBMs as analytically distinct from

[16] The entire SWtA project is framed, in policy terms, as an anti-car congestion measure designed to maintain accessibility for freight and passenger movements on the city-region's roads, and all of the MfM's projects are evaluated, in project materials, in terms of one key metric: the number of peak-hour automobile trips avoided (uitgespaarde autoverplaatsingen).

the BMC, and of these, those relating to urban contexts all insist on the role of the commons as the basis of that distinction.

This three-part division of interpretations of the CBM may be relevant for sustainable urban mobility researchers seeking to better understand how collaboration can be mandated as a governance approach for new mobility modes. In the case of cycling, which is appealing to urban decision-makers precisely because of the uncaptured positive externalities it produces for society, the Dutch case shows how difficult it can be to sustain a CBM where private risks remain high but the capture of private rewards (for service providers) is limited. Further, the few CBM sources that explicitly address the commons, and particularly the urban commons, suggest that public and private stakeholders in urban mobility could benefit by moving beyond a transactional logic in structuring mobility services, particularly where bikeshare is concerned. For example, purpose-driven urban entrepreneurship and Gyimóthy's (2017) account of commons or communitarian business models share a dual role for the commons as both the host and the recipient of concerted action. In business model terms, this could take the form, in MaaS, of proactive efforts by city government to offer MSPs and MaaS platforms a more stable, 'ring-fenced' stake in the physical or data commons. This is the case with Finland's TSA, which has given legal stability to a very new sector and produced a relatively mature and pioneering framework for innovation in bundled mobility services.

What is also striking in our cases is the extent to which 'collaboration' is imposed on MaaS platforms and MSPs by fiat of a city or regional government, acting as a commons gatekeeper or steward, without supporting interventions at other levels of government (especially national legislation). This is an underexplored avenue for further research into CBMs and, ultimately, for a more specific definition of the term 'Collaborative' in CBMs in opposition to closely related terms like coercion, coordination and cooperation. Public-sector decision-makers in cities contemplating the creation of a mobility services platform may take note of the difficulties that collaboration entails when it is imposed on different mobility modes. Analysis of the individual MSP business models reveals that these difficulties differ according to mode, and are therefore amplified in the case of a single-mode MSP, as in the Dutch case.

Our study is limited by the limited number of interviews carried out, as well as by a lack of comprehensive mapping of the business models of MaaS platforms, as well as MSPs. Future research on the fast-moving empirical field of MaaS platforms could better develop the theme of business model morphology among different types of MaaS platform, for example, as a function of high-margin, motorised, heavyweight mobility services, as opposed to low-margin, non-motorised modes, such as cycling and walking. Lastly, future research is likely to benefit from the growing number of MaaS platforms that offer services beyond wayfinding and information, thereby allowing for a richer comparison.

Addendum: Interviews

Interview Protocols

Q1–Q3: Please describe your (Q1) value proposition, (Q2) value creation mechanisms (prompt: resources, supplier and distribution channels and partners) and (Q3) value capture mechanisms (prompt: costs structures and revenue models) mechanisms *[interviewer presents two BM canvases to respondent: one blank, and one filled in with interviewer's projection of BM derived from grey literature]*.

Q4–Q6: Does your organisation (Q4) distinguish between commercial/for-profit and non-commercial/social elements of your value proposition? If so, please describe these (Q5) commercial and (Q6) non-commercial elements.

Q7–Q9: How does your organisation (Q7) mediate or limit the incentive to compete between participating service providers, and (Q8) between your organisation and participating service providers? What role does your organisation play in (Q9) mitigating or managing risks between service providers?

Q10: How did your platform come to be? What factors influenced its current design?

Q11: What limitations or barriers would you like to see removed? What forms of support would you like to receive now or in the future, and from whom?

List of Interviews, Presentations or Meetings, and Grey Literature Sources Per Case

	Case: The Netherlands (Deelfietsdashboard)	Case: Antwerp (Marketplace for Mobility)	Case: Helsinki (Whim app)
Interviews	Video interview with Sven Boor, 13/05/2020 and 16/07/2020, recorded and transcribed	Video interview with Stijn Vernaillen, 29/05/2020, recorded and transcribed	Video interview with Sampi Hietanen, 13/12/2017, recorded and transcribed Video interview with Paula Kivimaa, researcher on MaaS in Finland, 30/06/2020, recorded and transcribed
(Virtual) Presentations	Boor, Sven, and Hink Vincent. 'Deelfiets Dashboard voor gemeentes: Hoe krijgt een gemeente inzicht in (real-time) deelfietsgebruik?' Presented at the Lancering gemeentelijk Deelfiets dashboard, CROW-Fietsberaad, Utrecht, 25/04/2019 Haan, Dirk Jan de. 2018. 'Het Deelfietsconvenant Openbike Brengt MaaS Voor Deelfietsen Dichtbij'. Presented at meeting 'Aan de slag met deelfietsen', CROW-Fietsberaad, Utrecht, 13/11/2018	Maroey, Chris Van. 2019. 'Antwerp's Marketplace for Mobility'. Presented at the Polis Network, 27–28/11/2019, Brussels. https://www.polisnetwork.eu/wp-content/uploads/2019/11/4F-Chris-Van-Maroey.pdf City of Antwerp. 'Smart Ways to Antwerp/Slim naar Antwerpen – Webinar NXTMobility'. 29/04/2020 (https://www.youtube.com/watch?v=lgacUjyRISs)	Tuli, Apaar and Oxley, Brylie (MaaS Global/Whim). 'Designing the Future of Urban Mobility'. Presented at Data-Driven Design Day, 19/09/2018 (https://www.youtube.com/watch?v=8W5ljbKgjLQ)
Apps	–	Slim naar Antwerpen iOS app (https://apps.apple.com/be/app/slim-naar-antwerpen/id1343247830?l=nl)	Whim iOS app (https://apps.apple.com/fi/app/whim-all-your-journeys/id1110962965)

(*continued*)

(continued)

	Case: The Netherlands (Deelfietsdashboard)	Case: Antwerp (Marketplace for Mobility)	Case: Helsinki (Whim app)
Websites	Websites: CROW (crow.nl), Deelfietsdashboard (deelfietsdashboard.nl), Openbike (openbike.nl)	Smart Ways to Antwerp (slimnaarantwerpen.be)	Whim (whimapp.com), Helsinki Smart Region (helsinkismart.fi)
Grey literature (reports and corporate literature)	Mingardo, G., M. Streng, and J.J. Witte. 2017. 'Een deelfiets voor de Hele stad: Een onderzoek naar de kansen en uitdagingen voor Een Stadsbreed deelfietssysteem in Rotterdam'. RHV Erasmus Urban, Port and Transport Economics	Broer, Karin. 2016. 'Fietsdeelsystemen in Antwerpen: Het success van de Velo'. CROW-Fietsberaad (https://www.fietsberaad.nl/CROWFietsberaad/media/Kennis/Bestanden/CROW-Fietsberaad_notitie_excursie_huurfietsen_antwerpen_mei-2016.pdf?ext=.pdf)	Kanger, Laur, and Paula Kivimaa. 2017. 'Transformative Innovation Learning History: Finland - The Emergence and Consolidation of Mobility-as-a-Service in Finland'. Transformative Innovation Policy Consortium (http://www.tipconsortium.net/wp-content/uploads/2019/04/finland-TLHC-v5.pdf) Ramboll, and MaaS Global., 2019. 'WHIMPACT: Insights from the World's First Mobility-as-a-Service (MaaS) System'. Helsinki: Ramboll (https://ramboll.com/-/media/files/rfi/publications/Ramboll_whimpact-2019.pdf)
Academic sources	Petzer et al. (2020), van Zessen (2017)	Kishchenko et al. (2019)	Ache (2011), Audouin and Finger (2018), Heikkilä (2014), Kivimaa and Rogge (forthcoming), Surakka et al. (2018)

References

Aagaard, A. (Ed.). (2019). *Sustainable business models: Innovation, implementation and success*. Springer International Publishing. https://doi.org/10.1007/978-3-319-93275-0

Ache, P. (2011). "Creating futures that would otherwise not be"–Reflections on the greater Helsinki vision process and the making of metropolitan regions. *Progress in Planning, 75*(4), 155–192. Elsevier. https://doi.org/10.1016/j.progress.2011.05.002

Akyelken, N., Banister, D., & Givoni, M. (2018). The sustainability of shared mobility in London: The dilemma for governance. *Sustainability, 10*(2), 420. https://doi.org/10.3390/su10020420

Amaral, M. (2008). Public vs private management of public utilities–The case of urban public transport in Europe. *Research in Transportation Economics, 22*(1), 85–90. Elsevier. https://doi.org/10.1016/j.retrec.2008.05.021

Ambrosino, G., Nelson, J. D., Boero, M., & Ramazzotti, D. (2016). From the concept of flexible mobility services to the "Shared Mobility Services Agency". In C. Mulley & J. D. Nelson (Eds.), *Transport and sustainability* (Vol. 8, pp. 203–215). Emerald Group Publishing Limited. https://doi.org/10.1108/S2044-994120160000008010

Audouin, M., & Finger, M. (2018). The development of mobility-as-a-service in the Helsinki Metropolitan Area: A multi-level governance analysis. *Research in Transportation Business & Management, 27*(June), 24–35. https://doi.org/10.1016/j.rtbm.2018.09.001

Berger, G., Feindt, P. H., Holden, E., & Rubik, F. (2014). Sustainable mobility—Challenges for a complex transition. *Journal of Environmental Policy & Planning, 16*(3), 303–320. https://doi.org/10.1080/1523908X.2014.954077

Bleja, J., Grossmann, U., & Langer, H. (2018). A Collaborative System Business Model for Ambient Assisted Living Systems, IEEE 4th International Symposium on Wireless Systems within the International Conferences on Intelligent Data Acquisition and Advanced Computing Systems (IDAACS-SWS), pp. 78–81. https://doi.org/10.1109/IDAACS-SWS.2018.8525684

Bleja, J., Langer, H., & Grossmann, U. (2019). Business Models for Wireless AAL Systems — Financing Strategies, 10th IEEE International Conference on Intelligent Data Acquisition and Advanced Computing Systems: Technology and Applications (IDAACS), pp. 130–133. https://doi.org/10.1109/IDAACS.2019.8924437

Boor, S. (2020). Sven Boor interview 16072020Video Call.

Boor, S., & Vincent, H. (2019, April 25). Deelfiets Dashboard voor gemeentes: Hoe krijgt een gemeente inzicht in (real-time) deelfietsgebruik? Presented at the Lancering gemeentelijk Deelfiets dashboard, CROW-Fietsberaad, Utrecht. https://fietsberaad.nl/getmedia/44e5231a-9383-428f-8694-6b838449be75/Presentatie-25-4-2019-van-bijeenkomst-Lancering-gemeentelijk-Deelfietsdashboard.pdf.aspx?ext=.pdf

Botsman, R., & Rogers, R. (2011). What's mine is yours: How collaborative consumption is changing the way we live.

Brandajs, F., & Russo, A. P. (2019). Whose is that square? Cruise tourists' mobilities and negotiation for public space in Barcelona. *Applied Mobilities*, 1–25. https://doi.org/10.1080/23800127.2019.1576257

Broer, K. (2016). Fietsdeelsystemen in Antwerpen: Het success van de Velo. *CROW-Fietsberaad.* https://www.fietsberaad.nl/CROWFietsberaad/media/Kennis/Bestanden/CROW-Fietsberaad_notitie_excursie_huurfietsen_antwerpen_mei-2016.pdf?ext=.pdf

Carmona, M. (2015). Re-theorising contemporary public space: A new narrative and a new normative. *Journal of Urbanism: International Research on Placemaking and Urban Sustainability, 8*(4), 373–405. https://doi.org/10.1080/17549175.2014.909518

Cohen, B., & Kietzmann, J. (2014). Ride on! mobility business models for the sharing economy. *Organization & Environment, 27*(3), 279–296. https://doi.org/10.1177/1086026614546199

Cohen, B., & Muñoz, P. (2015). Toward a theory of purpose-driven urban entrepreneurship. *Organization and Environment, 28*(3), 264–285. https://doi.org/10.1177/1086026615600883

de Haan, D. J. (2018). Het Deelfietsconvenant Openbike Brengt MaaS Voor Deelfietsen Dichtbij. Presented at the Aan de slag met deelfietsen, CROW-Fietsberaad, Utrecht, November 13.

de Magalhães, C., & Freire Trigo, S. (2017). "Clubification" of urban public spaces? The withdrawal or the re-definition of the role of local government in the management of public spaces. *Journal of Urban Design, 22*(6), 738–756. https://doi.org/10.1080/13574809.2017.1336059

de Man, A.-P., & Luvison, D. (2019). Collaborative business models: Aligning and operationalizing alliances. *Business Horizons, 62*(4), 473–482. https://doi.org/10.1016/j.bushor.2019.02.004

Dreyer, B., Lüdeke-Freund, F., Hamann, R., & Faccer, K. (2017). Upsides and downsides of the sharing economy: Collaborative consumption business models' stakeholder value impacts and their relationship to context.

Technological Forecasting and Social Change, 125(December), 87–104. https://doi.org/10.1016/j.techfore.2017.03.036

Dyer, J. H. (1996). Does governance matter? Keiretsu alliances and asset specificity as sources of Japanese competitive advantage. *Organization Science, 7*(6), 649–666. INFORMS. https://doi.org/10.1287/orsc.7.6.649

EC DG MOVE. (2019). Transport in the European Union: Current trends and issues. In *Mobility and transport*. European Commission Directorate-General for Mobility and Transport. https://ec.europa.eu/transport/sites/transport/files/2019-transport-in-the-eu-current-trends-and-issues.pdf

Fietsberaad. (2018, January 30). Overal Een Deelfiets Met Één Account. *Nieuws*. http://www.fietsberaad.nl/?section=nieuws&mode=newsArticle&newsYear=2018&repository=Overal+een+deelfiets+met+%C3%A9%C3%A9n+account

Finnish Government. (2020, October 15). Numerous amendments proposed to taxi legislation. *Valtioneuvosto*. https://valtioneuvosto.fi/en/-/numerous-amendments-proposed-to-taxi-legislation

Fishman, E. (2016). Bikeshare: A Review of Recent Literature. *Transport Reviews, 36*(1), 92–11. https://doi.org/10.1080/01441647.2015.1033036

Gemeente Amsterdam. (2017). *Gemeente Amsterdam Nota Deelfiets (Concept)*. Gemeente Amsterdam.

Gemeente Amsterdam. (2019). *Deelmobiliteit, Kansen Voor de Stad: Beleid Voor Het Delen van Schone Vervoermiddelen Anders Dan de Auto*. Verkeer & Openbare Ruimte. https://www.amsterdam.nl/deelvervoer/documenten-deelvervoer/?PagClsIdt=15730633#PagCls_15730633

Gemeente Rotterdam. (2018). *Beleidsnotitie Deelfietsen Rotterdam*. Gemeente Rotterdam.

Gössling, S., Schröder, M., Späth, P., & Freytag, T. (2016). Urban space distribution and sustainable transport. *Transport Reviews, 36*(5), 659–679. https://doi.org/10.1080/01441647.2016.1147101

Grossmann, U., Horster, B., & Khess, I. (2017). Collaborative business models for AAL-services based on M2M-communication. In, 1:436–40. https://doi.org/10.1109/IDAACS.2017.8095119

Gyimóthy, S. (2017). Business models of the collaborative economy. In *Collaborative economy and tourism* (pp. 31–39). Springer. https://link.springer.com/chapter/10.1007/978-3-319-51799-5_3

Heikkilä, S. (2014). *Mobility as a service – A proposal for action for the public administration case Helsinki*. Aalto University School of Engineering. https://

aaltodoc.aalto.fi/bitstream/handle/123456789/13133/master_Heikkil%c3%a4_Sonja_2014.pdf?sequence=1&isAllowed=y

Hensher, D. A., Mulley, C., Ho, C., Smith, G., Wong, Y., & Nelson, J. D. (2020). *Understanding mobility as a service (MaaS): Past, present and future*. Elsevier.

Hietanen, S. (2017). Interview with Sampi Hietanen of MaaS Global/Whim.

Jittrapirom, P., Caiati, V., Feneri, A.-M., Ebrahimigharehbaghi, S., Alonso González, M. J., & Narayan, J. (2017). Mobility as a service: A critical review of definitions, assessments of schemes, and key challenges. *Urban Planning, 2*(2), 13. https://doi.org/10.17645/up.v2i2.931

Kamargianni, M., & Matyas, M. (2017). The business ecosystem of mobility-as-a-service. In, 14.

Karppanen, M. (2017). Regulating ridesourcing companies and the employment status of drivers in the sharing economy-A study on uber. Master's thesis in European Law, University of Helsinki. Retrieved from https://helda.helsinki.fi/bitstream/handle/10138/181492/Regulating%20Ridesourcing%20Companies%20and%20the%20Employment%20Status%20of%20Drivers%20in%20the%20Sharing%20Economy%20-%20A%20Study%20on%20Uber%20by%20Mira%20Karppanen.pdf

Kishchenko, K., De Roeck, M., Salens, M., & Van Maroey, C. (2019). The antwerp marketplace for mobility: Partnering with private mobility service providers as a strategy to keep the region accessible. *Transportation Research Procedia, 39*, 191–200. https://doi.org/10.1016/j.trpro.2019.06.021

Kivimaa, P., & Rogge, K. (forthcoming). Interplay of policy experimentation and institutional change in sustainability transitions: The case of mobility as a service in Finland.

Li, Y., Taeihagh, A., & de Jong, M. (2018). The governance of risks in ridesharing: A revelatory case from Singapore. *Energies, 11*(5), 1277. https://doi.org/10.3390/en11051277

Li, Y., & Voege, T. (2017). Mobility as a service (MaaS): Challenges of implementation and policy required. *Journal of Transportation Technologies, 07*(02), 95–106. https://doi.org/10.4236/jtts.2017.72007

Machado, C., de Salles Hue, N., Berssaneti, F., & Quintanilha, J. (2018). An overview of shared mobility. *Sustainability, 10*(12), 4342. https://doi.org/10.3390/su10124342

Meurs, H., Sharmeen, F., Marchau, V., & van der Heijden, R. (2020). Organizing integrated services in mobility-as-a-service systems: Principles of alliance formation applied to a MaaS-Pilot in the Netherlands. *Transportation Research*

Part A: Policy and Practice, 131, 178–195. Elsevier. https://doi.org/10.1016/j.tra.2019.09.036
Mulley, C. (2017). Mobility as a services (MaaS) – Does it have critical mass? *Transport Reviews, 37*(3), 247–251. https://doi.org/10.1080/01441647.2017.1280932
Muñoz, P., & Cohen, B. (2016). The Making of the Urban Entrepreneur. *California Management Review, 59*(1), 71–91. https://doi.org/10.1177/0008125616683953
Nieuwland, S., & van Melik, R. (2018). Regulating Airbnb: How cities deal with perceived negative externalities of short-term rentals. *Current Issues in Tourism*, 1–15. https://doi.org/10.1080/13683500.2018.1504899
Osterwalder, A. (2004). *The business model ontology: A proposition in a design science approach*. PhD. University of Lausanne. http://www.hec.unil.ch/aosterwa/PhD/Osterwalder_PhD_BM_Ontology.pdf
Pangbourne, K., Mladenović, M. N., Stead, D., & Milakis, D. (2020). Questioning mobility as a service: Unanticipated implications for society and governance. *Transportation Research Part A: Policy and Practice, 131*, 35–49. https://doi.org/10.1016/j.tra.2019.09.033
Petticrew, M., & Roberts, H. (2006). *Systematic reviews in the social sciences*. Blackwell.
Petzer, B. J. M., Wieczorek, A. J., & Verbong, G. P. J. (2019). Making sense of cycling-as-a-service in the Netherlands: A combined business models and transitions approach. *Environmental Innovation and Societal Transitions*. https://doi.org/10.1016/j.eist.2019.09.001
Petzer, B. J. M., Wieczorek, A. J., & Verbong, G. P. J. (2020). Dockless bike-share in Amsterdam: a mobility justice perspective on niche framing struggles. *Applied Mobilities*. https://doi.org/10.1080/23800127.2020.1794305
Petzer, B. J. M., Wieczorek, A. A. J., & Verbong, G. P. J. (2021). The legal street: A scarcity approach to urban open space in mobility transitions. *Urban Transformations, 3*(3), 1–24. https://doi.org/10.1186/s42854-021-00018-0
Poderi, G. (2019). Sustaining platforms as commons: Perspectives on participation, infrastructure, and governance. *CoDesign, 15*(3), 243–255. https://doi.org/10.1080/15710882.2019.1631351
Polydoropoulou, A., Pagoni, I., Tsirimpa, A., Roumboutsos, A., Kamargianni, M., & Tsouros, I. (2020). Prototype business models for mobility-as-a-service. *Transportation Research Part A: Policy and Practice, 131*, 149–162. Elsevier. https://doi.org/10.1016/j.tra.2019.09.035

Ramboll and MaaS Global. (2019). *WHIMPACT: Insights from the world's first mobility-as-a-service (MaaS) system.* Ramboll. https://ramboll.com/-/media/files/rfi/publications/Ramboll_whimpact-2019.pdf
Salazar, A. (2015). Platform competition: A research framework and synthesis of game-theoretic studies. *Available at SSRN 2565337.*
Shrivastava, P., & Kennelly, J. J. (2013). Sustainability and place-based enterprise. *Organization & Environment, 26*(1), 83–101. SAGE Publications. https://doi.org/10.1177/1086026612475068
Slütter, M. (2018). OpenBike, Op Weg Naar Één Account Voor Alle Deelfietsen. *Fietsverkeer*, November 29. https://www.fietsberaad.nl/Kennisbank/Magazine-Fietsverkeer-43
Smith, G., & Hensher, D. A. (2020). Towards a framework for mobility-as-a-service policies. *Transport Policy, 89*(April), 54–65. https://doi.org/10.1016/j.tranpol.2020.02.004
Smith, G., Sochor, J., & Karlsson, I. C. M. (2018). Mobility as a service: Development scenarios and implications for public transport. *Research in Transportation Economics, 69*, 592–599. https://doi.org/10.1016/j.retrec.2018.04.001
Surakka, T., Härri, F., Haahtela, T., Horila, A., & Michl, T. (2018). Regulation and governance supporting systemic MaaS innovations. *Research in Transportation Business & Management, 27*(June), 56–66. https://doi.org/10.1016/j.rtbm.2018.12.001
Van Maroey, C. (2019). Antwerp's marketplace for mobility. Presented at the Polis Network, November. https://www.polisnetwork.eu/wp-content/uploads/2019/11/4F-Chris-Van-Maroey.pdf
van Zessen, P. C. (2017). De Deelfiets in Nederland: Over De Potentie Van De Deelfiets in Nederland En De Ruimtelijke Effecten Van De Deelfiets in De Stad (HBO). Hogeschool Utrecht: Utrecht.
Vernaillen, S. (2020). Stijn Vernaillen interview 29052020.
Wells, P., Wang, X., Wang, L., Liu, H., & Orsato, R. (2020). More friends than foes? The impact of automobility-as-a-service on the incumbent automotive industry. *Technological Forecasting and Social Change, 154*, 119975. Elsevier. https://doi.org/10.1016/j.techfore.2020.119975
Wong, Y. Z., & Hensher, D. A. (2020). Delivering mobility as a service (MaaS) through a broker/aggregator business model. *Transportation.* https://doi.org/10.1007/s11116-020-10113-z
Yin, R. K. (2014). *Case study research design and methods* (5th ed.). SAGE Publications.

Upscaling Sustainable Niches: How a User Perspective of Organizational Value Logics Can Help Translate Between Niche and System

Alexandra Palzkill and Karoline Augenstein

1 Upscaling of Sustainable Niches: The Dilemma Faced by Sustainable Entrepreneurs

There are many sustainability-oriented organizations in the business field and beyond, that might play an important role in sustainability transitions, including all kinds of organizations, that deviate to a greater or lesser degree from a strictly commercial logic, and primarily focus on creating value based on sustainable business models (e.g. Bidmon & Knab, 2018; Boons & Lüdeke-Freund, 2013; Garud et al., 2011; Schaltegger et al., 2012, 2016). A key question of how to grow, increase their impact and defend their radically new organizational value

A. Palzkill (✉) • K. Augenstein
Center for Transformation Research and Sustainability (Transzent), University of Wuppertal, Wuppertal, Germany
e-mail: palzkill@uni-wuppertal.de; augenstein@uni-wuppertal.de

A. Aagaard et al. (eds.), *Business Models for Sustainability Transitions*,
https://doi.org/10.1007/978-3-030-77580-3_8

structures against dominant commercial structures arises especially for those organizations that seek a more radical and comprehensive approach to sustainability, deviating to a greater degree from traditional market and profit orientation. In principle, they can aim at achieving a balance between adaptation to existing structures, in order to be able to scale within existing economies, and simultaneously building a "resilient business model" (Palzkill-Vorbeck, 2018) to eventually introduce sustainability into the system from within (Wells, 2016: 5). However, in practice this is a delicate balance, where these organizations may feel the risk of compromising their sustainable values, leading many of them to avoid this risk by keeping their sustainability-oriented organizations relatively small (Hockerts & Wüstenhagen, 2010: 487). Against this background, Bidmon and Knab (2018) describe three roles of business models in sustainability transitions: (1) as a stabilizing part of the regime, understood as "industrial recipes" (p. 905) that follow a certain logic of economic activity; (2) as intermediaries between technological niche and regime, by disseminating technology via the market and thus translating it into regime logics; and (3) as non-technological niche innovations, following and introducing a different form of economic activity, that is, a different logic. This understanding is grounded in the basic framework of the multi-level perspective on sustainability transitions (Geels, 2011), which conceptualizes the transition of socio-technical systems, such as the transport or energy system, as a complex and profound process of change across different levels. Sociotechnical systems are characterized by three levels (landscape, regime, niche), each of which is characterized by a different degree of structuration, that is, the degree to which actors are more or less bound by dominant structures. The landscape level describes the broad, external developments and long-term trends that can hardly be influenced by individual actors or organizations. The regime is defined as a set of dominant structures, cultures and practices, with a high degree of structuration, thus reproducing existing structures. Niches, on the other hand, emerge where actors proactively try out new practices that differ from the prevailing rules and routines of the regime; protective spaces are being created for experimentation and for the development of technological innovations as well as alternative practices (Geels & Schot, 2007). A central research focus in transition studies is concerned with the question of how upscaling from sustainable niches can be promoted and eventually contribute to more sustainable regime structures. From the perspective of sustainability-oriented organizations, for example, those following a business model of non-technological niches as described by Bidmon and Knab, this question also presents itself as an organizational (rather than systemic) challenge. How can they persist in a market- and profit-oriented regime while following fundamentally different logics and eventually contributing to a more fundamental change in regime structures towards more sustainable systems? The challenges associated with upscaling efforts of sustainability-oriented organizations can be described as a fundamental dilemma (Augenstein, Bachmann, et al., 2020; Augenstein, Palzkill, et al., 2020). Developing an organization's activities from a radical niche towards a broader mainstream requires (at least to some degree) adapting to those same pressures and structural conditions it seeks to change. Huijben et al. (2016) and Wesseling et al. (2020) describe the possibilities for new business models to scale up successfully within the regime with the help of the concept of business model design space: niches can, for instance, aim to "fit and conform" within the space of given regime structures in order to scale up and become part of the regime. Or they can establish their own alternative values and logics aiming to "stretch and transform" the given space (Huijben et al., 2016: 2). However, both approaches are discussed as promising, especially under conditions of landscape pressure, where niches offer a better and sought-after new solution (Wesseling et al., 2020: 156). In the absence of this kind of landscape pressure, sustainability-oriented entrepreneurs are confronted with a trade-off between the radicality of their activities and opportunities to scale them from the niche (Smith & Raven, 2012: 1030). It is therefore imperative for sustainability-oriented organizations operating at niche level to find a productive way to deal with this dilemma. Considering the complexity of niche-regime dynamics affecting and challenging sustainability-oriented organizations, the user perspective of sustainable business models—or organizational value logics (Laasch, 2018)—will be used in this chapter as a specific approach to analyze the relations and translations between different logics at niche and regime levels and the way that organizations attempt to address and challenge systemic unsustainabilities (Augenstein, Bachmann, et al., 2020; Augenstein, Palzkill, et al., 2020).

2 Organizational Value Logics as Conceptual Link Between Sustainable Niches and Regime Structures

To address this relation and translation between different logics at regime and niche levels, this chapter uses the concept of organizational value logics and a user perspective on it to illustrate how organizations deal with different logics and how the dilemma of upscaling can be approached by them.

2.1 From Business Models to Organizational Value Logics

In order to analyze how organizations face the dilemma of upscaling and have to deal with conflicting logics, we use the concept of "organizational value logics" (Laasch, 2018) based on the concept of sustainable business models (e.g. Boons & Lüdeke-Freund, 2013; Schaltegger et al., 2012, 2016).

Basically, business models can be understood as a cognitive scheme or a narrative about how business works (or should work) (e.g. Casadesus-Masanell & Ricart, 2010; Chesbrough & Rosenbloom, 2002; Zott et al., 2011). Following this understanding, business models are culturally and socially determined, that is, they are shaped by certain institutional logics and are therefore potentially negotiable (Magretta, 2002) and can be described as performative social practices (Laasch, 2018; Perkmann & Spicer, 2010). At the same time, business models not only encompass the more intangible ideas of how business works, but also relate them to the concrete implementation in practice, in terms of value creation, value exchange and value capture (Demil & Lecocq, 2015; Doganova & Eyquem, 2009), leading to the respective positive or negative sustainability impacts. Research on sustainable business models explicitly integrates this dimension of impact, describing how different business models can contribute to generating systemic changes in production and consumption patterns (e.g. Lüdeke-Freund et al., 2018; Boons & Lüdeke-Freund, 2013; Schaltegger et al., 2016). And although mostly describing changing production and consumption patterns, business models are often analyzed from the production side (Bocken et al., 2014; Viciunaite & Alfnes, 2020). However, consumption patterns in particular are of course not determined solely by the organization: (because) which value proposition is successful is of course only determined in exchange with stakeholders and users.

Another fundamental shortcoming of business models in this context is discussed by Laasch, pointing out that the "value logic of business models is a purely commercial one" (Laasch, 2018: 158).

Hence, business models cannot conceptually capture radically different motivations and logics followed by organizations operating in niches. Thus, it is suggested here that understanding the role of business models in sustainability transitions can benefit from a broader perspective, as introduced in the concept of organizational value logics, based on Laasch (2018) and Randles and Laasch (2016) and the concept of institutional logics (Thornton et al., 2012). By broadening the debate in this way, organizations that can be described as sustainability-oriented entrepreneurs but fall outside narrower definitions of business organizations because they follow non-commercial logics can be examined in more adequate ways.

A broad variety of institutional logics can be observed guiding sustainability-oriented organizations (or organizations in general). Institutional logics are defined as "the socially constructed, historical patterns of material practices, assumptions, values, beliefs, and rules by which individuals produce and reproduce their material subsistence, organize time and space, and provide meaning to their social reality" (Thornton & Ocasio, 1999: 804). They are therefore socially accepted basic principles that help actors to interpret situations appropriately and to act successfully in a given system. They provide orientation that usually seems self-evident, so that they are often implemented without being questioned or even unconsciously. Institutional logics have a comprehensive effect and guide thinking (as basic assumptions and beliefs), feeling (as values and emotional occupation) and physical sensory experience (as practices and artefacts that manifest presumptions, values, etc.) in organizations (e.g. Besharov & Smith, 2014; Pache & Santos, 2013). Based on the duality of structure and agency (Giddens, 1984), the concept of institutional logics offers an analytical perspective on identifying the way that the behavior of different actors is grounded in underlying structures, on relating the structure and agency dimensions and tracing change in structuration processes (Thornton et al., 2012). The degree of structuration, that is, the degree to which agency is bound to dominant structures, is expressed by the strength of specific institutional logics (Fuenfschilling & Truffer, 2014), similar to how regime and niche levels are conceptualized in the MLP. In principle, actors and organizations can be grouped according to their roles in specific societal subsystems characterized by the respective institutional logics, for example, civil society initiatives following a social welfare or community-oriented logic and business actors following a commercial or market logic. In reality, these categorizations are rarely this clear-cut and unambiguous. Actors as well as organizations often find themselves struggling with multiple collective identities and sometimes conflicting logics influencing their behavior (Laasch, 2018; Thornton & Ocasio, 2008: 111). A growing body of literature explores the conflicting logics within social enterprises (e.g. Battilana & Dorado, 2010; Maibom & Smith, 2016; Mars & Lounsbury, 2009; Pache & Santos, 2013), analyzing different ways of balancing environmental, social and commercial logics.

The concept of organizational value logics thus represents a "full range and variety of organization types" (Randles & Laasch, 2016: 53) that combine different logics in their value logics. It is therefore particularly suitable for analyzing the more "radical" niche organizations, which do not primarily follow a commercial logic and explore alternative and innovative ways of creating value. This kind of organization in particular often faces an upscaling dilemma when confronted with a commercial logic in conflict with its own particular logic of creating value in alternative ways.

Broadening the concept of sustainable business models in this way offers the possibility to describe the duality of structure and agency (Giddens, 1984) and can be linked to an institutional logics perspective (Laasch, 2018)—thus including a more explicit reflection on the relation between an organization's activity and its sustainability-oriented impact. From an organizational perspective, organizational value logics thus describe the rules to which organizations refer in their actions and therefore offer a more systemic view of the organization in terms of its systemic concepts, the institutional logics it draws upon and potentially changes over time.

From an upscaling perspective, it is imperative to better understand what happens when value logics that do not operate according to commercial logics but follow other, alternative logics are confronted with the dominant logic of the market and thus have to combine or balance conflicting logics (e.g. Besharov & Smith, 2014; Pache & Santos, 2013).

2.2 User Perspective of Organizational Value Logics for a Better Understanding of Upscaling

In order to better understand the opportunities for organizations in such an upscaling situation, the user perspective is included here.

A company itself may be able to determine how value is created, but how and which value proposition is offered cannot be understood solely as a one-sided process on the part of the organization to a certain group of customers or recipients, but rather as a two-way process in which the various stakeholders create new realities through narratives and communication (Zerfaß, 2010: 141). And yet, sustainable business models are viewed particularly from the perspective of the production system (Bocken et al., 2014; Viciunaite & Alfnes, 2020). Of course, attention is also paid to the consumer system, but then it is primarily about how companies can use their influence to drive sustainable consumption (see, e.g. Boons & Lüdeke-Freund, 2013; Viciunaite & Alfnes, 2020) and less about how a consumer and user perspective can contribute to the further development of the business model. To adopt this perspective, it is rather necessary to adopt an "outside-in perspective" (Muff & Dyllick, 2014: 3). With the help of this perspective, Dyllick and Muff (2014) describe a "true business sustainability" (Muff & Dyllick, 2014: 3), arguing that the requirements for sustainable development of organizations can only to a limited extent be derived from their own internal logic (inside-out-perspective), but that it is actually the sustainability challenges themselves that provide the frame of reference for defining organizations (outside-in-perspective).

The starting point of their work is that although many companies are concerned with and implement sustainability from within their business logic, these efforts hardly contribute in a relevant way to a more sustainable development (Dyllick & Muff, 2016: 2). For sustainable organizations, which want to overcome this problem, it is important that the view of the relationship between business and sustainability is reversed to an outside-in-perspective: "True sustainability demands a radically different perspective. True business sustainability reverses the traditional inside-out logic and moves to an outside-in logic, using sustainability challenges as the starting point to define possible contributions by business that also make business sense" (Muff & Dyllick, 2014: 3). Such an outside-in-perspective focuses on the most pressing sustainability challenges and user needs and then analyzes how companies can help solving them with their specific resources and competences (Dyllick & Muff, 2016: 12). Such a perspective does not attempt to manage sustainable consumer behavior through business model strategies, but rather to shape one's own organization sustainably through an orientation outward, towards social problems and thus also to consumer needs (and sustainable value creation based on these).

It thus takes up the original idea of the "job to be done" business models (Johnson, 2010; Johnson et al., 2007), which cannot be addressed without the user perspective and, in the case of sustainable business models, without the perspective of the sustainability challenges. With the help and inclusion of the user perspective, the view on the complex transition dynamics and challenges will be broadened, and the user perspective will be discussed in relation to the upscaling challenge.

3 The Users' Perspective on the Organizational Value Logic of Utopiastadt

To illustrate a more user-oriented approach to investigating alternative organizational value logics emerging in niches, a case study is presented in the following. The example of a civil society initiative (Utopiastadt) in Wuppertal, Germany, is used to illustrate how an entrepreneurial, sustainability-oriented organization following a non-commercial logic of value creation approaches the dilemma of upscaling. In this exploratory case study, we used a user-focused approach to analyze what the users' expectations of the organization are, what value propositions an organization like Utopiastadt actually offers from the user's point of view and which logics it addresses and Utopiastadt is confronted with.

3.1 The Case of Utopiastadt

The initiative Utopiastadt[1] (translates to "Utopia City") is a civil society initiative that focuses on sustainable urban development; it is engaged in various cultural and social entrepreneurial activities in its surrounding neighborhood in the German city of Wuppertal. Since 2011, Utopiastadt's main activity has been the restoration of an old railway station building and developing it into a cultural center. Over the past years, cultural events, particularly sustainability-oriented activities, ranging from food-sharing, urban gardening, bike rental and repair to open workshops, co-working and a hacker space have been established. Recently, Utopiastadt has acquired a brownfield site adjacent to the old railway station and is in the process of developing it as a livable urban space, shielding it from gentrification processes and aiming to increase quality of life in the city and its particular neighborhood. Based on the work of Pache and Santos (2013), who identified the characteristics of organizations that operate according to social welfare logics and those that operate according to commercial logics, Utopiastadt's organizational value logic primarily

[1] https://clownfisch.eu/

follows the logic of a social welfare organization: the main purpose is to provide products or services to meet local social needs (Pache & Santos, 2013: 980). Utopiastadt can be described along these lines; it pursues a broad social, cultural and sustainability-oriented mission; and it is hardly possible to derive a single value proposition—especially not a commercial one (Palzkill et al., 2015: 72f). The self-determined organizational value logic of Utopiastadt can be described as follows: its value proposition is to contribute to sustainable urban development, to create livable urban space in cooperation with citizens and other organizations active in this field, providing space for a wide range of projects and ideas (value creation), in order to address local social needs. Utopiastadt creates this value as a non-profit association that has founded its own non-profit limited company and follows a more or less democratic control provided by the joint contribution of the active utopians (value capture). While Utopiastadt has so far hardly followed a commercial logic, more recent developments, such as the acquisition of the brownfield site, have confronted the organization with the need to develop its activities in such a way that they can also be sustained economically. Thus, on the one hand, Utopiastadt aims to be a "permanent social congress with ambition and impact"[2] which can be interpreted in terms of a social welfare logic (as described by Pache & Santos, 2013: 980); on the other hand, there is the need to ensure a stable financial basis for its activities, which makes an orientation towards a commercial logic necessary. In order to gain insights into the user perspective of the different expectations and the underlying logics, the following questions were addressed as part of a transdisciplinary research project in the real-world lab Wuppertal (Schneidewind et al., 2018), in which researchers and members of Utopiastadt jointly attempted to address the question, how Utopiastadt could realize its community-oriented vision while also dealing with economic pressures and commercial logics in its role as property owner and developer? To approach this question in a real-world lab setting, an intervention was conducted: on the grounds of the brownfield site, there had already been a number of activities and projects carried out in old shipping containers (e.g. bike rental and repair), and some food trucks were offering

[2] https://clownfisch.eu/utopiastadt/

gastronomic services. The idea for the intervention was to provide two old shipping containers and use them for short-term experimental uses to test different concepts for reviving the space. An open call for participation was communicated through various channels, offering anyone with a business, social, cultural, artistic or other ideas for the brownfield site the opportunity to use one of the containers for a period of up to eight weeks. The whole intervention ran from June to October 2019, and the containers were used by a variety of actors, ranging from local businesses, artists, start-ups, social entrepreneurs and a local politician. The aim was to find a balance between activities following a social welfare logic and dealing with demands following commercial logics. The perceptions of Utopiastadt's role and positioning in this endeavor and alternative and old logics introduced by participants of the container experiments were traced through interviews with participating actors and visitors of the site and evaluated using qualitative content analysis (Mayring, 2015).

The data for this exemplary case study in Wuppertal was thus collected via semi-structured interviews with participants of the container intervention and visitors of the site. In total, 39 interviews were conducted, with 9 container users being interviewed at the beginning and end of their period of use and 21 randomly selected visitors of the site (see Table 1).

The interviews provided insights into the different expectations of the value proposition that make Utopiastadt interesting for its users, the different logics that shape the value logic of Utopiastadt, the functions and conflicts attributed to Utopiastadt and the (conflicting) logics perceived by different actors.

Table 1 Interviews

Interviews 1–9	Container users at the beginning of their period of use
Interviews 10–18	Container users at the end of their period of use
Interviews 19–39	Visitors of the site

3.2 Results: Narratives Reflecting the Conflicting Logics Faced by Utopiastadt

This section presents results from the analyzed interviews conducted with participants of the container experiment and visitors to the Utopiastadt site. In order to better understand how different and partly contradictory logics influence Utopiastadt as an organization and at the same time shape Utopiastadt's activities, the user perspective representing the expectations of Utopiastadt offers relevant insights. This approach does not focus on the value proposition produced unilaterally by the organization itself but maps the joint development of it with the help of those who are involved in or addressed by the organization's activities.

The first step was to survey users' expectations of Utopiastadt, focusing on the question of what functions or services the Utopiastadt site offers users and what specific local social needs are addressed by Utopiastadt. The aim was to understand how the value of Utopiastadt is interpreted by its users and to derive from this the organizational value logics Utopiastadt perceives to follow and to balance out.

The coding and categorization of the material resulted in seven overarching categories that describe the specific values Utopiastadt offers its users:

1. a creative and free space, a "nucleus, *where things are simply tried out*" *(Interview 21)*,
2. a place to meet people that is open for everyone and contributes to social integration: "The atmosphere is just great. People meet here. I have already made many friends here" *(Interview 17)*,
3. a place to go out and enjoy gastronomic offers, as "the only place here in the area where you can meet people in public, have a drink, chill out together and from time to time there's music and a concert" *(Interview 25)*,
4. a central location for networking among artists, the cultural scene and local sustainability initiatives, a place "where this is centered somehow (…) and that's just very good, because you know, you come here and there is everything somehow, you don't have to search" *(Interview 21)*,

5. a place with high quality of stay without the need to engage in consumption activities (bringing your own food and drinks, no shops, no entrance fees) "where you can go and sit in a sun lounger without having to buy anything" *(Interview 39)*,
6. a place of retreat and rest for residents, "an oasis, in the positive sense of the word, to recharge, with the energy here" *(Interview 3)*,
7. a recreational area that attracts tourists and contributes to improving the city's overall image: "whenever you bring people here, they say, oooh Wuppertal is actually quite cool" *(Interview 33)*.

This brief overview shows that the values generated by Utopiastadt meet different local social needs. Overall, it can be said that Utopiastadt provides a specific type of "livable public space" that differs from the more consumption-oriented city center as well as the primarily nature- or entertainment-oriented recreational areas, such as parks or playgrounds. It is thus understood as a place that fulfills a public and particularly social function where people with different backgrounds meet, where people can engage in cultural or sustainability-oriented activities; it is "a possibility-creating space that somehow tries to fill a gap" *(Interview 20)*, "...but not city. If I want city, then I'll go down here" *(Interview 21)*.

These interpretations fit well with the way that Utopiastadt operates and finances its activities. The acquisition of the brownfield site can be viewed as a strategy to protect this space from traditional investment and gentrification by making it the private property of Utopiastadt. At the same time, it is then developed as a quasi-public space, oriented towards the well-being of the community and developed in cooperation with local partners. Accordingly, Utopiastadt finances its activities through a mix of public subsidies and volunteer work as well as through income generated from operating a gastronomic service on site. What can be observed here is a combination of different users' expectations of Utopiastadt and of different logics: the benefit of (3) providing a place to go out and enjoy gastronomic offers is very compatible with a commercial logic of selling goods and services to generate a surplus. At the same time, Utopiastadt is valued as a place (5) that is precisely not consumption-oriented but has a high quality of stay without the need to engage in consumption activities. These different expectations that shape the organizational value logic of Utopiastadt make the dilemma visible: commercial and social welfare logics have to be combined, which is at least a delicate balance or may even result in incompatible needs. While in some interviews it was emphasized that the quality of this place lies precisely in its beautiful ambience with gastronomic offers, many others visit the place mainly because it is perceived as free of consumption constraints: "when she heard the word 'money', there was a lady who just turned on her heel and left" *(Interview 11)*. In order to deal with this dilemma and contradictions, Utopiastadt relies on the help of users to balance social welfare and commercial logics in a hybrid logic of values. What makes their approach particularly innovative is the focus on collaboration and experimentation, as exemplified by the container intervention, where an open search process is used to experiment with ideas that might work and collaboratively develop the site, truly taking an outside-in-perspective.

Focusing on the experimental form of collaboration, the second step of the analysis was to examine how the participants of the container experiment perceive and deal with these hybrid value logics of Utopiastadt. The participants included businesses, political and cultural actors, and actors from civil society. Especially the participating local companies, which followed more of a commercial logic, understood the place as an alternative location and as a kind of alternative marketplace where they could sell their products outside of their normal business context, where they could "get out of the fixed store for a change; broaden their spectrum of both customers and range of economic activities" *(Interview 2)*. What all participants agreed on and what motivated them to participate was that the time in the container offered them an opportunity to experiment outside their usual circumstances. The experimental nature of the project proved to be particularly attractive because the project was associated with minimal costs and a time limit with low risks: "in such a tough business environment (…) so if I wanted to do this somewhere in the city center and had to go to a bank, borrow the money and somehow (…) I wouldn't feel like it" *(Interview 4)*. Especially in retrospect, most participants emphasized that participating in this experiment was useful for them to reflect on their goals and their normal way of doing things and doing business. Thus, local entrepreneurs found that the time spent in the container was a valuable experience, even if the experiment was rarely an economic success for them: "That's what inspired us to experiment here. Well, we wouldn't have done it in our (...) environment, because that's natural there, we would have thought much more economically" *(Interview 17)*.

The container users, who on the one hand are users of Utopiastadt and at the same time also have commercial concerns, confirmed that there were tensions emerging, but that these were not perceived as insoluble conflicts: "Of course you couldn't work there now as well as I can work here now. And of course it was a double burden, because I still had to work here. But basically I think it was a cool time. And in terms of turnover, yes, you can't measure it" *(Interview 11)*.

Summing up, the expectations of the users of Utopiastadt and of the containers on the brownfield side and the underlying value logics for Utopiastadt can be understood as a balancing act supported by a user perspective, experimental and collaborative way of doing things. In terms of translating and reinterpreting conflicting logics, this approach seems to prove useful when it comes to reflecting structural framework conditions and finding alternative approaches.

4 Discussion and Further Research on Organizational Value Logics in Sustainability Transitions

This chapter started with the question how sustainability-oriented organizations can develop and defend alternative organizational value logics against dominant logics of the regime, for example, in terms of commercial logic.

From a transitions perspective, this question may present a dilemma situation for sustainable entrepreneurs: many niche actors tend to keep their organizations small in order not to risk compromising their sustainable values (Hockerts & Wüstenhagen, 2010: 487). This dilemma of upscaling is faced by many organizations that follow an alternative organizational value logic: they are confronted with dominant market structures, commercial logics and current industrial recipes, and in order to be able to grow they need to adapt to some degree.

On the other hand, there are the expectations of the users, which can also be satisfied by a commercial logic, but often are not or are opposed to it.

There is an enormous challenge in dealing with this dilemma, which cannot be solved with economical, simple management and planning approaches, but requires at least an extension of the user perspective. Based on the case study of the civil society initiative Utopiastadt, these questions were illustrated with a practical example. Following a hybrid model that balances different expectations and underlying logics and approaching this as a collaborative and experimental process, Utopiastadt may be viewed as an "institutional entrepreneur" (e.g. DiMaggio, 1988), using its resources in such a way that it can further develop its activities without simply adapting to market or other structural constraints.

It achieves this by truly aligning its value proposition with the needs of its users and adopting an outside-in-perspective. In this way, it is able to experimentally develop its own organizational value logic together with the users, so that they can not only formulate expectations of the organization but also help to further develop the organizational value logic.

With the help of the organizational value logic perspective adopted here, it can be illuminated how sustainable entrepreneurs can proceed in cooperation with their users. And thus, with their help, challenge non-sustainable structures in order to maintain their specific value logics or to be able to develop them together with the customers in the first place.

The example of Utopiastadt was used to illustrate what hybrid organizational value logics might look like and what diverse expectations users have of the value proposition of radical niches like Utopiastadt.

An organizational value logic approach that explicitly includes a user perspective to describe the logics of organizations can be helpful in avoiding the dichotomy between established and niche actors. Instead, it focuses on the balancing act that sustainable entrepreneurs perform in dealing with conflicting logics. While this does not solve the dilemma of upscaling, it can generate options for action under these conditions. It can help to understand how certain organizations can establish themselves in the niche, how they understand and position themselves vis-à-vis the regime, how they develop and implement their organizational value logic and where there might be space for change and potential impact (precisely because the users are behind it).

References

Augenstein, K., Bachmann, B., Egermann, M., Hermelingmeier, V., Hilger, A., Jaeger-Erben, M., Kessler, A., Lam, D. P. M., Palzkill, A., Suski, P., & von Wirth, T. (2020). From niche to mainstream: The dilemmas of scaling up sustainable alternatives. *GAIA – Ecological Perspectives for Science and Society, 29*(3), 143–147. https://doi.org/10.14512/gaia.29.3.3

Augenstein, K., Palzkill, A., Hermelingmeier, V., Bachmann, B., Kessler, A., & Suski, P. (2020). The dilemma of upscaling. *Workingpaper, 2*.

Battilana, J., & Dorado, S. (2010). Building sustainable hybrid organizations: The case of commercial microfinance organizations. *Academy of Management Journal, 53*(6), 1419–1440. https://doi.org/10.5465/amj.2010.57318391

Besharov, M. L., & Smith, W. K. (2014). Multiple institutional logics in organizations: Explaining their varied nature and implications. *Academy of Management Review, 39*(3), 364–381. https://doi.org/10.5465/amr.2011.0431

Bidmon, C. M., & Knab, S. F. (2018). The three roles of business models in societal transitions: New linkages between business model and transition research. *Journal of Cleaner Production, 178*, 903–916. https://doi.org/10.1016/j.jclepro.2017.12.198

Bocken, N. M. P., Short, S. W., Rana, P., & Evans, S. (2014). A literature and practice review to develop sustainable business model archetypes. *Journal of Cleaner Production, 65*, 42–56. https://doi.org/10.1016/j.jclepro.2013.11.039

Boons, F., & Lüdeke-Freund, F. (2013). Business models for sustainable innovation: State-of-the-art and steps towards a research agenda. *Journal of Cleaner Production, 45*, 9–19. https://doi.org/10.1016/j.jclepro.2012.07.007

Casadesus-Masanell, R., & Ricart, J. (2010). From strategy to business models and onto tactics. *Long Range Planning, 43*, 195–215. https://doi.org/10.1016/j.lrp.2010.01.004

Chesbrough, H., & Rosenbloom, R. (2002). The role of the business model in capturing value from innovation: Evidence from Xerox Corporation's technology spin-off companies. *Industrial and Corporate Change, 11*. https://doi.org/10.1093/icc/11.3.529

Demil, B., & Lecocq, X. (2015). Crafting an innovative business model in an established company: The role of artifacts. *Advances in Strategic Management, 33*, 31–58. https://doi.org/10.1108/S0742-332220150000033003

Doganova, L., & Eyquem, M. (2009). What do business models do? Innovation devices in technology entrepreneurship. *Research Policy, 38*, 1559–1570. https://doi.org/10.1016/j.respol.2009.08.002

DiMaggio, P. J. (1988). Interest and agency in institutional theory. In Zucker, L. (Ed.), *Institutional Patterns and Culture*, (pp. 3–22). Cambridge, MA: Ballinger.

Dyllick, T., & Muff, K. (2014). *The Business Sustainability Typology*. https://doi.org/10.2139/ssrn.2368735

Dyllick, T., & Muff, K. (2016). Clarifying the meaning of sustainable business: Introducing a typology from business-as-usual to true business sustainability. *Organization & Environment, 29*(2), 156–174. https://doi.org/10.1177/1086026615575176

Fuenfschilling, L., & Truffer, B. (2014). The structuration of socio-technical regimes—Conceptual foundations from institutional theory. *Research Policy, 43*(4), 772–791. https://doi.org/10.1016/j.respol.2013.10.010

Garud, R., Dunbar, R. L. M., & Bartel, C. A. (2011). Dealing with unusual experiences: A narrative perspective on organizational learning. *Organization Science, 22*(3), 587–601. https://doi.org/10.1287/orsc.1100.0536

Geels, F. W. (2011). The multi-level perspective on sustainability transitions: Responses to seven criticisms. *Environmental Innovation and Societal Transitions, 1*(1), 24–40. https://doi.org/10.1016/j.eist.2011.02.002

Geels, F. W., & Schot, J. (2007). Typology of sociotechnical transition pathways. *Research Policy, 36*(3), 399–417. https://doi.org/10.1016/j.respol.2007.01.003

Giddens, A. (1984). *The constitution of society. Outline of the theory of structuration.* University of California Press.

Hockerts, K., & Wüstenhagen, R. (2010). Greening goliaths versus emerging Davids—Theorizing about the role of incumbents and new entrants in sustainable entrepreneurship. *Journal of Business Venturing, 25*(5), 481–492. https://doi.org/10.1016/j.jbusvent.2009.07.005

Huijben, J. C. C. M., Verbong, G. P. J., & Podoynitsyna, K. S. (2016). Mainstreaming solar: Stretching the regulatory regime through business model innovation. *Environmental Innovation and Societal Transitions, 20*, 1–15. https://doi.org/10.1016/j.eist.2015.12.002

Johnson, M. W. (2010). *Seizing the white space: Business model innovation for growth and renewal.* Harvard Business Press.

Johnson, G., Langley, A., Melin, L., & Whittington, R. (2007). *Strategy as practice: Research directions and resources.* Cambridge University Press. http://public.eblib.com/choice/publicfullrecord.aspx?p=802933

Laasch, O. (2018). Beyond the purely commercial business model: Organizational value logics and the heterogeneity of sustainability business models. *Long Range Planning, 51*(1), 158–183. https://doi.org/10.1016/j.lrp.2017.09.002

Lüdeke-Freund, F., Carroux, S., Joyce, A., Massa, L., & Breuer, H. (2018). The Sustainable Business Model Pattern Taxonomy—45 Patterns to Support Sustainability-Oriented Business Model Innovation. *Sustainable Production and Consumption, 15*, 145–162.

Magretta, J. (2002). Why business models matter. *Harvard Business Review, 80*, 86–92.

Maibom, C., & Smith, P. (2016). Symbiosis across institutional logics in a social enterprise. *Social Enterprise Journal, 12*(3), 260–280. https://doi.org/10.1108/SEJ-02-2016-0002

Mars, M. M., & Lounsbury, M. (2009). Raging against or with the private marketplace?: Logic hybridity and eco-entrepreneurship. *Journal of Management Inquiry, 18*(1), 4–13. https://doi.org/10.1177/1056492608328234

Mayring, P. (2015). *Qualitative Inhaltsanalyse: Grundlagen und Techniken* (12., überarbeitete Aufl.). Beltz Verlag.

Muff, K., & Dyllick, T. L. (2014). An organizational roadmap of business sustainability. *SSRN Electronic Journal*. https://doi.org/10.2139/ssrn.2442211

Pache, A.-C., Santos, F. (2013). Embedded in hybrid contexts: How individuals in organizations respond to competing institutional logics. In *Institutional logics in action*. Emerald.

Palzkill, A., Wanner, M., & Markscheffel, F. (2015). Suffizienz als Geschäftsmodell: Die Bedeutung von Social-Entrepreneurship-Initiativen am Beispiel von Utopiastadt Wuppertal. *uwf UmweltWirtschaftsForum, 23*(1–2), 69–76. https://doi.org/10.1007/s00550-015-0353-8

Palzkill-Vorbeck, A. (2018). *Geschäftsmodell-Resilienz: Bezugsrahmen für das strategische Verständnis von Unternehmen in gesellschaftlichen Umbruchprozessen*. Springer Gabler.

Perkmann, M., & Spicer, A. (2010). What are business models? Developing a theory of performative representations. *Research in the Sociology of Organizations, 29*. https://doi.org/10.1108/S0733-558X(2010)0000029020

Randles, S., & Laasch, O. (2016). Theorising the normative business model. *Organization & Environment, 29*(1), 1–21. https://doi.org/10.1177/1086026615592934

Schaltegger, S., Freund, F. L., & Hansen, E. G. (2012). Business cases for sustainability: The role of business model innovation for corporate sustainability. *International Journal of Innovation and Sustainable Development, 6*(2), 95. https://doi.org/10.1504/IJISD.2012.046944

Schaltegger, S., Hansen, E. G., & Lu deke-Freund, F. (2016). Business models for sustainability: Origins, present research, and future avenues. *Organization & Environment, 29*(1), 3–10. https://doi.org/10.1177/1086026615599806

Schneidewind, U., Augenstein, K., Stelzer, F., & Wanner, M. (2018). Structure matters: Real-world laboratories as a new type of large-scale research infrastructure: A framework inspired by Giddens' structuration theory. *GAIA – Ecological Perspectives for Science and Society, 27*(1), 12–17. https://doi.org/10.14512/gaia.27.S1.5

Smith, A., & Raven, R. (2012). What is protective space? Reconsidering niches in transitions to sustainability. *Research Policy, 41*(6), 1025–1036. https://doi.org/10.1016/j.respol.2011.12.012

Thornton, P. H., & Ocasio, W. (1999). Institutional logics and the historical contingency of power in organizations: Executive succession in the higher education publishing industry, 1958–1990. *American Journal of Sociology, 105*(3), 801–843. https://doi.org/10.1086/210361

Thornton, P. H., & Ocasio, W. (2008). Institutional logics. In *The SAGE handbook of organizational institutionalism* (pp. 99–128). SAGE Publications Ltd. https://doi.org/10.4135/9781849200387.n4

Thornton, P. H., Ocasio, W., & Lounsbury, M. (2012). *The institutional logics perspective: A new approach to culture, structure, and process.* Oxford University Press.

Viciunaite, V., & Alfnes, F. (2020). Informing sustainable business models with a consumer preference perspective. *Journal of Cleaner Production, 242*, 118417. https://doi.org/10.1016/j.jclepro.2019.118417

Wells, P. (2016). Economies of Scale Versus Small Is Beautiful: A Business Model Approach Based on Architecture, Principles and Components in the Beer Industry. *Organization & Environment, 29*(1), 36–52.

Wesseling, J. H., Bidmon, C., & Bohnsack, R. (2020). Business model design spaces in socio-technical transitions: The case of electric driving in the Netherlands. *Technological Forecasting and Social Change, 154*, 119950. https://doi.org/10.1016/j.techfore.2020.119950

Zerfaß, A. (2010). *Unternehmensführung und Öffentlichkeitsarbeit: Grundlegung einer Theorie der Unternehmenskommunikation und Public Relations* (3., aktualisierte Aufl.). VS, Verl. für Sozialwiss.

Zott, C., Amit, R., & Massa, L. (2011). The business model: Recent developments and future research. *Journal of Management, 37*(4), 1019–1042. https://doi.org/10.1177/0149206311406265

Part III

Being the Change: Transformative and Transformed Business Models in Selected Industries

IoT-Driven Reuse Business Models: The Case of Salesianer Textile Rental Services

Andres Alcayaga, Hanna Geyerlechner, and Erik G. Hansen

1 Introduction

The Industrial Revolution paved the way for a new mindset towards the concept of product lifetime. More product categories became subject to single use and were manufactured in ever-larger quantities to reduce production costs. Products were quickly discarded and, therefore, became disposables. This change in mentality has resulted in a throwaway economy and has generated severe environmental pollution (Lieder & Rashid, 2016). In such a linear economy, most products are lost to landfill, incinerated, or end up in downcycling schemes (e.g., House of Commons, 2019; Sanders et al., 2019).

A. Alcayaga (✉) • E. G. Hansen
Johannes Kepler University Linz (JKU), Linz, Austria
e-mail: andres.alcayaga@jku.at; erik.hansen@jku.at

H. Geyerlechner
Salesianer Miettex GmbH, Vienna, Austria
e-mail: h.geyerlechner@salesianer.com

A. Aagaard et al. (eds.), *Business Models for Sustainability Transitions*,
https://doi.org/10.1007/978-3-030-77580-3_9

In order to replace the prevalent linear economy, scholars, practitioners, and policymakers have increasingly embraced the concept of the *Circular Economy* (EMF, 2015; Kirchherr et al., 2017; Murray et al., 2017). In a circular economy (CE), products, in principle, are kept at their highest value during their entire lifetime, and materials are reused after end of life, allowing for a restorative system to thrive (Morseletto, 2020; Stahel, 2016). While both biological and technical cycles are covered by the CE, here we focus only on the technical cycles of maintenance, repair, reuse, refurbishing, and recycling (Hansen & Revellio, 2020). For instance, a circular textile industry would create safe materials and durable products, scale up service business models (SBMs), and increase product longevity and utilisation through reuse, repair, and recycling (EMF, 2017)—a system sometimes referred to as a "performance economy" (Stahel, 2010).

The transition to such a service-oriented economy requires organisations to invest in innovation to develop new service-oriented offerings (Hansen & Revellio, 2020) and drive changes in the broader socio-technical system (Geels, 2004; Markard, 2011). Firms with an SBM could alter the network of interdependent actors, technologies, business practices, cultural meanings, and policies around them. For example, specific business practices related to SBMs, such as organising the take-back of products, require a different relationship with the customer (Heyes et al., 2018). However, plenty of technical, organisational, and inter-organisational barriers exist, hindering the adoption of SBMs and the transition towards a CE. These barriers refer to missing collaboration, business model alignment, and cross-value chain information exchange (Hansen & Schmitt, 2021).

The use of digital technologies holds great potential to overcome such barriers and successfully implement circular SBMs (Hansen et al., 2020). Smart products connected through the Internet of Things (IoT) could facilitate closed-loop business processes, enabling firms to streamline a service architecture (EMF, 2016). Technologies could also enable longer lifetimes through product traceability and data sharing across the supply chain. For example, firms may tag textiles with Radio Frequency Identification (RFID) chips to improve quality testing and coordination with suppliers, thus fostering product longevity (Cooper et al., 2017). In addition, an IoT-enabled circular offer may alter the interactions of the firm with external entities. Understanding the effects of these interactions may reveal insights about broader socio-technical transitions. For example, a data-driven circular business model may transform the firm into a digital change-maker in the industry while motivating wider sustainability transformations for both the economy and society.

The shift towards services and the use of digital technologies to enable a CE could be analysed using the concept of the business model. The business model is understood as a new unit of analysis and a firm-centric, yet boundary-spanning, system (Zott et al., 2011). Research focused on the business model could offer insights into the effects of business activities across the organisational boundaries (e.g., Brehmer et al., 2018). However, there is a lack of empirical evidence of how the vision of a CE enabled by smart products and related service business models can become a reality (Alcayaga et al., 2019; Nobre & Tavares, 2017; Pagoropoulos et al., 2017). Therefore, the purpose of this research is to explore how practitioners are adopting smart products and related infrastructures to optimise use-oriented SBMs (Tukker, 2004) in the context of a reuse system.

With this objective in mind, we address the following overarching research question: *How do smart products and related infrastructures enable reuse service business models in the context of fast-cycling goods* (i.e., *textiles*)? This question is operationalised using the following sub-questions:

(a) *How do smart products enable reuse services?*
(b) *How can smart products enable product longevity through maintenance and repair?*
(c) *How can real-time life cycle data inform product procurement and related design?*

2 Literature Background

2.1 Circular Economy

The CE is understood as a cyclical closed-loop system (Murray et al., 2017) and has been proposed as an approach to replace our current "take-make-waste" system of production and consumption (EMF, 2013). The CE could be a solution for firms to engage in environmental protection and reduce the negative impacts of business operations (Ghisellini et al., 2016). Specifically, improving product longevity could considerably reduce waste while increasing the positive environmental impacts of the firm (Tietze & Hansen, 2016).

Blomsma and Brennan (2017) have framed the CE as an umbrella concept (Hirsch & Levin, 1999) that groups several circular strategies, that is, maintenance, repair, reuse, upgrade, remanufacturing, and recycling, among others. The adoption of circular strategies could transform the economy and lead to more sustainable practices and outcomes.

While sustainability improvements in the textile industry can be reached by switching to more circular (i.e., recycled) or sustainable (e.g., organic) fibres in product design (Hansen & Schaltegger, 2013), our main interest here lies in the servitisation of a given product design. In particular, reusing products could offer savings in energy and materials which would be otherwise required for the production of new goods (Cooper & Gutowski, 2017). For example, textile reuse in the healthcare industry has reported significant cost savings, reductions of waste, and a minimisation of the health consequences that residents near landfills and waste incinerators may experience (Zins, 2011). In addition, textile reuse could mitigate certain rebound effects by reducing the amount of resources needed by the customer. This could be achieved, for instance, by increasing the operational efficiency of the laundry cycle, increasing longevity due to reduced disposal of single-use textiles, or intensifying product usage due to reuse and sharing. However, rebound effects may still occur outside the domain of the service provider and can be difficult to mitigate (Kjaer et al., 2018).

2.2 The Performance Economy

It has been generally understood that improving the product life cycle requires product-service systems (Tukker, 2004, 2015) and, relatedly, new service business models (Hansen et al., 2009). In this respect, SBMs may allow firms to focus on maximising value over long periods of time, what Stahel (2010) refers to as a "performance economy". By internalising the costs of risks and waste, firms may integrate resilience, sufficiency, and redundancy into their practices (Stahel, 2010). Specifically, the concept of redundancy applied to business activities means having spare parts in order to keep the economic value of products for as long as possible. Redundancy also applies to life cycle management at end of life. Minimising disposals and fostering recycling to reuse materials entails the idea of redundancy (Stahel, 2016, 2019).

Furthermore, SBMs offer firms a strategic position of proximity to and more intense relationships with their customers. This position allows firms to influence the way products are used and circulated (Heyes et al., 2018). It also motivates firms to seek process and practice alignment between their suppliers and customers, thus working towards a circular infrastructure (Pedersen & Clausen, 2018).

2.3 Transitioning Towards a Service-Oriented CE

Sustainability transitions, including those targeted at a circular economy, are understood as long-term, multi-dimensional, and fundamental shifts of established *socio-technical systems* to more sustainable modes of production and consumption (Markard et al., 2012). They require the involvement of a broad range of stakeholders, business practices, cultural meanings, infrastructures, and policy environments, among others. Transitions are long-term processes that involve the development of multiple pathways for radical change. These pathways may contest established business models and bring uncertainty and disagreement among diverse stakeholders.

Successful transitions are driven by the introduction of technological and non-technological innovation from entrepreneurial ventures and pioneering incumbents, which ultimately drive changes in the broader socio-technical system (Geels, 2004; Markard, 2011). In the context of a CE, this requires the introduction and diffusion of service-oriented value propositions and offerings (Hansen & Revellio, 2020). Changes to the organisational value proposition (in concert with changes to other aspects of the business model) should be made to deliberately create social and ecological value in the long term and depart from the focus on solely financial value appropriation based on short-lived goods (Schaltegger et al., 2016). An alternative to traditional business models with a transactional approach are SBMs. These business models may offer a higher degree of interaction within the socio-technical system due to closer customer relationships and an emphasis on product lifetime optimisation (Stahel, 2010). Accordingly, the enhanced boundary-spanning nature of an SBM could play a key bridging role among the elements of the socio-technical system where the firm is embedded.

Against this background, understanding the interactions (and effects) of the different aspects of a circular business model (e.g., the take-back and reuse strategy) and the socio-technical system where the focal firm is embedded could shed light on the broader topic of sustainability transitions (Köhler et al., 2019; Markard et al., 2012).

2.4 Smart Products and the IoT as Enablers

To overcome barriers and enable a transition to a CE, smart products and the IoT could play a crucial role. Smart products can be considered as physical products amplified with distinctive physical and digital smart enablers, this is, hardware and software components (cf. Noll et al., 2016). Smart products are opening unprecedented opportunities for value creation (Porter & Heppelmann, 2014). These opportunities relate to the use of digital technologies to increase resource efficiency, extend product lifetime, and recover materials (EMF, 2016). Digital technologies and smart products can enable the CE as follows:

- They could support the optimisation of the *use phase* through product monitoring and tracking (Alcayaga et al., 2019).

- They may facilitate the provision of *maintenance* with new approaches such as predictive maintenance (Selcuk, 2016).
- Moreover, life cycle data could offer a better account of product condition before *reuse*, a reduction of process failures and losses, and improved output quality, among other benefits (Alcayaga et al., 2019, 2020). For instance, textiles and clothing powered by RFID tags and related readers could communicate their location remotely, enabling tracking and streamlining sorting, logistics, and analytics (Hansen & Gillert, 2008). Business analytics tools could generate insights into efficiency improvements or lifetime extension (EMF, 2017).
- They may enable *remanufacturing and recycling* by storing and updating condition and usage history of the product and its components, as well as instructions for disassembly or dismantling (Hansen et al., 2020).
- Finally, they may enhance circular *product (re)design* using life cycle data (e.g., Ingemarsdotter et al., 2020).

In addition, firms using SBMs could leverage smart products to optimise their circular value proposition (Alcayaga & Hansen, 2017). For example, RFID-tagged products in a closed-loop system allow optimal control and higher circulation speed (Leblanc, 2011). Additionally, a digital identity for textiles could connect the entire fashion value chain, facilitating the identification of products and materials for reuse, repair, or recycling (EON, 2020). Thus, smart products and IoT-enabled SBMs can be utilised to develop feedback-rich systems throughout the entire product life cycle, accelerating the scaling up of the CE (EMF, 2016).

3 Method

In this chapter, we present an in-depth case study (Yin, 2018) in which we analyse Salesianer Miettex GmbH (henceforth simply referred to as "Salesianer"), a firm that rents out and washes professional textiles. We choose a case study approach because of the uniqueness of the case that characterises an emergent and contemporary phenomenon (Eisenhardt & Graebner, 2007; Yin, 2018).

We select Salesianer because they have been operating a rental business model for several decades and have recently become a front-runner in using RFID-tagged textiles. We triangulate data from semi-structured and ethnographic interviews at various hierarchical levels, observations from on-site visits and industry events, as well as data from internal reports and databases.

4 Case Study: Salesianer Miettex

4.1 Case Overview

Salesianer operates facilities in several locations across Europe. The firm serves a range of industries, including healthcare, hospitality, manufacturing, pharmaceutical, and semiconductor industries. Salesianer services cover three product types: *flat textiles* (e.g., towels, bedsheets, and napkins), *surgical textiles* (e.g., surgical gowns, drapes, and towels), and *uniforms* (e.g., trousers, shirts, and other garments). Textiles are equipped with ultra-high frequency (UHF) tags, high-frequency (HF) tags, or barcodes. The main difference between UHF and HF technologies lies in their reading capabilities. Textiles powered with UHF tags are read in batches, whereas textiles with HF tags are read individually. Moreover, UHF tags can be read from longer distances than HF tags can. Salesianer also equips textiles owned by specific persons (i.e., patients) with tags so that they seamlessly circulate throughout the reuse loop.

This chapter focuses on a highly digitalised and automated laundry line at a location dedicated to the healthcare industry. The top management of Salesianer selected hospitals and nursing homes for this location to allow for productivity improvements. When compared to other customers (e.g., hotels), hospitals and nursing homes are more concerned about the cleanliness rather than the appearance of the textiles. This understanding of quality allows for faster but more intensive washing cycles, generating negative consequences for the fabrics and shorter product lifetimes.

The facilities at the location are distributed between two buildings and can process approximately 60–70 tonnes of textiles per day. The laundry line under study is located in one of the buildings and processes UHF-tagged flat textiles rented only to hospitals. Activities in the selected building are highly automated, whereas tasks in the other building are executed rather manually; this differentiation allows us to understand the impact of smart products combined with automated systems on circularity and SBMs. Besides the level of automation, both buildings differ in customer types, product types, and the IT infrastructure installed.

4.2 Smart Reuse of Fast-Cycling Goods

Smart rental textiles circulate in a closed-loop system between Salesianer and its customers. As seen in Fig. 1, the reuse loop starts with the take-back of dirty laundry that is collected by Salesianer employees. Then, the laundry cycle takes a predefined number of days to wash, prepare, and dispatch clean textiles. Finally, clean laundry is delivered to the customer to replenish their working stations. This delivery closes the reuse loop.

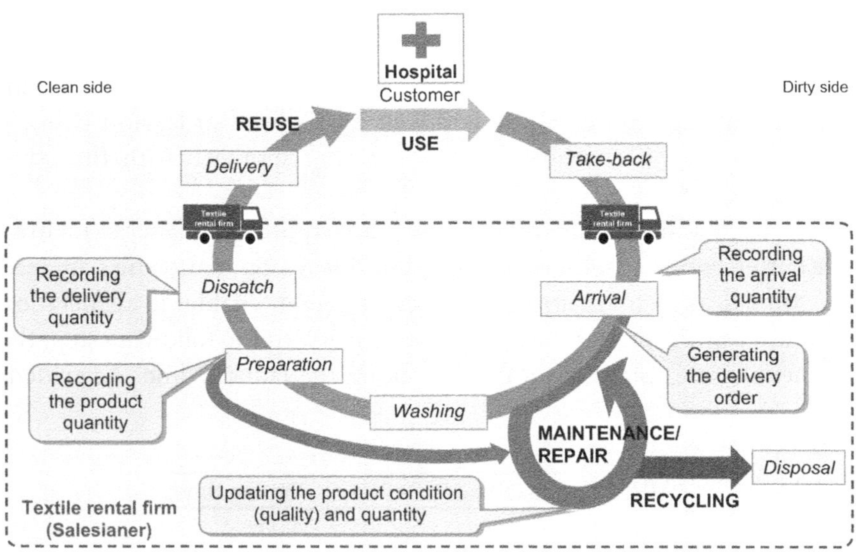

Fig. 1 Reuse loop

Textiles circulate several times per week between Salesianer and its customers in an overlapping manner, that is, some textiles are in the laundry cycle while others are at customer sites or in transit. Both the duration of the laundry cycle and the number of deliveries (and take-backs) per week are agreed upon with the customer in advance. For example, a laundry cycle may last four days, and the firm could do three deliveries per week (Table 1). Furthermore, flat textiles can circulate freely among customers. For instance, a towel could be used a few weeks at customer A, then at customer B, and then at customer A or C.

In order to ensure a continuous replenishment of the textile stock at customer sites, Salesianer offers its customers several alternatives for the order and delivery process. As a first option, UHF tags and their batch-enabled reading capabilities allow a process driven by the *current stock* approach. The number of textiles delivered by Salesianer is the difference between the required stock and the current stock at customer sites. The required stock per working station is agreed upon in the contract. Changes to the current stock are made at Salesianer in an Enterprise-Resource-Planning (ERP) system when the laundry arrives and when it is dispatched. As a second option, Salesianer and its customers can agree on the delivery of a fixed number of textiles at each delivery day. As a third and complementary option, customers may make additional requests via electronic orders or use a web portal to order clean textiles on-demand. The laundry line under study is driven by a mixed order and delivery process because it combines the *current stock* approach with the other alternatives.

The overlapping nature of the reuse loop requires Salesianer to identify the current stock as soon as possible. For this reason, flat textiles are read one time directly upon arrival. This reading point enables the generation and faster processing of the upcoming delivery. In the following step, the flat textiles are sorted automatically along the laundry line. As evident

Table 1 Laundry cycle of a single customer

Take-back	Delivery	Cycling time
Tuesday	Saturday	4 days
Thursday	Tuesday	4 days
Saturday	Thursday	4 days

Table 2 Laundry line of flat textiles with UHF tags for hospitals

Laundry line	Dirty side	Washing machine	Clean side	
Main stages	Arrival (collection, inspection and pre-sorting)	Washing (disinfection and drying)	Preparation (sorting, ironing and finishing)	Dispatch
Reading points	Two	None	Four	One

from Table 2, many reading points have been installed to ensure a highly accurate reading rate. Reading in batches may generate some discrepancies and several reading points may serve to correct them.

Rental textiles are assets, and a long-lasting lifetime is crucial for this business model. However, one of the main challenges for Salesianer involves losses (and higher costs) due to lost textiles. An approach to evaluate losses is the *speed of circulation*. The firm classifies textiles in four categories according to the speed of circulation (fast, slow, very slow, and non-circulating or lost). A highly accurate identification of textiles based on multiple reading points along the laundry line enables this categorisation. Textiles circulating between Salesianer and its customers within seven days are identified as fast circulating textiles. When textiles are not read within 90 days, they are considered lost. Lost textiles are either disposed of at customer sites or stolen by customers' employees (e.g., hospital staff) or final customers (e.g., patients). For several product types (e.g., towels), more than 50% of the textiles reach the non-circulating category within one year, that is, they have not returned to Salesianer 90 days after delivery within a specific year.

A shorter than expected product lifetime due to severe dirt and damages is a second (but minor) source of losses. Salesianer participates in public procurement tenders to obtain contracts for textile rental services. The expected lifetime of the textiles and the price per washed textile unit are set in the contract. However, some textiles may reach the end of their useful life before the agreed one, hence increasing costs. Textiles may be extremely dirty, even for an industrial laundry line, or may be damaged due to intensive usage, continual washing, or laundry line jams. Salesianer discards all these textiles because it is not possible to clean or repair them.

The use of RFID-tagged textiles has allowed Salesianer to generate accurate information regarding losses. The firm uses this information to raise awareness among its customers and perform better cost control.

4.3 Smart Maintenance and Repair

Customers send back textiles that may need to be repaired or have stains in special bags, separated from dirty textiles. These bags do not enter the laundry line and are sent to the repair crew, a dedicated team at Salesianer that manually analyses these textiles and decides on whether to repair, run an additional washing cycle, or dispose of them. After the team has performed the required repairs, they book the flat textiles into the ERP system allowing for full traceability of repair activities in the product life cycle. After that, textiles are sent to the dirty side for washing and they re-enter the reuse loop (Fig. 1).

4.4 (Smart) Recycling

Currently, at the end of their lifetime, flat textiles, surgical textiles, and uniforms are collected in large waste containers and then sold in the market for the highest economic value (or the least cost). Most flat textiles that have reached the end of their lifetime are downcycled into cleaning towels by an external firm. However, severely damaged or dirty textiles are utilised as inputs in waste-to-energy plants, for which Salesianer pays a fee. Further recycling opportunities, also in support of newly available life cycle data, have been investigated but have not been implemented so far. At the time of writing this document, recycling activities were not directly supported by digital technologies.

4.5 Smart Feedback into Procurement (and Product Design)

The data from the product life cycle allows the company to analyse product quality over time. This data is then used to inform the next procurement cycle by changing product specifications or switching to alternative products or suppliers. For instance, if a textile has a predefined duration of 50 washing cycles and holes appear in the fabric after 10 washing cycles, Salesianer can identify the supplier that delivered the product and assess the problem. Reasons behind the damage could relate to the supplier's reliability, the quality of the fabrics, or the specific usage by the customer, among others. Ultimately, it can be expected that life cycle data also has an indirect impact on product (circular) design for the suppliers' development teams. Overall, smart products and feedback systems enable a virtuous cycle of improved product quality and extended product lifetimes.

4.6 Case Summary

The use of smart textiles has allowed the implementation of value-chain measures that may improve circularity, sustainability performance, and the development of better relationships along the value chain:

- Firstly, before implementing RFID tags, the fast-cycling nature of rental textiles and their large quantity (several tonnes per day) made it practically impossible for Salesianer to perform a daily inventory of arrivals. In this sense, the implementation of smart textiles has allowed Salesianer to acquire accurate information on the condition and location of its textiles. This information has enabled an analysis of circulation, losses, and quality of specific product lines. For these reasons, the most remarkable benefit of using RFID-tagged textiles within the reuse loop for Salesianer is the gain in transparency. This enhancement of data analysis and transparency considerably improves the effectiveness of the reuse SBM.

- Secondly, Salesianer has capitalised on the use of RFID-tagged textiles to improve the overall service and gain a strategic position of proximity to its customers. The firm has used product lifetime data to raise customer awareness due to losses of rental textiles. Reducing losses at customer sites could bring cost savings and resource efficiencies for both parties. Moreover, Salesianer performs better inventory management and ensures a continuous replenishment of the textile stock.
- Thirdly, an analysis of product quality could improve product procurement decisions and enable proactive supplier management. Changes in product design and customer demands can be redirected to the supplier with the support of digital technologies and RFID tags. For instance, the amount of cotton (or other fibres) in the textile can be adapted to improve its durability.

5 Discussion: The Role of Smart Rental Textiles in the Transition to a Circular Economy

Transition scholars mainly take a holistic and systemic approach on major sectoral transformations or on how alterations to the business dimension affect political, institutional, or societal change (Köhler et al., 2019; Markard, 2017). However, looking into concepts such as the business model and the adoption of digital technologies from an organisational (micro) level could bring deeper insights into pathways and dynamics for sustainability transitions. Thus, we join the call for research by Köhler et al. (2019) on mobilising concepts from other social sciences to enable deeper insights into sustainability transitions. In particular, we refer to IoT-enabled circular service business models. Below, we discuss how the rental business model of Salesianer and the use of smart products may drive systemic and sustainable change.

5.1 Making Reuse Business Models Outperform Single Use

Firstly, the boundary-spanning nature of Salesianer's rental business model may have wider implications for the socio-technical system in terms of sustainability due to the involvement of other actors and changes in business practices. Salesianer's partnership with an external company that makes cleaning towels from discarded textiles could create a recycling niche in the industry for the reuse of materials. In addition, the business model based on textile reuse and rentals allows for a reduction of disposable, single-use textiles in the value chain of the healthcare industry and other business-to-business contexts. Relevant actors like municipalities or waste collection firms may profit from the use of reusable textiles by having to manage less hazardous waste from hospitals and nursing homes. Secondly, the firm has embraced multiple innovation pathways for its business model through an exploratory journey. For instance, managing textile stock is a key activity for the firm. Salesianer has developed different approaches for the order and delivery process to address challenges related to seasonal fluctuation, textile durability, and customer demand, among others. Finally, the activities of the firm may generate a wider impact on customer firms, final customers, employees, suppliers, policymakers, and other stakeholders due to the disruptive nature of the business model. For example, Salesianer's marketing, communication, and advertisement about the characteristics of the business model emphasise the reuse of rental textiles and may drive the industry towards more sustainable practices.

5.2 Digital Technologies as Enablers of Circular Innovation

As introduced in this chapter, Salesianer's journey towards a more efficient and transparent reuse business model has strongly benefited from the use of digital technologies. Firstly, the firm has made several internal changes to adapt to (and profit from) the pervasiveness of technological innovation. For instance, Salesianer has made changes to the IT infrastructure, human resources, and supplier base to integrate RFID technology into its operations. The firm has also used the transparency of location and condition of its textiles to improve the relationships with its customers, generate trust in the value chain, and facilitate managerial decision-making. Secondly, the use of data-based reports about textile circulation and losses has allowed the firm to explore alternative tendering procedures. In turn, this exploration has enabled an improvement of the definition of responsibilities and terms of agreement in new contracts. Finally, the firm has started to alter the configuration of the value chain through specific business practices based on data transparency. These activities could lead, in the long term, towards more effective product circulation (i.e., less losses) and a broader diffusion of reuse business models in the industry.

Acknowledgements This publication is part of the research project "Business Models for Extending Industry 4.0 towards the entire Product Life Cycle (I4L)" conducted at the Institute for Integrated Quality Design (IQD). The project is funded by Quality Austria (Quality Austria—Trainings, Zertifizierungs und Begutachtungs GmbH, Vienna, Austria). We would like to thank the quality and environmental management team—Michael Neumann, Arno Friedl, and Hanna Geyerlechner—at Salesianer Miettex GmbH for their trust and support.

References

Alcayaga, A., & Hansen, E. G. (2017). Smart-circular systems: A service business model perspective. In C. A. Bakker & R. Mugge (Eds.), *Vol. 9. Research in design series, PLATE 2017 conference proceedings* (pp. 10–13). IOS Press BV. https://doi.org/10.3233/978-1-61499-820-4-10

Alcayaga, A., Wiener, M., & Hansen, E. G. (2019). Towards a framework of smart-circular systems: An integrative literature review. *Journal of Cleaner Production, 221*, 622–634. https://doi.org/10.1016/j.jclepro.2019.02.085

Alcayaga, A., Hansen, E. G., & Koubek, A. (2020). *Quality in the age of Industry 4.0: From digital production to thinking in value chains.* Whitepaper "Digitalisation". Quality Austria – Trainings, Zertifizierungs und Begutachtungs GmbH.

Blomsma, F., & Brennan, G. (2017). The emergence of circular economy: A new framing around prolonging resource productivity. *Journal of Industrial Ecology, 21*(3), 603–614. https://doi.org/10.1111/jiec.12603

Brehmer, M., Podoynitsyna, K., & Langerak, F. (2018). Sustainable business models as boundary-spanning systems of value transfers. *Journal of Cleaner Production, 172*, 4514–4531. https://doi.org/10.1016/j.jclepro.2017.11.083

Cooper, D. R., & Gutowski, T. G. (2017). The environmental impacts of reuse: A review. *Journal of Industrial Ecology, 21*(1), 38–56. https://doi.org/10.1111/jiec.12388

Cooper, T., Oxborrow, L., Claxton, S., Goworek, H., Hill, H., & McLaren, A. (2017). New product development and testing strategies for clothing longevity: An overview of a UK research study. In C. A. Bakker & R. Mugge (Eds.), *Vol. 9. Research in design series, PLATE 2017 conference proceedings* (pp. 94–97). IOS Press BV. https://doi.org/10.3233/978-1-61499-820-4-94

Eisenhardt, K. M., & Graebner, M. E. (2007). Theory building from cases: Opportunities and challenges. *Academy of Management Journal, 50*(1), 25–32. https://doi.org/10.5465/amj.2007.24160888

Ellen MacArthur Foundation (EMF). (2013). *Towards the circular economy vol. 1: Economic and business rationale for an accelerated transition*. http://www.ellenmacarthurfoundation.org/publications

Ellen MacArthur Foundation (EMF). (2015). *Delivering the circular economy. A toolkit for policymakers*. http://www.ellenmacarthurfoundation.org/publications

Ellen MacArthur Foundation (EMF). (2016). *Intelligent assets: Unlocking the circular economy potential*. http://www.ellenmacarthurfoundation.org/publications

Ellen MacArthur Foundation (EMF). (2017). *A new textiles economy: Redesigning fashion's future*. http://www.ellenmacarthurfoundation.org/publications

EON Group Holdings Inc. (EON). (2020). *The Connected products economy – Powering fashion and retail's circular future*. Eongroup. https://www.eongroup.co/connected-products-economy

Geels, F. W. (2004). From sectoral systems of innovation to socio-technical systems. *Research Policy, 33*(6–7), 897–920. https://doi.org/10.1016/j.respol.2004.01.015

Ghisellini, P., Cialani, C., & Ulgiati, S. (2016). A review on circular economy: The expected transition to a balanced interplay of environmental and economic systems. *Journal of Cleaner Production, 114*, 11–32. https://doi.org/10.1016/j.jclepro.2015.09.007

Hansen, W.-R., & Gillert, F. (2008). *RFID for the optimization of business processes*. Wiley. https://doi.org/10.1002/9780470754160

Hansen, E. G., & Revellio, F. (2020). Circular value creation architectures: Make, ally, buy, or laissez-faire. *Journal of Industrial Ecology, 24*(6), 1250–1273. https://doi.org/10.1111/jiec.13016

Hansen, E. G., & Schaltegger, S. (2013). 100 per cent organic? A sustainable entrepreneurship perspective on the diffusion of organic clothing. *Corporate Governance: The International Journal of Business in Society, 13*(5), 583–598. https://doi.org/10.1108/CG-06-2013-0074

Hansen, E. G., & Schmitt, J. C. (2021). Orchestrating cradle-to-cradle innovation across the value chain: Overcoming barriers through innovation communities, collaboration mechanisms, and intermediation. *Journal of Industrial Ecology, 25*(3), 627–647. https://doi.org/10.1111/jiec.13081

Hansen, E. G., Grosse-Dunkler, F., & Reichwald, R. (2009). Sustainability innovation cube – A framework to evaluate sustainability-oriented innovations. *International Journal of Innovation Management, 13*(04), 683–713. https://doi.org/10.1142/S1363919609002479

Hansen, E. G., Wiedemann, P., Fichter, K., Lüdeke-Freund, F., Jaeger-Erben, M., Schomerus, T., Alcayaga, A., Blomsma, F., Tischner, U., Ahle, U., Büchle, D., Denker, A., Fiolka, K., Fröhling, M., Häge, A., Hoffmann, V., Kohl, H., Nitz, T., Schiller, C., … Kadner, S. (2020). *Circular Business Models: Overcoming barriers, unleashing potentials*. Series Circular Economy Initiative Deutschland, no. Working Group 1. acatech – Deutsche Akademie der Technikwissenschaften e.V.; SYSTEMIQ. https://www.circular-economy-initiative.de/publikationen

Heyes, G., Sharmina, M., Mendoza, J. M. F., Gallego-Schmid, A., & Azapagic, A. (2018). Developing and implementing circular economy business models in service-oriented technology companies. *Journal of Cleaner Production, 177*, 621–632. https://doi.org/10.1016/j.jclepro.2017.12.168

Hirsch, P. M., & Levin, D. Z. (1999). Umbrella advocates versus validity police: A life-cycle model. *Organization Science, 10*(2), 199–212.

House of Commons. (2019). *Fixing fashion: Clothing consumption and sustainability. (Sixteenth report of session 2017–19, HC 1952).* House of Commons, Environmental Audit Committee. https://publications.parliament.uk/pa/cm201719/cmselect/cmenvaud/1952/full-report.html

Ingemarsdotter, E., Jamsin, E., & Balkenende, R. (2020). Opportunities and challenges in IoT-enabled circular business model implementation – A case study. *Resources, Conservation and Recycling, 162*, 105047. https://doi.org/10.1016/j.resconrec.2020.105047

Kirchherr, J., Reike, D., & Hekkert, M. (2017). Conceptualizing the circular economy: An analysis of 114 definitions. *Resources, Conservation and Recycling, 127*, 221–232. https://doi.org/10.1016/j.resconrec.2017.09.005

Kjaer, L. L., Pigosso, D. C. A., Niero, M., Bech, N. M., & McAloone, T. C. (2018). Product/service-systems for a circular economy: The route to decoupling economic growth from resource consumption? *Journal of Industrial Ecology, 58*(3), 523. https://doi.org/10.1111/jiec.12747

Köhler, J., Geels, F. W., Kern, F., Markard, J., Onsongo, E., Wieczorek, A., Alkemade, F., Avelino, F., Bergek, A., Boons, F., Fünfschilling, L., Hess, D., Holtz, G., Hyysalo, S., Jenkins, K., Kivimaa, P., Martiskainen, M., McMeekin, A., Mühlemeier, M. S., … Wells, P. (2019). An agenda for sustainability transitions research: State of the art and future directions. *Environmental Innovation and Societal Transitions, 31*, 1–32. https://doi.org/10.1016/j.eist.2019.01.004

Leblanc, R. (2011). *Delhaize in Belgium confirms its innovating role in fresh produce logistics*. https://packagingrevolution.net/delhaize-in-belgium-confirms-its-innovating-role-in-fresh-produce-logistics/

Lieder, M., & Rashid, A. (2016). Towards circular economy implementation: A comprehensive review in context of manufacturing industry. *Journal of Cleaner Production, 115*, 36–51. https://doi.org/10.1016/j.jclepro.2015.12.042

Markard, J. (2011). Transformation of infrastructures: Sector characteristics and implications for fundamental change. *Journal of Infrastructure Systems, 17*(3), 107–117. https://doi.org/10.1061/(ASCE)IS.1943-555X.0000056

Markard, J. (2017). *Sustainability transitions: Exploring the emerging research field and its contribution to management studies* [33rd EGOS Colloquium, July 6–8, 2017]. Copenhagen.

Markard, J., Raven, R., & Truffer, B. (2012). Sustainability transitions: An emerging field of research and its prospects. *Research Policy, 41*(6), 955–967. https://doi.org/10.1016/j.respol.2012.02.013

Morseletto, P. (2020). Restorative and regenerative: Exploring the concepts in the circular economy. *Journal of Industrial Ecology, 24*(4), 763–773. https://doi.org/10.1111/jiec.12987

Murray, A., Skene, K., & Haynes, K. (2017). The circular economy: An interdisciplinary exploration of the concept and application in a global context.

Journal of Business Ethics, 140(3), 369–380. https://doi.org/10.1007/s10551-015-2693-2

Nobre, G. C., & Tavares, E. (2017). Scientific literature analysis on big data and internet of things applications on circular economy: A bibliometric study. *Scientometrics, 111*(1), 463–492. https://doi.org/10.1007/s11192-017-2281-6

Noll, E., Zisler, K., Neuburger, R., Eberspächer, J., & Dowling, M. (2016). *Neue Produkte in der digitalen Welt*. Münchner Kreis.

Pagoropoulos, A., Pigosso, D. C. A., & McAloone, T. C. (2017). The emergent role of digital technologies in the circular economy: A review. *Procedia CIRP, 64*, 19–24. https://doi.org/10.1016/j.procir.2017.02.047

Pedersen, S., & Clausen, C. (2018). Co-designing for a circular economy. In I. Bitran, S. Conn, E. K. Huizingh, O. Kokshagina, M. Torkkeli, & M. Tynnhammar (Eds.), *Proceedings of the XXIX ISPIM innovation conference 2018: Innovation, the name of the game* (pp. 1–11). The International Society for Professional Innovation Management Ltd.

Porter, M. E., & Heppelmann, J. E. (2014). How smart, connected products are transforming competition. *Harvard Business Review, 92*(11), 1–23.

Sanders, L., Mawson, J., Hart, C., Tatzenko, J., Hollister-Jones, A., Ryland, M., Medic, L., & Taylor, E. (2019). *The 2019 ethical fashion report: The truth behind the barcode*. https://baptistworldaid.org.au/resources/2019-ethical-fashion-report/

Schaltegger, S., Hansen, E. G., & Lüdeke-Freund, F. (2016). Business models for sustainability: Origins, present research, and future avenues. *Organization & Environment, 29*(1), 3–10. https://doi.org/10.1177/1086026615599806

Selcuk, S. (2016). Predictive maintenance, its implementation and latest trends. *Proceedings of the Institution of Mechanical Engineers, Part B: Journal of Engineering Manufacture, 231*(9), 1670–1679. https://doi.org/10.1177/0954405415601640

Stahel, W. R. (2010). *The performance economy* (2nd ed.). Palgrave Macmillan.

Stahel, W. R. (2016). Circular economy. *Nature, 531*(7595), 435–438. https://doi.org/10.1038/531435a

Stahel, W. R. (2019). *The circular economy: A user's guide*. Routledge.

Tietze, F., & Hansen, E. G. (2016). To own or to use? How product service systems facilitate eco-innovation behavior. *Centre for Technology Management Working Paper Series, 4*(June), 1–23.

Tukker, A. (2004). Eight types of product-service system: Eight ways to sustainability? Experiences from SusProNet. *Business Strategy and the Environment, 13*(4), 246–260. https://doi.org/10.1002/bse.414

Tukker, A. (2015). Product services for a resource-efficient and circular economy – A review. *Journal of Cleaner Production, 97*, 76–91. https://doi.org/10.1016/j.jclepro.2013.11.049

Yin, R. K. (2018). *Case study research and applications: Design and methods* (6th ed.). SAGE.

Zins, H. M. (2011). Reusable medical textiles. In V. T. Bartels (Ed.), *Handbook of medical textiles* (pp. 80–105). Woodhead Publishing. https://doi.org/10.1533/9780857093691.1.80

Zott, C., Amit, R., & Massa, L. (2011). The business model: Recent developments and future research. *Journal of Management, 37*(4), 1019–1042. https://doi.org/10.1177/0149206311406265

Business Models for Smart Sustainability: A Critical Perspective on Smart Homes and Sustainability Transitions

Lara Anne Blasberg

1 Introduction

Smart homes with digital technologies (i.e. sensors for CO_2, particulate matter, temperature, and automation) can be a potential pathway to sustainable transformation of the housing segment of the building industry. The sustainability efforts of the building industry—one of the most economically significant (Economist, 2020) and carbon-polluting (Christiansen & Andersen, 2013) sectors—align with innovations in digital technologies that can track energetic, environmental, and human health data, all of which are interdependent. The lack of sustainable housing, in particular, is a pervasive and very human problem, with 90% of our time spent indoors (U.S. Environmental Protection Agency, 1987)—and in the age of COVID-19, even more time spent at home with greater impact on society. While a long-standing issue, it also now coincides with sustainability and health being redefined as the ability to 'adapt and

L. A. Blasberg (✉)
Copenhagen Business School (CBS), Frederiksberg, Denmark
e-mail: lh.msc@cbs.dk

A. Aagaard et al. (eds.), *Business Models for Sustainability Transitions*,
https://doi.org/10.1007/978-3-030-77580-3_10

self-manage' (Huber et al., 2011), placing responsibility upon individuals to seek better lifestyles and environments, especially in the spaces we control like our homes. As Turits (2020: para. 21) indicates in a recent *BBC* article about working from home in the COVID-19 era, "the burden of carbon impact may inadvertently fall on employees as it becomes incumbent on individual workers to invest in their own lower-emission infrastructure." This turn towards everyday citizens arises against the backdrop of an industry that, despite decades of pressures to "green," resists change and only innovates towards sustainability in entrepreneurial niches (ONeill & Gibbs, 2014). Home-based digital technologies present disruptive innovations that can lead the building industry towards more sustainable development, from niches to shifted markets and user preferences (Geels, 2019). They invite for new business models, while creating new agency for building users to engage digitally in the sustainability performance of their houses and thus alter the "trajectory of practices" (McMeekin & Southerton, 2012). While the building industry is experimenting with business models through which they can employ these niche technological opportunities, connect with users, and stage sustainability transformations, the implications of business using technology to enter the home space and engage with users need to be explored.

Although socio-technical systems are considered to include user behaviour, practices, norms, and values (Geels, 2002; McMeekin & Southerton, 2012), challenges and opportunities for digital technology-driven, user-centred business models to improve sustainability are not yet well understood. As Geels et al. (2018: 24) point out in their work on demand-side energy innovations, change to the system "involves more than improving individual technologies or changing individual behaviours, but instead requires interlinked and potentially far-reaching changes in the systems themselves—or 'sociotechnical transitions.'" The housing segment of the building industry and shift towards smart homes present a glimpse into these intertwined dimensions during business model innovation and technological maturation. Homes are complex systems with linkages among building users, home technology, and the businesses that produce and service the structure. Especially in regions such as Europe, where the built environment is largely already extant, sustainability transitions relate to improving the use, maintenance, and renovation of already existing homes (Power, 2008). Shifting housing provision towards sustainability will require changes on the individual, organisational, and institutional levels (Hoffman & Henn, 2008). Whereas the building industry historically excels at applying technical solutions and framing sustainability in terms of resource efficiency, it has tended to overlook technical limitations and such sustainability drivers as behaviour, attitudes, and social agendas (Cooper, 2009). Gram-Hanssen and Georg (2018: 7) refer to building industry and policy efforts at reducing carbon impacts as "insufficient" due to the avoidance of the direct connection between resource use and building users. This is not least of all due to the disconnect among building clients, owners, and users in conventional building business models, which are employed without consideration of total lifecycle costs or impacts. Unfortunately, the neglect of social aspects interferes with the sustainability of buildings (Cole et al., 2010), as there are no built-in incentives for behavioural elements such as controlling indoor climate parameters (temperature, humidity, etc.), airing out practices, cleaning filters, or any other maintenance and care decisions. As such, business models that effectively drive sustainability transitions in the built environment necessitate innovation that incorporates economic, environmental, and social dimensions (Moschetti & Brattebø, 2016). This chapter examines the pros and cons of this form of driving sustainability in housing with a focus on the roles of digital technologies, businesses, and users. It poses the question: *What are the prerequisites in terms of digital technologies, business models, and user practices to support a sustainable trajectory of the housing segment?*

2 Theoretical Foundations

This research draws upon socio-technical perspectives and sustainability transitions, namely a combination of *user-technology interaction* and *business model innovation (BMI)*. The connections between these two relate to social practices as typically invisible (Hagendijk, 2004), whereas technology can serve to make the invisible visible (Flyverbom et al., 2016; Latour, 1991), giving rise to new agency and potential business areas. Sustainability transitions can be driven by "the development of new technologies and the formation of niches or innovation systems, or the re-orientation of industries" (Köhler et al., 2019: 12), while these technologies and systems are bounded in configurations with industry structures, policies, markets, and users (Geels et al., 2018). Science and Technology Studies (STS) is useful for examining the relationship between technical systems like buildings and social systems (Müller & Reichmann, 2015) like home-dwellers and for understanding how business models can support the "upgrading" of sustainability in mass markets (Schaltegger et al., 2016). As digital systems expand, STS points to a potential change in users' ability to be conscious of and influence their environments, thus redefining what a *user* is. Historically from the 1970s the user went from "a cog in a rational machine, became a source of error in the 1980s and then a social actor in the 1990s, and [was in the 2000s] a consumer" (McCarthy & Wright, 2007). There is a call to refocus attention from users as *consumers* to their potential to influence *production* (also referred to as *prosumers*) (Oudshoorn & Pinch, 2007). In the housing business, users are referred to in different ways, ranging from *occupants* (as if the building was involuntarily occupied), *inhabitants*, *residents*, to *end-users* (those who ultimately interact with the house and its parts), terminology which evolves along with changes to the perceived role of the user. STS is known for considering such co-evolution of artefacts and humans, for example Pinch and Bijker's (1984) oscillating interpretation and stabilisation of innovations' meanings. These co-adaptations can be seen among users, housing, and smart technology (Christiansen & Andersen, 2013; Hale, 2018). But reorientation of users towards being part of producing innovation involves engaging normative politics of technology and spanning levels of sustainability transitions (Köhler et al., 2019). It also involves trying to understand how the needs and behaviours that generate support for new business models are created in the first place.

In recent years, business model literature has developed beyond the landscape of the Business Model Canvas to consider businesses (like users) as embedded in larger systems or "business model ecosystems" (Boons & Bocken, 2018), which affect the nature of innovation and transitions (Zott & Amit, 2010). In this way, the business model concept can be examined from socio-technical transitions and practice-based perspectives, which "both offer accounts that emphasise significant societal change involving coordinated shifts in multiple and systemically interdependent elements" (McMeekin & Southerton, 2012: 353). This includes recognition of downstream customers as essential to business model innovation (Boons & Lüdeke-Freund, 2013); though little is known about *how* users engage with transitions in the wider systems that "service" them (Köhler et al., 2019). As such, theorising business models in the building sector is inherently grounded in socio-technical systems (Müller & Reichmann, 2015), sustainability transformations (Köhler et al., 2019), and the "wicked problems" of organising in urban settings (Whyte & Sexton, 2011). Buildings are treated as "embedded" in socio-ecological systems (Cole et al., 2013), wherein ecosystems of organisations and users undergo "complex multi-level processes that involve interactions and co-evolutionary alignments between socio-technical systems, landscapes, and niches" (Manning & Reinecke, 2016: 618). Within buildings, socio-technical agency (Müller & Reichmann, 2015) and co-evolution among producers, users, and objects (Shove et al., 2007) meet BMI's activity- and eco-system perspectives (Bouwman et al., 2018; Zott & Amit, 2010). Business models that offer active choice and engagement with users involve the co-creation of sustainability value (Aagaard & Ritzén, 2020). But these new business models also present risk: the risk of users consuming even more resources ('the rebound effect') with new technologies (Sovacool & Furszyfer Del Rio, 2020) and previously untried consumption systems (Boons & Bocken, 2018), and the risk of businesses being held accountable for measurable failures of product or process performance. Whereas sustainability pressures are stimulating the building industry to reject its former propensity for business models that prohibit user engagement (Åkerman et al., 2020), the implications of pointing towards complex relational sustainability (technology, business, users) are not yet understood.

3 Methodology

This chapter is based upon an organisational ethnography supported by field notes (Phillippi & Lauderdale, 2018) in the VELUX Group headquarters in Hørsholm, Denmark. Ethnography is significant for probing dynamics of norms, behaviours, and social practices (Wolcott, 1999), such as is needed for investigating user-centred, service business models. The focus on VELUX as an organisation and the Active House Alliance (AHA) as an industry platform serves to elucidate connections between the organisational and industry levels. This data has then been considered against technical data, as an extension of "sensory ethnography" (Pink, 2009) in that the sensing by digital devices builds upon and adds new dimensions to ethnographic data. The interpretation of sensor data in line with observations and notes was made possible in collaboration with business partners such as Renson (heating, ventilation, and air conditioning systems) and Leapcraft (sensor systems and data analysis). In conjunction with the ethnography, 61 interviews were conducted, 32 of which were in-depth, semi-structured interviews with building professionals (Table 1) surrounding building demonstration projects, and 29 of which were "mini" interviews with building users, reflecting such concerns as comfort, allergies, design preferences, and screen visibility. The interviews were thus useful for both exploring practitioner perceptions of sustainability and opportunities and barriers to utilisation of building data and to supplement feedback from sensor data with users' own reported experiences during building use.

4 Company and Business Context

The research focuses on the case of the VELUX Group, a manufacturer of rooftop windows and promoter of sustainable building, as well as VELUX partners and the broader industry, particularly through study of the Active House Alliance (AHA). This alliance works towards sustainable construction based on environmental, energetic, and comfort sustainability. In addition to the VELUX Group's 2018 launch of the smart product VELUX Active that regulates roof window operation based on indoor health conditions, VELUX has worked with the Active House alliance to construct innovative, technology-infused demonstration buildings around the world to push against current housing business models based on rapid construction with few or no maintenance offerings. Digital home technologies open for new ways of creating and

Table 1 In-depth interviews

Interview #	Date	Location	Company type	Title
1	06/09/2018	Toronto	Bldg. components	Technical Manager
2	06/09/2018	Toronto	Architects	Principal
3	10/09/2018	Toronto	University	Professor of Urban Studies
4	12/09/2018	Toronto	Bldg. components	President
5	13/09/2018	Hamilton	Government	Smart City Officer
6	17/09/2018	Toronto	University	Prof. of Architectural Science
7	17/09/2018	Toronto	Home builders	President and COO
8	18/09/2018	Toronto	Home builders	Senior Vice President
9	18/09/2018	Toronto	Building utilities	VP of Business Development
10	21/09/2018	Toronto	Building security	Director of Operations
11	22/09/2018	Toronto	Government	Chief Technology Officer
12	24/09/2018	Toronto	Home builders	VP of Sustainable Development
13	15/10/2018	Brussels	Ventilation systems	Public Affairs Manager
14	15/10/2018	Brussels	Ventilation systems	Research Manager
15	16/10/2018	Brussels	Ventilation systems	Group Product Manager
16	16/10/2018	Brussels	Ventilation systems	Digital Product Manager
17	16/10/2018	Brussels	Ventilation systems	Consulting Technician
18	17/10/2018	Kortrijk	Building renovation	Project Leader
19	18/10/2018	Leuven	Building engineers	Engineering Consultant
20	17/06/2019	Brussels	Prof. federation	Director General
21	17/06/2019	Brussels	Prof. federation	Smart Building Advisor
22	18/06/2019	Brussels	Building research	Senior Expert
23	18/06/2019	Brussels	Social housing	Project Manager
24	19/06/2019	Brussels	Building research	Head of Division
25	20/06/2019	Zaventum	Home automation	Training Manager
26	21/06/2019	Brussels	Social housing	Director of Real Estate
27	21/06/2019	Brussels	Social housing	Project Manager

(*continued*)

Table 1 (continued)

Interview #	Date	Location	Company type	Title
28	19/09/2019	Toronto	Smart city design	Urban Systems Consultant
29	19/09/2019	Toronto	Smart city design	Facilitator
30	20/09/2019	Toronto	Tech investors	Principal
31	20/09/2019	Toronto	Tech investors	Managing Partner
32	20/09/2019	Toronto	Tech investors	Principal

capturing value during use, such as through results-based product-service system business models. The building industry tests individual technologies and technological systems through demonstration projects—and in the case of Active House demonstrations, the experiments include so-called *post-occupancy studies*, wherein the buildings continue to be studied while in use. The research examines VELUX Active developments (e.g. increased interoperability, voice command option), applied smart technology in Active House demonstration buildings, and proptech (properties technologies) in Belgium and Canada.

The interviews revolve around two demonstration buildings, constructed in partnership among Active House Alliance member companies: RenovActive in Brussels, Belgium, and the Centennial Park Active House in Toronto, Canada. RenovActive is a social housing renovation project that includes building automation (Renson HealthBox-controlled ventilation and VELUX Active-controlled windows) and Raspberry Pi sensor-based performance monitoring. The AHA followed its performance while a low-income family lived in the house over a period of two years. The project exemplifies state-of-the-art building renovation in the very seat of the European Commission. The Centennial Park house utilises EcoBee smart systems, an automated heat pump, and Tesla energy storage with photovoltaic collection. The AHA monitored the house with a family of five over a period of six months, and it is now privately owned by a family of four. The Centennial Park house was also constructed against the backdrop of the contentious Quayside project, the smart city project spearheaded by Sidewalk Labs, a daughter company of Alphabet Inc., as well as extensive propagation of proptech startups in the Toronto area (as the fastest growing city in North America). These technological systems represent a fraction of potential offerings. Sovacool and Furszyfer Del Rio (2020) identified 267 different smart home products in 13 different categories (household appliances, lighting, energy and utilities, entertainment, health and wellness, safety and security, baby and pet monitors, clothes and accessories, vehicles and drones, home robots, gardening, integrated solutions, and "others"), provided by 113 different companies (p. 5). And it is worth noting that these offerings extend beyond devices—some examples from the building industry include technologies for building design processes (e.g. Building Information Modelling, BIM), mass timber construction, and pre-fabrication (such as used in companies like Ilke in the UK).

5 Sustainability Value as Visibility

One challenge is for businesses to capture value from sustainability factors that are intangible in such a way as users are not even aware of them. In the context of sustainable housing, sustainability transitions relate to the technologically modified link between producers and users, wherein the business model is a critical bridge between the creation and derivation of value. This holds true for building users, for whom the sustainability and health impacts of building use—beyond utility bills—remain invisible.

> If you are not aware of what is there and why it is there, then you don't use it. (Interview 19)

> Consumers are not really educated on what they should be looking for. (Interview 4)

Companies manufacturing home technologies do not necessarily see value as stemming from sustainability either, but more as business-as-usual profit rooted in either luxury or convenience (Sovacool & Furszyfer Del Rio, 2020). But for building organisations, who are under immense pressure to comply with increasingly stringent sustainability requirements in building codes and directives, smart technologies have the potential to further sustainability outcomes through product-service system models. Both building and utilities companies are considering the new opportunities:

> In the U.S., [utility companies] are now also thinking about whether or not cost-benefit analyses should include a quantitative measure for improved indoor air quality or improved health outcomes. (Interview 28)

Home technologies can cater real-time data on the contracted service and redefine acceptable metrics of service quality, including sustainability service. Based on this, the differences among sustainability for efficiency, sufficiency, and thriving become not only critical, but measurable and thus visible.

Measurement, particularly that of real-time information, is a key aspect of making the previously invisible actionable and capturable in new business models. As Nuñez-Cacho et al. (2018: 2340) phrase it, "what gets measured gets done" in reference to the need for concrete, validated scales of measurement for advancing sustainability in the building industry. And there is a growing debate in the building industry on the use of "measured data" versus "predicted data," as in previous years, construction projects relied upon calculations and modelling, as opposed to information from buildings in use:

> There is a gap between the theoretical calculation and real consumption, and the challenge if you have the monitoring is to have this link. (Interview 24)

> Robust in use as opposed to robust in theory. (Interview 31)

In addition to other forms of measurement (energy and resource consumption, details on materials used, etc.) such as are necessary for achieving voluntary sustainability standards like LEED, BREEAM, or DGNB, measures now extend to personal data in buildings. The commercialisation of personal data over the past decades has stimulated debate over control, fairness, and even an individual's data as a form of their labour

(Hirsch, 2019). Recent years have witnessed a growing sophistication in how organisations analyse and respond to new forms of measurement:

> Week, period, month, or year, and all this [building performance] information is being generated. (Interview 2)

> A lot of these companies are starting to collect data that didn't exist before. (Interview 30)

Of particular interest is what Flyverbom et al. (2016) coin as *visibility management*, wherein organisations exert technological control over what is transparent and what is opaque. Visibility management extends to automated or adaptive functions that shroud the basis of algorithmic decision-making, such as AI-delivered credit discrimination (Klein, 2019) and thermostat gender bias in both office buildings (Kingma & van Marken Lichtenbelt, 2015) and homes (Sintov et al., 2019). Control and even authoritarianism fears can at times overwhelm the potentially positive directions that visibility can drive business model innovation. One example of attempts to balance consumer data protection with the advancement of measured data arises from a Toronto-based home utilities company:

> We use [the metering data] internally to validate our own models and to verify the advocacy of measures that we are recommending. (Interview 9)

Hirsch (2019: 51) goes so far as to argue that business moving any direction other than transitioning to full individual ownership of the personal data from digital technologies would essentially be "killing the goose that laid the golden eggs" in so far as he predicts "great competitive advantage" derived from openness and transparency. Even if users are not given direct control over data from smart home devices (bearing their own burdens of education, analysis, and application), the enabling of transparency and facilitating of action can positively affect sustainability empowerment (Thøgersen, 2005). An example of this can also be seen with what Lupton (2020: 1) refers to as "forces gathering in human-nonhuman assemblages to create a set of key agential capacities" in the case of youth empowerment through FitBit communities in Australia. Even in this case, she says that the positive self-awareness and well-being effects of using digital technologies arise without consideration of potential benefit to third parties.

Is this just gadget fetishism? Is technology helping, or possibly hurting sustainability? There is no easy answer to these questions; and sustainability effects appear to depend on factors such as organisational intent, user motivation, and technological integration. The latter refers to integration of digital technologies for a higher-level, more synergistic performance. In their critical review of smart home technologies in Europe, Sovacool and Furszyfer Del Rio (2020) outline six different levels of technology in the home:

1. Basic analogue home;
2. Isolated smart technology;
3. Bundled and programmable smart technology;
4. Automated and anticipatory technology;
5. Integrated technology for learning, modifying, and adapting services;
6. Fully integrated, automated, and predictive technology; and intuitive or sentient homes linked with larger systems.

While the authors indicate that higher levels of integration demonstrate greater potential for sustainability value, they also indicate a need for government policy to guide organisational interest and lifestyle choices of users. Governmental involvement in smart technology tends towards "smart city" programmes, though these often entail public-private or private-public partnerships, as was the case for Quayside, with Sidewalk Labs as private leadership with Waterfront Toronto and City of Toronto as public partners. One would be hard-pressed to identify a truly successful "smart" transformation on the city level; and both the aims and metrics increasingly merge with the "sustainable cities" movement (Zheng et al., 2020). The Quayside business model fundamentally relied upon paying for construction with profits from selling personal data. Despite Sidewalk's later efforts to accommodate both citizen data protections and open protocols (Interviews 11, 28), the financial foundations of the model crumbled. Yet, the collection of measured data has itself become a rubric of smartness. Smart city expert Cha Chung-ha even criticises South Korea's "smartest" smart city Songdo: "Are they measuring metrics or data? Do they open the data and allow access to it to citizens or start-ups? No" (Dong-hwan, 2019: para. 6). As such, there is ample opportunity for governments to democratically, civically shape the development and implementation of smart home technologies, that is, mandating sustainability results from building technologies in government buildings, a strategy that has similarly been utilised to accelerate adoption of building energy performance standards. Though, arguably, businesses are best equipped to spearhead these changes, or as Wells (2018) notes, they remain "socially and politically unassailable as the primary organisational template" for innovating and scaling technologies for sustainability (p. 1705), even if entailing intrepid ventures into sacred spaces.

6 Home as Sacred

Another challenge is posed by the question of how building organisations can expand sustainability in the use of private homes while still respecting privacy. The home space was previously considered sacred, where privacy ruled, and businesses had limited research and marketing access. Product placement and advertising in movies and television was considered the pinnacle of marketing. Meanwhile, the building industry developed in such a way as to plan and construct homes and then "walk away," having a vague (if any) idea of how the houses performed, or if the building users were at all satisfied. The emergent access to this market through digital technologies is appealing to building companies:

> Imagine across Flanders 10,000 people click "Yes" [to renovation offers]. Then on the supply side, they have access to our digital marketplace, where 10,000 house owners say, "We want to change our glazing." Then you have a mass market. (Interview 22)

Yet, the aforementioned lack of awareness is also linked to a shortage of demand, or at least an initial unwillingness of the end-user to bear additional costs:

> [Quality housing] has a cost, and it is a buyer who is not prepared to pay for it. (Interview 7)

> [Homeowners] say, "Well, what will I save?" Maybe $50 a month. It is the equivalent of getting a better-quality phone package. (Interview 4)

But frontrunners are also perceived as shifting the market:

> I think that then you will start to see more monitoring of it, and that can drive the demand for it. [...] It has to be reciprocated on both sides that people care about it, that the tenants care about it, the home buyers care about it. And then the real estate companies can start to prioritize it. (Interview 30)

And health and comfort draw user interest in a more compelling way than energy savings (Interview 4). One interviewee describes the quest of pivoting business models towards user concerns:

> What are those points that we can connect with? Are they concerned about health? Are they concerned about productivity? [...] Does that resonate with people? (Interview 1)

These flows of data and personal information to business open the sanctity of private homes (Lindgreen et al., 2019). Smart home technologies have extended the reach of the corporate eye, enabling very personal data to be gathered and sent outside of the home, for example: who is in the house in which rooms, the contents of the refrigerator, and even how frequently and for how long the bathrooms are being used (Interview 13)—in other words, introducing a "higher level of intimacy" than previous forms of data (Hirsch 2019: 50). On the one hand, the North American interviewees cite privacy as a primary concern (Interviews 6, 9, 10) in the seemingly unstoppable smart home technology market—forecast to reach US $113 billion worth of value by 2024 (Research and Markets, 2020)—as governmental protections are considered largely insufficient and enforcement challenging under the reign of "data capitalism" (Flyverbom et al., 2019). On the other hand, European interviewees under the purview of the EU's General Data Protection Regulation (GDPR) refer to privacy regulations as an effective and absolutely critical factor shaping their business practice, but also as interfering with the innovative potential of technology (Interviews 14, 22). And still, under the arguably limited protections of GDPR, personal boundaries regarding smart homes seem to be determined on an entirely different basis, often convenience and a sense of control:

> You are not going to get anybody to use less energy by asking them, "Would you mind, today at 5:00 [PM] when you come home from work, do not turn on your lights." It is just like, "No." (Interview 28)

> In individual units, people want to have as much control as they can. Obviously you have to supply them with the means of controlling it, but we won't be making a decision if they will have a smart coffee maker that is going to make a coffee for them. (Interview 7)

Personalisation, control, and convenience all relate to behavioural relations between users and technologies, such as *appropriation* (users taking control of technologies) and *scripting* (redefining how technologies are used) (Akrich, 1992; Hale, 2018; Shove, 2003). There is a range of behavioural profiles in housing, from users who ignore building systems to users who actively engage:

> They [the users] should do it themselves, but most of the people forget it. (Interview 13)

> There are also people who may be more like me, who have a smart thermostat or maybe that have a smart climate device, and yes, sooner or later, they want to combine it and make it a real smart home. (Interview 15)

At the same time, the lack of smart home pedagogy, wildly varying levels of control, and domestic power imbalances have enabled individuals to seize control at the expense of others in the form, at times as a form of domestic abuse, as unveiled in a disturbing *The New York Times* feature (Bowles, 2018). Riley (2020), in a similar feature in *BBC Future*, argues that poor consumer awareness of potential uses and misuses of connected technologies is at the root of these troubles. The question remains open if greater personalisation of smart home technologies would (terrifyingly) exacerbate such abuses or perhaps offer better protections via each person owning the rights to their personal settings in the home. The most widely cited opportunity is that of automation (Interviews 1, 13, 14, 17, 19), wherein the system simultaneously removes personal controls, while automating based on personal preferences (levels 4–6 of smart home stages, Sovacool & Furszyfer Del Rio's, 2020):

> That is probably the future of smart home. That smart home will already be a smart home, and it is just there, and you do not have to think about how it works. (Interview 17)

> That is important that the building can be controlled so that you do not see it, that you do not feel it, that it is controlled in the way you want. (Interview 14)

Whereas these near-future solutions entail systems that can know the user and what the user wants, identity and preferences that feed into automation are affected by hyperconnected marketing and branding. Swaminathan et al. (2020) refer to these changes as "blurring of branding boundaries" (p. 25). They describe new modes of branding through connected technologies, where brands shift from individual to co-created. While acknowledging problems of information overload, they also refer to the heightened role of the prosumer, spanning supply and demand sides through digital technologies. The identity question arises as a significant factor in the apparent shift in near-future market demand for more technified buildings and expanded automation.

> Customers, I think, made it very clear through a lot of venues, through market research, that they expect these things [smart home technologies] to become standard. They are expecting this DNA: I want smart. (Interview 12)

Smart home technologies can go further to extend and alter one's sense of self, harking back to body politics and cyborg feminism, which portray technologies as affecting reimagination and reorganisation of body, home, and market (Haraway, 1991). For example, one of the Centennial Park home owners announced their intent to switch smart home platforms from Zigbee to Apple Homekit, explaining that the family is already "in the Apple ecosystem." What is less clear is whether business can shape sustainable consumption identities through technology, perhaps by employing brand relationships to further users' life goals (MacInnis & Folkes, 2017). Alternatively, Simons et al. (2020) suggest the use of social innovation in the design of digital technologies in order to balance power through equal contribution of knowledge. Pel et al. (2020) likewise indicate that social innovation can generate a kind of "network empowerment" that can generate the structures necessary for sustainability transitions, extending into the built environment via demonstration projects and living lab networks. The role of business in these networks is to make concrete the value created in the operationalisation of sustainable business models; but how such networks divide and share risk—also with users—is a new front in the building industry.

7 Networked Responsibilities

Yet another challenge is that of organisational and user responsibility for the sustainability performance of buildings. Business ecosystems and the creation of new awareness, needs, and markets in the home space bring to the forefront the disputed nature of object, human, and organisational *accountability* (not so distinct from the previously discussed measurement, or accounting) for the sustainability impacts. And although it is not uncommon for greening organisations to stress the unpredictability of user behaviour, the interrelations among consumption, business, and technology are often glazed over (McMeekin & Southerton, 2012). The vagueness surrounding responsibility can create tension in designing business models for smart homes. Users may demand that producers miraculously transform their homes from unsustainable to sustainable; and just as impossible to satisfy, producers may expect that users transform from convenience consumers into conscientious green prosumers (while still willing to buy their products). Further, there are very practical considerations regarding the physical set-up of smart homes, as well as different household cultures and levels of technological literacy among users. As many of us have experienced to a greater extent as work moves to the home space, seamlessly functioning technology is a myth; and even building engineers do not necessarily take responsibility for malfunctions.

> From time to time I measure my equipment is not working, and then I have to send in the mail [to technical support]. (Interview 19)

> There are the engineers, but they are not in charge of the maintenance of it, because all the technical staff in charge of the maintenance, they do not look into the data. (Interview 24)

The author of this chapter has on occasion found herself inexplicably responsible for checking sensor readings, restarting systems, or replacing batteries. Beyond these very basic functionalities, smart homes need to offer users both control and satisfaction (Fabi et al., 2017); and the technologies must provide options for both flexibility and adaptability to ensure long-term use (Gijsbers & Lichtenberg, 2014). However, there is no clear responsibility for ensuring any of these features. And whereas much of the narrative concerns the sustainability of the users and their behaviour, smart homes create a record of what is and is not working in the house. Building users may start to question the basis of prices, the energy and health effects of the buildings they rent or buy, or most importantly, why they should invest in businesses that demonstrably do not deliver what they promise.

As such, organisations perceive a great deal of risk in measuring the performance of smart homes:

> At some point you become responsible and much more responsible than before, because the end user can see how your product is performing. And not everybody is ready to do that. (Interview 13)

> I think the challenge has to do with coordinating and figuring out the risk in the business model. (Interview 30)

> You are confronted all the time, with all the measurements, all the equipment, you know that it is there. [...] I am willing to believe this can change something. (Interview 19)

As the performance of the building is inherently systematic—depending on the interoperability of multiple structures and components, building businesses increasingly perceive and attempt to capture value from partnership models. Partnership-based business models that integrate smart home systems are increasingly seen as the path forward (Interviews 4, 5, 12, 13, 16, 24, 30):

> If we do not do anything, we will be reduced to a components supplier, and we offer a commodity. That is definitely not our ambition. (Interview 16)

> Instead of us trying to reinvent the wheel and make a lot of mistakes in the process, we just partnered with someone who has that sort of capacity and then work with them. (Interview 12)

> I see a possibility because with this element [smart system integrators], we have access to everything else. If you buy into the connected elements, push it to connected elements. I see trends for the big tertiary building integrators, and especially business for it. (Interview 24)

The value from these interrelations can be better seen in social housing, where users possess limited financial resources, businesses seek value beyond pricing (i.e. selling anonymised user profile data to other companies or utility providers) (Interview 13), and governments as building owners are incentivised to demonstrate sustainability performance (Interviews 26, 27).

Networked responsibility is an inherent part of experimentation with sustainable business model innovation, though what this means in terms of implementation (together with users) is underexplored (Evans et al., 2017). In the BMI literature, product-service systems (PSS) are presented as promising, networked structuration for sustainable—even circular—business (Evans et al., 2017; Pieroni et al., 2019) and, for the building industry, are "identified as a paradigm for the development of integrated offers with interactions, creating more value" (Nuñez-Cacho et al., 2018). The automobile industry has extensively used PSS models, though in seeking sustainability transitions, the industry has similarly struggled with embedded social practices and structures (Wells & Nieuwenhuis, 2012). Interviewees in this project commonly compare with the automobile industry (Interviews 4, 7, 14, 25), as cars are also computerised, durable, expensive, complex products, with multiple stakeholders required for their production. But capturing value from building performance, like vehicle performance, requires a certain level of institutionalisation and literacy (Interview 19), as well as a certain kind of universality:

> The building manager is maybe very technical, but he is not a legal expert. And the people left to make the decisions, they want to know the legal aspects of the business. So that is, for me, so very complex. But the more end user, user-friendly that they are, the more viable your business models are. (Interview 22)

And although organisations can grasp the reduced risk and higher value involved in partnership-based business models, there is a struggle to navigate design for simplicity of use, based on understandings and consideration of human behaviour. This is no surprise, given the arguable impossibility of making that sacred home experience universal (precisely the behavioural, cultural, norm challenges cited in Geels et al., 2018).

> The awareness of what is going on inside homes—and how it relates to people in different information that they are looking to provide—is going to become uniquely different. [...] These cooperative technologies, the lights, motion detection, the time of the day, are just working together to form a very unique experience. (Interview 10)

Thus, the business drive to develop sustainability through user-centred housing is synonymous with the drive to better represent and mimic reality virtually.

> It is more and more about having run the same plan virtual as in reality. (Interview 22)

And while the model becomes more like the reality, the reality becomes more like the model. Hargreaves et al. (2018) categorise this "domestication" of smart homes (implying a taming process) into three areas: cognitive where users learn about the technology; practical where they learn to use it; and symbolic where they interpret meaning from the technologies and integrate this into their identities. The interpretation includes what users do or do not consider violating or invasive, a calculation that comes down to the value and the meaning of the products and services provided (i.e. if a user should share biometric data in order to ensure that his or her health is protected).

> [Users] do not seem to care that there is a microphone going on inside the house, that there are photos being taken inside the home, as opposed to outside the home. Security, to me, has to catch up with balancing that user experience. (Interview 10)

In addition to affecting the willingness of users to share data, the value of the experience also affects consumer choice and financial viability:

> They are willing to pay a bit extra if you give them something meaningful. (Interview 12)

The organisation creation of *meaning* is a crucial point in sharing responsibility between producers and users for the sustainability of buildings in use, as, aforementioned, there is both a risk in smart homes of the rebound effect—that users will inadvertently live less sustainably because of the convenience (be it buying more, or wasting more) (Herrero et al., 2018; Sovacool & Furszyfer Del Rio, 2020)—and that organisations reject business models for sustainability for fear of negative results (e.g. measured poor performance, privacy violations) (de Souza et al., 2019). It is just as important for business models to make responsibility meaningful as it is to make performance visible; so that the pathway towards sustainability transition is one walked hand-in-hand, producers and consumers.

8 Discussion and Conclusion

The prerequisites of digital technologies, business models, and user practices to support a sustainable trajectory of the housing segment are integrated building performance that can deliver measurable sustainability results, that is, through partnership models; balancing personal data usage with the personal meaning of services provided, thus sheltering the sanctity of the home; and modelling sustainability performance based on a shared responsibility between producers and consumers. In welcoming the building user as significant for business models for sustainability in houses, building organisations may perceive that they face the risk of losing power and control over the systems they produce. However, this power and control was always illusory. Users have always done as they please, as witnessed in the frequent appropriation of building technologies, be it stuffing rags into vents or outright breaking motors on automation systems. The opportunity for sustainability service is not necessary in directly influencing behaviour (as behavioural economists would urge), but in revamping organisational approaches to holistic sustainability; that is to say allowing for social influence on business practice (social innovation) combined with structuring education and practice in smart homes to facilitate sustainability. As similarly argued in Shove (2003), redefining normal (household) practice is more important than ecological improvement of the products themselves. And while user engagement, co-design, and co-creation are all challenges in their own rights, perhaps the loftiest challenge is to innovate business models that make sustainability value concrete, while retaining the adaptability essential to shared sustainability visions across diverse household identities. Taking responsibility for the social (whether referring to organisations or users) entails the "skilful task of reconstructing the boundaries of daily life, in partial connection with others, in communication with all of our parts" (Haraway, 1991: 181).

As aforementioned, shifting housing towards sustainability will involve changes on the individual, organisational, and institutional levels (Hoffman & Henn, 2008); and systems change requires the shift of interdependent elements, as is the basis of socio-technical transitions (Geels et al., 2018). Amongst other challenges, the needed changes to achieve the identified prerequisites include *individual* changes to relationship with technology (namely empowerment), improved housing literacy, and consumption behaviour (avoiding rebound effect); *organisational* changes to the attention to end-user experience, partnership-oriented practices, and expanded responsibility for both product performance and privacy protection; and *institutional* changes to the broader market, including a shift to profitisation based on quality (benefit to the end-user, durability, reusability, and recyclability) and performance (how well products or services are working during use) rather than pure focus on price and growth. The author conjectures that these latter elements will remain relevant but can be re-evaluated through accounting that reflects the human and environmental qualities of the buildings in use. Business models for sustainable transition act as the transcendent process among these three levels—business focused on end-users, performed as a service or product-service system, and structured within an institutional context that lifts value to include quality and performance. Technology serves to enable these business models through end-user contact with building organisations, real-time data on performance, and lower-cost building monitoring—not to mention the disruptive influence of the technology sector on the building industry. In the pursuit of service business models as modes of jointly interpreting the meaning of sustainability in homes, smart home technologies can serve as agency-infused objects that drive a landscape shift, gradually strengthening behavioural and values relations between producers and users. They can work to make visible both the sustainability impacts of smart homes and make meaningful the responsibility for sustainability performance—a shift that, ideally, affects the institutional context itself.

Because of the extent of the building industry's negative impacts, even minor sustainability improvements can have significant consequences on a global scale. Though considered rather conservative, the building industry has gone through landscape sustainability improvements stemming from technological innovation before, most notably with the rolling out of mandatory building codes, including recent building energy performance regulations. For example, no household situated in Europe today would consider single-pane glass windows standard, having been uniformly overtaken by double- or even triple-pane with their excellent comfort provisions and winter heating bill savings. Such alterations have similarly been rooted in demonstration projects and "best cases" and have involved incremental changes to norms that unfold over time and unevenly by different geographic and cultural contexts. For business models, this implies a necessity of fluidity, the ability of not just companies, but whole networks to be able to adapt, learn from, and continuously interpret how to turn sustainability value into something real and meaningful for society.

In considering the sustainability implications of business models for smart homes, this chapter faces limitations that future research could improve upon, such as research based on a wider representation of the building industry and other types of buildings (shopping malls, cinemas, universities); case studies of co-created business processes; smart technology applications in manufacturing and circularity; and an exploration of smart technology-driven business models in other industries (the automobile, pharmaceutical, and agriculture industries come to mind). As the dynamics among digital technologies, business models, and users emerge, we need industry to embrace social and behavioural aspects of innovative business models to initiate sustainability transitions as much as we need to embrace our roles as building users in making those business models viable.

References

Aagaard, A., & Ritzén, S. (2020). The critical aspects of co-creating and co-capturing sustainable value in service business models. *Creativity and Innovation Management, 29*(2), 292–302.

Åkerman, M., Halonen, M., & Wessberg, N. (2020). Lost in building design practices: The intertwining of energy with the multiple goals of home building in Finland. *Energy Research and Social Science, 61*(April 2019), 101335.

Akrich, M. (1992). The description of technical objects. In W. E. Bijker & J. Law (Eds.), *Shaping technology/building society: Studies in sociotechnical change*. MIT Press.

Boons, F., & Bocken, N. (2018). Towards a sharing economy – Innovating ecologies of business models. *Technological Forecasting and Social Change, 137*(April), 40–52.

Boons, F., & Lüdeke-Freund, F. (2013). Business models for sustainable innovation: State-of-the-art and steps towards a research agenda. *Journal of Cleaner Production, 45*(April), 9–19.

Bouwman, H., Nikou, S., Molina-Castillo, F. J., & de Reuver, M. (2018). The impact of digitalization on business models. *Digital Policy, Regulation and Governance, 20*(2), 105–124.

Bowles, N. (2018). Thermostats, locks and lights: Digital tools of domestic abuse. *The New York Times*. https://www.nytimes.com/2018/06/23/technology/smart-home-devices-domestic-abuse.html. Accessed 24 Aug 2020.

Christiansen, E., & Andersen, P. V. K. (2013). Digital living at home – User voices about home automation and a home-keeping design discourse. In M. Aanestad & T. Bratteteig (Eds.), *Nordic contributions in IS research* (SCIS 2013. Lecture notes in business information processing) (Vol. 156). Springer.

Cole, R. J., Brown, Z., & McKay, S. (2010). Building human agency: A timely manifesto. *Building Research and Information, 38*(3), 339–350.

Cole, R. J., Oliver, A., & Robinson, J. (2013). Regenerative design, socio-ecological systems and co- evolution. *Building Research and Information, 41*(2), 237–247.

Cooper, I. (2009). Comfort in a brave new world. *Building Research and Information, 37*(1), 95–100.

de Souza, V., Bloemhof-Ruwaard, J., & Borsato, M. (2019). Exploring ecosystem network analysis to balance resilience and performance in sustainable supply chain design. *International Journal of Advanced Operations Management, 11*(1–2), 26–45.

Dong-hwan, K. (2019). [Interview] Smart city expert unimpressed with Songdo. *The Korea Times*. https://www.koreatimes.co.kr/www/nation/2020/02/371_278300.html. Accessed 24 Aug 2020.

Economist. (2020). Tearing down the house: Technology is poised to upend America's property market. https://www.economist.com/finance-and-economics/2020/02/15/technology-is-poised-to-upend-americas-property-market. Accessed 10 Mar 2020.

Evans, S., Vladimirova, D., Holgado, M., Van Fossen, K., Yang, M., Silva, E. A., & Barlow, C. Y. (2017). Business model innovation for sustainability: Towards a unified perspective for creation of sustainable business models. *Business Strategy and the Environment, 26*, 597–608.

Fabi, V., Spigliantini, G., & Corgnati, S. P. (2017). Insights on smart home concept and occupants' interaction with building controls. *Energy Procedia, 111*(September 2016), 759–769.
Flyverbom, M., Deibert, R., & Matten, D. (2019). The governance of digital technology, big data, and the internet: New roles and responsibilities for business. *Business and Society, 58*(1), 3–19.
Flyverbom, M., Leonardi, P. M., Stohl, C., & Stohl, M. (2016). The management of visibilities in the digital age. *International Journal of Communication, 10*, 98–109.
Geels, F. W. (2002). Technological transitions as evolutionary reconfiguration processes: A multi-level perspective and a case-study. *Research Policy, 31*(8–9), 1257–1274.
Geels, F. W. (2019). Socio-technical transitions to sustainability: A review of criticisms and elaborations of the multi-level perspective. *Current Opinion in Environmental Sustainability, 39*, 187–201.
Geels, F. W., Schwanen, T., Sorrell, S., Jenkins, K., & Sovacool, B. K. (2018). Reducing energy demand through low carbon innovation: A sociotechnical transitions perspective and thirteen research debates. *Energy Research & Social Science, 40*, 23–35.
Gijsbers, R., & Lichtenberg, J. (2014). Demand driven selection of adaptable building technologies for flexibility-in-use. *Smart and Sustainable Built Environment, 3*(3), 237–260.
Gram-Hanssen, K., & Georg, S. (2018). Energy performance gaps: Promises, people, practices. *Building Research and Information, 46*(1), 1–9.
Hagendijk, R. P. (2004). The public understanding of science and public participation in regulated worlds. *Minerva, 42*(1), 41–59.
Hale, L. (2018). Anthropocentric urban sustainability: Human significance in building automation. *Sustainable Cities and Society, 42*, 423–433.
Haraway, D. (1991). A cyborg manifesto: Science, technology, and socialist feminism in the late twentieth century. In *Simians, cyborgs and women: The reinvention of nature* (pp. 149–181). Routledge.
Hargreaves, T., Wilson, C., & Hauxwell-Baldwin, R. (2018). Learning to live in a smart home. *Building Research and Information, 46*(1), 127–139.
Herrero, S. T., Nicholls, L., & Strengers, Y. (2018). Smart home technologies in everyday life: Do they address key energy challenges in households? *Current Opinion in Environmental Sustainability, 31*, 65–70.
Hirsch, P. B. (2019). The goose that laid the golden eggs: Personal data and the internet of things. *Journal of Business Strategy, 40*(1), 48–52.

Hoffman, A. J., & Henn, R. (2008). Overcoming the social and psychological barriers to green building. *Organization & Environment, 21*(4), 390–419.

Huber, M., Knottnerus, J. A., Green, L., van der Horst, H., Jadad, A. R., Kromhout, D., et al. (2011). How should we define health? *BMJ, 343*, d4163.

Kingma, B., & van Marken Lichtenbelt, W. (2015). Energy consumption in buildings and female thermal demand. *Nature Climate Change, 5*(12), 1054–1056.

Klein, A. (2019). Credit denial in the age of AI. *The Brookings Institution*. https://www.brookings.edu/research/credit-denial-in-the-age-of-ai/. Accessed 20 Aug 2020.

Köhler, J., Geels, F. W., Kern, F., Markard, J., Onsongo, E., Wieczorek, A., … Wells, P. (2019). An agenda for sustainability transitions research: State of the art and future directions. *Environmental Innovation and Societal Transitions, 31*, 1–32.

Latour, B. (1991). Technology is society made durable. In J. Law (Ed.), *A sociology of monsters: Essays on power, technology and domination*. Routledge.

Lindgreen, A., Vallaster, C., Yousafzai, S., & Hirsch, B. (Eds.). (2019). *Measuring and controlling sustainability: Spanning theory and practice*. Routledge.

Lupton, D. (2020). 'Better understanding about what's going on': Young Australians' use of digital technologies for health and fitness. *Sport, Education and Society, 25*(1), 1–13.

MacInnis, D. J., & Folkes, V. S. (2017). Humanizing brands: When brands seem to be like me, part of me and in a relationship with me. *Journal of Consumer Psychology, 27*(3), 355–374.

Manning, S., & Reinecke, J. (2016). A modular governance architecture in-the-making: How transnational standard-setters govern sustainability transitions. *Research Policy, 45*(3), 618–633.

McCarthy, J., & Wright, P. (2007). *Technology as experience*. MIT Press.

McMeekin, A., & Southerton, D. (2012). Sustainability transitions and final consumption: Practices and socio-technical systems. *Technology Analysis and Strategic Management, 24*(4), 345–361.

Moschetti, R., & Brattebø, H. (2016). Sustainable business models for deep energy retrofitting of buildings: State-of-the-art and methodological approach. *Energy Procedia, 96*(1876), 435–445.

Müller, A., & Reichmann, W. (2015). *Architecture, materiality and society: Connecting sociology of architecture with science and technology studies*. Palgrave Macmillan.

Nuñez-Cacho, P., Górecki, J., Molina-Moreno, V., & Corpas-Iglesias, F. A. (2018). What gets measured, gets done: Development of a circular economy measurement scale for building industry. *Sustainability (Switzerland), 10*(7), 2340.

ONeill, K. J., & Gibbs, D. C. (2014). Towards a sustainable economy? Socio-technical transitions in the green building sector. *Local Environment, 19*(6), 572–590.

Oudshoorn, N., & Pinch, T. (2007). User-technology relationships: Some recent developments. In E. J. Hackett & M. E. Lynch (Eds.), *The handbook of science and technology studies* (pp. 541–566). MIT Press.

Pel, B., Wittmayer, J., Dorland, J., & Søgaard Jørgensen, M. (2020). Unpacking the social innovation ecosystem: An empirically grounded typology of empowering network constellations. *Innovations, 33*(3), 311–336.

Phillippi, J., & Lauderdale, J. (2018). A guide to field notes for qualitative research: Context and conversation. *Qualitative Health Research, 28*(3), 381–388.

Pieroni, M. P. P., McAloone, T. C., & Pigosso, D. C. A. (2019). Business model innovation for circular economy and sustainability: A review of approaches. *Journal of Cleaner Production, 215*, 198–216.

Pinch, T., & Bijker, W. (1984). The social construction of facts and artefacts: Or how the sociology of science and the sociology of technology might benefit each other. *Social Studies of Science, 14*(3), 399–441.

Pink, S. (2009). *Doing sensory ethnography*. SAGE Publications.

Power, A. (2008). Does demolition or refurbishment of old and inefficient homes help to increase our environmental, social and economic viability? *Energy Policy, 36*, 4487–4501.

Research and Markets. (2020). Global smart home market forecast to 2024 – $113 billion opportunity assessment by technology, application and region. https://www.globenewswire.com/news-release/2020/07/01/2056219/0/en/Global-Smart-Home-Market-Forecast-to-2024-113-Billion-Opportunity-Assessment-by-Technology-Application-and-Region.html. Accessed 20 Aug 2020.

Riley, A. (2020). How your smart home devices can be turned against you. *BBC Future*. https://www.bbc.com/future/article/20200511-how-smart-home-devices-are-being-used-for-domestic-abuse. Accessed 24 Aug 2020.

Schaltegger, S., Hansen, E. G., & Lüdeke-Freund, F. (2016). Business models for sustainability. *Organization & Environment, 29*(1), 3–10.

Shove, E. (2003). Users, technologies and expectations of comfort, cleanliness and convenience. *Innovation: The European Journal of Social Science Research, 16*(2), 193–206.

Shove, E., Watson, M., & Ingram, J. (2007). Products and practices: Selected concepts from science and technology studies and from social theories of consumption and practice. *Design Issues, 23*(2), 3–16.

Simons, R. N., Fleischmann, K. R., & Roy, L. (2020). Leveling the playing field in ICT design: Transcending knowledge roles by balancing division and privileging of knowledges. *Information Society, 36*(4), 183–198.

Sintov, N. D., White, L. V., & Walpole, H. (2019). Thermostat wars? The roles of gender and thermal comfort negotiations in household energy use behaviour. *PLoS One, 14*(11), e0224198.

Sovacool, B. K., & Furszyfer Del Rio, D. D. (2020). Smart home technologies in Europe: A critical review of concepts, benefits, risks and policies. *Renewable and Sustainable Energy Reviews, 120*(May 2019). https://doi.org/10.1016/j.rser.2019.109663

Swaminathan, V., Sorescu, A., Steenkamp, J. B. E. M., O'Guinn, T. C. G., & Schmitt, B. (2020). Branding in a hyperconnected world: Refocusing theories and rethinking boundaries. *Journal of Marketing, 84*(2), 24–46.

Thøgersen, J. (2005). How may consumer policy empower consumers for sustainable lifestyles? *Journal of Consumer Policy, 28*(2), 143–177.

Turits, M. (2020). Why working from home might be less sustainable. https://www.bbc.com/worklife/article/20200218-why-working-from-home-might-be-less-sustainable. Accessed 2 Nov 2020.

U.S. Environmental Protection Agency. (1987). *The total exposure assessment methodology (TEAM) study: Summary and analysis* (EPA/600/6-87/002a). Office of Research and Development, U.S. Environmental Protection Agency.

Wells, P. (2018). Degrowth and techno-business model innovation: The case of Riversimple. *Journal of Cleaner Production, 197*, 1704–1710.

Wells, P., & Nieuwenhuis, P. (2012). Transition failure: Understanding continuity in the automotive industry. *Technological Forecasting and Social Change, 79*(9), 1681–1692.

Whyte, J., & Sexton, M. (2011). Motivations for innovation in the built environment: New directions for research. *Building Research & Information, 39*(5), 473–482.

Wolcott, H. F. (1999). *Ethnography: A way of seeing*. Altamira Press.

Zheng, C., Yuan, J., Zhu, L., Zhang, Y., & Shao, Q. (2020). From digital to sustainable: A scientometric review of smart city literature between 1990 and 2019. *Journal of Cleaner Production, 258*, 120689.

Zott, C., & Amit, R. (2010). Business model design: An activity system perspective. *Long Range Planning, 43*(2–3), 216–226.

Business Models for Energy Efficiency Services: Four Archetypes Based on User-Centeredness and Dynamic Capabilities

Ruth Mourik, Carolina Castaldi, and Boukje Huijben

1 Introduction

Estimates indicate that by 2035 two-thirds of the total potential for energy savings in transport, industry, power generation and buildings will remain unexploited (IEA, 2014). For 2018 the energy efficiency target for total

R. Mourik
Duneworks, Eindhoven, The Netherlands
e-mail: ruth.mourik@duneworks.nl

C. Castaldi (✉)
Department of Human Geography and Planning, Utrecht University, Utrecht, The Netherlands
e-mail: c.castaldi@uu.nl

B. Huijben
Department of Industrial Engineering and Innovation Sciences, Eindhoven University of Technology, Eindhoven, The Netherlands
e-mail: b.huijben@tue.nl

A. Aagaard et al. (eds.), *Business Models for Sustainability Transitions*,
https://doi.org/10.1007/978-3-030-77580-3_11

domestic energy demand in the European Union (EU) was still almost 5% off from 2020 targets and more than 20% from 2030 targets (Eurostat, 2020). There is no lack of technological solutions to increase the energy efficiency of buildings. These range from low-tech solutions like roof and wall insulation material to more complex and high-tech solutions such as 'smart' meter devices (i.e. connected and sharing data) and other energy management systems for households and industry (Technopedia, 2020). Some argue that the key to their diffusion could lie in the further development of Energy Efficiency Services (EES) (Kindström et al., 2017). Such services can have a major impact on energy use, both directly, for instance by facilitating the adoption of energy saving technology, and indirectly, for example, by providing end users with information on their energy consumption patterns. For this study we will focus on the end users of energy efficiency technologies and related services. These end users may or may not be the ones paying for the offer. Examples of EES, which we focus on in this chapter, include integrated or one-stop shops, bundled offerings around retrofitting, smart (grid) services, lighting-as-a-service, heating-as-a-service, smart energy management as a service and the more common Energy Service Company (ESCo) and Energy Performance Contracts (EPC). The target group for EES is both households and companies.

Unfortunately, EES remain underdeveloped and the companies delivering them struggle to remain viable. A major weakness of EES firms is their struggle in defining and implementing viable business models (IEA, 2014). Business models represent how a focal firm and its partners create and capture value, for example for new, more sustainable technologies (Boons & Lüdeke-Freund, 2013; Chesbrough, 2010; Osterwalder & Pigneur, 2010; Zott et al., 2011). The traditional business model related to energy efficiency is focused on the commercialization of energy efficiency technologies; hence it is a product-based rather than a service-based model. Such a technology-centered business model often fails to define the value being created for users (Gentile et al., 2007) and tends to focus on economic value only instead of broader notions of value. Several studies (Arevalo et al., 2011; Hienerth et al., 2011; Tolkamp et al., 2018) claim that a more user-centered approach has the potential to be more effective in creating market uptake of Energy Efficiency Services.

However, it remains unclear how to implement and further develop more effective user-centered business models.

A recent study on North American and European utilities demonstrates that some utilities are indeed investing significantly in the energy efficiency market and realize that EES play a key role in the uptake of user-centered solutions (Bigliani et al., 2015). This move appears to be a response to increasing competition from non-utility companies including tech companies, energy equipment manufacturers and even companies from the automotive industry (Vahidi & Sciarretta, 2018). Such companies offer a richer user experience than traditional energy companies thanks to innovative business models, exploiting new uses of ICT to shift energy consumption patterns (Bastida et al., 2019). In Europe, new business models are therefore high on the strategy agenda of some utility executives (Richter, 2013), in particular service-based business models covering PV charging, HVAC services, rooftop solar, bundled home services, community energy and data management. Some of these utilities even decouple the service from the sale of a commodity supply contract (Bigliani et al., 2015).

Our study aims to analyze current business models for EES with respect to two conceptual dimensions, borrowed from the management literature on business models. A *first* dimension relates to the level of user-centeredness of the business models. We expect that more service-based business models can create greater value for users, both by lowering energy bills and by improving experience indicators like comfort (Calabrese, Castaldi, Forte, & Levialdi, 2018). At the same time, a viable business model is one that creates value for the company itself. Thereby a *second* dimension is the EES suppliers' overall dynamic capabilities. These capabilities not only entail excellent sensing of user needs but also seizing of opportunities and reconfiguring activities in dynamic contexts (Teece, 2007; Teece, 2010).

These two conceptual dimensions form the basis for analyzing a set of 46 business models for EES targeted to both households and industry. The empirical material was collected as part of the International Energy Agency Demand Side Management (IEA DSM) project Task 25, focusing on five European countries and South Korea and their EES markets. The project and case study analysis will be described extensively in the methodological section.

Our study has important managerial and policy implications. A capability framework has proven useful not only to understand the determinants of organizational success with business models but also to provide a rationale for policy development (Janssen & Castaldi, 2018). Hence our detailed investigation of which specific capabilities matter for the development of the different elements of a business models offers relevant clues for businesses and policymakers to facilitate the market uptake of EES.

The outline of the paper is as follows. We begin by reviewing current research on business models to justify our selection of theoretical dimensions for investigating EES. Here we take stock of recent research on business models for sustainability, focusing especially on the shift to service-based business models. We then describe the methods used in our empirical analysis and present the results. We conclude with a discussion of our main results and the general lessons from our study: we provide managerial and policy implications as well as directions for further research.

2 Theoretical Framework

2.1 Service-Based Business Models and Sustainability

Servitization is not new and has taken place throughout the economy for several decades (Vandermerwe & Rada, 1988). Servitization is also seen as a possible solution to sustainability challenges (Bocken et al., 2014; Calabrese, Castaldi, Forte, & Levialdi, 2018; Tukker & Tischner, 2006) given that the focus shifts toward fulfilling needs and functions like energy or mobility and away from the sale and ownership of goods. Throughout these processes, the availability of Information and Communication Technologies (ICT) has played a key role in fueling the growth of services (Miozzo & Soete, 2001). Thanks to advances in ICT and the use of Big Data, customized output and economies of scale in service provision can be realized at the same time. However the overall net effect of the implementation of these new technologies on energy demand remains to be seen, as rebound effects may play a role in certain contexts (Steg et al., 2015).

Vargo and Lusch (2008, p. 4) define a 'service' as 'the application of competencies for the benefit of another party'. Their definition stresses that a service is not actually the goal in itself, but a delivery mechanism or a process. Two key elements stand out in this definition and resonate with the archetypical differences between goods and services. *First*, goods and technologies become secondary for the provision of valuable services, while more intangible competences take the center stage. In the case of energy efficiency, physical goods like smart meters, algorithms, smart home devices, appliances and solar panels become enabling tools; they help to provide benefits, but the focus is on how they realize benefits for users. A *second* key element is that services should create value for users. A firm's main goal is therefore to facilitate outcomes that users value and that only materialize in the use phase. From this perspective, the user has a dominant role in creating value as well as in creating business (Aagaard & Ritzén, 2020; Tolkamp et al., 2018). This means that user-centeredness is by definition more important when delivering a service than when merely delivering goods. Additionally, this requires the development of an accompanying business model with a strong focus on user needs. Essentially, business models are a way of creating and capturing value for various stakeholders, including end users (Zott et al., 2011). New sustainability-driven business models aim at balancing the value exchange between various stakeholders in terms of social, environmental and economic value (Boons & Lüdeke-Freund, 2013; Gentile et al., 2007). They can help in overcoming the barriers for the adoption of new, more sustainable technologies like energy efficiency-related technologies. For example, a business model for solar panels including a financing service was found to attract new types of users with limited cash flow (Rai & Sigrin, 2013). Additionally, Huijben and Verbong (2013) found new types of business models for households without a suitable roof for solar. These households could buy shares in collective projects. Hence, smart design of the business model removes barriers for investment and enables further market uptake. For EES such barriers include lack of financial means and low levels of knowledge and conflicting interests (Kindström et al., 2017; Chowdhury et al., 2018). Previous research on user-centered business models for EES in the Netherlands shows various types of interaction with the end user ranging from sending or receiving information to co-production and co-innovation (Tolkamp et al., 2018). However, no definitive conclusions could be drawn on whether the success rate of companies would increase in case of a higher level of user-centeredness nor on which specific capabilities were needed.

Below we will further discuss the need for development of specific capabilities for service-based business models as well as what these capabilities would entail.

2.2 Dynamic Capabilities for Service-Based Business Models

Business models can be considered as 'a reflection of the firm's realized strategy' (Casadesus-Masanell & Ricard, 2010, p. 195). Developing new business models therefore is a challenging endeavor for companies, since it requires entirely rethinking several elements of their strategy (Teece, 2018). The business model is not fixed and finding the right business model requires experimentation (Achtenhagen et al., 2013; McGrath, 2010). Business model research has shed light on the need for and type of capabilities required to develop new business models in general (Achtenhagen et al., 2013; Foss & Saebi, 2017) and service-based business models specifically (Janssen & den Hertog, 2016). The reference model is the dynamic capabilities framework (Teece, 2007). This framework has also been translated to the case of firms engaged in developing new services (Janssen et al., 2016) and for sustainability-oriented services (Calabrese, Forte, & Levialdi, 2018). What emerging research is finding is that companies moving from a goods-based to a service-based business model face challenges in understanding users' unique buying reasons, due to their focus on unique selling propositions and technical possibilities instead of appreciating users' overall needs.

For the specific case of service innovation, Den Hertog et al. (2010) and Janssen et al. (2016) found the following dynamic capabilities to significantly matters for firms to thrive:

- Sensing capabilities to identify user needs and (technological) options in specific market segments through meaningful engagement and co-learning with users and other stakeholders to design the best match between their needs and the service.

- Conceptualizing capabilities to process the knowledge sourced from the sensing activities to identify patterns for continuous innovation. This capability is key for overall learning and scaling-up activities.
- Co-producing and orchestrating capabilities to align all the relevant actors and providers working toward a seamless and coherent end-user experience.
- Scaling and internal stretching capabilities in relation to the service providers' marketing capabilities to facilitate their ability to create a smooth and aligned service-oriented company structure.

These capabilities are not independent; rather they form a coherent set of elements reinforcing each other. They can also be explicitly linked to the elements of sustainability-driven service innovations (Calabrese, Forte, & Levialdi, 2018), of which EES can be seen as a specific example. Research on dynamic capabilities has highlighted how these capabilities are higher-level capabilities that firms only develop through deliberate investment (Zollo & Winter, 2002). Simple accumulation of experience, which will grow along the service journey, needs to be complemented with purposeful articulation and codification of knowledge, to reflect and recognize patterns, and then develop new organizational routines (Janssen et al., 2016). As such, we expect that firms will vary in the degree to which they will master each dynamic capability, with some firms struggling and others thriving. This is also in line with the idea that firms develop new business models in an exploratory and evolutionary fashion (McGrath, 2010).

3 Methodology

For this study we followed an exploratory, multiple case study design and analyzed 46 business models in the Netherlands, Sweden, Norway, Austria, Switzerland and South Korea as part of the IEA DSM Task 25 (Seawright & Gerring, 2008; Yin, 2003). Four cases from South Korea were added as outsiders to the European context to further increase the external validity of the results. Together with national experts, we first compiled a long list of more than 350 energy efficiency initiatives in the participating countries, through online search and by leveraging the networks of the energy agencies involved. We focused on a mix of retrofitting, lighting, smart solutions and total solution (one-stop-shop) products and services, categories that emerged from a first shortlisting of available cases in the participating countries. Based on initial information collected in this long list, and based on availability of material and access, we selected 46 initiatives for further analysis of their business models. The selected initiatives were all commercially implemented EES, but they represented variety in success (i.e. in terms of market share and market uptake). The diverse sampling strategy matched the explorative nature of this study (Seawright & Gerring, 2008). The data was collected through at least one in-depth interview with all businesses, mostly several interviews. We interviewed the owners of the company, or the developers of the value proposition when dealing with a larger company.

The interviews relied on a semi-structured list of questions, covering the initial business model (all nine building blocks) and how and why it changed over time, but also about the positioning of the business model in the market, the intended user of the proposition, and the influence of context factors on the business model. The information from the interviews was also complemented with information available in reports and online.

The comparative analysis of the 46 business models leveraged our conceptual framework as a template. We started mapping the business model canvas and user value canvas designed by Osterwalder and Pigneur (2010). They defined a business model as consisting of nine building blocks: partners, activities, resources, value proposition, user relationships, channels, user segments, cost structure and revenue streams. We specifically focused on the development of the business model, its degree of user-centeredness and the dynamic capabilities they could demonstrate. Another key element concerned the (type of) user and their (type of) involvement in the business model development. We worked with qualitative scales and reconstructed user propositions for each case. For the measurement of the dynamic capabilities we relied on the measurement tool developed by Janssen et al. (2016) This measurement scale explicitly considers the micro-foundations of capabilities (Teece, 2007), hence lists measurable activities that one can trace back in actual organizational routines. Each capability is measured through three items (two for co-producing and orchestrating) that were validated in a large-scale study covering firms engaged in service innovation (Janssen et al., 2016). After measuring the strength of capability development we plotted the combinations of dynamic capabilities for all cases and mapped them to the to business model canvas and user involvement dimension to inductively construct categories of business models. Table A in Appendix provides an overview of all cases, classified by energy solution type and business model archetype.

Our analysis of the 46 cases revealed four types of business models, with varying degrees of user-centeredness and service orientation, as well as different combinations of dynamic capabilities which will be further discussed below. To define the archetypes, we exploited methods from qualitative research, in particular grounded theory (Corbin & Strauss, 1990). We engaged in an iterative inductive process, where independent researchers grouped the cases according to the chosen analytical dimensions until we converged to a shared grouping.

To further validate our findings, we organized a workshop in each of the participating countries, except for South Korea. The workshops engaged the entrepreneurs and other stakeholders from industry, academia and the policy arena to discuss the initial findings. In this way, we were able to triangulate our findings based on a combination of self-reported information from the interviews, collective reflections within the workshops and material collected from a range of other sources, either public or provided by the companies (including strategic information on turnover, client bases and other firm-level data).

4 Results: Business Model Archetypes in EES

Table 1 summarizes our findings by showing the key properties of the four business model archetypes in terms of business model dimensions, user-centeredness and dynamic capabilities. The archetypes clearly

Table 1 Business model archetypes for Energy Efficiency Services, their level of user-centeredness and the dynamic capabilities involved

BM elements	BM1: Pushing technology harder	BM2: Reframing what you propose	BM3: Pushing something else—the use phase model	BM 4: Servicing
Value proposition	Functional benefits and technical specs are the core of the proposition	By acknowledging that energy efficiency is low on purchasers' priority list	Delivering multiple benefits (other than energy efficiency) in an integrated way	Fluid value proposition, customized
User segment	Industrial/ commercial	Consumers, industrial, commercial	Expanding B2C segments with B2B2C segments	Users as partners
User relationship	Distant, not personal, no focus on user needs/ barriers	Standardized. More personal and tailored	Explicitly and actively creating partnerships with users. Entering new niches	Built on trust and long term
Channels	Traditional, focus on cold acquisition	Traditional. Word of mouth	Direct and personalized. Word of mouth	Multichannel. Tailored. Word of mouth
Key activities	Focus on hardware and software, develop reseller channels, train resellers and users	Focus on hardware and software, tackle fragmentations, process optimization	Collecting and handling user and usage data	Build relationships across the user lifecycle. Tracking changes in value
Key partners	Hierarchical/value chain. Resellers and intermediaries for sales purposes	More equal. Focus on co-creation. Choice of partners based on branding quality and matching	Explicitly service-oriented partners that help deliver complex packages. Partners who can also be a launching user	Equal partnerships, user is considered a partner
Key resources	Technical and sales knowledge	Technical and sales knowledge. Partners become resources	Data and ICT become enablers of delivering value	User, use phase, data
Costs	Traditional, focus on personnel and material	Traditional, focus on personnel and material	Personnel and material. Technological innovation	Investment in 'vision'

Revenue streams	One-off, transaction-based maintenance fee	Transaction based. Create goodwill	Subscription fee. User retention and goodwill	Crowdfunding, memberships, goodwill
User-centeredness	Low	Medium	Medium	High
Dynamic capabilities	**User sensing** Not in a structured way	**User sensing** Weakly developed. Collecting user insights up to transaction. Strong focus on specific details in transaction journey (like decision-making, info needed or simplifying process, trust building)	**User sensing** Well developed. Systematic. Active co-creation becomes key activity	**User sensing** Core capability
	Conceptualizing Not in a structured way	**Conceptualizing** Shifting focus from delivery process toward tailoring value proposition and buyer satisfaction	**Conceptualizing** Active conceptualizing; however, technological barriers are inhibiting. Moving toward multiple benefit innovation	**Conceptualizing** Co-creating. Growth of user base is inhibiting the aim to expand
	Orchestrating Not in a structured way. Focus on the supply chain side	**Orchestrating** Public-private partnerships to boost sales and trust	**Orchestrating** Problem solvers. Delivering complex services. Or become original equipment manufacturer (OEM)	**Orchestrating** Aimed at serving the user during the use phase
	Scaling and stretching Outsourcing the sales skills	**Scaling and stretching** Branding to create competitive edge. Quality and ease as differentiating elements	**Scaling and stretching** Tech barriers still hard to overcome	**Scaling and stretching** Aimed at continuous innovation

differed regarding the selected dimensions, which validates the relevance of our theoretical lens.

4.1 BM1: Pushing Technology Harder

This first business model type has a strong technology driven start and stems directly from new laws, regulations or directives. Nine cases fell under this archetype. Usually a very passionate and skilled engineer developed a concept and proceeded to market it. Typically, the initial target users were industrial users. These entrepreneurs developed their business around one technology or product, for example, a smart plug, smart algorithm, insulation and Heating Ventilation and Air Conditioning (HVAC) system or earth leak detectors. The selling proposition revolved around stressing the technological and energy-related functions and performance characteristics of the product, such as figures on energy saved, insulation quotients, safety, reliability, control, optimization and verification to their users, rather than more qualitative notions about the benefits of the product to users. To some extent, many of the industrial users did demand a very specific performance requirement. Yet, the initiatives reported that their user base was too small and the competition too high; hence they were experiencing stagnation in sales. Partners were usually on the technology side, often co-developers of the product. This type of business did not really focus on sensing user needs, certainly not in a systematic manner, nor during the use of the product. The goal was to sell a one-off product. Hence, the cost structure was very traditional and included personnel and product component costs. The revenue structure was also mostly product oriented, with one-off payments and hardly any recurring fees. If the companies had recurring (monthly) fees or subscriptions, this was at most 20% of their revenues, with 80% one-off payments for the product sales.

Once businesses started experiencing that the market of early adopters was saturated, their response was to focus on strengthening marketing and sales. To this end, they developed new relations to specific intermediaries: they approached consultants, installers or even original equipment manufacturers (OEMs). They paid them to resell or refer the product, or they trained them to better understand the product and as such become better able to refer it to potential users. The training focused on the technical characteristics of the product, whereas the capability of sensing user needs remained undeveloped. There were still no activities aimed at sensing user needs systematically and adapting the value proposition to these needs. Instead, sensing technological options came naturally to this type of business model.

A key capability was orchestration: these initiatives invested in relationships with retailers to get them to consider offering their product as part of their packages. Yet, this focus of orchestration also revealed an important limitation in other capabilities, specifically conceptualizing capabilities. Any innovation or shift in offerings was incidental and incremental. They did not aim to radically innovate their product or develop a set of new services. In fact, all initiatives focusing on this business model were facing stagnation in their user base and increasing difficulties securing enough revenues by product sales. Actually, they mentioned themselves that a potential future strategy would involve conceptualizing services around the product to facilitate its further uptake.

In sum, this 'pushing technology harder' model was about keeping a strong focus on technology but pushing harder and using other channels to increase the market potential. Examples of cases falling into this first archetype were a developer of a smart algorithm that could tell households what appliances needed replacement with more energy efficient ones, or a provider of insulation measures. Importantly, some of the companies in this category went bankrupt or decided to stop. However, some of them tried to turn their business model into the next model by reframing their offer. This shows the highly exploratory and evolutionary character of the business model development process (McGrath, 2010).

4.2 BM2: Reframing What You Propose

This business model was typically developed by companies that, having experienced the limitations of just selling products, started reframing the value of their products. Nineteen cases fitted this archetype, including insulation companies that switched their selling strategy to offering energy benefits such as comfort, or an easy implementation, but also builders of nearly zero energy buildings (NZEB) that started promoting their houses as designer homes. The key difference between this business model and the first archetype is that these initiatives took users and their needs into account when (re)defining their propositions. Such a strategy added extra value to existing services and led to the development of further services focusing more on the use phase. At the same time, this business model still focused on one-off transactions with users. Companies did not consider user relations during the use phase of a proposition to be relevant.

In terms of capabilities, it was clear that these business models involved developing a capability of sensing user needs through personal contacts, training potential users, tailored quotes, personal telephone calls and follow-up talks. In response to this deeper understanding, companies came to realize that energy efficiency or a product's specific technical characteristics were not a top priority for users. The value proposition changed to reflect this. Nevertheless, no systematic and pro-active sensing of user needs occurred in the use phase as all efforts would channel into influencing the purchasing decision.

The capability of conceptualizing also further developed, however not toward technological innovation but rather toward process innovation aimed at building a trust relationship with users. The technologies were still at the core of the value proposition. For example, some companies conducted process innovation, and then delivered the process as a service to households, as in the case of insulation companies delivering timely quotes and a no-hassle process around retrofitting. Their business models then became focused on delivering ease and comfort instead of energy efficiency alone. The technologies or products do not change, only the process to deliver them.

Partners for these types of initiatives were usually technical and mostly co-developers of the proposition. However, these partners explicitly played a role in underpinning the branding of the product and were selected based on excellence and quality. Follow-up was carried out to make sure the process was a pleasant experience for users and to solve potential technical matters. That was also where the companies stopped.

The actual use phase of the home or insulation method did not represent a gateway to deliver more services, for example, smart home services.

As with the first model, the revenue structure was also mostly product oriented, with one-off payments and hardly any recurring fees. If the companies had recurring fees or subscriptions, that was at most 20% of their revenue, with 80% one-off payments for the sale of a product. A few companies also mentioned more intangible revenues in the form of goodwill. These companies implemented their energy efficiency product or service as a means of fulfilling other goals such as gaining a competitive edge in their respective market (e.g. rental or retail).

To sum up, this business model was very much about reframing what was proposed. It represented a first consistent step toward servitization, focusing on user needs, collaborating with excellent partners and increasing value. However, this model still lacked a comprehensive focus on the use phase, and on delivery of services around the product, which would enable an extended relationship with users beyond the purchasing phase.

4.3 BM3: Pushing Something Else—The Use Phase Model

The third archetype was about pushing something else and exactly about focusing on the use phase that was neglected in the previous archetype. The ten cases falling in this archetype demonstrated a shift from pushing a solution, to becoming problem solvers. This often happened in response to reaching a ceiling in terms of number of clients, but also after unsolicited feedback from users. This unsolicited feedback then triggered a company to reflect on its value proposition and start focusing more actively on user needs. The main difference with the second archetype was that essential elements in the proposition changed, not merely the framing in terms of language and branding. The main change was the awareness that the client was in fact a 'user' and use was not limited to a single moment in time, but was instead a whole process. As such the use phase, starting after the first sale transaction, could provide key insights for innovation. Companies opting for this model still had a strong technology push start, but were not afraid to develop a very new package around that technology or even adapt their technology to meet new user needs, especially once the technologies become part of a larger package. These companies had typically started by developing specific technologies in the smart metering, solar business, smart ICT and feedback sectors, but were trying to steer away from direct consumer sales toward a business-to-business partner relationship. They aimed to partner with a bigger company to jointly offer a larger and more complex value proposition to end consumers, sometimes not directly related to energy efficiency at all. Often, these complex value propositions revolved around delivering health or safety benefits, comfort and much more. In this archetype all elements of the business model differed to some extent, but mostly the users, the value proposition, resources and the partners appeared significantly different, as compared to the first two archetypes. Activities focused on data handling and analysis, instead of developing soft and hardware; typical activities included data mining of user profiles to allow for systematic monitoring while still tailoring to personal user needs and profiles.

Opting for this type of business model clearly indicated a stronger sensing of user needs and capabilities than previous archetypes. Companies realized that their specific technology, focusing on energy, energy efficiency or conservation, was not valuable to their users as such. What significantly differentiated this model from the first two was the emphasis on extending and deepening the relationship with the end users of the package, focusing on the use phase. Companies had a clear aim of not only collecting data that could be valuable from a business perspective but also as source for further improvements and better responses to user needs. In the case of companies moving into the B2B segment, they aided clients to develop a relationship with their own users, thus moving from being B2C to B2B2C companies. Another clear difference was that this model was about delivering multiple values to both the user and to partners. The systematic analysis of user needs was center stage. These companies made considerable efforts to develop the capability of sensing user needs, and mediating between both the primary businesses they delivered to as users and their users being final (residential) users.

These initiatives also developed strong orchestration capabilities. They explicitly aimed to align with providers for a larger, more complex value proposition, and correspondingly developed their conceptualizing capability, making sure they innovated their product sufficiently to match their partner's technological system. For some of the businesses in Sweden, for example, this meant that their value proposition was adapted from providing a metering device to delivering a platform to users, a hub where various complex datasets could be merged and offer the basis for simple and actionable feedback on energy use for different users. By becoming part of a network delivering multiple values, the initiatives in this archetype engaged in complex problem solving as their main strategy.

4.4 BM4: Servicing Model

A fourth and final business model type matched eight of our cases that all started with an explicit service orientation, typically in response to a deep concern about available options and often as a result of collective action by user groups. One example is a case in Sweden, where a magazine dedicated to sustainable technologies developed a total solution around testing, choosing, financing, implementing and maintaining solar systems for households. Their users (readers) asked for help in testing and identifying the best solar system and related financing and this magazine developed a business to meet these needs. The unmet needs were well known and researched, and the initial value proposition was explicitly developed for a small group of specific users. An iterative process of build-test-learn in co-creation with users and partners led to a network type of enterprise, where a proposition was the result of intensive cooperation between more or less equal partners and with (at least a representative group of) users. The idea was to extend their business gradually with new or extra benefits that in some way naturally matched the needs and lives of the users. The main difference between this model and the other ones was that the users and their needs and lives were at the core of the business model at every stage (from orientation to transaction, to use and even end of use). Some entrepreneurs did not even start with energy efficiency:

they just ended up there because it was instrumental for achieving their goals.

The key dynamic capabilities of sensing, conceptualizing and orchestrating all needed to be highly developed for this business model to be viable. The trust relationship with users and partners was an essential resource in facilitating all activities related to sensing, innovation and collaboration, but also in allowing experimentation with unconventional funding options, including crowdfunding and membership support options.

5 Discussion and Conclusions

In this final section we highlight and critically discuss the main findings of our study and reflect upon the implications for managers, policymakers and for further research.

5.1 The Road to Becoming More User Centered and Service Oriented

The richness of our qualitative data, including in-depth interviews with the companies, allowed us to capture the entire process of how the different business models emerged. We managed to do so by reconstructing the journeys of the extensive set of initiatives we were able to select thanks to strong networks of national agencies committed to understanding the challenges for further uptake of energy efficiency markets.

An initial insight was that the transition to a more service-oriented approach often only started as a reaction to the absence of market growth or a disappointing market uptake. Consequently, the sale of energy efficiency goods and technology was 'enriched' with add-on services. At the same time, we also observed cases of companies that did not go through the whole journey but started with a clear service proposition from the start. Secondly, companies typically changed their business models in incremental ways, starting with small, often intuitive, changes to the business model and tackling only the dynamic capabilities they needed to align their business more with user needs. This was in line with the idea that dynamic capabilities only emerge through a painstaking process of deliberate investment in understanding what works and what does not. A third main insight was that when the transition was really pushed through, new business models emerged where energy efficiency was no longer the primary value delivered, but a secondary outcome of other value delivery, such as designing near-zero energy homes, safety, control, ease or values such as user retention and access. Overall, our study has contributed to the emerging theoretical discussion on linking service business model development and dynamic capabilities, by suggesting user-centeredness as the space where companies can be challenged on whether their service propositions and organizational capabilities align.

5.2 Clues to Potential Success Factors

When analyzing the cases and the reported success of the companies representative of the four business model types, the companies that were more user centered had more success at delivering energy efficiency in terms of market uptake, growth of user base and market share. However, this was particularly the case for business models with a parent company providing startup capital, which allowed for effective sensing of user needs or becoming service and user centered, for example, through co-creation. Such parent companies often provided two further valuable elements: an existing user base and branding. Perhaps most importantly, these parent companies had a patient attitude with respect to how long companies could experiment. They gave their subsidiaries time to experiment, learn and adapt the services, before becoming commercially viable. General Electric for example launched Current, a company that blended advanced energy technologies like LED and solar with networked sensors and software to make commercial buildings and industrial facilities more energy efficient and productive. Current soon had 1 billion dollars in revenue. Especially the spin-offs from universities, utilities and distribution system operators were doing better than smaller and standalone businesses because they had a parent company providing protected space for experimentation or niche and further development of the business model without too much financial constraint, which was essential for their further development and up-scaling (Sarasini & Linder,

2018; Smith & Raven, 2012). Building of strong actor coalitions including actors with high levels of power and resources is considered an essential strategy for developing such niches in order for them to become mainstream and (partially) replacing the status quo (Kemp et al., 1998; Schot & Geels, 2008).

Another finding was that those business models that delivered value to multiple stakeholders and gave end users the opportunity to experience the value of energy efficiency after the initial transaction (i.e. during use) were also more successful in terms of market share. This again indicates that energy efficiency may not be a reason for buying, as it often only proves to be of value in the use phase. Delivering value to multiple stakeholders and end users required companies to have excellent conceptualizing and orchestration capabilities. Experiencing energy efficiency in use was mostly realized where it was related to other values being delivered such as comfort, safety, convenience, or control or a combination. The business models that successfully delivered this experience of energy efficiency shared the focus on the total end-user journey, from the orientation phase, through transaction, to the use phase and beyond. The focus on the use phase also required businesses and entrepreneurs to be able to really sense user needs on a continuous basis and adjust (conceptualize) the value proposition in response to changing needs in different use phases of the (buying, using). Hence, the conceptualizing capability also needed to be rather well developed.

These insights offer very hands-on recommendations for companies entering or already engaged in the energy efficiency market. Our message is that striving for a user-centered model and investing in the capabilities needed to deliver a thriving service-based business model are powerful enablers of organizational success. At the same time, not all companies are able to embrace and realize a servicing business model type. Hence, we also see space for policy interventions to facilitate current initiatives in specific ways.

5.3 Implications for Management, Policy and for Further Research

This study offered a first comprehensive overview of business model archetypes for EES. We have argued that understanding how companies account for users and how they develop related organizational dynamic capabilities provides important insights to facilitate the further uptake of EES. An important question when it comes to a goal like energy efficiency, which is desirable from a societal perspective, is the extent to which policy initiatives should be geared to facilitate the underlying processes. We can use our framework to shed light on this policy question.

A key consideration is that most firms providing EES are very small (often under ten employees). These firms have a very hard time becoming truly service oriented. These companies often opt for a push technology harder or smart matcher strategy. Most SMEs have hardly any capacity and resources to experiment and develop the capabilities required to shift from a product and technology push approach. SMEs may lack both the experience and the resources to invest in learning, both fundamental to develop dynamic capabilities (Zollo & Winter, 2002). However, existing policy frameworks do not sufficiently facilitate this experimentation or responsiveness. Many have argued that (innovation) policy is about creating conducive context for organizations to engage in experimentation (Metcalfe, 1995; Smith & Raven, 2012). Public authorities could do more to nurture energy efficiency service entrepreneurs, than simply financing (Borgeson et al., 2012). Rubalcaba et al. (2010) and Janssen and Castaldi (2018) stress the relevance of using capability failure arguments to make a case for policy intervention, starting from the observation that many firms lack dynamic capabilities and competences to realize new services. Importantly, companies may also 'borrow' experience from others if they lack their own (Janssen et al., 2018), for instance by joining initiatives where entrepreneurs share their journeys or by getting advice rather than finance from support organizations. For entrepreneurs using the 'push technology harder' business model, the biggest barrier seems to be their own lack of awareness of where they are positioned on the product-service shift and how that relates to the other stakeholders (Mont & Lindhqvist, 2003). These entrepreneurs would for instance benefit from self-assessment information tools, to increase awareness of service value.

The 'reframing what you propose' business model already entails awareness about how to create a longer-term relationship with users. The entrepreneurs need resources to be able to experiment conceptualization and co-creation with users. Policy support for this type of entrepreneur can take the form of SME subsidies to support co-creation and other sensing activities, or grants to enable experimentation with delivering multiple value and more collaborative and sustainable types of business models. However, support can and should take the form of training in dynamic capabilities such as conceptualizing in incubators or in Chamber of Commerce types of network. Public-private partnerships such as the European innovation intermediary InnoEnergy have an important role to play here, not only in providing business modeling training and support but also with a clear focus on delivering service and value in the use phase.

Initiatives falling under the third business model archetype need well-developed orchestration capabilities and experimental space to learn about user needs. These entrepreneurs could use policy support that opens up user relations and quantitative and qualitative data on users that can help businesses identify valuable user segments. Many public authorities have very relevant open data about home energy labels, infrastructure and so on that SMEs can use to perform an initial sensing of user needs, for example, finding out which homes are in dire need of insulation. Policy instruments that support the development of the orchestration capabilities these entrepreneurs need are for example collaboration platforms focused on linking businesses with consumer organizations, governmental agencies, NGOs and other businesses. Facilitating partnerships across sectors and including public-private partnerships with, for example, NGOs, creating trust by endorsing a type of service (brand independent) and certification, labels and codes (if standardized and provided by trusted institutions) are potentially powerful market changers supporting this third type of businesses. Yet another type of support is through public procurement. This could be launching customers for SMEs focused on delivering services. These contracts should then be opened up to serve as demonstration sites for others to learn from and experiment.

The fourth business model hardly needs policy support, but more research on success factors could help entrepreneurs opting for this strategy. For example, what type of regulation can support the provision of feedback on energy consumption, and what type of feedback generates behavioral change and energy conservation; what type of regulation can improve billing, and what type of billing and its frequency best create demand for energy efficiency; also research on the best type of Energy Performance Contracting for the residential sector, in order to overcome challenges such as the lack of user trust and financial drivers. Other interesting foci to investigate are the internalization of externalities in electricity or gas prices, thus making energy efficiency more attractive pricewise, or investigating and consequently revisiting the system where the price of electricity decreases with increased use and understanding what type of use behavior this evokes. Other research could focus on generating multiple and sustainable values, such as could be the case in the sharing economy, and regulations that help to create a healthy indoor climate, both for residential and buildings in general, or reduce sick leave for companies through better working environments (lighting, heating, acoustics, ventilation). In sum, acknowledging the existence of different business model archetypes can inform the targeted design of policy instruments to facilitate the uptake of EES.

We should conclude with two important considerations. First, further research could test the determinants of success for the identified business model archetypes in a quantitative large-scale study, complementary to our exploratory, case-based analysis. It remains challenging to define the success of entrepreneurial ventures, even more so of business models. Success can be captured by market uptake, growth of user base and market share, but also by measuring user satisfaction or the environmental benefits in terms of energy efficiency gains. A discourse analysis of the storylines used by companies, users and other stakeholders could investigate how the different actors frame the success of the business models and how this shapes the EES market. These further analyses of success will be more relevant if they embrace a holistic consideration of sustainability, including social sustainability (the value created for individuals), economic sustainability (the value created for businesses) and environmental sustainability (the value created for the environment) (see Maltz et al., 2018). Second, it remains unclear what the actual impact of the uptake of EES on energy demand is. Studies on energy rebound effects have warned that energy savings in one domain might trigger increased demand in other domains. Further research could look into these effects, by leveraging insights from the psychology of energy use (Steg et al., 2015).

Acknowledgments This work was supported by the Technology Collaboration Programme User-Centred Energy Systems by the International Energy Agency. We thank the national experts involved in the project for their support in the analysis and data gathering. We are also grateful to the editors of this book, in particular Peter Wells, for their suggestions.

Appendix

Table A Overview of cases, classified by energy solution type (rows) and business model archetypes (columns)

Energy solution type/ business model archetype	BM1: Pushing harder	BM2: Reframing what you propose	BM3: Pushing something else	BM4: Servicing
Total solutions		GroupE Tygr Ench, Switzerland SIG Commun d'immeuble, Switzerland BAS, Netherlands Click for Climate, Austria LSI Leistungsgruppe, Austria Friendly buildings, Sweden		Buurkracht, Netherlands ETC, Sweden Filago, Norway Hvaler, Norway

(*continued*)

Table A (continued)

Energy solution type/ business model archetype	BM1: Pushing harder	BM2: Reframing what you propose	BM3: Pushing something else	BM4: Servicing
Retrofitting	Cremab, Sweden	Reimarkt, Netherlands Nederland Isoleert, Netherlands EPC+, Austria Ahlsell, Sweden Humlagadan, Sweden Bolig Enøk, Norway	Otovo, Norway Samchully ES, South Korea SIG Eco-social, Switzerland	Meshcrafts, Norway
Smart energy solutions	Greeniant, Netherlands Mywarm, Austria Messpunkt, Austria Netconnect, Austria Climacheck, Sweden Megacon, Sweden	HyttaMi, Norway Sikom, Norway Gridwiz, South Korea E-smart, Sweden	Eneco Toon, Netherlands Woonconnect, Netherlands Exibea, Sweden Ferro amp, Sweden Serinus, Norway Tiny Mesh, Norway Future home, Norway	BEN Energy, Switzerland Evalo, Switzerland
Lighting and heating	Led design Holland, Netherlands Eco solution, South Korea	Julia Dusche, Switzerland Withlight, South Korea GroupE Lighting, Switzerland		Philips Light as a service, Netherlands

References

Aagaard, A., & Ritzén, S. (2020). The critical aspects of co-creating and co-capturing sustainable value in service business models. *Creativity and Innovation Management, 29*(2), 292–302.

Achtenhagen, L., Melin, L., & Naldi, L. (2013). Dynamics of business models – Strategizing, critical capabilities and activities for sustained value creation (2015). *Long Range Planning, 46*(6), 427–442.

Arevalo, J. A., Castelló, I., de Colle, S., Lenssen, G., Neumann, K., & Zollo, M. (2011). Introduction to the special issue: Integrating sustainability in business models. *Journal of Management Development, 30*, 941–954.

Bastida, L., Cohen, J. J., Kollmann, A., Moya, A., & Reichl, J. (2019). Exploring the role of ICT on household behavioural energy efficiency to mitigate global warming. *Renewable and Sustainable Energy Reviews, 103*, 455–462.

Bigliani, R., Eastman, R., Segalotto, J., Feblowitz, J., & Gallotti, G. (2015). *Designing the new utility business models* (White paper). Energy Insights IDC.

Bocken, N. M. P., Short, S. W., Rana, P., & Evans, S. (2014). A literature and practice review to develop sustainable business model archetypes. *Journal of Cleaner Production, 65*, 42–56.

Boons, F., & Lüdeke-Freund, F. (2013). Business models for sustainable innovation: State-of-the-art and steps towards a research agenda. *Journal of Cleaner Production, 45*, 9–19.

Borgeson, M., Zimring, M., & Goldman, C. (2012). *The limits of financing for energy efficiency*. Lawrence Berkeley National Laboratory. https://escholarship.org/uc/item/10b8d9zs

Calabrese, A., Castaldi, C., Forte, G., & Levialdi, N. G. (2018). Sustainability-oriented service innovation: An emerging research field. *Journal of Cleaner Production, 193*, 533–548.

Calabrese, A., Forte, G., & Levialdi, N. G. (2018). Fostering sustainability-oriented service innovation (SOSI) through business model renewal: The SOSI tool. *Journal of Cleaner Production, 201*, 783–791.

Casadesus-Masanell, R., & Ricard, J. E. (2010). From strategy to business models and onto tactics. *Long Range Planning, 43*, 195–215.

Chesbrough, H. (2010). Business model innovation: Opportunities and barriers. *Long Range Planning, 43*(2–3), 354–363.

Chowdhury, J. I., Hu, Y., Haltas, I, Balta-Ozkan, N., & Liz Varga, G. Jr. M. (2018). Reducing industrial energy demand in the UK: A review of energy efficiency technologies and energy saving potential in selected sectors. *Renewable and Sustainable Energy Reviews, 94*, 1153–1178.

Corbin, J. M., & Strauss, A. (1990). Grounded theory research: Procedures, canons, and evaluative criteria. *Qualitative Sociology, 13*(1), 3–21.

Den Hertog, P., Van der Aa, W., & De Jong, M. W. (2010). Capabilities for managing service innovation: Towards a conceptual framework. *Journal of Service Management, 21*(4), 490–514.

Eurostat. (2020). Energy consumption in 2018: Primary and final energy consumption still 5% and 3% away from 2020 targets. *Newsrelease*. Retrieved September 11, 2020, from https://ec.europa.eu/eurostat/documents/2995521/10341545/8-04022020-BP-EN.pdf/39dcc365-bdaa-e6f6-046d-1b4d241392ad

Foss, N. J., & Saebi, T. (2017). Fifteen years of research on business model innovation: How far have we come, and where should we go? *Journal of Management, 43*(1), 200–227.

Gentile, C., Spiller, N., & Noci, G. (2007). How to sustain the user experience: An overview of experience components that co-create value with the user. *European Management Journal, 25*, 395–410.

Hienerth, C., Keinz, P., & Lettl, C. (2011). Exploring the nature and implementation of user-centred business models. *Long Range Planning, 44*, 344–374.

Huijben, J. C. C. M., & Verbong, G. P. J. (2013). Breakthrough without subsidies? PV business model experiments in the Netherlands. *Energy Policy, 56*, 362–370.

International Energy Agency (IEA). (2014). *Capturing the multiple benefits of energy efficiency: Executive summary*. International Energy Agency. Retrieved September 11, 2020, from https://webstore.iea.org/download/direct/375?fileName=Multiple_Benefits_of_Energy_Efficiency.pdf

Janssen, M. J., & Castaldi, C. (2018). Services, innovation, capabilities, and policy: Toward a synthesis and beyond. *Science and Public Policy, 45*(6), 863–874.

Janssen, M. J., Castaldi, C., & Alexiev, A. (2016). Dynamic capabilities for service innovation: Conceptualization and measurement. *R&D Management, 46*(4), 797–811.

Janssen, M. J., Castaldi, C., & Alexiev, A. S. (2018). In the vanguard of openness: Which dynamic capabilities are essential for innovative KIBS firms to develop? *Industry and Innovation, 25*(4), 432–457.

Janssen, M. J., & den Hertog, P. (2016). Developing service-based business models: Which innovation capability for which innovation dimension? In *Service innovation* (pp. 97–128). Springer Japan.

Kemp, R., Schot, J., & Hoogma, R. (1998). Regime shifts to sustainability through processes of niche formation: The approach of strategic niche management. *Technology Analysis & Strategic Management, 10*(2), 175–198.

Kindström, D., Ottosson, M., & Thollander, P. (2017). Driving forces for and barriers to providing energy services. A study of local and regional energy companies in Sweden. *Energy Efficiency, 10*, 21–39.

Maltz, E., Bi, H. H., & Bateman, M. (2018). Benchmarking sustainability performance: The next step in building sustainable business models. *Journal of Public Affairs, 18*(3), e1606.

McGrath, R. G. (2010). Business models: A discovery driven approach. *Long Range Planning, 43*(2–3), 247–261.
Metcalfe, J. S. (1995). Technology systems and technology policy in an evolutionary framework. *Cambridge Journal Economics, 19*(1), 25–46.
Miozzo, M., & Soete, L. (2001). Internationalization of services: A technological perspective. *Technological Forecasting and Social Change, 67*(2–3), 159–185.
Mont, O., & Lindhqvist, T. (2003). The role of public policy in advancement of product service systems. *Journal of Cleaner Production, 11*(8), 905–914.
Osterwalder, A., & Pigneur, Y. (2010). *Business model generation: A handbook for visionaries, game changers, and challengers*. Wiley.
Rai, V., & Sigrin, B. (2013). Diffusion of environmentally-friendly energy technologies: Buy versus lease differences in residential PV markets. *Environmental Research Letters, 8*(1), 1–8.
Richter, M. (2013). German utilities and distributed PV: How to overcome barriers to business model innovation. *Renewable Energy, 55*, 456–466.
Rubalcaba, L., Gallego, J., & Den Hertog, P. (2010). The case of market and system failures in services innovation. *Service Industries Journal, 30*(4), 549–566.
Sarasini, S., & Linder, M. (2018). Integrating a business model perspective into transition theory: The example of new mobility services. *Environmental Innovation and Societal Transitions, 27*, 16–31.
Schot, J., & Geels, F. W. (2008). Strategic niche management and sustainable innovation journeys: Theory, findings, research agenda, and policy. *Technology Analysis & Strategic Management, 20*(5), 537–554.
Seawright, J., & Gerring, J. (2008). Case selection techniques in case study research: A menu of qualitative and quantitative options. *Political Research Quarterly, 61*(2), 294–308.
Smith, A., & Raven, R. (2012). What is protective space? Reconsidering niches in transitions to sustainability. *Research Policy, 41*(6), 1025–1036.
Steg, L., Perlaviciute, G., & van der Werff, E. (2015). Understanding the human dimensions of a sustainable energy transition. *Frontiers in Psychology, 6*, 805.
Technopedia. (2020). Smart device. Retrieved July 27, 2020, from https://www.techopedia.com/definition/31463/smart-device
Teece, D. J. (2007). Explicating dynamic capabilities: The nature and microfoundations of (sustainable) enterprise performance. *Strategic Management Journal, 28*, 1319–1350.
Teece, D. J. (2010). Business models, business strategy and innovation. *Long Range Planning, 43*, 172–194.

Teece, D. J. (2018). Business models and dynamic capabilities. *Long Range Planning, 51*(1), 40–49.

Tolkamp, J., Huijben, J. C. C. M., Mourik, R. M., Verbong, G. P. J., & Bouwknegt, R. (2018). User-centred sustainable business model design: The case of energy efficiency services in the Netherlands. *Journal of Cleaner Production, 182*, 755–764.

Tukker, A., & Tischner, U. (Eds.). (2006). *New business for old Europe. Product services, sustainability and competitiveness*. Greenleaf Publishing Ltd.

Vahidi, A., & Sciarretta, A. (2018). Energy saving potentials of connected and automated vehicles. *Transportation Research Part C: Emerging Technologies, 95*, 822–843.

Vandermerwe, S., & Rada, J. (1988). Servitization of business: Adding value by adding services. *European Management Journal, 6*(4), 314–324.

Vargo, S. L., & Lusch, R. F. (2008). Service-dominant logic: Continuing the evolution. *Journal of the Acad. Marketing Science, 36*, 1–10.

Yin, R. K. (2003). *Case study research: Design and methods*. Sage Publications.

Zollo, M., & Winter, S. G. (2002). Deliberate learning and the evolution of dynamic capabilities. *Organization Science, 13*(3), 339–351.

Zott, C., Amit, R., & Massa, L. (2011). The business model: Recent developments and future research. *Journal of Management, 37*(4), 1019–1042.

Reverse Logistics Process for Business Transitions: An Example from the Clothing Industry

Ignes A. Castro Contreiras de Carvalho, Pascale Schwab Castella, and Marcos Queiroz

1 Introduction

The clothing industry accounts for numerous environmental and health impacts. This includes the water consumption and contamination with pesticides used in the agriculture to produce cotton, the toxic chemicals used in its manufacturing process (Kooistra et al., 2006) and the embodied energy consumption in the fibre production, consuming fuel for crops machinery and electricity for heating water and air in laundering (Rana et al., 2015).

I. A. Castro Contreiras de Carvalho (✉) • P. Schwab Castella
Institute of Earth Surface Dynamics, University of Lausanne, Lausanne, Switzerland
e-mail: ignes.contreiras@unil.ch; pascale.schwabcastella@alumnil.unil.ch

M. Queiroz
Refazenda, Recife, Brazil
e-mail: marcos@refazenda.net

A. Aagaard et al. (eds.), *Business Models for Sustainability Transitions*,
https://doi.org/10.1007/978-3-030-77580-3_12

The fast-fashion brings an overproduction of new fabric wastes during production stage, and used clothing is also considered as waste. This important waste volume of fabric and used clothes in developed countries cannot be ignored, besides the relatively high rate of clothing reuse by low-income countries. The US and China are in the ranking of the underutilization of clothing and textiles (Ellen MacArthur Foundation, 2017), and the UK sent around 30 kg per capita to landfill each year (Allwood et al., 2006). Social impacts on the labour force with low-paid workers, working hours, safety and use of child labour in developing countries and on the health of employees also cannot be ignored (Desore & Narula, 2018).

However, instead of the stimulation of the over-consumption and its high volumes of waste as a consequence of fast-paced fashion practices with cheaper options, it is possible to transform the perceived obsolescence culture to offer newness in a more sustainable form. There are some positive examples of innovations able to deal with impacts as poor working conditions, greenhouse effects and how to dispose used old clothes.

This study analyses ways to transform the development of the textile industry, exploring options to improve lifetime and social practices. This includes slowing down the production and consumption of clothes and the generation of waste, changing the way clothes are made and used, choosing different fibres and farming practices, paying attention to the washing process and disposing them in a distinct form (Allwood et al., 2006).

Due to the qualitative and exploratory nature of this research, the method includes a process that consists in the literature review, practice review and analysis of conceptual framework with a single-case company, Refazenda. The case study was chosen to support the generation of ideas that are able to answer the questions 'how' and 'why' in exploratory researches, especially those where there is little or absence of control over behavioural events (Yin, 2017).

In the single-case study, only one case is examined, for example, a specific organization (Verschuren & Doorewaard, 2010). The important aspect here is to illustrate theories using an 'analytic generalization' approach, not to achieve 'statistical generalization' (Bocken et al., 2020).

This single-case study approach explores the application of concepts and frameworks previously exposed and seeks to understand how the development of a new business model for the clothing industry can encourage sustainable production and consumption processes and lead transitions using different organizational and resources strategies. The key data sources were semi-structured interviews and review of the company's organization documents, international reports and observations.

In other words, how it is possible to go to the direction of slow-paced fashion practices, prioritizing social and ecological issues instead of industrial ones. The reduction in the resource flow depends on the customer support and education to improve mindfulness and the focus on durability instead of fashion.

A holistic and systemic perspective can improve the understanding of opportunities for socio-technical transitions and explain how changes in the organizational and business dimensions can affect transitions more broadly to promote sustainable production and consumption. This exploratory research aims to analyse Refazenda from the perspective of its business model and see how this enables it to propose different practices favouring the sustainability of the sector. This also enables to see if the existing literature helps to organize a company's actions to understand whether they are moving in this direction.

This can require the support of new business models, the second-purchasing culture and eco-taxation to promote better use of resources and efficient production, distribution, use and disposal (Allwood et al., 2008). These strategies can avoid waste of fabric, energy and water, reduce the need of more materials and reuse what would be disposed. It also brings better jobs, with higher added value, opening up a perspective towards the social opportunities.

The development of this case study can contribute to fill the current gap in the development of new business models and demonstrate solutions that can respond to demands to understand, analyse and manage sustainability dynamics, considering business and industries as agents of change (Köhler et al., 2019; Markard, 2017).

This chapter starts by presenting the role of sustainability transitions. This is an effort to explain transformations, or what have been changed from these emergent patterns through different processes and dynamics the outcomes at systemic level (Hölscher et al., 2018).

It continues by exposing a literature review with some frameworks able to support the understanding and development of new business models through sustainable archetypes based on technological, social and organizational dimensions. This also presents a life-cycle perspective connected to open innovation strategies.

Afterwards, a single-case study approach is presented. This explores the application of concepts and frameworks previously exposed to promote more sustainable practices at Refazenda, a Brazilian company from the clothing sector.

1.1 The Role of Sustainability Transitions

The current networked society is facing an environmental crisis that requires the development of solutions able to lead transformations in the long term. This demands fundamental changes in a highly sophisticated and complex environment to modify consumption practices, lifestyles, business models, value chains, technologies, organizational infrastructures and policies (Markard, 2017; Markard et al., 2012). The adoption of a systemic view is crucial to understand the relations and possibilities that can arise inside the networks.

This context demands a social-technical transition process and dynamics to achieve sustainability goals, encouraging different dimensions for the organization of sustainable production and consumption systems. To open up opportunities is necessary to promote resilience thinking and breakthrough of niche innovations (Schilling et al., 2018).

The sustainability transitions occur along certain pathways of change that emerge due to the systemic interactions between multiple different agents or causal forces (Geels & Schot, 2007). This includes business and industries and explains what have been changed from transition pathways.

In order to be successful, the systems need to maintain their functionality and, at the same time, develop internal and external resilience in front of shocks and challenges (Binder et al., 2017). The development of business models can deal with constant changes and pressures and lead transitions able to promote sustainable patterns (Markard, 2017).

1.2 The Role of Business and Industries for Sustainability Transitions

The sustainability transitions require transformations in the industries and the emergence of new products, services and organizations, including the ability to complement or substitute current practices or to radically change them (Markard et al., 2012). This means doing business in another way, turning challenges into opportunities.

The businesses and industries have an important role to provide enduring significance for social-technical transition and contribute to the design of innovation systems for sustainability. They can be able to develop and legitimate technologies, to facilitate institutional change and to manage collective expectations between newcomers and incumbents' actors and to deal with the struggle for public policies (Köhler et al., 2019). This can set up a system capable to promote an environment for the emergence of innovative industries and the transformation or decline of current ones.

With regard to the clothing sector, the need to prioritize social and ecological issues requires the reduction in the flow of energy and resources. The technological innovation is crucial to improve environmental performance related to the better use of resources and efficient production, distribution, use and disposal. This can also avoid toxic chemicals and lower energy consumption and promote extended product life.

However, behavioural innovations are also important to promote durability (Beton et al., 2014), for example, transforming and reusing clothes, using fewer and more durable options, leasing what would not wear, washing less often, repairing them when some damages occurred, returning them for second-hand sale or recycling the yarn or fibres (Allwood et al., 2006).

The social-technical innovations and institutional and organizational changes can consider different business models and user experience. This can encourage technology development, economic growth decoupled from increased material flow, consumer education and durability. These solutions can respond to demands to understand, analyse and manage sustainability dynamics in daily practices through adaptation and resilience (Köhler et al., 2019; Markard, 2017).

The development of new business models for sustainability can encourage a more environmentally friendly sustainable production and consumption, going beyond profit maximization and industrial convergence (Battilana & Dorado, 2010; Markard, 2017). The understanding of all the types of innovations that are emerging in rapidly changing environments and the solutions provided to face ecological pressures require a dedicated attention to explain how firms can follow a hybrid path, maintaining their business while leading and promoting sustainability transitions (Markard, 2017; Markard et al., 2012).

2 New Business Models: Going Beyond the Traditional Scope of the Firms

2.1 New Business Models for the Sustainability Transition

The development of more sustainable business models can encourage more environmentally friendly production and consumption (Battilana & Dorado, 2010; Markard, 2017). They are able to deal with environmental pressures and promote sustainability transitions (Markard, 2017; Markard et al., 2012).

The social-technical innovations and institutional and organizational changes can consider different business models and user experience through adaptation and resilience (Köhler et al., 2019; Markard, 2017). In this context, it is important to develop sustainable option to offer solutions based on technology development, economic growth decoupled from increased material flow, consumer education and durability.

The business model innovation for sustainability offers opportunities to shape transitions towards more sustainable strategies and practices (Huijben et al., 2016; van Waes et al., 2018; Wainstein & Bumpus, 2016). The firms and industries can go beyond the traditional scope of and develop sustainable business models. They are able to expand boundaries and activities to offer flexibility in rapid changing environments, provide solutions based on sufficiency and promote technical, social and organizational innovations (Bocken & Short, 2016; Brehmer et al., 2017).

Bocken et al. (2014) and Richardson (2008) go towards a conceptual framework for the development of sustainable business models, as shown in Table 1. This is organized in some core elements, value proposition, value creation, value delivery and capture value, taking into consideration how they affect companies, societies and the environment.

This framework can offer a basis to seek solutions able to promote societal changes towards more sustainable practices. Together, they offer an overview about how to develop the sustainability inside different businesses. It can support different understandings, that is, value proposition and type of values provided, the value creation and delivery and its practices and how the company is able to capture values. This analysis will be used to understand some aspects of the sustainability embedded in the case study.

The value proposition can consider the sustainability in an ecological and social form underlying the offering, the target customer segment and the basic strategy of the organization. The value creation and delivery system can build up a value network among the key stakeholders to provide resources and capabilities while arranging the value chain, activity system and corporate processes (Richardson, 2008; Bocken et al., 2013,

Table 1 Conceptual sustainable business model framework (Bocken et al., 2014; Richardson, 2008)

Value proposition	Value creation and delivery	Value capture
Product/service Customer segments and relationships Value for customer, society and environment	Activities Resources Distribution channels Partners and suppliers Technology and product features	Cost structure and revenue streams Value capture for key actors, incl. environment and society Growth strategy/ethos
What value is provided and to whom?	How is value provided?	How does the company make money and capture other forms of value?

2015). This highlights which kind of value is provided to both economic, ecological and social spheres.

Finally, the value capture focuses on how the business model is able to contemplate environmental and social values, growth strategy and ethos (Bocken et al., 2014). This offers a more sustainable vision connected to its economics (Richardson, 2008), that is, revenue and cost structure.

In order to give assist the design of sustainable business models, Bocken et al. (2014) developed eight archetypes using a value-network perspective. They are structured in three dimensions: technological, social and organizational. Together, they cover micro and macro aspects. The sustainable archetypes are presented in Fig. 1. This research also uses this framework as a reference to observe the sustainability strategies and practices embedded in the business case.

The first dimension, technological, favours the maximization of material and energy efficiency, creation of value from waste and substitution

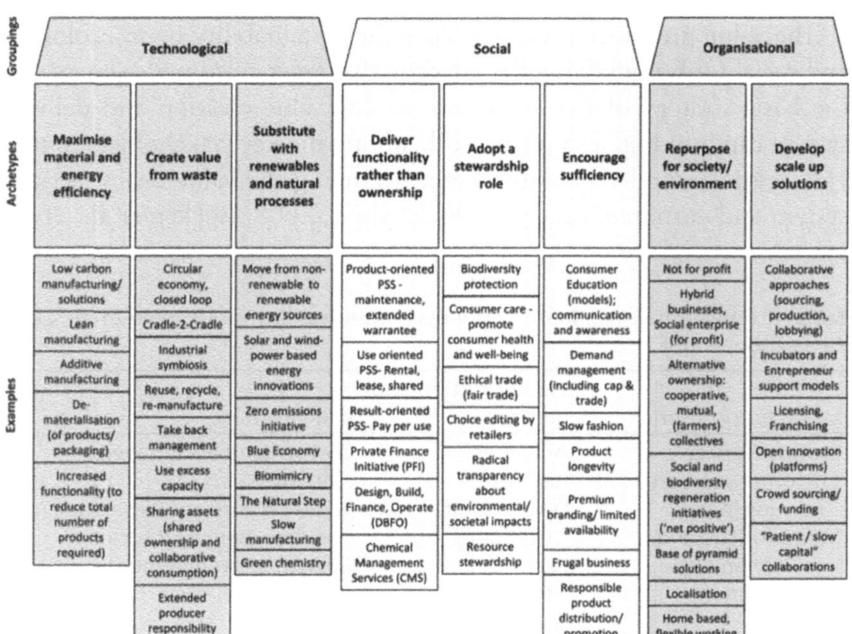

Fig. 1 The sustainable business model archetypes (Bocken et al., 2014)

with renewable and natural processes. The second, social, seeks the delivery of functionality rather than ownership, adoption of a stewardship role and promotion of the sufficiency. The functionality option includes pay per use strategy, and it is important to highlight that this may act in direct conflict with product longevity (part of the sufficiency approach). The intensive use of an asset can go in the opposite direction of durability, generating a reduced functional lifespan.

Despite the focus of this study being the promotion of the slow fashion, an option encompassed in the sufficiency approach, what is just one element in all of framework, firms need also to practise other strategies in order to develop a sustainable business model. Finally, the third, organizational, focuses on value propositions able to account for economy, environment and society and the development of scale-up solutions. Nonetheless, this last approach can be suspicious and go in the opposite direction of sustainable practices towards degrowth perspectives.

The design of business models using the archetypes can offer clues to the emergence of new products and services, promoting organizational changes able to partially or radically transform business strategies and practices. If these strategies can endorse some important shifts favouring the sustainability, it is necessary to point out that together they may not work. Some archetypes need to be used carefully, as the scale-up, whose effects may go in an opposite direction.

2.2 The Use of a Life-Cycle Perspective

An important aspect in the design of new business model is the need to consider the main components linked to sustainable business models and a life-cycle perspective of the products and services offered by a firm. This is embedded in some of the sustainable archetypes to deal with end-to-end environmental impacts related to business decisions to create, deliver and capture economic, environmental and social value. This vision is important to distinguish challenges and opportunities in the value chain to promote practices for sustainable production and consumption.

The life cycle of a material goes from its extraction until its disposal. When recyclable, the waste can be reintroduced in the cycle, instead of being disposed, reusing it to make the same product. However, there are other ways to convert materials, as downcycling or upcycling.

The former gives a different purpose while reusing them as it is, but removing value and delivering something with lower quality and functionality. In the opposite direction, the latter adds value and/or quality in the second life (Braungart & McDonough, 2002; Sung et al., 2019). The upcycling can also offer the possibility of downcycling or regular recycling later. This promotes the continuous reuse of products and material in technical systems.

These strategies are designed to improve environmental performance. Other strategies over the entire life cycle are the maximization of material productivity and energy efficiency, product design and promotion of the substitution with renewable and natural processes, cited as eco-design patterns by Lüdeke-Freund et al. (2018). Considering the materials and energy flows, this author establishes as core elements the co-product generation, industrial symbiosis, waste exchange platform, product recycling, remanufacturing/next life sales, repair, reuse, take back management and upgrading.

2.3 Going Beyond Boundaries with Open Innovation Networks

Open innovation refers to the creation, development and maintenance of channels to access external sources of knowledge, reducing the barriers to the exchange in a set of more open principles. Although the origin of the term comes from high-tech industries (Chesbrough, 2003), it has been developed into a widely innovation practice (Gassmann et al., 2010).

The collaborative production of knowledge across open innovation networks can facilitate sustainability transitions. This democratization of the access to knowledge and the development of trust and consensus structure is able to seize multiple sustainable opportunities (Narayan & Tidström, 2019).

The main idea behind its principle is to allow people to collaborate at scale, crowdsourcing the best ideas from the public to tackle challenging problems (Boudreau & Lakhani, 2013). This emphasizes a collaborative design to unlock ideas and boost organizational performance going beyond traditional corporate borders.

The peer-to-peer platforms for sharing resources are examples of solutions for today's rapidly moving world and the expansion of new types of processes and models for industry organizations. They can offer important strategies to the conduction of sustainability transitions (Dahlander & Gann, 2010; Kivimaa et al., 2019; Köhler et al., 2019; Hyysalo, Juntunen, & Martiskainen, 2018; Hyysalo, Perikangas, et al., 2018).

Open innovation offers customer participation and involvement and can be incorporated in business models to support the life-cycle analysis for the development of collaborative production and consumption systems. This can allow the importation of low-cost and high-quality ideas from a wide array of agents to identify the best ideas (King & Lakhani, 2013). This can improve speed, quality and cost of innovation through a strong collaboration between different actors while arranging a form of co-evolution.

The life-cycle perspective integrated to an open innovation approach for the fashion industry can assess the environmental aspects and potential impacts associated with a product, process or service. They can also provide managerial solutions since significant overlaps and interconnections are presented across different stages and promote more sustainable practices.

The life-cycle and the open innovation approaches can give support to reveal the advantages of a close collaboration in a co-creation and co-production process that can impact business decision on overall value creation, deliver and capture. This is crucial for the transformation and development of strategies and activities in order to complement or substitute existing practices and conceive new ones. This research also analyses the open innovation strategies and practices embedded in the business case and how it can seek solutions able to promote societal changes towards more sustainable practices.

3 The Case: Going Beyond the Traditional Scope in the Clothing Industry

Refazenda is a Brazilian company from both clothing and textile reverse logistics sectors. The company was chosen based on its sustainability purpose from the outset, using leftover fabric scraps as raw materials for the design of new items, a strategy evolved to the almost complete utilization of the textile waste.

The firm focus on the 'sustainable growth' considers two main strategies, Realce ('fashion upgrades') and Reouse (i.e., to dare, offering services to improve the modular use of pieces of clothes). They are based on practices for slowing down the production and consumption of clothes and the generation of waste, changing the way clothes are made and used.

The corporation has a small size (according to its annual income in the Brazilian categorization). The main physical deliverables are clothes and accessories with 90% of natural fabric (such as cotton—10% is organic—silk and linen) and lower use of chemical dyes (40% of the production). The main inputs and outputs are shown in Fig. 2. The organization has 38 employees and work directly with 10 local cooperatives to make clothes that will be sold in three stores in Recife, in the state of Pernambuco, Brazil.

The business strategy for product lifetime extension is considered as upcycling and reuse and the firm sector as textile reverse logistics by

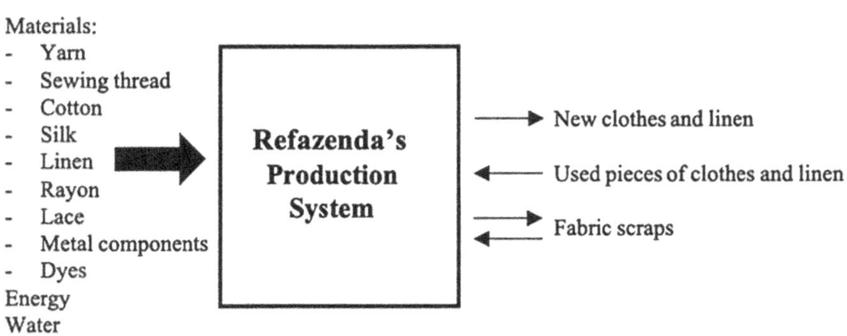

Fig. 2 Main inputs and outputs in the production system of Refazenda

UNEP[1] studies (Akatu Institute et al., 2017; Bakker & Schuit, 2017). The basic operations of the company include the purchase of the fabric and weaves of the clothes, before selling them. They are reassembled as secondary materials to be embedded in the production of smaller pieces or reinforce bigger ones.

However, this also provokes waste as small patchworks that are subsequently employed to manufacture accessories (brooches, bracelets, earrings, necklaces and scarfs) or sent to the cooperatives associated with the organization that reused it to produce fabric and clothes and from whom they rebuy it as new, restarting the cycle. Each piece of leftover from the cuts is transformed into raw material for the design of new items using almost the entire amount of the textile waste.

On the consumption side, two projects focus on the extended product lifetime. One is called Realce and coordinates a series of workshops that happens each three months in the stores to stimulate consumers to do upcycling in their clothes while modifying them, a service offered by the organization. It is part of a co-production process that gives a second life to used pieces.

This activity includes the awareness about different utilizations of worn-out pieces to reinforce others, suggesting innovative ways of wearing them or the redesign to be transformed into new ones (adding details or transforming them, e.g., a long skirt that can be adapted to be used as strapless dress or a jumpsuit as trouser and blouse, as well as the reinforcement making double-sided options).

This process allows the opportunity of maintaining the value of clothes and fabrics while preserving a level of newness but with less perceived obsolescence and waste. It is possible to affirm that they can improve adaptability and promote life extended to avoid premature discarding.

The second project, Reouse, focuses on the customer and supplier's education, and not physical transformation, focusing on the importance to rethink the use of the clothes and their versatility through meetings and conferences with companies from the textile sector. The main idea is to design them in distinct forms, changing the perceptions in order to boost different ways of wearing them.

---

[1] United Nations Environment Programme (UNEP).

The motivations behind these strategies are cost-saving and marketing differentiation while offering a more environmentally friendly practice. Both focuses on the promotion of 'slow fashion' practices and possibilities to make less purchases, at the same time that is able to provide the feeling of getting something new, the development of a community of users and to increase the sense of belonging between stakeholders.

3.1 The Sustainability in the Business Model Case

The development of more sustainable business models is able to encourage sustainable production and consumption (Battilana & Dorado, 2010; Markard, 2017). Hence, this offers opportunities to promote sustainability transitions through social-technical innovations and institutional and organizational changes (Markard, 2017; Markard et al., 2012).

The business model of the firm is based in a value proposition that considers both ecological and social aspects for suppliers, partners and clients. The initial idea was a result of cost reduction while keeping a higher level of quality as part of a textile reverse logistics strategy in connection with artisanal weavers to offer handcrafted work based on unused materials (i.e., scraps) to make other products. However, the link with environmental and social concerns also evolved towards a transition to slow-paced fashion and sustainable practices.

The scraps started being used to reinforce new and old clothes, providing a higher-quality finishing, that is, reinforcement in the seams to increase the life cycle, and a higher added value. They also are used to transform used ones, evolving to a more sophisticated process. The slowing down consumption strategies include customers and partners support and education for more durability and sufficiency; reduced use of auxiliary materials and production; processes efficiency for lower use of material, energy and water; reuse of waste; and offer of a second life to used options.

The company also support some cultural aspects and maintain regional characteristics in their products. The clients have the opportunity to maintain a longer relationship with the organization, buying not just the products but also services promoting changes and, at the same time, a diversified wardrobe.

The value creation and delivery system, that is, the coordination of activities, resources and capabilities, are designed focusing on a socio-technical circularity inside the value network, taking into consideration both suppliers and the final users. This spiral motivates them to change boundaries in order to extend the lifetime of the textile products and maintain added value.

The value capture embeds economic value in terms of revenues and reduction in some costs for the acquisition of the textiles and possibilities of a more emotional and stable relationship with partners and customers. The environmental value is linked to the minimization of fabric waste and the apparent need to purchase more clothes.

Finally, the social value is connected to the support to local artisans, information and education of value network to rethink the use of the fabrics and clothes, growth strategy based in frugality and ethos maintaining the initial approach over decades.

3.2 Business Model Archetypes Case

The firm encompasses several archetypes of sustainable business models (Bocken et al., 2014) using a value-network perspective. Table 2 summarizes the strategy adopted on the technological side.

The firm maximizes material and energy efficiency through low carbon manufacturing solutions. The use of handcrafted work instead of big textile machines is possible to make the same product, that is, technology applied for the production. The higher cost per unit is compensated with the cost reduction offered by the reuse of scraps, a relative lower cost of labour in the country and a higher price offered to a niche market. The dematerialization strategy is employed with less utilization of natural resources to have fabrics and clothes, not employing plastics in the packaging and small adoption of metal components.

It is also possible to point out the increased functionality, reducing the total amount of fabric required from suppliers and clothes from final customers. The production process does not necessitate the utilization of

Table 2 Technological aspects of business model archetypes for the case study (based on Bocken et al., 2014)

Technological aspects				
Maximize material and energy efficiency	Low carbon manufacturing solutions (handcrafted work, instead of the use of textile machines)	Dematerialization (less use of natural resources to have fabrics and clothes, no use of plastics in the packaging, no use of metal components in clothing)	Increased functionality reducing the total amount of fabric and clothes required by both suppliers and customers	No use of industrial water
Create value from waste	Circular economy promoting closed loops (upcycling) in a zero-waste politics	Reuse and a cradle-to-cradle approach (waste of fabrics is transformed to be kept inside the cycle)	Taking back management of the waste or old pieces of clothes to reuse, recycle and remanufacture (a level of industrial symbiosis with local partners and customers)	Redesigning of pieces and parts of new and old clothes, which includes the reuse of excess capacity of production to reach no waste of fabric scraps (extended producer responsibility)
Substitution with renewable and natural processes	Slow manufacturing (artisanship production technique and quality over quantity)	Access to the national electrical grid (86% of renewables)	Use of natural colorants and natural fibres	50% of the delivery is made using bicycles

industrial water because it does not operate laundry. For energy efficiency purposes, they use LED lamps and the sewing machines with reduced energy needs.

The firm also creates value from waste towards a circular economy promoting closed-loops patterns by reuse and a cradle-to-cradle approach, where the scraps of fabrics are transformed to be kept inside the cycle. The scraps are used to reinforce new and old clothes to provide a higher-quality finishing and to transform used ones, offering a second life, besides the creation of new products. This is part of reuse and repair systems that allow upgrading and product recycling.

Other important strategies include customers' and partners' support and education for more durability and sufficiency; reduced use of auxiliary materials and production; processes efficiency for lower use of material, energy and water; reuse of waste; and offer of a second life to used options.

The company also considers some cultural aspects, maintain regional characteristics in their products. The clients have the opportunity to maintain a longer relationship with the organization, buying not just the products but also services promoting changes and, at the same time, a diversified wardrobe.

There are also some clues about industrial symbiosis for the reduction of the ecological impact of the industrial processes characterized by connecting flows of material, water and energy among the actors (Boons et al., 2017). Almost the total amount of the leftovers from raw material is kept by the firm and its partners.

The customers can maintain the lifetime for their clothes with the possibility to go to the store to repair or transform them and give a new kind of use to old purchases which reveals activities such as taking back management of the waste or old pieces to reuse, recycle and remanufacture. The extended producer responsibility is practised with different forms. The Realce and Innovative Production strategies are able to redesign the excess capacity of production (fabrics), including using it to give a new aspect to old clothes, or to apply the mindset offered by Reouse, in order to transform the pieces to be used in different forms.

With regard to the substitution with renewable energy, the firm operates using the regional electrical grid based on hydroelectric sources that is connected to 86% of the total electric generation mix of the country.

Table 3 Organizational aspects of business model archetypes for the case study (based on Bocken et al., 2014)

Social aspects				
Delivery of functionality rather than ownership	Offer of services focusing on the extended product lifetime as part of a product-oriented strategy	Offer of services for consumers	Support the services of suppliers	
Adopt a stewardship role	Strategies towards a sustainable and responsible resource management	Income distribution and provision of jobs to skilled artisans	Women and minorities empowerment, social inclusion	Support to the local identity and culture
Encourage sufficiency	Consumer education models to improve communication and awareness to promote 'slow fashion' and extended lifetime of clothes	Promotion of product longevity with limited use of high-quality materials and small and original production	Organization of a responsible product acquisition, distribution and promotion process	Frugal business strategy maintaining a small size of the business and collaborative work for more than 30 years

The link with natural processes is highlighted by an artisanship technique and focus in the quality over the quantity, even if the slow manufacturing means longer production time. The delivery of the products uses bicycles that respond to 50% of the total quantity shipped. The adoption of natural colourants and natural fibres go to the green chemistry strategies.

On the social side, as shown in Table 3, the firm encourages the delivery of functionality rather than ownership. This is highlighted by the offer of services focusing on the extended product lifetime as part of a product-oriented approach embedded in the Realce strategy.

The stewardship role adoption is revealed in the design of systems towards a sustainable and responsible approach to resource management. This takes in consideration the share of responsibility with clients and partners across the chain of custody of products. These ecological and social aspects include frugal strategies for the business and are able to maintain a small size production and co-production with partners and clients.

The partnership with local lace makers provides direct and indirect jobs to skilled artisans who had fallen out of favour because of new technologies. Besides the income distribution, this also promotes women's empowerment and social inclusion with a total of 90% of women as employees and 65% of black or mixed origin. These actions can also translate the support to the local identity and culture.

The social strategies also consider sufficiency through consumer education models to improve communication and awareness to advocate 'slow fashion' and an extended lifetime of a cloth, encouraging eco-consciousness and co-participation in the sustainability process from suppliers and consumers. The adoption of labels and partnership with agencies that promote sustainable issues enable to advertise the subject and assume a marketing strategy.

The incentives for product longevity through a premium branding consider limited availability and use of high-quality materials. The handmade processes offer pieces with greater durability and original design.

It is also possible to identify a responsible product acquisition, distribution and promotion process. The firm runs workshops for customer support and education to show them how to upcycle clothes and, subsequently, to extend the lifetime of wardrobes.

Table 4 explores the organizational side. The company has a purpose embracing ecological and social concern with the economic ones from the beginning of its activities. The direct work with local cooperatives and collectives engages strategies to acquire fibres that are mostly produced in the country and transform textile waste.

The organization develops scale-up solutions in order to keep its environmental and social strategies through a collective approach for sourcing, production and final user consumption. This also supports frugality, giving double uses, second utilization and life to products in order to

Table 4 Organizational aspects of business model archetypes for Refazenda (based on Bocken et al., 2014)

Organizational		
Repurpose for society/environment	Environment and social concerns are in the heart of the strategy	Direct partnership with local cooperatives and collectives. Acquisition of fibres that are mostly produced in the country
Develop scale-up solutions	Solutions based on environmental and social strategies through a collaborative approach for sourcing and production	Use of open innovation platforms for sharing knowledge. Seeking of 'patient/slow capital' collaborations

Table 5 Open innovation projects

Open innovation project	Innovative production	Realce	Reouse
Focus of the knowledge shared	Amount and types of leftovers, fabric waste	Redesigning and recreating pieces and accessories from other worn-out clothes, leftovers and waste	Information and education towards versatility and multi-use of pieces

maintain a slow-paced growth. It still coordinates forms to make use of open innovation platforms for sharing knowledge and seek 'patient/slow capital' collaborations.

3.3 Open Innovation Projects

The firm has three online open innovation projects to build platforms for feeding and sharing information through the organization of value networks as demonstrated in Table 5. The first is innovative production and is focused on the textile leftovers from suppliers and other brands to do upcycling in their production and creative processes.

The second targets new ways to redesign and recreate pieces and accessories from other worn-out clothes, including possibilities to offer a second utilization and life of clothes. This is part of the Realce strategy with a focal point on a co-product generation. If the workshops and ateliers require subscription and payment of the service, the online projects are based in the free access.

The third is focused on the versatility and multi-use of the same piece. It promotes different ways to use and wear it, such as a jumpsuit that is adaptable to become trousers and blouses and/or as double-sided clothes, as part of the Reouse strategy. This organizes a waste exchange platform that is also going to be launched online in order to scale up opportunities for sharing knowledge.

In common, all these strategies are able to lead a sustainability transition changing operations towards slow-paced fashion practices and conduct more environmental-friendly production and consumption processes. The performance is connected to the amount of information and knowledge provided by the partners in an open-source form, revealing a co-creation and collaborative mechanisms.

4 Discussion and Conclusion

The clothing industry is responsible for several environmental impacts. The inefficiency and unsustainability of its systems generates overconsumption and high volumes of waste. This context demands a social-technical transition process and dynamics to encourage sustainable production and consumption systems (Schilling et al., 2018).

The sustainability transitions reveal pathways of change that emerge out of the systemic interactions between multiple different agents (Geels & Schot, 2007). This can offer understanding about how to maintain functionality and, at the same time, develop internal and external resilience in front of shocks and challenges (Binder et al., 2017).

The development of new business models is important to handle the constant changes and pressures and promote transitions based on sustainable patterns (Markard, 2017) and inspire a more environmentally friendly production and consumption (Battilana & Dorado, 2010; Markard, 2017).

4.1 Unveiling the Sustainability of the Case

4.1.1 The Use of the Conceptual Sustainable Business Model Framework

The analysis of conceptual sustainable business model framework aspects developed by Bocken et al. (2014) and Richardson (2008) reveals some practices in the business model of the Refazenda. Its value proposition considers both ecological and social aspects for suppliers, partners and clients, while remaining economically viable and even more profitable. The value creation and delivery system are designed promoting different levels of circularity inside the value network, taking into consideration both suppliers and the final users.

The firm captures economic value in terms of revenues and cost reduction while managing waste and encouraging slow-paced fashion and sustainable practices. The social value of its economic strategy is reflected by the support to local artisans, information and education within the value network to rethink the use of the fabrics and clothes and a slow growth strategy.

4.1.2 The Use of the Sustainable Archetypes

The investigation of some sustainable archetypes based in the work of Bocken et al. (2014) gives the opportunity to observe sustainability strategies practised by business case. They can endorse some important shifts, although it is necessary to point out that together they may not work because of certain effects that may go in an opposite direction.

On the technological side, the simple reuse of the fabric waste can lead to an increased production of new clothes and higher levels of consumption, despite the possibility to offer a more efficient practice. The reuse as reinforcement of new and old clothes and transformation of used one to give a second life are able to slower the consumption or, at least, to endorse a reduction.

The pay per use strategy, part of the social side, may act in direct conflict with product longevity. The asset intensive use can reduce its functional lifespan and durability. On the organizational side, the development of scale-up solutions needs to take into account can be contradictory with degrowth perspectives.

Although the focus of this research is the promotion of slow fashion, and one of the elements in all of framework in the sufficiency approach, the case study showed that other archetypes are equally important for the development of a sustainable business model. This can lead to the emergence of new products and services and organizational changes towards partial or radical innovations through different strategies and practices.

The development of some sustainable business model archetypes describes opportunities for products and services able to complement the practices of the clothing industry to transform leftovers in a partial or profound form. This does not require radical changes but a different mindset in order to rethink the structural design of clothes towards an extended lifetime.

If the strategies of this organization are being implemented in a tropical country, where a warm climate demands light-weighted clothes, it is possible to imagine that temperate regions could offer a bigger market. The leftover fabric straps could be applied to thicken vestments and to promote various uses in different seasons through layers and changeable structures.

As some of the fabrics are acquired in other Latin America countries, as organic cotton, this reveals a level of higher carbon practice. Especially when considering that the company is located in a tropical region that allows the growth of this type of material. However, this requires more political support in terms of regulations and subsides.

4.1.3 The Use of Open Innovation Strategies

Another relevant aspect for the sustainability embedded in the case is the open innovation projects for the creation, development and maintenance of channels to access external sources of knowledge in order to reduce barriers to the exchange of information, development of trust and consensus and seizing multiple sustainable opportunities while creating value with and for customers and partners (Gassmann et al., 2010; Narayan & Tidström, 2019).

This collaborative production can facilitate sustainability transitions and allow the crowdsourcing of the best ideas able to tackle challenging problems (Boudreau & Lakhani, 2013). The democratization of the access to knowledge offered by the projects of Refazenda supports the different forms to reuse waste through possibilities of co-creation and co-production.

The organization of platforms to organize the amount and types of leftovers, fabric waste, and to redesigning and recreating pieces and accessories from other waste and worn-out clothes is a strategy that affects the physical part of the products. However, the success of this action is strictly linked to the offer of information and education projects able to stimulate customers and partners.

4.2 Other Implications

The concern in the offer of more sustainable practices requires a more sophisticated process and structure. On one hand this can generate extra costs, but on the other hand can take into consideration some reductions offered by the reuse of waste and the possibility of a higher price paid by a niche market.

They offer a more systemic view of the impacts and opportunities, including collaborations through the value network and ways to unlock ideas and promote actions able to boost organizational performance going beyond traditional corporate borders. This can avoid overlaps and reveal interconnections across different stages to promote more sustainable practices.

The application of the conceptual framework and the archetypes for the development of sustainable business models can explore options and limits to the improvement of lifetime social practices in the clothing industry. Refazenda organized different processes and practices able to slow down the production and consumption and the generation of waste.

The company applies some strategies highlighted by Allwood et al. (2006), offering different forms to change the way clothes are made and used, including behavioural approaches for the promotion of durability. These strategies can avoid waste of fabric, energy and water and reduce the need and the cost of materials and waste. The efficiency gains in the use of material and in the production, distribution, use and disposal can allow, at the same time, the reduction in the flows with the support of partners and customers.

In common, all these managerial strategies are able to lead a sustainability transition changing operations towards slow-paced fashion practices and conduct more environmental-friendly production and consumption processes. The performance is connected to the amount of information and knowledge provided by the partners in an open-source form, revealing a co-creation and collaborative mechanisms able to open up opportunities in a process that promotes resilience and adaptation inside a value network.

Considering the role of sustainability transitions, analysing patterns of change produced by processes and dynamics, the case study can reveal some transformations and outcomes at systemic level to avoid to let clothes being discarded before reaching the end of their lifetime, dealing with textile leftover problems.

The eco-design and closing-the-loop and open innovation patterns can integrate important contributions into value propositions, partnerships, key activities and customer channels to integrate ecological and social aspects through the support of business models to promote better use of resources and efficient production, distribution, use and disposal.

This can encourage technology development and economic growth decoupled from increased material flow coupled with services, such as repair, novel coatings, other maintenance options, remanufacturing or fashion upgrades, to give a second life to used products. The infrastructure of clothing collection with the support of public policies can promote bigger reduction of total or embedded impacts in clothes for the promotion of environmental and social responsibility.

This chapter offers some possibilities to develop sustainable strategies by organizations to slow down the textile and clothing consumption based on frameworks and archetypes for the development of sustainable business models. However, further research could focus in the influences in the entire cloth and fibres industry.

In order to transform all the current clothing economy, based in waste and pollution, it is also necessary to analyse the agriculture and fibre production, the amount of water and energy used for laundry by final users, the different ways to dispose discarded products and the integration between companies in local regions to balance production and consumption and their environmental and social impacts. Finally, it requires the coordination of the entire value network, including organizations from both public and private sectors.

References

Akatu Institute, One Planet Network Consumer Information Programme, & UN Environment. (2017). *Product lifetime extension case study: Refazenda*. United Nations Environment Programme.

Allwood, J., Laursen, S., Rodríguez, C., & Bocken, N. (2006). *Well dressed? The present and future sustainability of clothing and textiles in the United Kingdom*. University of Cambridge, Institute of Manufacturing.

Allwood, J., Laursen, S., Russel, S., Rodríguez, C., & Bocken, N. (2008). An approach to scenario analysis of the sustainability of an industrial sector applied to clothing and textiles in the UK. *Journal of Cleaner Production, 16*, 1234–1246.

Bakker, C., & Schuit, C. (2017). *The long view: Exploring product lifetime extension*. United Nations Environment Programme.

Battilana, J., & Dorado, S. (2010). Building sustainable hybrid organizations: The case of commercial microfinance organizations. *The Academy of Management Journal, 53*(6), 1419–1440.

Beton, A., Dias, D., Farrant, L., Gibon, T., Le Guem, Y., Desaxc, M., Perwuelty, A., & Boufateh, I. (2014). *Environmental improvement potential of textiles (IMPRO Textiles)* (JRC Scientific and policy reports). European Commission's Joint Research Centre (JRC).

Binder, C., Mühlemeier, S., & Wyss, R. (2017). An indicator-based approach for analyzing the resilience of transitions for energy regions. Part I: Theoretical and conceptual considerations. *Energies, 10*, 36.

Bocken, N., Morales, L., & Lehner, M. (2020). Sufficiency business strategies in the food industry—The case of Oatly. *Sustainability, 12*(3), 824.

Bocken, N., Rana, P., & Short, S. (2015). Value mapping for sustainable business thinking. *Journal of Industrial and Production Engineering, 32*(1), 1–15.

Bocken, N., & Short, S. (2016). Towards a sufficiency-driven business model: Experiences and opportunities. *Environmental Innovation and Societal Transitions, 18*, 41–61.

Bocken, N., Short, S., Rana, P., & Evans, S. (2013). A value mapping tool for sustainable business modelling. *Corporate Governance, 13*(5), 482–497.

Bocken, N., Short, S., Rana, P., & Evans, S. (2014). A literature and practice review to develop sustainable business model archetypes. *Journal of Cleaner Production, 65*, 42–56.

Boons, F., Chertow, M., Park, J., Spekkink, W., & Shi, H. (2017). Industrial symbiosis dynamics and the problem of equivalence: Proposal for a comparative framework. *Journal of Industrial Ecology, 21*(4), 938–952.

Boudreau, K., & Lakhani, K. (2013). *Using the crowd as an innovation partner*. Harvard Business Review.

Braungart, M., & McDonough, W. (2002). *Cradle to cradle. Remaking the way we make things*. North Point Press.

Brehmer, M., Podoynitsyna, K., & Langerak, F. (2017). Sustainable business models as boundary-spanning systems of value transfers. *Journal of Cleaner Production, 172*, 4514–4531.

Chesbrough, H. (2003). *Open innovation, the new imperative for creating and profiting, from technology*. Harvard Business School Press.

Dahlander, L., & Gann, D. (2010). How open is innovation? *Research Policy, 39*(6), 699–709.

Desore, A., & Narula, S. (2018). An overview on corporate response towards sustainability issues in textile industry. *Environmental Development and Sustainability, 20*, 1439–1459.

Ellen MacArthur Foundation. (2017). A new textiles economy: Redesigning fashion's future. http://www.ellenmacarthurfoundation.org/publications

Gassmann, O., Enkel, E., & Chesbrough, H. W. (2010). The future of open innovation. *Research-Technology Management, 60*(1), 35–38.

Geels, F., & Schot, J. (2007). Typology of sociotechnical transition pathways. *Research Policy, 36* (3), 399–417.

Hölscher, K., Wittmayer, J., & Loorbach, D. (2018). Transition versus transformation: What's the difference? *Environmental Innovation and Societal Transitions, 27*, 1–3.

Huijben, J., Verbong, G., & Podoynitsyna, K. (2016). Mainstreaming solar: Stretching the regulatory regime through business model innovation. *Environmental Innovation and Societal Transitions, 20*, 1–15.

Hyysalo, S., Juntunen, J., & Martiskainen, M. (2018). Energy internet forums as acceleration phase transition intermediaries. *Research Policy, 47*(5), 872–855.

Hyysalo, S., Perikangas, S., Marttila, T., & Auvinen, K. (2018). Catalysing pathway creation for transition governance. In *Proceeding of the design research society 51st international conference – Volume 3, Limerick, Ireland, 25–28 June*. Design Research Society.

King, A., & Lakhani, K. R. (2013). Using open innovation to identify the best ideas. *MIT Sloan Management Review, 55*(1), 41–48.

Kivimaa, P., Boon, W., Hyysalo, S., & Klerkx, L. (2019). Towards a typology of intermediaries in sustainability transitions: A systematic review and a research agenda. *Research Policy, 48*(4), 1062–1075.

Köhler, J., Geels, F. W., Kern, F., Markard, J., Wieczorek, A., Alkemade, F., Avelino, F., Bergek, A., Boons, F., Fünfschilling, L., Hess, D., Holtz, G., Hyysalo, S., Jenkins, K., Kivimaa, P., Martiskainen, M., McMeekin, A., Mühlemeier, M. S., Nykvist, B., Onsongo, E., Pel, B., Raven, R., Rohracher, H., Sandén, B., Schot, J., Sovacool, B., Turnheim, B., Welch, D., & Wells, P. (2019). An agenda for sustainability transitions research: State of the art and future directions. *Environmental Innovation and Societal Transitions, 31*, 1–32.

Kooistra, K., Termorshuizen, A., & Pybum, R. (2006). *The sustainability of cotton. Consequences for man and environment* (Report 223). Science Shop Wageningen. University & Research Centre.

Lüdeke-Freund, F., Carroux, S., Joyce, A., Massa, L., & Breuer, H. (2018). The sustainable business model pattern taxonomy – 45 patterns to support sustainability-oriented business model innovation. *Sustainable Production and Consumption, 15*, 145–162.

Markard, J. (2017). Sustainability transitions: Exploring the emerging research field and its contribution to management studies. *Conference paper*. July 2017, 33rd EGOS Colloquium Copenhagen, July 6–8.

Markard, J., Ravenb, R., & Truffera, B. (2012). Sustainability transitions: An emerging field of research and its prospect. *Research Policy, 41*, 955–967.

Narayan, R., & Tidström, A. (2019). Blockchains for accelerating open innovation systems for sustainability transitions, world scientific book chapters. In M. Swan, J. Potts, S. Takagi, F. Witte, & P. Tasca (Eds.), *Blockchain economics: Implications of distributed ledgers markets, communications networks, and algorithmic reality*, Chapter 5 (pp. 85–101). World Scientific Publishing Pte. Ltd.

Rana, S., Pichandi, S., Moorthy, S., Bhattacharyya, A., Parveen, S., & Fangueiro, R. (2015). Carbon footprint of textile and clothing products. In S. Muthu (Ed.), *Handbook of sustainable apparel production*. CRC Press Research Centre.

Richardson, J. (2008). The business model: An integrative framework for strategy execution. *Strategic Change, 17*(5–6), 133–144.

Schilling, T., Wyss, R., & Binder, C. (2018). The resilience of sustainability transitions. *Sustainability, 10*, 4593.

Sung, K., Cooper, T., & Kettley, S. (2019). Factors influencing upcycling for UK makers. *Sustainability, 11*(3), 870.

Van Waes, S., De Maeyer, S., Moolenaar, N. M., Van Petegem, P., & Van den Bossche, P. (2018). Strengthening networks: A social network intervention among higher education teachers. *Learning and Instruction, 53*, 34–49.

Verschuren, P., & Doorewaard, H. (2010). *Designing a research project* (2nd ed.). Eleven International Publishing.

Wainstein, M., & Bumpus, A. (2016). Business models as drivers of the low-carbon power system transition: A multi-level perspective. *Journal of Cleaner Production, 126*, 572–585.

Yin, R. K. (2017). *Case study research and applications: Design and methods*. Sage Publications.

Index[1]

[1] Note: Page numbers followed by 'n' refer to notes.

A. Aagaard et al. (eds.), *Business Models for Sustainability Transitions*,
https://doi.org/10.1007/978-3-030-77580-3

The manufacturer's authorised representative in the EU is Springer Nature Customer Service Centre GmbH, Europaplatz 3, 69115 Heidelberg, Germany. If you have any concerns regarding our products, please contact ProductSafety@springernature.com

Printed and bound by CPI Group (UK) Ltd, Croydon, CR0 4YY
30/09/2026
02225311-0016